OFDM Wireless LANs: A Theoretical and Practical Guide

John Terry and Juha Heiskala

SAMS

800 East 96th St., Indianapolis, Indiana, 46240 USA

OFDM Wireless LANs: A Theoretical and Practical Guide

Copyright © 2002 by Sams Publishing

International Standard Book Number: 0-672-32157-2

Library of Congress Catalog Card Number: 00-112047

Printed in the United States of America

First Printing: December 2001

Second printing with corrections: September 2002

04   03   4   3

Figures 2.4, 6.7, 6.8, 6.11, and 6.13–6.16 have material in part or full reproduced with permission from IEEE Std. 802.11a-1999, Copyright © 1999, by IEEE. The IEEE disclaims any responsibility or liability resulting from the placement and use in the described manner.

Trademarks

All terms mentioned in this book that are known to be trademarks or service marks have been appropriately capitalized. Sams Publishing cannot attest to the accuracy of this information. Use of a term in this book should not be regarded as affecting the validity of any trademark or service mark.

Warning and Disclaimer

Every effort has been made to make this book as complete and as accurate as possible, but no warranty or fitness is implied. The information provided is on an "as is" basis. The authors and the publisher shall have neither liability nor responsibility to any person or entity with respect to any loss or damages arising from the information contained in this book.

ACQUISITIONS EDITOR
Dayna Isley

DEVELOPMENT EDITOR
Rebecca Greenberg

MANAGING EDITOR
Charlotte Clapp

PROJECT EDITOR
Carol Bowers

COPY EDITOR
Michael Henry

INDEXER
Ron Strauss

TECHNICAL EDITORS
Tony Reid, Douglas B. Williams

TEAM COORDINATOR
Pamalee Nelson

MEDIA DEVELOPER
Dan Scherf

INTERIOR DESIGNER
Anne Jones

COVER DESIGNER
Aren Howell

PAGE LAYOUT
Octal Publishing, Inc.

Contents at a Glance

Preface   ix

1   Background and WLAN Overview   1

2   Synchronization   47

3   Modulation and Coding   87

4   Antenna Diversity   123

5   RF Distortion Analysis for OFDM WLANs   171

6   Medium Access Control (MAC) for IEEE 802.11 Networks   215

7   Medium Access Control (MAC) for HiperLAN/2 Networks   257

8   Rapid Prototyping of WLANs Using FPGA   277

Index   299

Contents

Preface   ix

1   Background and WLAN Overview   1

Review of Stochastic Processes and Random Variables..........................2

Random Variables...3

Ensemble Averages...3

Review of Discrete-Time Signal Processing 6

Discrete-Time Signals 6

Discrete-Time Systems...7

Filtering Random Processes 9

Discrete Fourier Transform (DFT)..11

Components of a Digital Communication System 12

Source Formatting 13

Source Coding 18

Channel Coding..19

Modulation 25

Multiple Access Techniques 25

Channel Model 28

OFDM WLAN Overview 31

MAC for WLAN Standards...32

Physical Layer Specifications for WLAN Standards 36

Single Carrier Versus OFDM Comparison 38

Synchronization Errors...40

Effects of Frequency Errors 41

Bibliography 45

2   Synchronization   47

Timing Estimation 49

Packet Detection..49

Symbol Timing..57

Sample Clock Tracking 62

Frequency Synchronization 66

Post DFT Approach to Frequency Error Estimation 70

Comments on Frequency Error Estimation Algorithms...................72

Alternative Techniques for Frequency Error Estimation..................73

Carrier Phase Tracking 73

Channel Estimation..77

Frequency Domain Approach for Channel Estimation 77

Time Domain Approach for Channel Estimation............................79

Analysis of the Time Domain and Frequency Domain
   Approaches for Channel Estimation..80

Enhancing the Channel Estimate...81

Clear Channel Assessment 81

Signal Quality 82

Bibliography 83

3   Modulation and Coding   87

Modulation 88

    Coherent Modulations 90

    Detection of Coherent Modulations 97

    Non-Coherent Modulations 98

    Linear and Nonlinear Modulation 101

Interleaving 102

    Block Interleaver 103

    Convolutional Interleaver 104

    Interleaving in IEEE 802.11a 104

Channel Codes 106

    Performance of IEEE 802.11a 114

    Trellis Coded Modulation 118

    Block Codes 119

    Turbo Codes 119

Bibliography 120

4   Antenna Diversity   123

Background 124

    Limits of Capacity in Fading Environments 125

    Channel Model for Multiple-Input/Multiple-Output

      (MIMO) Systems 129

    Introducing Diversity 130

Receive Diversity 131

    Selection Diversity 131

    Maximal Ratio Combining 133

Transmit Diversity 136

    Transmit Diversity Design Criteria for Fading Channels 136

    Delay Diversity 139

    Trellis Space-Time Codes 140

    Layered Space-Time Codes 146

    Block Space-Time Codes 148

    Multidimensional Space-Time Codes 151

    Spherical Coding 151

    SSTC in OFDM Framework 152

    Water-Filling for Single Antenna Systems 154

    Water-Filling for Multi-Antenna Systems 157

    Adaptive Modulation 158

Bibliography 163

5   RF Distortion Analysis for OFDM WLAN   171

Components of the Radio Frequency Subsystem 172

Amplifier Classification and Distortion 173

Predistortion Techniques for Nonlinear Distortion Mitigation 178

A Decision-Aided Method for Clipping
   Amplitude Recovery 181

Bayesian Inference Method for Clipping Amplitude Recovery 184

Effects of Amplifier Nonlinearities Without Amplitude Clipping . 187

Adaptive Predistortion Techniques 190

Coding Techniques for Amplifier Nonlinear Distortion Mitigation 197

Partial Transmit Sequence Techniques 198

Modification of the PTS Algorithm 199

Selective Mapping 202

Phase Noise 205

IQ Imbalance 208

Bibliography 210

6   Medium Access Control (MAC) for IEEE 802.11 Networks   215

MAC Overview 216

MAC Services 217

MAC Frames 218

MAC Information Management 219

MAC System Architecture 219

Basic Service Sets 219

Extended Service Sets 221

MAC Frame Formats 222

IEEE 802.11 Frame Format 222

MAC Frame Subtypes 227

Frame Fragmentation 229

MAC Data Services 231

Distributed Coordination Function 231

Point Coordination Function 234

Frame Exchange with RTS/CTS 238

MAC Management Services 239

Power Management 239

Synchronization 243

Session Management 246

Privacy 250

MAC Management Information Base 251

Station Management Attributes 251

MAC Attributes 254

Bibliography 256

7 Medium Access Control (MAC) for HiperLAN/2 Networks 257

Network Architecture 259

DLC Functions 260

MAC Overview 261

Basic MAC Message Formats 262

Transport Channels 264

PDU Trains 266

Logical Channels 268

MAC Frame Structure 269

Order of the Transport Channels... 271

Schedule Addressing 271

Building a MAC Frame 273

MAC Frame Processing 274

Access Point... 274

Mobile Terminal.. 275

Bibliography 275

8 Rapid Prototyping for WLANs 277

Introduction to Rapid Prototype Design... 278

An Example of a Rapid Prototype Design Flow 280

Good Digital Design Practices 284

Rapid Prototyping of a WLAN System... 290

IEEE 802.11a Transmitter.. 292

IEEE 802.11a Receiver 293

IEEE 802.11a Baseband Demonstrator.. 295

Bibliography 298

Index 299

Preface

This book will address the subject of broadband communications using orthogonal frequency division multiplexing (OFDM). OFDM is a special case of multicarrier modulation (MCM), which is the principle of transmitting data by dividing the stream into several parallel bit streams and modulating each of these data stream onto individual carriers or subcarriers. Although the origin of MCM dates back to the 1950s and early 1960s with military high frequency (HF) radio links, R.W. Chang in the mid 60s first published a paper demonstrating the concept we today call OFDM. Chang demonstrated the principle of transmission of multiple messages simultaneously through a linear band-limited channel without *interchannel interference* (ICI) and *intersymbol interference* (ISI). The multichannel or OFDM system developed by Chang differed from traditional MCM in that the spectra of the subcarriers were allowed to overlap under the restriction they were all mutually orthogonal. This characteristic of OFDM systems required the abandonment of steep bandpass filters used in older MCM systems to separate the spectra of the individual subcarriers.

Weinsten and Ebert were the first to suggest using the *discrete Fourier Transform* (DFT) and *inverse discrete Fourier Transform* (IDFT) to perform baseband modulation and demodulation in 1971. Currently, OFDM systems utilize the Fast Fourier Transform (FFT) and Inverse FFT to perform modulating and demodulating of the information data. Saltzberg performed a performance analysis of OFDM, shortly after Chang published his paper, and concluded that the dominate impairment in OFDM is ICI. To combat ICI and ISI, Peled and Ruiz introduced the concept of a cyclic prefix (CP). Rather than using an empty guard space, a cyclic extension of the OFDM symbol is used instead. This effectively simulates a channel performing circular convolution as long as the CP is longer than the impulse response of the channel. The penalty of using a CP is loss of signal energy proportional to the length of the CP, yet the benefits of using a CP generally outweighs any loss of signal energy.

Presently, OFDM appears in several standards relating to wireless communications at high data rates such as terrestrial digital audio broadcasting (DAB) and digital video broadcasting (DVB-T) in Europe. Presumably, one of the reasons OFDM was chosen as the DAB standard is that it is possible to deploy single frequency subnetworks within its main networks. Hence, main and relay broadcast transmitters may use the same set of subcarriers. In areas with reception from multiple transmitters, receive diversity gains are experienced. Based on coded OFDM, DVB-T is the youngest and most sophisticated of the three core DVB systems. Combining channel coding with OFDM permits reliable transmission over dispersing channels. Furthermore, the inherent structure of OFDM allows for flexible transmission rates.

Finally, WLAN, the main subject of this book, is another application for OFDM technology. For instance, next generation wireless LAN standards such as IEEE 802.11a, High Performance Local Area Network type 2 (HiperLAN/2), and Mobile Multimedia Access Communication

(MMAC) system have accepted OFDM as their physical layer specifications. These WLAN systems also incorporate coding with OFDM to combat dispersing channels. It has been shown that coded OFDM modulation over modest dispersing channels can improve, rather than deteriorate, the reliability of the transmission. This interesting counterintuitive phenomenon can be attributed to the inherent frequency diversity provided by OFDM. Arguably, this characteristic is the most attractive feature of OFDM.

Interactive Learning

Clearly with the growing in interest in OFDM for high data rate wireless communications, in particular WLANs, there is a need in the technical community for a book that reviews the subject of OFDM WLANs. Typically, this is accomplished in a classroom setting. Unfortunately, many engineers and scientists today cannot afford the time required to attend classes at a university. What is needed is a tool to allow each reader to learn each of the concepts presented in the chapters at his/her own pace. We have provided that by means of an interactive simulation environment. Please visit our Web site at http://www.samspublishing.com and search for the OFDM book. More specifically, the site contains a complete OFDM WLAN physical layer simulation developed in MATLAB. We developed the simulation tool to illustrate the concepts discussed in Chapters 2–5.

To aid in the learning process, exercises are provided in each of these chapters. The exercises require the use of the OFDM system simulation tool and the simple programs you develop. Most of the examples given in this book are reproducible with the simulation program. The OFDM system simulation is executed through a graphical user interface (GUI) to facilitate system reconfigurability. The GUI is called from the MATLAB command window, which allows users to test quickly and easily many of the concepts in this book with a few clicks of the mouse. The novice and expert alike will thoroughly enjoy the endless combinations of test conditions available to them. With this learning tool, readers can further improve their understanding of the concepts presented in this book. In addition, readers interested in testing their algorithms over a WLAN environment will save months of software development time by using the simulation program located at our Web site.

Intended Audience

The primary audiences for this book are engineers and scientists without prior knowledge of OFDM. In the development of the text, we consider our primary audience to fall within two broad categories of readers: novice and advanced. For the novice, we envision someone with a background in engineering, mathematics, and some knowledge of communication theory. For that audience, this book provides the basics of OFDM theory with many examples and illustrations demonstrating concepts. An example novice reader might be a researcher in digital image processing, who is in interested in understanding what effects does an OFDM WLAN network might have on the quality of the video. Another example of the novice reader could be a radio frequency (RF) engineer, who is interested in the additional requirements imposed by OFDM modulation on the RF subsystems in the access point (AP) and mobile terminal (MT).

An example of an advanced reader is an engineer or scientist familiar with basic OFDM concepts. For those individuals, this book is intended as a source for practical guidelines as well as introductory material of advanced research topics in OFDM.

The secondary audiences for this book include individuals, such as network system engineers, product engineers, or managers, for whom some of the mathematical development presented in this text is slightly beyond their scope of understanding. For those individuals, explanatory text is provided throughout this book to give an intuitive feel of many of the concepts discussed.

It is assumed that the all audiences have a background in calculus, physics, and random and stochastic processes. Thus, the majority of the text in this book is written at the undergraduate level, with the exception of the advanced research topics, which are written at the first-year graduate level. In addition, the reader will be provided in each chapter all the relevant mathematical foundations necessary to understand the OFDM principles discussed. As mentioned earlier, explanatory text is also given to provide a better understanding of these OFDM principles from the mathematical expressions.

A final point concerning the audience: to reap the fullest benefit of this book, it is advantageous to the reader to become proficient in the use of MATLAB.

We expect this book to attract a broad range of readers, as it is written to do so. Certainly, no book can be all things to everyone. However, no matter your interest level in OFDM WLANs, this book has some insight to offer.

Organization of this Book

This book is organized as follows. Chapter 1, "Background and WLAN Overview," is dedicated to background material as well as an overview of OFDM WLANs. The background material covers relevant concepts in digital signal and stochastic processing. It expected that readers will refer to this chapter as needed to understand the concepts in latter chapters. Chapters 2–5 focus on the physical layer specifications of OFDM WLAN. Chapter 2, "Synchronization," provides a detailed discussion of many of the popular synchronization algorithms used in OFDM networks. Specifically, timing synchronization algorithms, which include packet detection, symbol timing recovery, and sample clock tracking, are covered. Also covered are frequency, channel estimation, and clear channel assessment (CCA) algorithms. Chapter 3, "Modulation and Coding," provides a brief overview of modulation and coding techniques. In particular, the phase-shift keying (PSK) and quadrature amplitude modulations (QAM) found in OFDM WLAN standards are covered. With respect of channel coding, discussions on block and convolutional codes are provided. Performance evaluation of several operational modes of the IEEE 802.11a physical specification are given. Chapter 3 can be thought of as the central theme or key technology area of current OFDM WLAN systems.

Chapter 4, "Antenna Diversity," is dedicated to the central theme or key technology area of future OFDM WLAN, antenna diversity. Several popular transmit and receive diversity schemes are discussed in their context to OFDM systems. Examples show that drastic improvement in error rate performance is achievable when these techniques are deployed. Chapter 5, "RF Distortion Analysis for OFDM WLANs," focuses on the system impairments of the OFDM system resulting from RF nonlinearities. Particularly attention is given to the peak-to-average power (PAPR) problem present in all OFDM systems. In this chapter, a survey of the more popular techniques to handle this problem is analyzed. In addition, other system impairments such as phase noise and in-phase and quadrature (IQ) imbalances are covered.

In Chapters 6 and 7, an introduction of the medium access control (MAC) layer is given. Chapter 6, "Medium Access Control (MAC) for IEEE 802.11 Networks," summarizes the IEEE 802.11a MAC, while Chapter 7, "Medium Access Control (MAC) for HiperLAN/2 Networks," summarizes the HiperLAN/2 MAC. Both chapter details of the interaction between the MAC layer and the physical layer.

Interestingly, a major criticism of OFDM has been the complexity issues associated with real-time implementation of the FFT and IFFT. However, steady improvements in semiconductor process technology has allowed for real-time prototyping of OFDM systems with Field Programmable Gate Array (FPGA) technology and cost effective solutions with Application Specific Integrated Circuit (ASIC) technology. Chapter 8, "Rapid Prototying of WLANs Using FPGA," is dedicated to the issues associated with real-time prototyping of an IEEE 802.11a radio using FPGA technology.

About the Authors

John Terry, Ph.D., is a senior research engineer at Nokia Research Center in Dallas, TX. He is currently managing the OFDM modulation and coding project in the High Speed Access (HSA) group. Dr. Terry has published several conference and journal papers, given numerous presentations on wireless communications, and generated six pending patents related to OFDM wireless LANs. He has 12 years of experience working in wireless communications, including tenures at NASA Glen Research Center and Texas Instruments, Inc. In addition, Dr. Terry is the vice-chair of the IEEE 802.11 Task Group g and serves as a technical reviewer for several conference and journal publications of the IEEE in wireless communications. Dr. Terry was the recipient of the 2002 Black Engineer of the Year Award for Outstanding Technical Contributions in Industy.

Juha Heiskala is a senior research engineer at Nokia Research Center in Dallas, TX. He is active in the IEEE 802.11 standards bodies and has been tasked with developing the 802.11a system simulation on several software platforms. He is the inventor/co-inventor of three pending patents in the area of OFDM LANs and co-designed with Dr. John Terry the modulation and coding scheme for achieving 100 Mbps speeds within currently allocated bandwidth specifications for OFDM wireless LANs.

About the Technical Editors

Douglas Williams received B.S.E.E., M.S., and Ph.D. degrees in electrical and computer engineering from Rice University, Houston, Texas, in 1984, 1987, and 1989, respectively. In 1989, he joined the faculty of the School of Electrical and Computer Engineering at the Georgia Institute of Technology, Atlanta, Georgia, where he is currently an Associate Professor. There he is also affiliated with the Center for Signal and Image Processing and teaches courses in signal processing and telecommunications. Dr. Williams has served as an Associate Editor of the IEEE Transactions on Signal Processing and is a member of the IEEE Signal Processing Society's Signal Processing Theory and Methods technical committee. He was co-editor of the *Digital Signal Processing Handbook* published in 1998 by CRC Press and IEEE Press. Dr. Williams is a member of the Tau Beta Pi, Eta Kappa Nu, and Phi Beta Kappa honor societies.

Anthony Reid received his B.S.E.E. (cum laude), from Rensselaer Polytechnic Institute, Troy, New York, M.S.E.E., from Stanford University, Palo Alto, California and Ph.D., from Southern Methodist University (S.M.U.), Dallas, Texas. Dr. Reid is currently a Principal Research Scientist at Nokia Research Center doing applied research in modulation, coding and equalization for 3-G (third generation) wireless systems. He also worked at Nortel Networks on Advanced Network Architectures for 3-G wireless networks. Before joining Nortel and Nokia, Tony was an Engineering Fellow and Branch Manager of Advanced Signal Processing in the Systems Technology Center in Raytheon Systems Corp. (RSC). This group developed broadband communications systems capability for both military and commercial applications. In the commercial arena capabilities were developed for high-speed SATCOM modems. In the past, this group developed image and signal processing algorithms for autonomous detection/tracking of military targets in infrared imagery and radar.

Dedication

To my son Amiel Terry and the fond memory of my grandfather, John D. Terry, both of whom made it possible for this work to be completed.

—John

To my parents.

—Juha

Acknowledgments

The authors of this book will like to thank the reviewers, Dr. Tony Reid from Nokia Research Center in Dallas and Prof. Douglas Williams from Georgia Institute of Technology, for their invaluable comments, which greatly improved the content of this book. Finally, the authors would like to express their deepest gratitude to Nokia, Inc. for providing the opportunity to work in this new and exciting area of wireless communications.

Tell Us What You Think!

As the reader of this book, *you* are our most important critic and commentator. We value your opinion and want to know what we're doing right, what we could do better, what areas you'd like to see us publish in, and any other words of wisdom you're willing to pass our way.

As an associate publisher for Sams Publishing, I welcome your comments. You can e-mail or write me directly to let me know what you did or didn't like about this book—as well as what we can do to make our books stronger.

Please note that I cannot help you with technical problems related to the topic of this book, and that due to the high volume of mail I receive, I might not be able to reply to every message.

When you write, please be sure to include this book's title and author as well as your name and phone or fax number. I will carefully review your comments and share them with the author and editors who worked on the book.

Email: `feedback@samspublishing.com`

Mail: Michael Stephens
          Executive Editor
          Sams Publishing
          800 East 96th Street
          Indianapolis, IN 46240 USA

Background and WLAN Overview

IN THIS CHAPTER

- Review of Stochastic Processes and Random Variables   2

- Review of Discrete-Time Signal Processing   6

- Components of a Digital Communication System   12

- OFDM WLAN Overview   31

- Single Carrier Versus OFDM Comparison   38

- Bibliography   45

Before delving into the details of orthogonal frequency division multiplexing (OFDM), relevant background material must be presented first. The purpose of this chapter is to provide the necessary building blocks for the development of OFDM principles. Included in this chapter are reviews of stochastic and random process, discrete-time signals and systems, and the Discrete Fourier Transform (DFT). Tooled with the necessary mathematical foundation, we proceed with an overview of digital communication systems and OFDM communication systems. We conclude the chapter with summaries of the OFDM wireless LAN standards currently in existence and a high-level comparison of single carrier systems versus OFDM.

The main objective of a communication system is to convey information over a channel. The subject of digital communications involves the transmission of information in digital form from one location to another. The attractiveness of digital communications is the ease with which digital signals are recovered as compared to their analog counterparts. Analog signals are continuous-time waveforms and any amount of noise introduced into the signal bandwidth can not be removed by amplification or filtering. In contrast, digital signals are generated from a finite set of discrete values; even when noise is present with the signal, it is possible to reliably recover the information bit stream exactly. In the sections to follow, brief reviews of stochastic random processes and discrete-time signal processing are given to facilitate presentation of concepts introduced later.

Review of Stochastic Processes and Random Variables

The necessity for reviewing the subject of random processes in this text is that many digital communication signals [20, 21, 22, 25] can be characterized by a *random or stochastic process*. In general, a signal can be broadly classified as either *deterministic* or *random*. Deterministic signals or waveforms can be known precisely at instant of time, usually expressed as a mathematical function of time. In constrast, random signals or waveforms always possess a measure of uncertainty in their values at any instant in time since random variables are rules for assigning a real number for every outcome ξ of a probabilistic event. In other words, deterministic signals can be reproduced exactly with repeated measurements and random signals cannot.

A stochastic or random process is a rule of correspondence for assigning to every outcome ξ to a function $X(t, \xi)$, where t denotes time. In other words, a stochastic process is a family of time-functions that depends on the parameter ξ. When random variables are observed over very long periods, certain regularities in their behavior are exhibited. These behaviors are generally described in terms of probabilities and statistical averages such as the mean, variance, and correlation. Properties of the averages, such as the notion of stationarity and ergodicity, are briefly introduced in this section.

Random Variables

A random variable is a mapping between a discrete or continuous random event and a real number. The *distribution function, $F_X(\alpha)$,* of the random variable, X, is given by

$$F_X(\alpha) = \Pr(X \le \alpha) \tag{1.1}$$

where $\Pr(X \le \alpha)$ is the probability that the value taken on by the random variable X is less than or equal to a real number α. The distribution function $F_X(\alpha)$ has the following properties:

- $0 \le F_X(\alpha) \le 1$
- $F_X(\alpha) \le F_X(\beta)$ if $\alpha \le \beta$
- $F_X(-\infty) = 0$
- $F_X(+\infty) = 1$

Another useful statistical characterization of a random variable is the *probability density function* (pdf), $f_X(\alpha)$, defined as

$$f_X(\alpha) = \frac{\partial}{\partial \alpha} F_X(\alpha) \tag{1.2}$$

Based on properties of $F_X(\alpha)$ and noting the relationship in Equation 1.2, the following properties of the pdf easily deducted:

- $f_X(\alpha) \ge 0$

- $\int_{-\infty}^{\infty} f_X(\alpha)\partial\alpha = F_X(+\infty) - F_X(-\infty) = 1$

Thus, the pdf is always a nonnegative function with unit area.

Ensemble Averages

In practice, complete statistical characterization of a random variable is rarely available. In many applications, however, the average or *expected value* behavior of a random variable is sufficient. In latter chapters of this book, emphasis is placed on the expected value of a random variable or function of a random variable. The mean or expected value of a continuous random variable is defined as

$$m_X = E\{X\} = \int_{-\infty}^{\infty} \alpha f_X(\alpha)\partial\alpha \tag{1.3}$$

and a discrete random variable as

$$m_X = E\{X\} = \sum_k \alpha_k \Pr(X = \alpha_k) \tag{1.4}$$

where $E\{\cdot\}$ is called the expected value operator. A very important quantity in communication systems is the *mean squared value* of a random variable, X, which is defined as

$$E\{X^2\} = \int_{-\infty}^{\infty} \alpha^2 f_X(\alpha)\partial\alpha \qquad (1.5)$$

for continuous random variables and

$$E\{X^2\} = \sum_k \alpha_k^2 \Pr(X = \alpha_k) \qquad (1.6)$$

for discrete random variables. The mean squared value of a random variables is a measure of the average power of a random variable. The *variance* of X is the mean of the second central moment and defined as

$$\sigma_X^2 = E\{(X - m_X)^2\} = \int_{-\infty}^{\infty} (\alpha - m_X)^2 f_X(\alpha)\partial\alpha \qquad (1.7)$$

Note a similar definition holds for the variance of discrete random variables by replacing the integral with a summation. The variance is a measure of the "random" spread of the random variable X. Another well-cited characteristic of a random X is its *standard deviation* σ_X, which is defined as the square root of its variance. One point worth noting is the relationship between the variance and mean square value of a random variable, i.e.,

$$\begin{aligned}
\sigma_X^2 &= E\{X^2 - 2Xm_X + m_X^2\} \\
&= E\{X^2\} - 2E\{X\}m_X + m_X^2 \\
&= E\{X^2\} - m_X^2
\end{aligned} \qquad (1.8)$$

In view of Equation 1.8, the variance is simply the difference between the mean square value and the square of the mean.

Two additional ensemble averages importantance in the study of random variables are the correlation and covariance. Both quantities are expressions of the interdependence of two or more random variables to each other. The correlation between complex random variables X and Y, r_{XY}, is defined as

$$r_{XY} = E\{XY^*\} \qquad (1.9)$$

where * denotes the complex conjugate of the complex random variable. A closely related quantity to the correlation of between random variables is their covariance c_{XY}, which it is defined as

$$c_{XY} = E\{[X - m_X][Y - m_Y]^*\} = E\{XY^*\} - m_X m_Y^* \tag{1.10}$$

Clearly, if either X or Y has zero mean, the covariance is equal to the correlation. The random variables X and Y need not stem from separate probabilistic events; in fact, X and Y can be samples of the same event A observed at two different time instants t_1 and t_2. For this situation, the correlation r_{XY} and covariance c_{XY} become the autocorrelation $R_X(t_1, t_2)$ and autocovariance $C_X(t_1, t_2)$, respectively, which are defined as

$$R_X(t_1, t_2) = E\{X(t_1)X^*(t_2)\}$$
$$C_X(t_1, t_2) = E\{[X(t_1) - m_X(t_1)][X(t_2) - m_X(t_2)]^*\} \tag{1.11}$$

Thus, the autocorrelation and autocovariance are measures of the degree to which two time samples of the same random process are related.

There are many examples of random variables that arise in which one random variable does not depend on the value of another. Such random variables are said to be statistically independent. A more precise expression of the meaning of statistical independence is given in the following definition.

Definition 1 *Two random variables X and Y are said to be statistically independent if the joint probability density function is equal to the product of the individual pdfs, i.e.,*

$$f_{XY}(\alpha, \beta) = f_X(\alpha) f_Y(\beta) \tag{1.12}$$

A weaker form of independence occurs when the correlation r_{XY} between two random variables is equal to the product of their means, i.e.,

$$r_{XY} = E\{XY^*\} = m_X m_Y^* \tag{1.13}$$

Two random variables that satisfy Equation 1.13 are said to be *uncorrelated*. Note that since

$$c_{XY} = r_{XY} - m_X m_Y^* \tag{1.14}$$

then two random variables X and Y will be uncorrelated if their covariance is zero. Note, statistically independent random variables are always uncorrelated. The converse, however, is usually not true in general.

Up to this point, most of the discussions have focused on random variables. In this section, we focus on random processes. Previously, we stated that a random process is a rule of correspondence for assigning to every outcome ξ of a probabilistic event to a function $X(t, \xi)$. A collection of $X(t, \xi)$ resulting from many outcomes defines an ensemble for $X(t, \xi)$. Another, more useful, definition for a random process is an indexed sequence of random variables. A random process is said to be *stationary* in the *strict-sense* if none of its statistics are affected by a shift in time origin. In other words, the statistics depend on the length of time it is observed and not when it is started. Furthermore, a random process is said to be *wide-sense stationary* (WSS) if its mean and variance do not vary with a shift in the time origin, i.e.,

$$m_X = E\{X(k)\} = a \; constant, \quad \forall k$$

and

$$R_X = (\tau + k, k) = R_X(\tau)$$

Strict-sense stationarity implies wide-sense stationary, but not vice versa. Most random processes in communication theory are assumed WSS. From a practical view, it is not necessary for a random process to be stationary for all time, but only for some observation interval of interest. Note that the autocorrelation function for a WSS process depends only on time difference τ. For zero mean WSS processes, $R_X(\tau)$ indicates the time over which samples of the random process X are correlated. The autocorrelation of WSS processes has the following properties:

- $R_X(\tau) = R_X(-\tau)$
- $R_X(\tau) \le R_X(0)$ for all τ
- $R_X(0) = E\{X^2(t)\}$

Unfortunately, computing m_X and $R_X(\tau)$ by ensemble averaging requires knowledge of a collection realizations of the random process, which is not normally available. Therefore, time averages from a single realization are generally used. Random processes whose time averages equal their ensemble averages are known as *ergodic processes.*

Review of Discrete-Time Signal Processing

In this brief overview of discrete-time signal processing, emphasis is placed on the specification and characterization of discrete-time signals and discrete-time systems. The review of stochastic processes and random variables was useful to model most digital communication signals. A review of linear discrete-time signal processing, on the other hand, is needed to model the effects of the channel on digital communication signals. Digital-time signal processing is a vast and well-documented area of engineering. For interested readers, there are several excellent texts [7, 10, 18] that give a more rigorous treatment of discrete-time signal processing to supplement the material given in this section.

Discrete-Time Signals

A discrete-time signal is simply an indexed sequence of real or complex numbers. Hence, a random process is also a discrete-time signal. Many discrete-time signals arise from sampling a continuous-time signal, such as video or speech, with an analog-to-digital (A/D) converter. We refer interested readers to "Discrete-Time Signals" for further details on A/D converters and sampled continuous-time signals. Other discrete-time signals are considered to occur naturally such as time of arrival of employees to work, the number of cars on a freeway at an instant of time, and population statistics. For most information-bearing signals of practical interest, three simple yet important discrete-time signals are used frequently to described them. These are the unit sample, unit step, and the complex exponential. The *unit sample,* denoted by $\delta(n)$, is defined as

$$\delta(n) = \begin{cases} 1, & n = 0 \\ 0, & n \neq 0 \end{cases} \qquad (1.15)$$

The unit sample may be used to represent an arbitrary signal as a sum of weighted sample as follows

$$x(n) = \sum_{k=-\infty}^{\infty} x(k)\delta(n-k) \qquad (1.16)$$

This decomposition is the discrete version of the *sifting property* for continuous-time signals. The *unit step,* denoted by $u(n)$, defined as

$$u(n) = \begin{cases} 1, & n \geq 0 \\ 0, & n < 0 \end{cases} \qquad (1.17)$$

and is related to the unit sample by

$$u(n) = \sum_{k=-\infty}^{\infty} \delta(k) \qquad (1.18)$$

Finally, the *complex exponential* is defined as

$$e^{jn\omega_0} = \cos(n\omega_0) + j\sin(n\omega_0) \qquad (1.19)$$

where ω_0 is some real constant measured in radians. Later in the book, we will see that complex exponentials are extremely useful for analyzing linear systems and performing Fourier decompositions.

Discrete-Time Systems

A discrete-time system is a rule of correspondence that transforms an input signal into the output signal. The notation $T[\cdot]$ will be used to represent a general transformation. Our discussions shall be limited to a special class of discrete-time systems called *linear shift-invariant* (LSI) systems.

As a notation aside, discrete-time systems are usually classified in terms of properties they possess. The most common properties include linearity, shift-invariance, causality, and stability, which are described below.

Linearity and Shift-Invariance

Two of the most desirable properties of discrete-time system for ease of analysis and design are *linearity* and *shift-invariance*. A system is said to be *linear* if the response to the superposition of weighted input signals is the superposition of the corresponding individual outputs weighted in accordance to the input signals, i.e.,

$$y = T[\alpha x_1 + \beta x_2] = \alpha T[x_1] + \beta T[x_2] \tag{1.20}$$

A system is said to be shift-invariant if a shift in the input by n_0 results in a shift in the output by n_0. In other words, shift-invariance means that the properties of the system do not change with time.

Causality

A very important property for real-time applications is *causality*. A system is said to be *causal* if the response of the system at time n_0 does not depend of future input values, i.e.,

$$y(n_0) = T[x(n - \tau)], \qquad 0 \le \tau \le \infty \tag{1.21}$$

Thus, for a causal system, it is not possible for changes in the output to precede changes in the input.

Stability

In many applications, it is important for a system to have a response that is bounded in amplitude whenever the input is bounded. In other words, if the unit sample response of LSI system is absolutely summable, i.e.,

$$\sum_{n=-\infty}^{\infty} |h(n)| < \infty \tag{1.22}$$

then for any bounded input $|x(n)| \le A < \infty$ the output is bounded $|y(n)| \le B < \infty$. This system is said to be *stable* in the Bounded-Input Bounded-Output (BIBO) sense. There are many other definitions for stability for a system, which can be found in [7, 18]; however, BIBO is one of the most frequently used.

Thus far, we have discussed only the properties of LSI systems without providing an example of it. Consider an LSI system whose q coefficients are contained in the vector h. The response of the system to an input sequence $x(n)$ is given by the following relationship

$$y(n) = \sum_{k=0}^{q} x(k)h(n-k) \tag{1.23}$$

is referred to as a *Finite length Impulse Response* (FIR) system. Notice that the output depends only on the input values in the system. It is possible, however, for the output of the system to depend on past outputs of the system as well as the current inputs, i.e.,

$$y(n) = \sum_{k=0}^{q} x(k)h(n-k) - \sum_{k=1}^{p} y(k)g(n-k) \tag{1.24}$$

This type of system is referred to as an *Infinite length Impulse Response* (IIR) system.

Filtering Random Processes

Earlier we have mentioned that all digital communication signals can be viewed as random processes. Thus, it is important to qualify the effects filtering has on the statistics of a random process. Of particular importance are LSI filters because of their frequent use in signal representation, detection, and estimation. In this section, we examine the effects of LSI filtering on the mean and autocorrelation of an input random process.

Let $x(n)$ be a WSS random process with mean m_x, and autocorrelation $R_x(n)$. If $x(n)$ is filtered by a stable LSI filter having a unit sample response $h(n)$, the output $y(n)$ is a random process that is related to input random process $x(n)$ via the convolution sum

$$y(n) = x(n) * h(n) = \sum_{k=-\infty}^{\infty} h(k)x(n-k) \tag{1.25}$$

The mean of $y(n)$, m_y, is found by taking the expected value of Equation 1.25 as follows,

$$E\{y(n)\} = E\left\{ \sum_{k=-\infty}^{\infty} h(k)x(n-k) \right\} = \sum_{k=-\infty}^{\infty} h(k)E\{x(n-k)\}$$

$$m_y = E\{y(n)\} = m_x \sum_{k=-\infty}^{\infty} h(k) = m_x H\!\left(e^{j0}\right)$$

where $H(e^{j0})$ is the zero-frequency response, or non-time varying response for the filter. Hence, the mean of $y(n)$ is a constant equal to the mean $x(n)$ scaled by the sample average of the unit sample response.

The autocorrelation of $y(n)$, is derived and understood best by first proceeding with the cross-correlation r_{yx} between $x(n)$ and $y(n)$, which is given by

$$r_{yx}(k) = E\{y(n+k)x^*(n)\} = E\left\{\sum_{l=-\infty}^{\infty} h(l)x(n+k-l)x^*(n)\right.$$

$$= \sum_{l=-\infty}^{\infty} h(l)E\{x(n+k-l)x^*(n)\} \qquad (1.26)$$

$$= \sum_{l=-\infty}^{\infty} h(l)r_x(k-l) = R_x(k) * h(k)$$

Recall, under the assumption of WSS, the cross-correlation r_{xy} depends only on the difference between sampling instants. It is interesting to note that the cross-correlation r_{xy} as defined in Equation 1.26 is just the convolution of the input autocorrelation $R_x(n)$ with the channel impulse response $h(n)$. We will use this result, shortly, to relate the output autocorrelation $R_y(n)$ to input autocorrelation $R_x(n)$.

The output autocorrelation is defined as

$$R_y(n) = E\{y(n+k)y^*(k)\} = E\left\{y(n+k)\sum_{l=-\infty}^{\infty} x^*(l)h^*(k-l)\right\}$$

$$= \sum_{l=-\infty}^{\infty} h^*(k-l)E\{y(n+k)x^*(l)\} \qquad (1.27)$$

$$= \sum_{l=-\infty}^{\infty} h^*(k-l)r_{yx}(n+k-l)$$

Inspection of Equation 1.27 reveals that the autocorrelation of $y(n)$, is really a convolution sum. Changing the index of summation by setting $m = l - k$, we obtain

$$R_y(n) = \sum_{l=-\infty}^{\infty} h^*(-m)r_{yx}(n-m) = r_{yx}(n) * h^*(-n) \qquad (1.28)$$

Combining Equations 1.26 and 1.28 we have

$$R_y(n) = R_x(n) * h(n) * h^*(-n) \qquad (1.29)$$

Equation 1.29 is a key result exploited often in the reception of wireless communication signals. Figure 1.1 illustrates the concepts expressed in Equations 1.26 and 1.28.

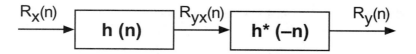

FIGURE 1.1

Input-output autocorrelation for filtered random processes.

Discrete Fourier Transform (DFT)

The Discrete Fourier Transform (DFT) is, arguably, the most widely used design and analysis tool in electrical engineering. For many situations, frequency-domain analysis of discrete-time signals and systems provide insights into their characteristics that are not easily ascertainable in the time-domain. The DFT is a discrete version of the discrete-time Fourier transforms (DTFT); that is, the DTFT is a function of a continuous frequency variable, whereas the DFT is a function of a discrete frequency variable. The DFT is useful because it is more amenable to digital implementations. The *N-point* DFT of a finite length sequence $x(n)$ is defined as

$$X(k) = \sum_{n=0}^{N-1} x(n)e^{-j2\pi kn/N} \qquad DFT \qquad (1.30)$$

Clearly, it can be seen from Equation 1.30 that the DFT is a sample version of the DTFT, i.e.,

$$X(k) = X(\omega)\big|_{\omega=2\pi k/N} \qquad (1.31)$$

where

$$X(\omega) = \sum_{n=-\infty}^{\infty} x(n)e^{-jn\omega} \qquad (1.32)$$

The DFT has an inverse transformation called the *inverse DFT* (IDFT). The IDFT provides a means of recovering the finite length sequence $x(n)$ through the following relationship,

$$x(n) = \frac{1}{N} \sum_{k=0}^{N-1} X(k)e^{j2\pi kn/N} \qquad IDFT \qquad (1.33)$$

Let's now consider the DFTs of the discrete-time signals given in "Discrete-Time Signals," since they form the basic building blocks to generate more complex signals. Using the definition in Equation 1.15, the DFT of the unit sample $\delta(n)$ becomes

$$X(k) = \sum_{n=0}^{N-1} \delta(n)e^{-j2\pi kn/N} = 1 \qquad (1.34)$$

Using the definition of the unit step given in Equation 1.17, its DFT is given by

$$X(k) = \sum_{n=0}^{N-1} e^{-j2\pi kn/N} = N\delta(k)$$

(1.35)

The result in Equation 1.35 follows directly since, with the exception of the $n = 0$ term, each of the complex exponentials sums to zero over the sample period of length N. Finally, the DFT of the complex exponential is given by

$$X(k) = \sum_{n=0}^{N-1} e^{jn\omega_0} e^{-j2\pi kn/N} = N\delta(k - \frac{N\omega_0}{2\pi})$$

(1.36)

Besides the DFTs given above, some useful properties of the discrete Fourier transforms that facilitate communication system analysis are summarized in Table 1.1. where ⊛ denotes circular convolution, $(\cdot)_N$ denotes modulo-N operation, and * denotes the complex conjugate as previously defined. This concludes the review of the mathematical background material.

TABLE 1.1 Some Useful Properties of the DFT

Discrete-Time Signal		DFT
$x(n)$	↔	$X(k)$
$x(n - n_0)$	↔	$X(k)e^{-j2\pi kn_0/N}$
$\alpha x_1(n) + \beta x_2(n)$	↔	$\alpha X_1(k) + \beta X_2(k)$
$x^*(n)$	↔	$X((-k))_N$
$y(n) \circledast x(n)$	↔	$Y(k)X(k)$
$x^*((-n))_N$	↔	$X^*(k)$
$e^{-j2\pi mn/N} x(n)$	↔	$X((k - m))_N$

Components of a Digital Communication System

In this section, the basic elements of a digital communication system are reviewed. The fundamental principle that governs digital communications is the "divide and conquer" strategy. More specifically, the information source is divided into its smallest intrinsic content, referred to as a *bit*. Then each bit of information is transmitted reliably across the channel. In general, the information source may be either analog or digital. Analog sources are considered first since they require an additional processing step before transmission. Examples of analog sources used in our everyday lives are radios, cameras, and camcorders. Each of these devices is capable of generating analog signals, such as voice and music in the case of radios and video images in the case of camcorders. Unfortunately, an analog signal can not be transmitted directly by means of digital communications; it must be first converted into a suitable format. With reference to the top chain of Figure 1.2, each basic element and its corresponding receiver function will be reviewed in the order they appear left to right.

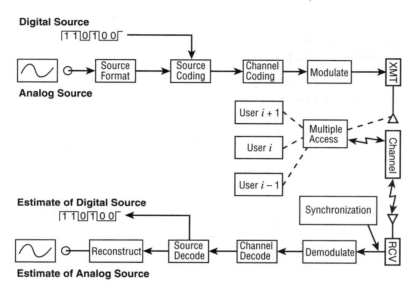

FIGURE 1.2

Basic elements of a digital communication system.

Source Formatting

Source formatting is the process by which an analog signal or continuous-time signal is converted into a digital signal. The device used to achieve this conversion is referred to as an *analog-to-digital (A/D)* converter. The basic elements of an A/D converter shown in Figure 1.3 consists of a sampler, quantizer, and encoder. The first component, the sampler, extracts sample values of the input signal at the sampling times. The output of the sampler is a discrete-time signal but with a continuous-valued amplitude. These signals are often referred to as *sampled data signals*; refer to Figure 1.4 for an illustration. Digital signals, by definition, are not permitted to have continuous-valued amplitudes; thus, the second component, the quantizer, is needed to quantize the continuous range of sample values into a finite number of sample values. Finally, the encoder maps each quantized sample value onto a digital word.

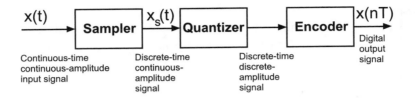

FIGURE 1.3

Basic elements of A/D converter.

Sampling and Reconstruction

To model the sampling operation of a continuous-time signal, we make use of a variant of the unit sample function $\delta(n)$ defined in "Discrete-Time Signals." An ideal sampler is a mathematical abstraction but is useful for analysis and given by

$$p(t) = \sum_{n=-\infty}^{\infty} \delta(t - nT_s) \tag{1.37}$$

where T_s is the sampling interval. Now, the sampled data signal $x_s(t)$ can be expressed as

$$x_s(t) = x(t)p(t) \tag{1.38}$$

where $x(t)$ is the continuous-time continuous-amplitude input signal as seen in Figure 1.4. Obviously, the more samples of the $x(t)$ we have, the easier it will be to reconstruct the signal. Each sample will be eventually transmitted over the channel. In order to save bandwidth, we would like to send the bare minimum number of samples needed to reconstruct the signal. The sampling rate that produces this is called the *Nyquist rate*. Nyquist sampling theorem states that samples taken at a uniform rate $2f_h$ where f_h is the highest frequency component of a band-limited signal $x(t)$, is sufficient to completely recover the signal. The Nyquist Sampling Theorem is conceptually illustrated in Figure 1.5. Notice first that sampling introduces periodic spectral copies of the original spectrum center at the origin. Second, the copies are sufficiently spaced apart such that they do not overlap. This simple principle is the essence of the Nyquist Sampling Theorem. If the spectral copies of the spectrum were permitted to overlap, aliasing of the spectral copies would occur. It would then be impossible to recover the original spectrum by passing it through a low-pass filter whose ideal frequency response is represented by the dashed box.

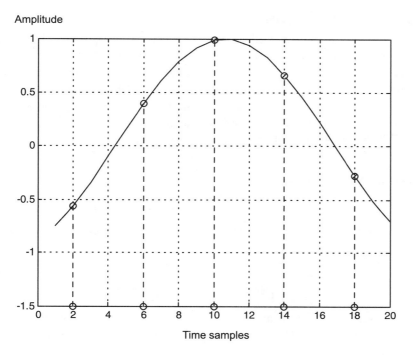

FIGURE 1.4

An example of a discrete-time continuous amplitude signal $X_s(t)$.

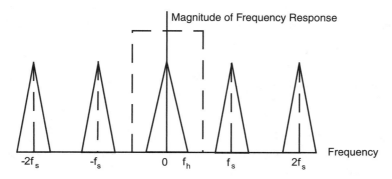

FIGURE 1.5

Spectrum of a sampled waveform.

Quantization and Encoding

After the signal has been sampled, the amplitude values must be quantized into a discrete set of values. The process of quantization entails rounding off the sample value to the nearest of a finite set of permissible values. Encoding is accomplished by assigning a digital word of length k, which represents the binary equivalent for the numerical value of the quantization level, as depicted in Figure 1.6. For example, at sampling time T, the amplitude of the signal lies within quantization level 12, which has a binary representation of 1101. Furthermore, the number of quantization levels q and the digital word length k are related by

$$q = 2^k$$

Another key observation that should be taken from Figure 1.6 is that the quantization process introduces an error source usually referred to as *quantization noise*. When decoding, it is usually assumed the amplitude falls at the center of the quantization level. Hence, the maximum error which can occur is $\pm \frac{1}{2} \Delta L$, where

$$\Delta L = \frac{A}{2^k} \tag{1.39}$$

and A is the difference between the maximum and minimum values of the continuous-time signal. If we assume a large number of quantization levels, error function is nearly linear within the quantization level, i.e.,

$$e(t) = \frac{\Delta L}{2\tau} t \tag{1.40}$$

where 2τ is the time the continuous-time signal remaining within the quantization level. The mean-square error P_n is thereby given by

$$P_n = \frac{1}{2\tau} \int_{-\tau}^{\tau} e^2(\lambda) \partial \lambda = \frac{\Delta L^2}{4\tau^3} \int_0^{\tau} \lambda^2 \partial \lambda \tag{1.41}$$

$$P_n = \frac{\Delta L^2}{12} \tag{1.42}$$

The quantity of most interest, however, is the *signal-to-noise ratio* (SNR) at the output of the A/D converter, which is defined as

$$SNR = \frac{P_s}{P_n} \tag{1.43}$$

where P_s and P_n are the power in the signal and noise, respectively. The signal power for an input sinusoidal signal is defined as

$$P_s = \frac{(A/2)^2}{2} = \Delta L^2 \left(2^{2k-3}\right) \tag{1.44}$$

which leads to a SNR of

$$SNR = \frac{12\Delta L^2 \left(2^{2k-1}\right)}{\Delta L^2} = \frac{3}{2}\left(2^{2k}\right) \tag{1.45}$$

or, in decibels,

$$SNR(dB) = 10\log_{10}(SNR) = 1.76 + 6.02k$$

Thus, the SNR at the output of the A/D converter increases by approximately 6 dB for each bit added to the word length, assuming the output signal is equal to the input signal to the A/D converter.

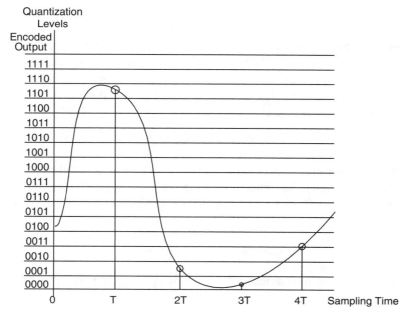

FIGURE 1.6

Quantization and digital encoding.

Source Coding

Source coding entails the efficient representation of information sources. For both discrete and continuous sources, the correlations between samples are exploited to produce an efficient representation of the information. The aim of source coding is either to improve the SNR for a given bit rate or to reduce the bit rate for a given SNR. An obvious benefit of the latter is a reduction in the necessary system resource of bandwidth and/or energy per bit to transmit the information source.

A discussion on source coding requires the definition of a quantity, which measures the average *self-information* in each discrete alphabet, termed *source entropy* [14]. The self-information $I(x_j)$ for discrete symbol or alphabet x_j is defined as

$$I(x_j) = -\log_2(p_j) \tag{1.46}$$

where p_j is the probability of occurrence for x_j. The source entropy $H(x_j)$ is found by taking the statistical expectation of the self-information, i.e.,

$$H(x_j) = E\{I(x_j)\} = -\sum_{j=1}^{M} p_j \log_2(p_j) \tag{1.47}$$

where M is the cardinality of the discrete alphabet set and the units of measure for $H(x_j)$ are bits/symbol. The source entropy can also be thought of as the average amount of uncertainty contained in the alphabet x_j. Therefore, the source entropy is the average amount of information that must be communicated across the channel per symbol. It can be easily shown that $H(x_j)$ is bounded by the following expression

$$0 \leq H(x_j) \leq \log_2 M \tag{1.48}$$

In other words, the source entropy is bounded below by zero if there is no uncertainty, and above by $\log_2 M$ if there is maximum uncertainty. As an example, consider a binary source x_j that generates independent symbols 0 and 1 with respective probabilities of p_0 and p_1. The source entropy is given by

$$H(x_j) = -\left[p_1 \log_2(p_1) + p_0 \log_2(p_0)\right] \tag{1.49}$$

Table 1.2 lists the source entropy as the probabilities of p_0 and p_1 are varied between 0 and 1.

TABLE 1.2   Source Entropy

p_0	p_1	$H(x_j)$
0.5	0.5	1.00
0.1	0.9	0.47
0.2	0.8	0.72

Table 1.2 illustrates that as the relative probabilities vary, the number of bits/symbol needed to transmit the information vary as well. One might wonder what information source would have such probabilistic distribution. English text, for instance, is known to have unequal probability for its alphabet; in other words, some letters appear in English text more frequently than others. Another key consideration when determining the source entropy is whether the source is *memoryless*. A discrete source is said to be memoryless if the sequence of symbols is statistically independent. The readers should refer to "Review of Stochastic Processes and Random Variables" for a definition of statistical independence. In contrast, if a discrete source is said to have memory, the sequence of symbols is not independent. Again, consider English text as an example. Given that the letter "q" has been transmitted, the next letter will probably be a "u." Transmission of the letter "u" as the next symbol resolves very little uncertainty from a communication perspective. We can thus conclude that the entropy of an *M*-tuple from a source with memory is always less than the entropy of a source with the same alphabet and symbol probability without memory, i.e.,

$$H_M(x_j)_{with\ memory} < H_M(x_j)_{without\ memory} \tag{1.50}$$

Another way to interpret the relationship in Equation 1.50 is that the average entropy per symbol of an *M*-tuple from a source with memory decreases as the length *M* increases. Hence it is more efficient to encode symbols from a source with memory three at a time than it is to encode them two at a time or one at a time. Encoder complexity, memory constraints, and delay considerations require that practical source encoding be performed on finite-length sequences. Interested readers are encouraged to examine References [8, 13, 15, 25] dealing with source coding.

Channel Coding

Channel coding refers to the class of signal transformations designed to improve communications performance by enabling the transmitted signal to better withstand the effects of various channel impairments, such as noise, fading, and jamming. The goal of channel coding is to improve the bit error rate (BER) performance of power-limited and/or bandwidth limited channels by adding structured redundancy to the transmitted data. The two major categories of channel coding are block coding and convolutional coding. In the following sections, we describe the fundamental principles governing each of these two types of codes.

Linear Block Codes

Linear block codes are a class of parity check codes that can be characterized by an integer pair (n, k). As such, the parity bits or symbols are formed by a linear sum of the information bits. In general, the encoder transforms any block of k message symbols into a longer block of n symbols called a *codeword*. A special class of linear block codes called systematic codes append the parity symbols to the end of the k symbol message to form the coded sequence. These codes are of particular interest since they result in encoders of reduced complexity.

For binary inputs, the k-bit messages, referred to as *k-tuples,* form 2^k distinct message sequences. The n-bit blocks, referred to as n-tuples, form 2^k distinct codewords or message sequences out of 2^n possible n-tuples in the finite dimensional vector space.

Hence, one can view linear block codes as a finite dimensional vector subspace defined over the extended Galois fields $GF(2^p)$. The transformation from a k-dimensional to an n-dimensional vector space is performed according to a linear mapping specified in the generator matrix $\mathbf{G}$. In other words, an (n, k) linear block code $\mathbf{C}$ is formed by partitioning the information sequence into message blocks of length k. Each message block $\mathbf{u}_i$ is encoded or mapped to a unique codeword or vector $\mathbf{v}_i$ in accordance with $\mathbf{G}$

$$\mathbf{v}_i = \mathbf{u}_i\mathbf{G} \tag{1.51}$$

Another useful matrix, often defined when describing linear block codes, is the parity-check matrix $\mathbf{H}$. The parity check matrix has the property that it generates code words that lie in the null space of $\mathbf{G}$. Mathematically, we describe this relationship as

$$\mathbf{G}\mathbf{H}^T = \mathbf{0}_{n-k} \tag{1.52}$$

where $\mathbf{0}_{n-k}$ is the zero vector of length $n - k$. As we will see in the following paragraphs, $\mathbf{H}$ plays an integral part in the detection process for linear block codes.

Consider a code vector $\mathbf{v}_i$ transmitted over a noisy channel. Denote the received vector from the channel as $\mathbf{r}_i$. The equation relating $\mathbf{r}_i$ to $\mathbf{v}_i$ is

$$\mathbf{r}_i = \mathbf{v}_i + \mathbf{e} \tag{1.53}$$

where $\mathbf{e}$ is an error pattern or vector from the noisy channel. At the receiver, the decoder tries to determine $\mathbf{v}_i$ given $\mathbf{r}_i$. This decision is accomplished using a two-step process: one, compute the *syndrome*; and two, add the *coset leader* corresponding to the syndrome to the received vector. We have just introduced two new terms that need defining. The syndrome $\mathbf{s}$ is defined as the projection of the received vector onto the subspace generated by $\mathbf{H}$

$$\mathbf{s}_i = \mathbf{r}_i\mathbf{H}^T \tag{1.54}$$

Using Equations 1.51–1.53, we see that Equation 1.54 simplifies to

$$\mathbf{s}_i = \mathbf{e}\mathbf{H}^T \tag{1.55}$$

The foregoing development is evidence that the syndrome test, whether performed on a corrupted codeword or on the error pattern that caused it, yields the same syndrome. An important property of linear block codes, fundamental in the decoding process, is the one-to-one mapping between correctable error patterns and the associated syndrome. This equivalence leads us to our discussion on coset leaders.

The coset leaders consist of all the correctable error patterns. A correctable error pattern is one whose *Hamming weight* is less than or equal to $\lfloor (d_{min} - 1)/2 \rfloor$, where $\lfloor x \rfloor$ means the largest integer not to exceed x, and d_{min} is defined as the minimum *Hamming distance* between any two code words for an (n, k) linear block code. For binary vectors, the Hamming weight is defined as the number of non-zero elements in a vector, and the Hamming distance between two code vectors is defined as the number of elements in which they differ. It is interesting to note that d_{min} for a linear block code is equal to the non-zero codeword with minimum Hamming weight. These concepts are easily generalized to the extended Galois field.

Note that there are exactly 2^{n-k} coset leaders for the binary case. Now, let's form a matrix as follows: first, list all the coset leaders in the first column; second, list all the possible code words in the top row; and, last, form the (i, j) element of the matrix from the sum of ith element of the first column with the jth element of the top row. The resulting matrix represents all possible received vectors and is often referred to as the *standard array*.

Now, we will relate how all the above fits into the decoding process. As stated earlier, the task of the decoder is to estimate the transmitted code vector, $\mathbf{v}_i$ from the received vector $\mathbf{r}_i$. The maximum likelihood solution $\hat{\mathbf{v}}_{ML}$ found by maximizing the conditional probability density function for the received vector for all possible code vectors $\mathbf{v}_j$; namely,

$$\hat{\mathbf{v}}_{ML} = \arg \max_{\mathbf{v}_j} \Pr\left(\mathbf{r}_i \big| \mathbf{v}_j\right) \tag{1.56}$$

The optimization criterion for Equation 1.56 over a binary symmetric channel (BSC) is to decide in favor of the code word that is the minimum Hamming distance from the received vector

$$d\left(\mathbf{r}_i, \mathbf{v}_i\right) = \min d\left(\mathbf{r}_i, \mathbf{v}_j\right) \quad \forall \mathbf{v}_j \tag{1.57}$$

A systematic procedure for the decoding process proceeds as follows:

1. Calculate the syndrome of $\mathbf{r}$ using $\mathbf{s} = \mathbf{r}\mathbf{H}^T$.
2. Locate the coset leader whose syndrome equals $\mathbf{r}\mathbf{H}^T$ from the standard array table.
3. This error pattern is added to the received vector to compute the estimate of $\mathbf{v}$ or read directly from the corresponding column in the standard array table.

Convolutional Codes

Another major category of channel coding is convolutional coding. An important characteristic of convolutional codes, different from block codes, is that the encoder has memory. That is, the n-tuple generated by the convolutional encoder is a function of not only the input k-tuple but also the previous $K - 1$ input k-tuples. The integer K is a parameter known as the *constraint length*, which represents the number of memory elements in the encoder. A shorthand convention typically employed in the description of a convolutional encoder is (n, k, K) for the integers defined above.

To understand the fundamental principles governing the convolutional codes, we direct our attention to the $(2,1,2)$ convolutional encoder depicted in Figure 1.7. This encoder, at any given sampling time instant, accepts k input bits, makes a transition from its current state to one of the 2^K possible successor states, and outputs n bits.

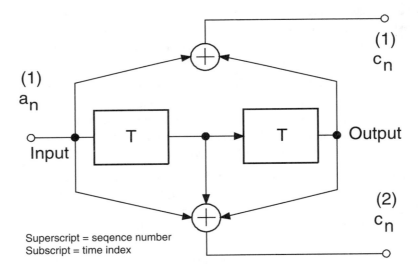

FIGURE 1.7
Four state convolutional encode.

The two noteworthy characteristics of a convolutional encoder are the tap connections and the contents of the memory elements. For the tap connections of the encoder, the generator polynomial representation is commonly used. Yet, for the state information as well as the output codewords, a state diagram or trellis diagram is typically employed.

With the generator polynomial representation, the taps for each output of the encoder are specified by a polynomial $g_i(D)$ where the coefficients of $g_i(D)$ are taken from $GF(2^p)$. Note, p equal to one corresponds to the binary field. For this case, a 1 coefficient denotes a connection and a 0 coefficient denotes no connection. The argument of the polynomial, D, denotes a unit time delay. In other words, we represent two unit time delays as D^2. The coded bits are formed by computing the sum over $GF(2^p)$ dictated by the tap coefficients. The two components of the sum are the current state of memory elements and the k input bits. To clarify these concepts, again consider the encoder shown in Figure 1.7. The generator polynomials for the outputs of this encoder are

$$g_1(D) = 1 + D^2 \tag{1.58}$$

$$g_2(D) = 1 + D + D^2 \tag{1.59}$$

We now briefly describe a method for viewing the state information as well as the output bits: the trellis diagram. We noted earlier that the convolutional encoder is a finite state machine. Thus, a natural way to describe its behavior is to view its state transition at each time instant. The state of the encoder is considered to be the contents of its memory elements. For a convolutional code with K memory elements, there are 2^K states. Each state is assigned a number from 0 to $2^K - 1$, which is obtained from the binary representation of its memory elements. The trellis diagram shows the state transitions and associated outputs for all possible inputs as seen in Figure 1.8. For binary inputs, solid and dashed lines are used, respectively, to represent a 0 or 1 input into the encoder. We also notice in the figure that there are two branches entering and leaving each state at every time instant. In general, there are 2^k branches emanating from each state and 2^k branches merging to each state. Each new sequence of k input bits causes a transition from an initial state to 2^k states at the next node in the trellis or time instant. Note, the encoder output is always uniquely determined by the initial state and the current input. Additionally, the trellis diagram shows the time evolution of the the states. Later, we will see that the trellis diagram is also very useful for evaluating the performance of these codes.

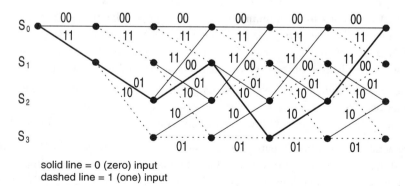

solid line = 0 (zero) input
dashed line = 1 (one) input

FIGURE 1.8

Trellis diagram for the four state convolutional encoder.

Note that after three stages into the trellis diagram, each node at subsequent stages has two branches entering and leaving it. Furthermore, it can be shown that the branches originate from a common node three stages back into the trellis. In general, for any constraint length (n, k, K) convolutional code, every K stages into the trellis diagram mark the point where 2^k branches merge and diverge at each node. Furthermore, the merging branches in a node can be traced back K stages into the past to the same originating node. This observation led to the development of a systematic approach for the optimum decoding of convolutional codes.

Decoder

As was the case for linear block codes, the decoder task is to estimate the transmitted code word from a received vector. It was shown that the optimum decoder strategy for linear block codes is to select the codeword with the minimum distance metric, the Hamming distance. The same is true for convolutional codes as well. Recall that an encoder for a convolutional code has memory. Thus, it is a reasonable approach to use all codewords associated with a particular symbol in the decision determination for it. Hence, for convolutional codes a sequence of codewords, or paths through the trellis, are compared to determine the transmitted codeword. In 1967, Viterbi [25] developed an algorithm that performs the maximum likelihood decoding with reduced computational load by taking advantage of the special structure of the code trellis.

The basis of *Viterbi decoding* is the following observation. If any two paths in the trellis merge to a single state, one of them can always be eliminated in the search for the optimum path. A summary of the Viterbi decoding algorithm proceeds as follows:

- Measure the similarity or distance between the received signals at each sampling instant t_i and all the paths entering each state or node at time t_i.

- The Viterbi algorithm eliminates from consideration the paths from the trellis whose distance metrics are not the minimum for a particular node. The distance metric can be either the Hamming distance or Euclidean distance. In other words, when two paths enter the same state, the one having the best distance metric is chosen. This path is called the *surviving path*. The selection of the surviving paths is performed for all the states.

- The decoder continues in this way, advancing deeper in the trellis and making decisions by elimination of least likely paths. In the process, the cumulative distance metric for each surviving path is recorded and used later to determine the maximum likelihood path.

The early rejection of the unlikely paths reduces the decoding complexity. In 1969, Omura [25] demonstrated that the Viterbi algorithm is, in fact, the maximum likelihood estimator. For a discussion of more advance of coding techniques, the reader is referred to Chapter 3, "Modulation and Coding," of this book.

Modulation

Modulation is the process by which information signals, analog or digital, are transformed into waveforms suitable for transmission across channel. Hence, digital modulation is the process by digital information are transform into digital waveforms. For baseband modulation, the waveforms are pulses; but for band-pass modulation, the information signals are transformed into radio frequency (RF) carriers, which have embedded the digital information. Since RF carriers are sinusoids, the three salient features are its amplitude, phase, and frequency. Therefore, digital band-pass modulation can be defined as the process whereby the amplitude, phase, or frequency of an RF carrier, or any combination of them, is varied in accordance with the digital information to be transmitted. The general form of a complex RF carrier is given by

$$s(t) = A(t)\exp(\omega_c t + \theta(t)) \tag{1.60}$$

where ω_c is the *radian frequency* of the carrier and $\theta(t)$ is the time-varying phase. The radian frequency of the RF carrier is related to its frequency in Hertz by

$$\omega_c = 2\pi f_c \tag{1.61}$$

At the receiver, the transmitted information embedded in the RF carrier must be recovered. When the receiver uses knowledge of the phase of the carrier to detect the signal, the process is called *coherent detection;* otherwise, the process is known as *non-coherent detection.* The advantage of non-coherent detection over coherent detection is reduced complexity at the price of increased probability of symbol error (P_E).

Whether the receiver uses coherent or non-coherent detection, it must decide which of the possible digital waveforms most closely resembles the received signal, taking into account the effects of the channel. A more rigorous treatment of common digital modulation formats and demodulation techniques is given in Chapter 3 of this book.

Multiple Access Techniques

Multiple access refers to the remote sharing of a fixed communication resource (CR), such as a wireless channel, by a group of users. For wireless communications, the CR can be thought of as a hyperplane in frequency and time. The goal of multiple access is to allow users to share the CR without creating unmanageable interferences with each other. In this section, we review the three most basic multiple access techniques for wireless communications: frequency division multiple access (FDMA), time division multiple access (TDMA), and code division multiple access (CDMA). Other more sophisticated techniques are combinations or variants of these three.

FDMA

In FDMA systems, the frequency-time plane is partitioned into non-overlapping frequency bands. The top graph in Figure 1.10 illustrates the FDMA concept. Each RF carrier in the FDMA system is assigned a specific frequency band within the allocated bandwidth specified by the

Federal Communications Commission (FCC). The spectral regions between adjacent channels are called guard bands, which help reduce the interferences between channels. As a result of the non-linearities of the power amplifier (PA) at the transmitter, signals experience spectral spreading—broadening of the bandwidth of the signal. The situation worsen when multiple RF carriers are present simultaneously in the PA, as in the case with OFDM, and adjacent channel interference may result. Another source of frequency domain distortions is co-channel interference.

Co-channel interference results when frequency reuse is employed in wireless communication systems as depicted in Figure 1.9. A frequency band is said to be reused when it is shared by two or more downlinks[*] of the base station. The co-channel reuse ratio (CRR) is defined as the ratio the distance d between cells using the same frequency to the cell radius r. The capacity of the cellular network can be increased by splitting existing cells into smaller cells but maintain the same d/r ratio. CRR is chosen to provide adequate protection against co-channel interference from neighboring sites. However, Jakes [12] shows that the interference protection degenerates in the presence of Rayleigh fading.

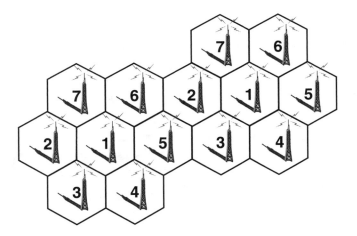

FIGURE 1.9

A macrocell layout using reuse factor of 7.

TDMA

In TDMA, sharing of the CR is accomplished by dividing the frequency-time plane into non-overlapping time slots which are transmitted in periodic bursts to the satellite. During the period of transmission, the entire allocated bandwidth is available to an user as illustrated in the middle graph of Figure 1.10. Time is segmented into intervals called frames. Each frame is further

---

[*]*The downlink transmission is the communication link originating from the base station and terminating at the mobile.*

partitioned into user assignable time slots. An integer number of time slots constitute a burst time or burst. Guard times are allotted between bursts to prevent overlapping of bursts. Each burst is comprised of a preamble and the message portion.

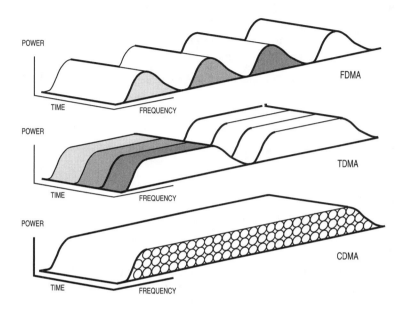

FIGURE 1.10

Communication resource hyperplane.

The preamble is the initial portion of a burst used for carrier and clock recovery and station-identification and other housekeeping tasks. The message portion of a burst contains the coded information sequence. In some systems, a training sequence is inserted in the middle of the coded information sequence. The advantage of this scheme is that it can aid the receiver in mitigating the effects of the channel and interferers. The disadvantage is that it lowers frame efficiency; that is, the ratio of the bit available for messages to the total frame length.

A point worth noting is that both FDMA and TDMA system performances degrade in the presence of the multipath fading. More specifically, due to the high transmission rates of the TDMA systems, the time dispersive channel (a consequence of delay spread phenomenon) causes inter-symbol interference (ISI). This is a serious problem in TDMA systems thus requiring adaptive techniques to maintain system performance.

CDMA

Unlike FDMA and TDMA who share only a portion of the frequency-time, CDMA systems share the entire frequency-time plane. Sharing of the CR is accomplished by assigning each user a unique quasi-orthogonal code as illustrated by the bottom graph of Figure 1.10.

Generally, CDMA is regarded as an application of direct sequence spread-spectrum techniques; a technique whereby the information signal is modulated by a high-speed (wideband) spreading signal and the resulting baseband signal is modulated onto an RF carrier. For digital communications, pseudonoise or pseudorandom (PN) signals are used as the spreading signals. Pseudonoise or pseudorandom signals are deterministic signals whose statistical properties are similar to sampled white noise. At the receiver in a CDMA system, the information signal is recovered by correlating the received spread signal with a synchronized replica of the spreading signal.

The ratio of the code chip rate and the data rate is called the processing gain GP. The processing gain represents the amount of interference protection provided by the code. Sklar [22] demonstrates that CDMA systems provide immunity to frequency selective fading and interferers by virtue of correlation property of the codes. Unfortunately, each additional user increases the overall noise level thus degrading the quality for all the users. In the next section, we describe the various impairments caused by the channel on the digital waveform.

Channel Model

In mobile wireless communications, the information signals are subjected to distortions caused by reflections and diffractions generated by the signals interacting with obstacles and terrain conditions as depicted in Figure 1.11. The distortions experienced by the communication signals include delay spread, attenuation in signal strength, and frequency broadening. Bello [1] shows that the unpredictable nature of the time variations in the channel may be described by narrowband random processes. For a large number of signal reflections impinging at the receiver, the central limit theorem can be invoked to model the distortions as complex-valued Gaussian random processes. The envelope of the received signals is comprised of two components: rapid-varying fluctuations superimposed onto slow-varying ones. When the mean envelope suffers a drastic reduction in signal strength resulting from "destructive" combining of the phase terms from the individual paths, the signal is said to be experiencing a *fade* in signal strength.

Multipath

In this section, we will develop a model to predict the effects of *multipath* on the transmitted communication signal. Multipath is a term used to describe the reception of multiple transmission paths to the receiver. As mentioned above, the channel can be accurately described by a random process; hence, the state of the channel will be characterized by its channel correlation function. The baseband transmit signal s(t) can be accurately modeled as narrowband process related to information bearing signal $x(t)$ by

$$s(t) = x(t)e^{-j2\pi f_c t} \tag{1.62}$$

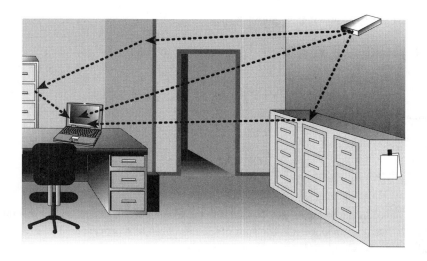

FIGURE 1.11

Multipath scattering in mobile communications.

Under the assumptions of Gaussian scatters and multiple propagation paths to the receiver, the channel is characterized by time-varying propagation delays, attenuation factors, and Doppler shifts. Proakis [21] shows that the time-variant impulse response is given by

$$c(\tau_n, t) = \sum_n \alpha_n(\tau_n(t)) e^{-j2\pi f_{D_n} \tau_n(t)} \delta[t - \tau_n(t)] \tag{1.63}$$

where

- $c(\tau_n, t)$ is the response of the channel at time t due to an impulse applied at time $t - \tau_n(t)$
- $\alpha_n(t)$ is the attenuation factor for the signal received on the nth path
- $\tau_n(t)$ is the propagation delay for the nth path
- f_{D_n} is the Doppler shift for the signal received on the nth path

The Doppler shift from relative motion between the vehicle and the receiver can be expressed as

$$f_{D_n} = \frac{v \cos(\phi_n)}{\lambda} \tag{1.64}$$

where v is the relative velocity of the vehicle, λ is the wavelength of the carrier, and ϕ_n is a random phase angle uniformly distributed from 0 to 2π.

Therefore, the output of the channel is simply the convolution of Equations 1.62 and 1.63, i.e.,

$$z(t) = c(\tau_n, t) * s(t) \tag{1.65a}$$

$$z(t) = \sum_n \alpha_n(\tau_n(t)) e^{-j2\pi(f_c + f_{D_n})\tau_n(t)} x[t - \tau_n(t)] e^{-j2\pi f_c t} \tag{1.65b}$$

$$z(t) = \sum_n \beta_n x[t - \tau_n(t)] e^{-j2\pi f_c t} \tag{1.65c}$$

where

$$x[t - \tau_n(t)] = \delta[t - \tau_n(t)] * x(t) \tag{1.66}$$

$$e^{-j2\pi(f_c + f_{D_n})\tau_n(t)} e^{-j2\pi f_c t} = \delta[t - \tau_n(t)] * e^{-j2\pi f_c t} e^{-j2\pi f_{D_n}\tau_n(t)} \tag{1.67}$$

and β_n is a Gaussian random process. Notice that the envelope of $c(\tau_n, t)$, at any instant t, exhibits a Rayleigh distribution since it is the sum of Gaussian random processes. The probability density function for a Rayleigh fading channel is given by

$$f_Z(Z) = \frac{Z}{\sigma^2} e^{-\frac{Z^2}{2\sigma^2}} \tag{1.68}$$

A channel with this distribution is typically termed a Rayleigh fading channel. In the event that there are fixed scatterers and a line of sight (LOS) path to the receiver, the envelope of $c(\tau_n, t)$ has a Rice distribution whose density is given by

$$f_Z(Z) = \frac{Z}{\sigma^2} I_0\left(\frac{Z\eta}{\sigma^2}\right) e^{-\frac{Z^2 + \eta^2}{2\sigma^2}} \tag{1.69}$$

where I_0 is the modified Bessel function of the zeroth kind and η is the mean due to the fixed scatters or LOS path. In this case, the channel is said to be a Rician fading channel.

Proakis [21] shows that the autocorrelation function for $c(\tau, t)$,

$$\Lambda_c(\tau, \Delta t) = E\{c(\tau, t) c^*(\tau, t + \Delta t)\}$$

can be measured in practice by transmitting very narrow pulses and cross correlating the received signal with a conjugate delayed version of itself. Also, the average power output of the channel is found by setting $\Delta t = 0$; i.e., $\Lambda_c(\tau, 0) \equiv \Lambda_c(\tau)$. This quantity is called the *multipath intensity profile* or the *delay power spectrum* of the channel. The range of values of τ over which $\Lambda_c(\tau)$ is essentially nonzero is called the *multipath spread* of the channel, denoted by T_m. The reciprocal of the multipath spread is a measure of the *coherence bandwidth* of the channel, i.e.,

$$B_m \approx \frac{1}{T_m} \tag{1.70}$$

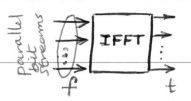

$f_i = f_c + \dfrac{i}{T}$

$i = 0, 1, \cdots, N-1$

1

Information bearing signals whose bandwidth is small compared to the coherence bandwidth of the channel experience frequency nonselective or flat fading. However, if the information bearing signals have bandwidth greater than the coherence bandwidth of the channel, then the channel is said to be frequency-selective. Channels whose statistics remain fairly constant over several symbol intervals are considered slowly fading in contrast to channels whose statistics changes rapidly during an symbol interval. Such channels are considered fast fading. In general, indoor wireless channels are well-characterized by frequency-selective slowly fading channels.

OFDM WLAN Overview

Orthogonal frequency division multiplexing (OFDM) is a promising technique for achieving high data rate and combating multipath fading in wireless communications. OFDM can be thought of as a hybrid of multi-carrier modulation (MCM) and frequency shift keying (FSK) modulation. MCM is the principle of transmitting data by dividing the stream into several parallel bit streams and modulating each of these data streams onto individual carriers or subcarriers; FSK modulation is a technique whereby data is transmitted on one carrier from a set of orthogonal carriers in each symbol duration. Orthogonality amongst the carriers is achieved by separating the carriers by an integer multiple of the inverse of symbol duration of the parallel bit streams. With OFDM, all the orthogonal carriers are transmitted simultaneously. In other words, the entire allocated channel is occupied through the aggregated sum of the narrow orthogonal subbands. By transmitting several symbols in parallel, the symbol duration is increased proportionately, which reduces the effects of ISI caused by the dispersive Rayleigh-fading environment. Here we briefly focus on describing some of the fundamental principles of FSK modulation as they pertain to OFDM. The input sequence determines which of the carriers is transmitted during the signaling interval, that is,

$$\mathbf{s}_i(t) = A\exp(2\pi f_i t)\,\prod(t/T) \tag{1.71}$$

where

$$f_i = f_c + \frac{i}{T}, \qquad i = 0,1,\ldots,N-1 \tag{1.72}$$

$$\prod(t/T) = \begin{cases} 1, & for \quad -T/2 \le t \le T/2 \\ 0, & otherwise \end{cases} \tag{1.73}$$

N is the total number of subband carriers, and T is the symbol duration for the information sequence. In order that the carriers do not interfere with each other during detection, the spectral peak of each carrier must coincide with the zero crossing of all the other carriers as depicted in Figure 1.12. Thus, the difference between the center lobe and the first zero crossing represents the minimum required spacing and is equal to $1/T$. An OFDM signal is constructed by assigning parallel bit streams to these subband carriers, normalizing the signal energy, and extending the bit duration, i.e.,

$$\widetilde{s}(n) = \frac{A}{N} \sum_{i=0}^{N-1} \mathbf{x}_i(n) \exp(2\pi f_i n), \quad for \quad 0 \leq n \leq N; 0 \leq i \leq N \tag{1.74}$$

where $\mathbf{x}_i(n)$ is the nth bit of the ith data stream. Recall from "Discrete Fourier Transform (DFT)," Equation 1.74 is just the IDFT of $\mathbf{x}_i(n)$ scaled by A. The output sequence $\widetilde{s}(n)$ is transmitted one symbol at a time across the channel. Prior to transmission, a cyclic prefix (CP) is prepended to the front of the sequence to yield $s(n)$. A cyclic prefix is a copy of the last part of the OFDM symbol. This makes a portion of the transmitted signal periodic with period N, i.e.,

$$s(n - m) = s(N + n - m), \quad for \quad n - m \leq p \tag{1.75}$$

where p is length of the CP. Hence, the received signal using vector notation is given by

$$\mathbf{r}(n) = \mathbf{s}(n) \circledast \mathbf{h}(n) + \mathbf{v}(n) \tag{1.76}$$

where $\circledast$ denotes circular convolution, $\mathbf{h}$ is the channel impulse response vector, and $\mathbf{v}$ is the additive noise vector. Now, if length of CP is longer than the delay spread of the channel, the linear convolution in Equation 1.76 becomes a circular one. Note the DFT transform pair for the convolution theory given Table 1.1 is based on circular convolution. Hence, the demodulated received signal is

$$\mathbf{R}(k) = \mathbf{S}(k)\mathbf{H}(k) + \mathbf{V}(k) \tag{1.77}$$

where $\mathbf{R}$, $\mathbf{S}$, and $\mathbf{H}$ are the respective DFTs of $\mathbf{r}$, $\mathbf{s}$, and $\mathbf{h}$. Henceforth, for notation simplicity, when Equation 1.76 is satisfied, the channel shall be referred to as *circulant*.

MAC for WLAN Standards

Currently, there are three approved world WLAN standards that utilize OFDM for their physical layer specifications, which are listed in Table 1.3, where HiperLAN/2 stands for High Performance Local Area Network type 2 and MMAC stands for Mobile Multimedia Access Communications. Each standard offers data rates ranging from 6 Mbps to 54 Mbps in the 5 GHz band. The major difference between the standards is the medium access control (MAC) used by each. IEEE 802.11a uses a distributed MAC based on Carrier Sense Multiple Access with Collision Avoidance (CSMA/CA); HiperLAN/2 uses a centralized and scheduled MAC based on wireless asynchronous transfer mode (ATM); and MMAC supports both of these MACs. In the remaining portion of this section, brief summaries of these MAC protocols are given. Although we would like to provide a thorough treatment of each of these MACs, we focus our attention on the most widely used MAC, the IEEE 802.11 MAC. Further treatment of this protocol is given in Chapter 6, "Medium Access Control (MAC) for IEEE 802.11 Networks," for interested readers.

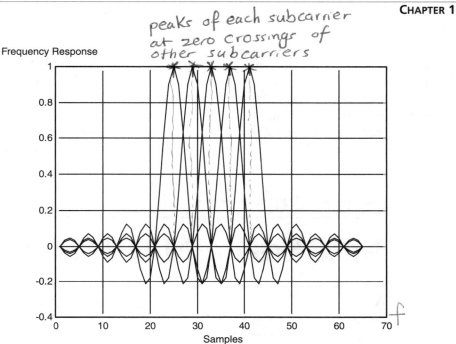

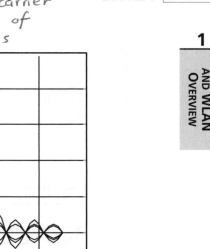

Figure 1.12

Overlapping orthogonal carriers.

Table 1.3 World Standards for OFDM WLANs

Standard	Region of Operation
IEEE 802.11a	Europe and North America
HiperLAN/2	Europe and North America
MMAC	Japan

The MAC frame structure for HiperLAN/2 shown in Figure 1.13 comprises time slots for broadcast control (BCH), frame control (FCH), access feedback control (ACH), and data transmission in downlink (DL), uplink (UL), and direct link (DiL) phases. These control frames are allocated dynamically depending on the need for transmission resources. To access the network, a mobile terminal (MT) first has to request capacity from the access point (AP) in order to send data. Access is granted via the random access channel (RCH), where contention for the same time slot is allowed. Downlink, uplink, and direct link phases consists of two types of protocol data units (PDUs): long PDUs and short PDUs. The long PDUs shown in Figure 1.14 have a size of 54 bytes and contain control or user data. They may contain resource requests, automatic repeat request (ARQ) messages, and so on, and they are referred to as the short transport channel (SCH). The payload is 49.5 bytes and the remaining 4.5 bytes are used for the 2 bits PDU type, 10 bits sequence number (SN), 24-bit cyclic redundancy check (CRC-24). Long PDUs are referred to as the long transport channel (LCH). Short PDUs contain only control data and have a size of 9 bytes. Traffic from multiple connections to/from one MT can be multiplexed onto one PDU train, which contains long and short PDUs. A physical burst shown in Figure 1.15 is composed of the PDU train payload and a preamble and is the unit to be transmitted via the physical layer.

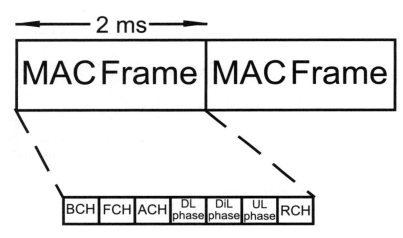

FIGURE 1.13
The HiperLAN/2 MAC frame.

PDU Type (2 bits)	SN (10 bits)	Payload (49.5 bytes)	CRC (3 bytes)

FIGURE 1.14
Format of the long PDU.

Preamble	PDU Train

FIGURE 1.15
HiperLAN/2 physical burst format.

The MAC frame structure for IEEE 802.11a is shown in Figure 1.16. As stated earlier, the IEEE 802.11a uses a CSMA/CA protocol. An MT must sense the medium for specific time interval and ascertain whether the medium is available. This process is referred as *clear channel assessment* (CCA). Algorithms for performing CCA are described in Chapter 2, "Synchronization." If the channel is unavailable, the transmission is suspended and a random delay for re-assessing the channel is assigned. After the delay expires, the MT can access the channel again. Once a packet has been transmitted, the MT waits for an acknowledgement (ACK) frame. Unlike wireline communications, collisions are undetectable in a wireless environment since corruptions of the data can be caused by either collisions or fading. Thus, an ACK frame is necessary. If an ACK frame is not received, the MT retransmit the packet. Figure 1.16 shows the format of a complete packet. The header contains information about the length of the payload and the transmission rate, a parity bit, and six zero tail bits. The header is transmitted using binary phased shifted keying (BPSK), the lowest rate transmission mode, to ensure reliable reception. The rate field conveys information about the type of modulation and coding rate used in the rest of the packet. The length field takes a value between 1 and 4095 and specifies the number of bytes in the Physical Layer Service Data Unit (PSDU). The six tail bits are used to flush the convolutional encoder and terminate the code trellis in the decoder. The first 7 bits of the service field are set to zero and are used to initialize the descrambler. The remaining nine bits are reserved for future use.

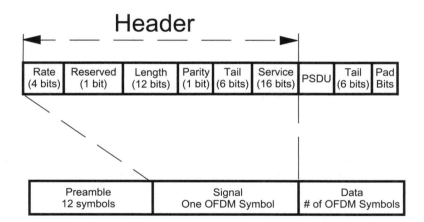

FIGURE 1.16

(PPDU) in 802.11a, including the preamble, header, and PSDU.

At the time this book was published, members of IEEE 802.11 and ETSI/BRAN standard committees were working to form a global 5 GHz WLAN standard. The task group within IEEE responsible for the harmonization process is 5GSG. The issues being addressed by the committee are co-existence, interworking, a single global standard, and regulatory issues. Co-existence issues are focused on frequency sharing and interference robustness. Interworking pertains to the ability of the two standards to communicate to each other. The new jointly developed global standard is being developed based on scenarios and application functional requirements. Finally, regulatory issues are centered around HiperLAN/2 need to restrict the frequency range and power to be compliant with the FCC regulations; for IEEE 802.11, what additional adoptions are needed for it to be operable outside of the USA.

Physical Layer Specifications for WLAN Standards

The physical layers of all the standards are very similar and are based on an OFDM baseband modulation. A list of the key parameters for the system is listed in Table 1.4. With each of the standards, OFDM was selected to combat frequency selective fading and to randomize the burst errors caused by a wideband fading channel. Selection of the transmission rate is determined by a *link adaptation scheme*, a process of selecting the best coding rate and modulation scheme based on channel conditions. The WLAN standards, however, do not explicitly specify the scheme. Data for transmission is supplied to the physical layer via a PDU train. The PDU train contains a sequence of 1s and 0s. Preparation for transmission and data recovery are performed by the functional blocks shown in Figure 1.17. Mux is a serial to parallel operation; demux (demultiplex) is a parallel to serial operation. It should be noted a length 127 pseudo random sequence is used to scramble the data out of the binary source prior to the convolutional encoder although it is not explicitly shown in the Figure. The purpose of scrambler is to prevent a long sequence of 1s or 0s. This helps with the timing recovery at the receiver. Besides that, the remaining functions in the transceiver are unaffected by the scrambling operation.

TABLE 1.4 Key Parameters of the OFDM Standards

Data Rate	*6, 9, 12, 18, 24, 36, 48, 54 Mbps*
Modulation	BPSK, QPSK, 16-QAM, 64-QAM
Coding Rates	1/2, 9/16, 2/3, 3/4
Number of Subcarriers	52
Number of Pilot Tones	4
OFDM Symbol Duration	$4\,\mu$ sec
Guard interval	800 η sec, 400 η sec (optional)
Subcarrier Spacing	312.5 kHz
Signal Bandwidth	16.66 MHz
Channel Spacing	20 MHz

BACKGROUND
AND WLAN
OVERVIEW

HiperLAN/2 and IEEE 802.11a standards specify different initialization for the scrambler. The scrambled data sequence is encoded with a de facto standard (2,1,7) convolutional encoder. The other rates shown in Table 1.4 are achieved by puncturing the output of this encoder. Puncturing involves deleting coded bits from output data sequence such that the ratio of uncoded bits to coded bits is greater than the mother code. For example, to achieve a 2/3 code rate one bit out of every four bits is deleted from the coded sequence. Next, the coded bits are interleaved to prevent error bursts from being fed into the convolutional decoder since the decoder does not work very well with burst errors. The interleaved coded bits are grouped together to form symbols. The symbols are modulated with one of the scheme given in Table 1.4. A BPSK symbol is comprised of one bit per symbol; a QPSK symbol is comprised of two bits per symbol; a 16-QAM symbol is comprised of four bits per symbol; and a 64-QAM symbol is comprised of 6 bits per symbol. The interested reader is referred to Chapter 3 for more details on modulation scheme mentioned here.

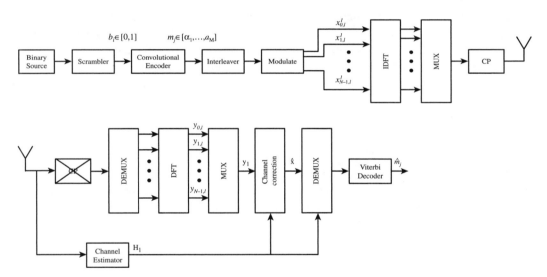

FIGURE 1.17

A simplified block diagram of the IEEE 802.11a transceiver.

The modulation symbols are mapped to the subcarrier of the 64 point IDFT, hence creating an OFDM symbol. Note that because of bandwidth limitations, only 48 subcarriers are used for modulation and four subcarriers are reserved for pilot tones.The remaining 12 subcarriers are not used. The pilot tones are used at the receiver to estimate any residual phase error. The output of the IDFT is converted to a serial sequence and a guard interval or CP is added. Thus, total duration of the OFDM symbol is the sum of the CP or guard duration plus the useful symbol duration. The guard or CP is considered overhead in the OFDM frame along with the preamble. After the CP has been added, the entire OFDM symbol is transmitted across the channel. As long as the duration of the CP is longer than the channel impulse response, ISI is eliminated, which is evident from Equation 1.77 in the previous section.

After the CP has been removed, the receiver is responsible for performing the inverse operations of the transmitter in reverse order. Before any receiver algorithms can be employed, timing must first be recovered; that is, the system clock at the receiver must become synchronized with that at the transmitter while taking into account the delay associated with propagation across the channel. Chapter 2 provides a full treatment of synchronization algorithms used to recovery timing in OFDM systems.

In addition to timing recovery, the receiver must also compute *automatic gain control* (AGC) for the A/D converter. The purpose of the AGC is to maintain a fixed signal power to the A/D converter to prevent signals from saturating or clipping the output of the A/D converter. Since OFDM is a frequency domain modulation technique, it is essential to have accurate estimates of the frequency offset, caused by oscillator instability, at the receiver. It is obvious from Equation 1.77 that channel estimation is needed as well to demodulate the symbols. Training sequences are provided in the preamble for these specific functions mentioned above. To reduced the uncertainty in the channel estimation, two OFDM symbols containing training sequences are provided: short training and long training. The short training is used to provide coarse and fine estimation of time and frequency errors. The long training sequence is used to estimate the channel impulse response or *channel state information* (CSI). With the CSI, the received signal can be demodulated, de-interleaved, and fed to a Viterbi algorithm for decoding. As far as the physical layer specifications are concerned, there are only a few minor differences between the standards. These differences are

- HiperLAN/2 uses extra puncturing to accommodate the tail bits in order to keep an integer number of OFDM symbols in 54 byte packets required for ATM transmission. For example, the 16-QAM mode of HiperLAN/2 uses a rate 9/16 convolutional encoder rather than the rate 1/2 convolutional encoder used by IEEE 802.11a and MMAC. The rate 9/16 is generated by puncturing 2 out of every 18 coded bits.

- HiperLAN/2 uses different training sequences. The long training is the same as IEEE 802.11, but the preceding sequence of short training symbols is different. A downlink transmission starts with 10 short symbols as IEEE 802.11, but the first 5 symbols are different in order to detect the start of the downlink frame. Uplink packets may use 5 or 10 identical short symbols, with the last short symbol inverted.

- HiperLAN/2 has an optional mode that uses a 400 η sec cyclic prefix.

Single Carrier Versus OFDM Comparison

We conclude this chapter with a comparison of single carrier systems versus OFDM systems with the same data rate. The main difference between the systems are their robustness to fading and synchronization errors—both frequency and timing. Under the assumption of perfect synchronization, the performance of a single carrier system and an OFDM system is equivalent for AWGN and flat or frequency non-selective channels. Consider a received signal for a single carrier system

$$r_i = \gamma s_i + n(i), \quad 0 \le i \le L-1 \tag{1.78}$$

where γ is a complex random variable, s_i is the baseband representation of the ith modulation symbol, and n_i is complex additive white Gaussian noise sample in the ith signal interval. The equivalent OFDM received signal for a circulant channel is

$$R_k = \gamma S_k + V_i, \quad 0 \le k \le L-1 \tag{1.79}$$

where R_k, X_k, and N_k are the frequency domain representations of r_i, x_i, and n_i respectively. Since the noise power of n_i and N_k are equivalent by Parseval's Theorem [7, 10, 18], there is no inherent advantage in detecting the signal using either Equation 1.78 or Equation 1.79. Now, consider reception of a signal over a circulant frequency-selective channel. For the single carrier system, the received signal becomes

$$\mathbf{r}(i) = \Gamma(i) \circledast \mathbf{s}(i) + \mathbf{n}(i) \tag{1.80}$$

where

$$\mathbf{r}(i) = \left[r_i, r_{i+1}, \cdots, r_{L+i-1} \right]^{\dagger}$$

$$\Gamma(i) = \left[\gamma_i, \gamma_{i+1}, \cdots, \gamma_{p+i-1} \right]^{\dagger}$$

$$\mathbf{s}(i) = \left[s_i, s_{i+1}, \cdots, s_{L+i-1} \right]^{\dagger}$$

$$\mathbf{n}(i) = \left[n_i, n_{i+1}, \cdots, n_{L+i-1} \right]^{\dagger}$$

and † denotes vector transpose. To recover s_i, the single carrier system requires an equalizer $\mathbf{g}(i)$ to compensate for the channel effect. The equalizer performs deconvolution on the received signal, i.e.,

$$\mathbf{r}_{eq}(i) = \mathbf{g}(i) \circledast \mathbf{r}(i) = \mathbf{g}(i) \circledast (\Gamma(i) \circledast \mathbf{s}(i) + \mathbf{n}(i))$$
$$\mathbf{r}_{eq}(i) = \mathbf{s}(i) + \Gamma(i) \circledast \mathbf{n}(i) \tag{1.81}$$

In practical systems, the equalizer does not perfectly inverse the effects of the channel, there is always some residual error $\varepsilon(i)$,

$$\mathbf{r}_{eq}(i) = \mathbf{s}(i) + \Gamma(i) \circledast \mathbf{n}(i) + \varepsilon(i) \tag{1.82}$$

In addition to the residual error term $\varepsilon(i)$, the deconvolution process correlates the noise samples and enhances the noise amplitude in some samples. Further discussion of equalization shall be limited since equalization is well researched in the literature. An excellent text [11] summarizes some of the popular equalization techniques used in systems. In comparison, the OFDM system performs equalization in the same manner as the case of the frequency non-selective channel, i.e.,

$$R(k) = \Gamma(k)S(k) + V(k)$$ (1.83)

$$R_{eq}(k) = S(k) + \Psi(k)V(k)$$ (1.84)

where

$$\Psi(k) = \left[1/\gamma_i, 1/\gamma_{i+1}, \cdots, 1/\gamma_{p+i-1}\right]^\dagger$$

why complexity for the OFDM system is less than for the single carrier system?

Equalization in OFDM systems is subject to the same impairments such as residual error and noise enhancement as the single carrier system; thus, theoretically, the two systems have equivalent performance. Yet, the complexity of the equalizer for the OFDM system is substantially less than that for the single carrier system. The reason is that OFDM systems employ a bank of single-tap equalizers while single carrier systems employ multi-tap equalizers. Further, the complexity of the equalizer grows as the square of the number of taps.

Synchronization Errors

Synchronization errors can be either timing, frequency, or both. The single carrier system is much more sensitive to timing errors than the OFDM system. On the other hand, the OFDM system is more sensitive to frequency errors. In the paragraphs to follow, the synchronization error performance for both systems will be examined.

Timing Errors

Even with the training interval, the demodulator reference circuitry may not be able to recover completely the timing at the transmitter. When the receiver is not symbol synchronized to the incoming data stream, the SNR at the output of the detection filter is degraded. In other words, for a particular sampling time $T_{optimal}$, the output SNR is given by [22]

$$\zeta = \Lambda(\tau)/\Lambda(0)$$ (1.85)

where Λ is the autocorrelation function and τ is the delay between the optimum sampling instance $T_{optimal}$ and the associated symbol timing for the received signal. Note that the parameter τ is random variable since it is estimated in the presence of noise and the variability of τ is usually referred to as *timing jitter*. The two special cases of interest, baseband time-limited signals and band-limited signals with normalized autocorrelation functions [26], are shown in Equations 1.86 and 1.87, respectively,

$$\Lambda(\tau) = \left(1 - \frac{|\tau|}{T_{Symbol}}\right) \tag{1.86}$$

$$\Lambda(\tau) = \frac{1}{N}\left(\frac{\sin(\pi NW\tau)}{\sin(\pi W\tau)}\right), \tag{1.87}$$

where W is the bandwidth of the band-limited signal. For the purpose of our discussion, the single carrier system is best described as a band-limited signal while the OFDM system is best described as a time-limited signal. For single carrier systems, the timing error or jitter manifests as a noisy phase reference for the bandpass signal. In the case of OFDM systems, pilot tones are transmitted along with the data bearing carrier to estimate residual phase errors. Chapter 2 outlines algorithms for estimating residual phase and compensation for the distortion. The single carrier system does not have a mechanism to achieve this compensation. The degradation resulting from phase error is developed later in this section.

Effects of Frequency Errors

When there is relative motion between the transmitter and receiver, a Doppler shift of the RF carrier results and introduces a frequency error. Also, there can be a residual frequency error caused by frequency instabilities in the oscillators at the transmitter and receiver. In either case, there are well-known carrier recovery scheme available for single carrier system such as a first order Costa loop [5]. The interested reader is encouraged to review [2], for more details. The important result is that although the carrier is recovered, the phase may be unknown and random.

Effects of Noisy Phase References

The effects of noisy phase references on the performance of the demodulator is developed in this section. We limit our treatment to binary phase shift keying (BPSK), quaternary phase shift keying (QPSK) modulation, and offset-QPSK. Consider first the baseband representation of a BPSK signal received in additive Gaussian noise

$$r(t) = \sqrt{2}\sum_n a_n h(t - nT)\cos\omega_c t + v(t) \tag{1.88}$$

where the signal amplitude has been normalized for unity power, $h(t)$ is the pulse shaping filter used at the transmitter, a_n refers to the binary digit transmitted in the nth interval, and $v(t)$ is the additive white Gaussian noise component. In general, $h(t)$ can be any band-limited shaping filter; however, for the sake of simplicity, we consider a finite duration unity amplitude rectangular pulse defined over the interval $(0, T]$. The receiver provides a reference carrier

$$R(t) = \sqrt{2}\cos(\omega_c t + \theta) \tag{1.89}$$

where θ is the phase error. Multiplying Equation 1.88 by Equation 1.89 and ignoring double-frequency terms yields

$$y(t) = r(t)R(t) = \sum_n a_n h(t - nT)\cos\theta + v(t)R(t) \qquad (1.90)$$

For the case of rectangular pulse shaping, the optimum matched filter is an integrate and dump, and its output corresponding to the nth bit is

$$y_n(T) = \frac{1}{T}\int_0^T y(t)\partial t = a_n \cos\theta + \frac{1}{T}\int_0^T v(t)R(t)\partial t \qquad (1.91)$$

The noise component of Equation 1.91 can be shown to be Gaussian with zero mean and variance $\sigma^2 = N_0/2$. The probability of error $P_b(\theta)$ conditioned on θ is easily derived and equal to

$$P_b(\theta) = Q\left[\sqrt{\frac{2E_b}{N_0}}\cos\theta\right] \qquad (1.92)$$

where Q is complementary error function. The average error rate is obtained by integrating $P_b(\theta)$, i.e.,

$$P_{BPSK} = \int_{-\pi}^{\pi} P_b(\theta)f(\theta)\partial\theta \qquad (1.93)$$

where $f(\theta)$ is the pdf of θ. For the case of timing jitter, the phase error is modelled as a uniform distribution between $[-\omega_c\Delta t_1, -\omega_c\Delta t_2]$, where Δt_1 and Δt_2 are the minimum and maximum timing errors, respectively. The average error rate must be evaluated numerical. For first order Costa loops, Viterbi showed in [26] that the pdf with an unmodulated carrier input is given by

$$f(\theta) = \frac{\exp(\alpha\cos\theta)}{2\pi I_0(\alpha)} \qquad (1.94)$$

where α is the phase reference signal-to-noise ratio (SNR) and $I_0(\alpha)$ refers to the modified Bessel function of order zero and argument α. For large SNR, Equation 1.94 is well approximated by

$$f(\theta) \approx \frac{\exp[\alpha(\cos\theta - 1)]}{(2\pi/\alpha)^{1/2}} \qquad (1.95)$$

Next, we consider a noisy phased corrupted QPSK signal. Recall that for QPSK, data is transmitted on quadrature channels; thus, the receiver must provide two local references

$$R_I(t) = \sqrt{2}\,\cos(\omega_c t + \theta)$$
$$R_Q(t) = \sqrt{2}\,\sin(\omega_c t + \theta)$$
(1.96)

for the receiver filters. For any nonzero phase error θ, each channel interferes with the other. An analysis similar to that for BPSK shows that the conditional error for QPSK is given by

$$P_q(\theta) = 1/2\left\{Q\left[\sqrt{\frac{2E_b}{N_0}}(\cos\theta + \sin\theta)\right] + Q\left[\sqrt{\frac{2E_b}{N_0}}(\cos\theta + \sin\theta)\right]\right\}$$
(1.97)

With offset QPSK one channel is offset with respect to the other channel by T, where T is the bit duration. As a result, a transition in one channel occurs at the midpoint of the signaling interval of the other channel. So, if a data transition occurs, the mutual interference from the first half interval exactly cancels the interference from the second half interval. If no transition occurs, the interference remains constant and the conditional is the same as that for QPSK. Thus, the conditional error rate for offset QPSK is

$$P_{O_q}(\theta) = 1/2[P_b(\theta) + P_q(\theta)]$$
(1.98)

For OFDM systems, the frequency offset error must be estimated with training sequence. Unfortunately, a residual frequency error might exist even after frequency correction has been applied. In the following development, we qualify the effects of frequency offset error in OFDM systems. Since the sampled output of the (I,Q) match filters are sufficient statistics for the receiver, it is instructive to examine these in the presence of frequency errors. Again assuming no timing error, the noiseless output values of the I channel and Q channel match filters are

$$y_n^I = \sqrt{E_b}\,h(\cos[2\pi\Delta ft + \theta])|_{t=nT}$$
$$y_n^Q = \sqrt{E_b}\,h(\sin[2\pi\Delta ft + \theta])|_{t=nT}$$
(1.99)

For time-limited signals or rectangular pulse shaping, $h(t)$ is an integration over one symbol period. Hence, the expressions in Equation 1.88 expand to

$$y_n^I = \frac{\sqrt{E_b}}{T}\int_0^T \cos[2\pi\Delta ft + \theta]\partial t$$
$$y_n^Q = \frac{\sqrt{E_b}}{T}\int_0^T \sin[2\pi\Delta ft + \theta]\partial t$$
(1.100)

which have closed form solutions

$$y_n^I = \sqrt{E_b}\left(\frac{\sin(2\pi\Delta fT)\cos\theta}{2\pi\Delta fT} + \frac{[-1+\cos(2\pi\Delta fT)]\sin\theta}{2\pi\Delta fT}\right)$$

$$y_n^Q = \sqrt{E_b}\left(\frac{[1-\cos(2\pi\Delta fT)]\cos\theta}{2\pi\Delta fT} + \frac{\sin(2\pi\Delta fT)\sin\theta}{2\pi\Delta fT}\right)$$

(1.101)

Thus, the signal power at the output of the matched filters is

$$Z = \left(y_n^I\right)^2 + \left(y_n^Q\right)^2$$

(1.102)

which simplifies to

$$Z = E_b\left(\frac{\sin(2\pi\Delta fT)}{2\pi\Delta fT}\right)^2 + E_b\left(\frac{[1-\cos(2\pi\Delta fT)]}{2\pi\Delta fT}\right)^2$$

$$Z = E_b\frac{2-2\cos(2\pi\Delta fT)}{(2\pi\Delta fT)^2}$$

$$Z = E_b\left(\frac{\sin(2\pi\Delta fT)}{\pi\Delta fT}\right)^2$$

(1.103)

Hence, the degradation of the signal due to a frequency error of Δf hertz is

$$L(\Delta f) = \left(\frac{\sin(\pi\Delta fT)}{\pi\Delta fT}\right)^2$$

(1.104)

Equation 1.104 can also be used to compute the intercarrier interference (ICI) from adjacent carriers. Thus, frequency offset errors not only result in a loss in SNR, but also create ICI, which can severely degrade the performance of the system.

To summarize, single carrier systems are fairly robust to frequency offset errors and are more appropriate for mobile environments that experience large frequency offset errors. Yet, the performance of single carrier systems is degraded as a result of SNR loss caused by timing errors. In constrast, OFDM systems are fairly robust to timing errors compared to single carrier systems, yet their performance is similarly affected by the loss in SNR caused by frequency offset errors. Intuitively, this is easily understood from the fact that the OFDM symbol duration is N times longer than its single carrier counterpart operating at the same data rate. In terms of fading, the performances of the two systems are similar. The complexity of the equalizer for single carrier systems, however, is much greater than OFDM systems.

Bibliography

[1]   P. A. Bello, "Characterization of randomly time-variant linear channels," *IEEE Trans. on Communication Systems,* vol. CS-11, Dec. 1963.

[2]   V. K. Bhargava, D. Haccoun, R. Matyas, and P. P. Nuspl, *Digital Communications by Satellite: Modulation, Multiple Access, and Coding.* Krieger Publishing Company, 1991.

[3]   R.W. Chang, "Synthesis of band-limited orthogonal signals for multichannel data transmission, *Bell System Tech. Journal,* 45:1775–1796, Dec. 1966

[4]   E. P. Cunningham, *Digital Filtering: An Introduction,* Houghton Mifflin Company, 1992.

[5]   A. N. D'Andrea and U. Mengali, *Synchronization Techniques for Digital Receivers,* Plenum Press, New York, 1997.

[6]   O. Edfors, M. Sandell, J. van de Beek, D. Landström, and F. Sjöberg, *An introduction to orthogonal frequency-division multiplexing,* Technical Report, September 1996, Division of Signal Processing, Luleå University.

[7]   D. R. Fannin, W. H. Tranter, and R. E. Ziemer, *Signal and Systems: Continuous and Discrete,* MacMillian Publishing Co., New York, 1983.

[8]   J. L. Flanagan, M. R. Schroeder, B. S. Atal, R. E. Crochiere, N. S. Jayant, and J. M. Tribolet, "Speech coding," *IEEE Trans. on Commun.,* COM-27, 1979, pp. 710–737.

[9]   S. Hara and J.P. Linnartz, *Wireless Personal Communication,* No.1-2, Kluwer, 1996.}

[10] M. H. Hayes, *Statistical Digital Signal Processing and Modeling,* John Wiley & Sons, Inc, New York, 1996.

[11] S. S. Haykin, *Adaptive Filtering Theory*: Fourth Editions, Prentice Hall, Inc., Englewood Cliffs, N.J., 1995.

[12] W. C. Jakes, *Microwave Communications,* IEEE Press, N.J. 1974.

[13] N. S., Jayant, and P., Noll, *Digital Coding of Waveforms,* Prentice-Hall, Inc., Englewood Cliffs, N.J., 1984.

[14] Cover and Thomas, *Elements of Information Theory,* JohnWiley & Sons, Inc, New York, 1991.

[15] T. J. Lynch, *Data Compression Techniques and Applications,* Lifetime Learning Publications, New York, 1985.

[16] E. Lutz, D. Cygan, M. Dippold, F. Dolainsky and W. Papke, "The land mobile satellite communication channel - recording, statistics, and channel model," *IEEE Trans. Veh. Tech.*, vol. 40, no. 2, May 1991.

[17] B. Noble and J. Daniel, *Applied Linear Algebra Third Edition*, Prentice Hall, Englewood Cliffs, New Jersey, 1988.

[18] A. V. Oppenheim and R. W. Schafer, *Discrete-Time Signal Processing*, Prentic Hall, Englewood Cliffs, New Jersey, 1989.

[19] A. Peled and A. Ruiz, "Frequency domain data transmission using reduced computational complexity algorithms, *In Proc. IEEE Int. Conf. Acoust., Speech, Signal Processing*, pp. 964–967, 1980.

[20] A. Papoulis, *Probability, Random Variables, and Stochastic Processes, 2nd Edition*, McGraw-Hill, 1984.

[21] J. G. Proakis, *Digital Communications Fourth Edition*. New York, McGraw-Hill, 2000

[22] B. Sklar, *Digital Communications: Fundamental and Applications*, Prentice Hall, Englewood Cliffs, New Jersey, 1988.

[23] B. R. Saltzberg, "Performance of an efficient parallel data transmission system," IEEE *Trans. on Commun.*, COM-15(6), Dec., 1967, pp. 805–811.

[24] J. D. Terry, *Blind Adaptive Array Techniques for Mobile Satellite Communications*, UMI Company, Ann Arbor, MI, 1999.

[25] A. J. Viterbi, and J. K. Omura, *Principles of Digital Communication and Coding*, McGraw-Hill Book Company, New York, 1979.

[26] A. J. Viterbi, *CDMA: Principles of Spread Spectrum Communication*. Addison Wesley Publishing Company, 1996.

[27] ETSI TS 101 761-1 V1.2.1 (2000-11), Broadband Radio Access Networks (BRAN); HIPERLAN Type 2; Data Link Control (DLC) Layer; Part 1: Basic Data Transport Functions

[28] ETSI TS 101 761-2 V1.2.1 (2001-04), Broadband Radio Access Networks (BRAN); HIPERLAN Type 2; Data Link Control (DLC) Layer; Part 2: Radio Link Control (RLC) sublayer

[29] ETSI TS 101 475 V1.2.2 (2001-02), Broadband Radio Access Networks (BRAN); HIPERLAN Type 2; Physical (PHY) layer

Synchronization

IN THIS CHAPTER

- Timing Estimation   49
- Frequency Synchronization   66
- Channel Estimation   77
- Clear Channel Assessment   81
- Signal Quality   82
- Bibliography   83

Synchronization is an essential task for any digital communication system. Without accurate synchronization algorithms, it is not possible to reliably receive the transmitted data. From the digital baseband algorithm design engineer's perspective, synchronization algorithms are the major design problem that has to be solved to build a successful product.

OFDM is used for both broadcast type systems and packet switched networks, like WLANs. These two systems require somewhat different approach to the synchronization problem. Broadcast systems transmit data continuously, so a typical receiver, like European Digital Audio Broadcasting (DAB) or Digital Video Broadcasting (DVB) system receivers, can initially spend a relatively long time to acquire the signal and then switch to tracking mode. Speth et al. [24] and [25] analyze synchronization techniques for broadcast receivers. On the other hand, WLAN systems typically have to use so called "single-shot" synchronization; that is, the synchronization has to be acquired during a very short time after the start of the packet. This requirement comes from the packet switched nature of WLAN systems and also from the high data rates used. To achieve good system throughput, it is mandatory to keep the receiver training information overhead to the minimum. To facilitate the single-shot synchronization, current WLAN standards include a preamble, like the IEEE 802.11a [9] preamble shown in Figure 2.4 or the various HiperLAN/2 [7] preambles shown in Figure 2.7, in the start of the packet. The length and the contents of the preamble have been carefully designed to provide enough information for good synchronization performance without any unnecessary overhead.

The OFDM signal waveform makes most of the synchronization algorithms designed for single carrier systems unusable, thus the algorithm design problem has to be approached from the OFDM perspective. This distinction is especially visible on the sensitivity difference to various synchronization errors between single carrier and OFDM systems. The frequency domain nature of OFDM also allows the effect of several synchronization errors to be explained with the aid of the properties of the Discrete Fourier Transform (DFT). Another main distinction with single carrier systems is that many of the OFDM synchronization functions can be performed either in time- or frequency-domain. This flexibility is not available in single carrier systems. The trade-offs on how to perform the synchronization algorithms are usually either higher performance versus reduced computational complexity.

The scope of this book is WLAN systems; hence this chapter concentrates on WLAN synchronization algorithms. Occasionally we comment on differences between WLAN and broadcast system synchronization algorithms.

The order of the algorithms described in this chapter follows to some extent the order of how an actual receiver would perform the synchronization. The main assumption usually made when WLAN systems are designed is that the channel impulse response does not change significantly during one data burst. This assumption is justified by the quite short time duration of transmitted packets, usually a couple milliseconds at maximum and that the transmitter and receiver in most applications move very slowly relatively to each other. Under this assumption most of the synchronization for WLAN receivers is done during the preamble and need not be changed during the packet.

Timing Estimation

Timing estimation consists of two main tasks: packet synchronization and symbol synchronization.

The IEEE 802.11 MAC protocol is essentially a random access network, so the receiver does not know exactly when a packet starts. The first task of the receiver is to detect the start of an incoming packet. HiperLAN/2 medium access architecture is a hybrid of both random access and time scheduled networks. Thus HiperLAN/2 receivers also have to be able to reliably detect the start of incoming packets, without prior knowledge.

Broadcast systems naturally do not require packet detection algorithms, because transmission is always on. However, for a packet oriented network architecture, finding the packets is obviously of central importance for high network performance.

Packet Detection

Packet detection is the task of finding an approximate estimate of the start of the preamble of an incoming data packet. As such it is the first synchronization algorithm that is performed, so the rest of the synchronization process is dependent on good packet detection performance. Generally packet detection can be described as a binary hypothesis test. The test consists of two complementary statements about a parameter of interest. These statements are called the null hypothesis, H_0, and the alternative hypothesis, H_1. In the packet detection test, the hypotheses assert whether a packet is present or not. The test is set up as shown below.

$$H_0 : \ Packet\ not\ present$$
$$H_1 : \ Packet\ present$$

The actual test is usually of the form that tests whether a decision variable m_n exceeds a predefined threshold Th. The packet detection case is shown below.

$$H_0 : m_n < Th \Rightarrow Packet\ not\ present$$
$$H_1 : m_n \geq Th \Rightarrow Packet\ present$$

The performance of the packet detection algorithm can be summarized with two probabilities: probability of detection P_D and probability of false alarm P_{FA}. P_D is the probability of detecting a packet when it is truly present, thus high P_D is a desirable quality for the test. P_{FA} is the probability that the test incorrectly decides that a packet is present, when actually there is none, thus P_{FA} should be as small as possible. In general, increasing P_D increases P_{FA} and decreasing P_{FA}

decreases P_D, hence the algorithm designer must settle for a some balanced compromise between the two conflicting goals. The general hypothesis test problem is discussed in several statistical inference and detection theory books [3, 10].

Generally it can be said that a false alarm is a less severe error than not detecting a packet at all. The reason is that after a false alarm, the receiver will try to synchronize to nonexistent packet and will detect its error at the first received data integrity check. On the another hand, not detecting a packet always results in lost data. A false alarm can also result in lost data, in case an actual data packet starts during the time the receiver has not yet detected its mistake. In this case, the receiver will not be able to catch that packet. The probability of this occurring depends on several issues like the network load and the time it takes for the receiver to detect its mistake. In conclusion, a little higher P_{FA} can be tolerated to guarantee good P_D. In the next sections, we introduce several approaches to the packet detection test design problem.

Received Signal Energy Detection

The simplest algorithm for finding the start edge of the incoming packet is to measure the received signal energy. When there is no packet being received, the received signal r_n consists only of noise $r_n = w_n$. When the packet starts, the received energy is increased by the signal component $r_n = s_n + w_n$, thus the packet can be detected as a change in the received energy level. The decision variable m_n is then the received signal energy accumulated over some window of length L to reduce sensitivity to large individual noise samples.

$$m_n = \sum_{k=0}^{L-1} r_{n-k} r_{n-k}^* = \sum_{k=0}^{L-1} |r_{n-k}|^2 \tag{2.1}$$

Calculation of m_n can be simplified by noting that it is a moving sum of the received signal energy. This type of sum is also called a sliding window. The rationale for the name is that at every time instant n, one new value enters the sum and one old value is disgarded. This structure can be used to simplify the computation of Equation 2.1. Equation 2.2 shows how to calcute the moving sum recursively.

$$m_{n+1} = m_n + |r_{n+1}|^2 - |r_{n-L+1}|^2 \tag{2.2}$$

Thus the number of complex multiplications is reduced to one per received sample; however, more memory is required to store all the values of $|r_n|^2$ inside the window. The response of this algorithm is shown in Figure 2.1. The figure shows the value m_n for IEEE 802.11a packet with 10dB Signal to Noise Ratio (SNR) and sliding window length $L = 32$. The true start of the packet is at $n = 500$, thus in this case the threshold could be set between 10 and 25. The value of the threshold defines the P_D and P_{FA} of the test.

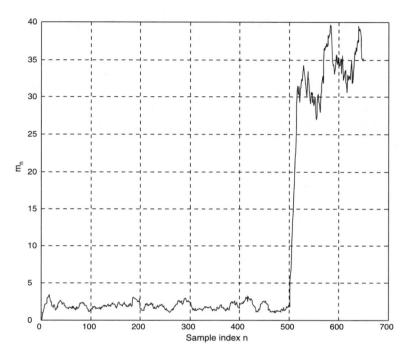

FIGURE 2.1

Received signal energy based packet detection algorithm.

This simple method suffers from a significant drawback; namely, the value of the threshold depends on the received signal energy. When the receiver is searching for an incoming packet, the received signal consists of only noise. The level of the noise power is generally unknown and can change when the receiver adjusts its Radio Frequency (RF) amplifier settings or if unwanted interferers go on and off in the same band as the desired system. When a wanted packet is incoming, its received signal strength depends on the power setting of the transmitter and on the total path loss from the transmitter to the receiver. All these factors make it quite difficult to set a fixed threshold, which could be used to decide when an incoming packet starts. The next section describes an improvement to the algorithm that alleviates the threshold value selection problem.

Double Sliding Window Packet Detection

The double sliding window packet detection algorithm calculates two consecutive sliding windows of the received energy. The basic principle is to form the decision variable m_n as a ratio of the total energy contained inside the two windows. Figure 2.2 shows the windows A and B and the response of m_n to a received packet. In Figure 2.2, the A and B windows are considered stationary relative to the packet that slides over them to the right. It can be seen that when only noise is received the response is flat, since both windows contain ideally the same amount of noise energy. When the packet edge starts to cover the *A* window, the energy in the *A* window gets higher until the point where *A* is totally contained inside the start of the packet. This point is the peak of the triangle shaped m_n and the position of the packet in Figure 2.2 corresponds to this sample index *n*. After this point *B* window starts to also collect signal energy, and when it is also completely inside the received packet, the response of m_n is flat again. Thus the response of m_n can be thought of as a differentiator, in that its value is large when the input energy level changes rapidly. The packet detection is declared when m_n crosses over the threshold value *Th*.

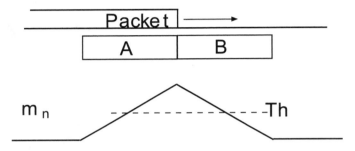

FIGURE 2.2

The response of the double sliding window packet detection algorithm.

Equation 2.3 shows the calculation of the *A* window value and Equation 2.4 the calculation for *B* window.

$$a_n = \sum_{m=0}^{M-1} r_{n-m} r_{n-m}^* = \sum_{m=0}^{M-1} |r_{n-m}|^2 \tag{2.3}$$

$$b_n = \sum_{l=1}^{L} r_{n+l} r_{n+l}^* = \sum_{l=0}^{L} |r_{n+l}|^2 \tag{2.4}$$

Both a_n and b_n are again sliding windows, thus the computation can be simplified in the same recursive manner as for the energy detection window. Then the decision variable is formed by dividing the value of the a_n by b_n

$$m_n = \frac{a_n}{b_n} \tag{2.5}$$

A simulated response of the variable m_n is shown in Figure 2.3. The figure is again for the IEEE 802.11a preamble with 10dB SNR. The figure clearly shows how the value of m_n does *not* depend on the total received power. After the peak, the response levels off to the same value as before the peak, although the received energy level is much higher. An additional benefit of this approach is that, at the peak point of m_n the value of a_n contains the sum of signal energy S and noise energy N and the b_n value is equal to noise energy N, thus the value of m_n at the peak point can be used to estimate the received SNR. Equation 2.6 is the ratio a_n and b_n at the peak point and Equation 2.7 is the SNR estimate calculated from the ratio.

$$m_{peak} = \frac{a_{peak}}{b_{peak}} = \frac{S+N}{N} = \frac{S}{N} + 1 \tag{2.6}$$

$$\widehat{SNR} = m_{peak} - 1 \tag{2.7}$$

2

SYNCHRONIZATION

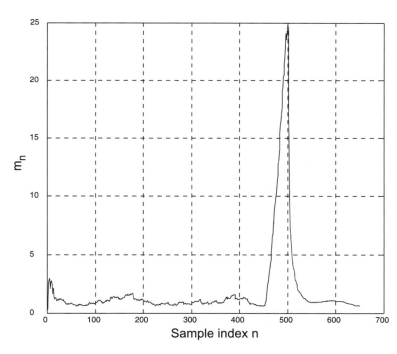

FIGURE 2.3
Double sliding window packet detection.

Using the double sliding window algorithm is a good approach, if the receiver does not have additional information about the received data. However, if the receiver does have additional information, more can be done as is explained in the following section.

Using the Structure of the Preamble for Packet Detection

A general communications system engineering principle is that the receiver should use all the available information to its advantage. In the packet detection algorithm, this means that the known structure of the preamble should be incorporated into the algorithm. The preambles of both the IEEE 802.11a and HiperLAN/2 systems have been designed to help the detection of the start edge of the packet. The IEEE 802.11a standard gives guidelines on how to use the various segments of the preamble to perform the necessary synchronization functions. The preamble structure and the guidelines are illustrated in Figure 2.4. The parts from A_1 to A_{10} are short training symbols, that are all identical and 16 samples long. CP is a 32-sample cyclic prefix that protects the long training symbols C_1 and C_2 from intersymbol interference (ISI) caused by the short training symbols. The long training symbols are identical 64 samples long OFDM symbols. However, the guidelines are not binding requirements of the standard. The design engineer has the freedom to use any other available method or develop new algorithms.

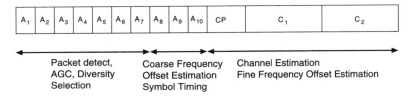

FIGURE 2.4

The IEEE 802.11a standard preamble.[*]

The structure of the WLAN preamble enables the receiver to use a very simple and efficient algorithm to detect the packet. The following approach was presented in Schimdl and Cox [21] for acquiring symbol timing, but the general method is applicable to packet detection. Overall the method resembles the double sliding window algorithm introduced in the previous section, but it takes advantage of the periodicity of the short training symbols at the start of the preamble. This approach is called the delay and correlate algorithm. The name and the relation to the double sliding window method is illustrated in Figure 2.5, which shows the signal flow structure of the delay and correlate algorithm. The Figure shows two sliding windows C and P. The C window is a crosscorrelation between the received signal and a delayed version of the received signal, hence the name delay and correlate. The delay z^{-D} is equal to the period of the start of the preamble; for example, IEEE 802.11a has $D = 16$, the period of the short training symbols. The P window calculates the received signal energy during the crosscorrelation window. The value of the P window is used to normalize the decision statistic, so that it is not dependent on absolute received power level.

The value c_n is calculated according to Equation 2.8, and the value of p_n according to Equation 2.9.

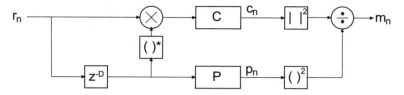

FIGURE 2.5

Signal flow structure of the delay and correlate algorithm.

$$c_n = \sum_{k=0}^{L-1} r_{n+k} r_{n+k+D}^* \tag{2.8}$$

$$p_n = \sum_{k=0}^{L-1} r_{n+k+D} r_{n+k+D}^* = \sum_{k=0}^{L-1} |r_{n+k+D}|^2 \tag{2.9}$$

Then the decision statistic m_n is calculated from Equation 2.10

$$m_n = \frac{|c_n|^2}{(p_n)^2} \tag{2.10}$$

c_n and p_n are again sliding windows, so the general recursive procedure can be used to reduce computational workload.

Figure 2.6 shows an example of the decision statistic m_n for IEEE 802.11a preamble in 10dB SNR. The overall response is restricted between $[0,1]$ and the step at the start of the packet is very clear. The difference of the response to the double sliding window response in Figure 2.3 can be explained with the behavior of the c_n value. When the received signal consists of only noise, the output c_n of the delayed crosscorrelation is zero-mean random variable, since the crosscorrelation of noise samples is zero. This explains the low level of m_n before the start of the packet. Once the start of the packet is received, c_n is a crosscorrelation of the identical short training symbols, which causes m_n to jump quickly to its maximum value. This jump gives a quite good estimate of the start of the packet.

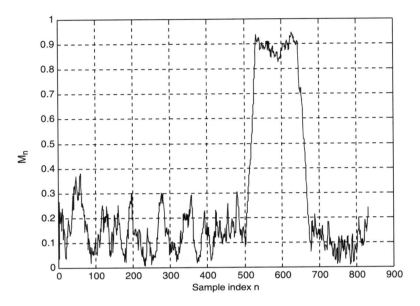

FIGURE 2.6
Response of the delay and correlate packet detection.

Exercise 1 *The simulation tool implements the delay- and correlate packet detection algorithm. Write a Matlab script for the double sliding window algorithm and compare its performance with the original algorithm.*

HiperLAN/2 Preambles

HiperLAN/2 has been designed with several different preambles, in contrast to the IEEE 802.11a that has only one preamble. The rationale for HiperLAN/2's several preambles is the different MAC architecture of HiperLAN/2. The centralized control approach of HiperLAN/2 enables some optimizations of the preamble design; namely, the preamble length is variable. This reduces overhead for some packets, which in turn increases system capacity. The different preamble structures of HiperLAN/2 are shown in Figure 2.7. The letters inside the figure designate different waveforms that are used during the preamble, the *I* preceding a letter means that the signal is inverted; for example *IA* is equal to *–A*. Preamble (a) is used for broadcast packets from the Access Point (AP); it is a full-length structure, since all the stations have to be able to receive the packet. The preamble (b) is a downlink preamble; it does not contain the short training symbols, because the all the stations know the starting point of the packet and frequency synchronization information. Preamble (c) is intented for general uplink use. Preamble (d) can be used instead of (c), if the AP supports it. The main reason for the longer (d) preamble is a possibility to use switch antenna diversity, this technique is discussed in more detail in Chapter 4, "Antenna Diversity." The longer short training symbol section allows the receiver to measure the received signal power for two antennas before the long training symbols, and make a decision of which antenna to use.

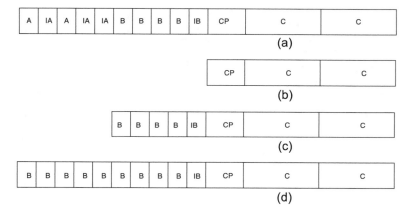

FIGURE 2.7
Different preambles of the HiperLAN/2 standard.[*]

The different patterns for the short training symbols, when used with the delay and correlate algorithm, allow the receiver to distinguish between the different types of bursts. The response of m_n to preambles (c) and (d) is the same as for the IEEE 802.11a preamble, and is shown in Figure 2.8 (b). The response to preamble (a), however, is a zig-zag curve as the windows slide through multiple sections A, IA, B, and BI, this is shown in Figure 2.8 (a). This zig-zag response designates the broadcast packets that every station should decode. However, if a station receives a flat response, and it is not expecting a packet, decoding is not necessary.

Symbol Timing

Symbol timing refers to the task of finding the precise moment of when individual OFDM symbols start and end. The symbol timing result defines the DFT window; i.e., the set of samples used to calculate DFT of each received OFDM symbol. The DFT result is then used to demodulate the subcarriers of the symbol. The approach to symbol timing is different for WLAN and broadcast OFDM systems. A WLAN receiver cannot afford to spend any time beyond the preamble to find the symbol timing, whereas a broadcast transmission receiver can spend several symbols to acquire an accurate symbol timing estimate.

---

[*] *© ETSI 2000. Further use, modification, redistribution is strictly prohibited. ETSI standards are available from publication@etsi.fr and http://www.etsi.org/eds/home.htm.*

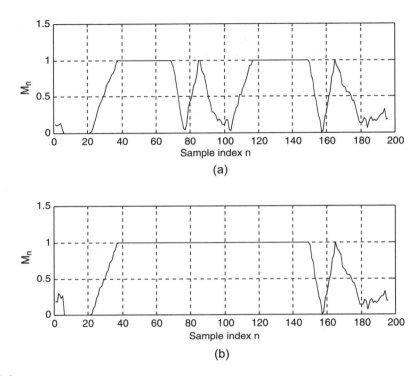

FIGURE 2.8
Response of delay and correlate to HiperLAN/2 preambles (a) and (d).

Symbol Timing for a WLAN Receiver

WLAN receivers have knowledge of the preamble available to them, which enables the receiver to use simple crosscorrelation based symbol timing algorithm. After the packet detector has provided an estimate of the start edge of the packet, the symbol timing algorithm refines the estimate to sample level precision. The refinement is performed by calculating the crosscorrelation of the received signal r_n and a known reference t_k; for example, the end of the short training symbols or the start of the long training symbols, to find the symbol timing estimate. Equation 2.11 shows how to calculate the crosscorrelation. The value of n that corresponds to maximum absolute value of the crosscorrelation is the symbol timing estimate.

$$\hat{t}_s = \arg\max_n \left| \sum_{k=0}^{L-1} r_{n+k} t_k^* \right|^2 \tag{2.11}$$

In Equation 2.11, the length L of the crosscorrelation determines the performance of the algorithm. Larger values improve performance, but also increase the amount of computation required.

In hardware implementations, it is possible to use only the sign of the reference and received signals, effectively quantizing them to one-bit accuracy. This greatly simplifies the hardware implementation, since no actual multiplications are necessary. Figure 2.9 shows the output of the crosscorrelator that uses the first 64 samples of the long training symbols of the IEEE 802.11a standard as the reference signal. The simulation was run in Additive White Gaussian Noise (AWGN) channel with 10dB SNR. The high peak at $n = 77$ clearly shows the correct symbol timing point.

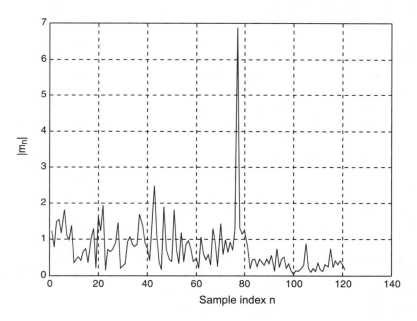

FIGURE 2.9
Response of the symbol timing crosscorrelator.

Optimization of Symbol Timing in a Multipath Channel

The performance of the symbol timing algorithm directly influences the effective multipath tolerance of a OFDM system. Characteristics of multipath channels were introduced in Chapter 1, "Background and WLAN Overview." An OFDM receiver achieves maximum multipath tolerance when symbol timing is fixed to the first sample of an OFDM symbol. Figure 2.10 shows three consecutive OFDM symbols, their respective cyclic prefixes (CP), and the effect of symbol timing on the DFT window. The ideal timing for symbol 2 is shown as the ideal DFT window in Figure 2.10 (a). In this case the DFT window does not contain any samples from the CP, hence the maximum length of the channel impulse response (CIR) that does not cause intersymbol interference (ISI) is equal to the CP length. This is the maximum possible ISI free multipath length for an OFDM system. In practice, it is impossible to fix the symbol timing point perfectly to the first sample of the OFDM symbol. There will always be some variability in the symbol timing estimate around its mean value. In addition to the ideal symbol timing, Figure 2.10 (a) shows the probability density function (PDF) of a realistic symbol timing estimate with the mean value equal to the ideal symbol timing. The PDF shows how the actual symbol timing estimate can be before or after the ideal value. The effect on the DFT window is shown as the DFT window range; that is, the range within which the DFT window will fall. When the symbol timing point is estimated before the ideal value, the start of the DFT window will contain samples from the CP and the last samples of the symbol are not used at all. This case does not cause serious problems, because the CP is equal to the last samples of the symbol the circular convolution property of DFT is still satisfied as shown in Equation 1.74. It is possible that some ISI is caused by the early symbol timing estimate, if the CIR is long enough to reach the first samples of the DFT window. For a properly designed OFDM system, the amount of this interference is negligible, because the last taps of the CIR are small. Next consider the case when the symbol timing estimate is after the ideal value. In this case, the start of the DFT window will be after the first sample of the symbol and the last samples are taken from the beginning of the CP of the next symbol. For example, in Figure 2.10 (a), this would mean the the DFT window for symbol 2 would contain samples from the CP 3. When this happens, significant ISI is created by the samples form CP of the next symbol. Additionally the circular convolution property required for the orthogonality of the subcarriers is no longer true, hence intercarrier interference is generated. The end result of a late symbol timing estimate is a significant performance loss. Fortunately, there is a simple solution for this problem. Since early symbol timing does not create significant problems, the mean value of the symbol timing point can be shifted inside the CP. This is shown in Figure 2.10 (b). After the shift, the PDF of the symbol timing estimate is entirely contained inside the CP 2, hence the DFT range is also within CP 2 and symbol 2. This means that the circular convolution is preserved and no ISI is caused by the samples from CP 3. The optimal amount of the shift depends on the OFDM system paremeters and the performance of the symbol timing algorithm. A rule of thumb for an IEEE 802.11a system is 4-6 samples. The drawback of the shift of the mean symbol timing point is reduced multipath tolerance of the OFDM system. The shift effectively shortens the CP by the amount of the shift, because some samples of the CP are always used for the DFT window. This means that a CIR shorter that the CP can cause ISI; however, as was mentioned earlier, the last taps of the CIR are quite small, so the effect on performance is not serious. Nevertheless the OFDM system designer should keep the symbol timing in mind and put some samples in to the CP in addition to the maximum expected CIR length.

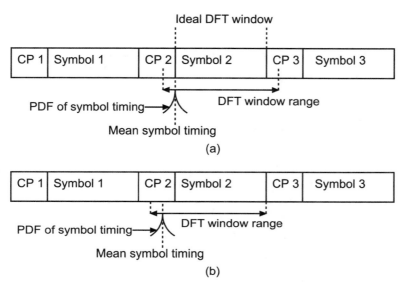

FIGURE 2.10

Effect of variance in symbol timing.

Exercise 2 *The simulation tool allows you to change the amount of the symbol timing shift. Experiment with different values with a multipath channel model, and observe the performance difference.*

In a multipath environment, the symbol timing can be further optimized, if an estimate of the multipath taps h_n of the channel impulse response is available to the receiver. This approach is discussed in more detail in [15]. Figure 2.11 shows a sample of a channel impulse response. In the sample, the strongest tap occurs several taps later than the first one. The crosscorrelation symbol timing estimator would pick the strongest tap 3 as the timing point; however, this will mean that the taps 0 to 2 will not contribute to the signal energy inside the DFT window. This means that some signal energy is lost due to the symbol timing estimate. This loss can be recovered by changing the timing point such that the energy of h_n inside the DFT window is maximized. For the CIR sample in Figure 2.11, this would mean shifting the timing point to the left to cover the taps that occur before the strongest tap.

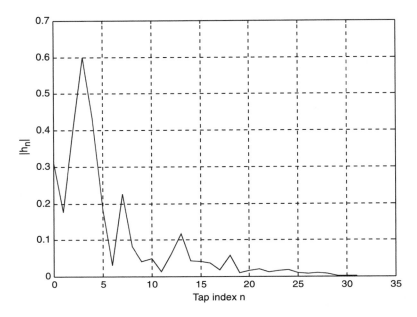

FIGURE 2.11
A sample of a channel impulse response.

Continuous Transmission System Symbol Timing

The different symbol timing algorithms for continuous transmission receivers can coarsely be divided into data-aided and nondata-aided methods. To facilitate data-aided methods broadcast OFDM systems like DVB, periodically insert known training symbols into the transmitted signal. These symbols are called *pilot symbols*. The nondata-aided methods use the cyclic prefix structure of OFDM waveform to perform symbol timing. In this sense, they are similar to the preamble structure packet detection algorithm; the algorithm presented in Schimdl and Cox [21] was developed for symbol timing, but the approach could also be used packet detection. Several authors have investigated symbol timing based on the cyclic prefix [1, 2]. Okada et al. [16] develop a technique for jointly estimating the symbol timing and frequency offset of the received signal. The underlying theme in all these techniques is the use of correlation to detect the repetition of the cyclic prefix in the received signal.

Sample Clock Tracking

A quite different timing estimation problem is tracking the sampling clock frequency. The oscillators used to generate the Digital to Analog Converter (DAC) and Analog to Digital Converter (ADC) sampling instants at the transmitter and receiver will never have exactly the same period.

Thus the sampling instants slowly shift relative to each other. The problem has been analyzed by several authors [6, 11, 17, 19].

The sampling clock error has two main effects: A slow shift of the symbol timing point, which rotates subcarriers, and a loss of SNR due to the intercarrier interference (ICI) generated by the slightly incorrect sampling instants, which causes loss of the orthogonality of the subcarriers. In [23] the normalized sampling error is defined as

$$t_\Delta = \frac{T' - T}{T} \tag{2.12}$$

where T and T' are the transmitter and receiver sampling periods, respectively. Then the overall effect, after DFT, on the received subcarriers $R_{l,k}$ is shown as

$$R_{l,k} = e^{j2\pi kt_\Delta l \frac{T_s}{T_u}} X_{l,k} \operatorname{sinc}(\pi kt_\Delta) H_{l,k} + W_{l,k} + N_{t_\Delta}(l,k) \tag{2.13}$$

where l is the OFDM symbol index, k is the subcarrier index, T_s and T_u are the duration of the total OFDM symbol and the useful data portion, $W_{l,k}$ is additive white noise and the last term $N_{t_\Delta}(l,k)$ is the additional interference due to the sampling frequency offset. The power of the last term is approximated by

$$P_{t_\Delta} \approx \frac{\pi^2}{3}(kt_\Delta)^2 \tag{2.14}$$

hence the degradation grows as the square of the product of the offset t_Δ and the subcarrier index k. This means that the outermost subcarriers are most severely affected. The degradation can also be expressed directly as SNR loss in decibels. The following approximation [19] is derived

$$D_n \approx 10\log_{10}\left(1 + \frac{\pi^2}{3}\frac{E_s}{N_0}(kt_\Delta)^2\right) \tag{2.15}$$

WLAN OFDM systems typically have relatively small number of subcarriers and quite small t_Δ, hence $kt_\Delta \ll 1$, so the interference caused by sampling frequency offset can usually be ignored. Equation 2.13 also shows the more significant problem caused by the offset, namely the term

$$e^{j2\pi kt_\Delta l \frac{T_s}{T_u}} \tag{2.16}$$

This term shows the amount of rotation angle experienced by the different subcarriers as an OFDM signal is received. The angle depends on both the subcarrier index k and the OFDM symbol index l. Hence the angle is largest for the outermost subcarriers and increases with consecutive OFDM symbols. The term t_Δ is usually quite small, but as l increases, the rotation will eventually be so large that correct demodulation is no longer possible. This necessitates tracking the sampling frequency offset.

Estimating the Sampling Frequency Error

The majority of the published approaches to estimating the sampling frequency offset rely on *pilot subcarriers*. The pilot subcarriers are used to transmit known data, called *pilot symbols*, that the receiver can use to perform synchronization functions. Sampling frequency error estimation algorithms usually assume the pilots to be symmetrically distributed around a middle subcarrier. The following method was presented in Speth et al. [25] and Fechtel [6]. The pilot subcarriers are divided into two sets; C_1 corresponds to pilots on negative subcarriers, and C_2 to pilots on positive subcarriers. The sampling frequency offset is estimated by using the knowledge of the linear relationship between the phase rotation caused by the offset and the pilot subcarrier index. The received pilot subcarriers, in a simplified form, are

$$R_{l,k} = H_k P_{l,k} e^{j2\pi k t_\Delta l \frac{T_s}{T_u}} \tag{2.17}$$

Then calculate the rotation of the pilots from one symbol to the next

$$Z_{l,k} = R_{l,k} R_{l-1,k}^* \tag{2.18}$$

$$= H_k P_{l,k} e^{j2\pi k t_\Delta l \frac{T_s}{T_u}} \left(H_k P_{l-1,k} e^{j2\pi k t_\Delta l \frac{T_s}{T_u}} \right)^* \tag{2.19}$$

$$= |H_k|^2 |P_{l,k}|^2 e^{j2\pi k t_\Delta l \frac{T_s}{T_u}} e^{-j2\pi k t_\Delta (l-1) \frac{T_s}{T_u}} \tag{2.20}$$

$$= |H_k|^2 |P_{l,k}|^2 e^{j2\pi k t_\Delta l \frac{T_s}{T_u}} \tag{2.21}$$

Next calculate the cumulative phases of $Z_{l,k}$ for the two sets C_1 and C_2 as

$$\phi_{1,l} = \angle \left[\sum_{k \in C_1} Z_{l,k} \right] \tag{2.22}$$

$$\phi_{2,l} = \angle \left[\sum_{k \in C2} Z_{l,k} \right] \tag{2.23}$$

The sampling frequency offset is then estimated by

$$\hat{t}_\Delta = \frac{1}{2\pi} \frac{T_u}{T_s} \frac{1}{\min_{k \in C_2}(k) + \max_{k \in C_2}(k)} \left(\phi_{2,l} - \phi_{1,l} \right) \tag{2.24}$$

where the normalization factor $\min_{k \in C_2}(k) + \max_{k \in C_2}(k)$ assumes that the pilot indexes k are evenly distributed.

Correcting the Sampling Frequency Error

The rotation caused by the sampling frequency offset can be corrected with two main approaches. Namely, the problem can be corrected at its source by adjusting the sampling frequency of the receiver DAC—the receiver structure is shown on top of Figure 2.12. Secondly, the rotation can be corrected after the DFT processing by derotating the subcarriers, the lower receiver structure in Figure 2.12. Both of these solutions are analyzed in Pollet et al. [19], where the first method is referred to as synchronized sampling and the second as non-synchronized sampling.

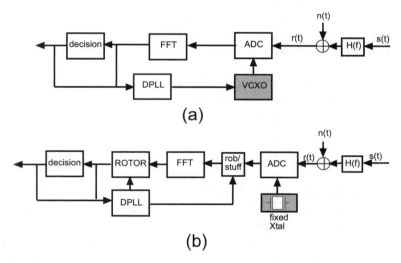

2

SYNCHRONIZATION

FIGURE 2.12

Adapted from Pollet et. al. [19]: Receiver structures for correcting sampling frequency error. © 1994 IEEE.

The adjustment of the clock of the ADC naturally perfectly removes the sampling frequency offset, provided the estimate of the offset is accurate. In this sense, it is the optimal way of performing the correction. However, during recent years, the trend in receiver design has been towards all digital receivers, that do not attempt to adjust the sampling clock. This is illustrated in the lower receiver structure in Figure 2.12 by the fixed crystal that controls the ADC. The rationale for this trend is the desire to simplify the analog part of the receiver, as the analog components are relatively costly compared to digital gates. Hence by using a fixed crystal, instead of a controllable one, the number of analog components can be reduced, and as a result the cost of the receiver can be decreased. The non-synchronized sampling receiver in Figure 2.12 (b) shows an additional block named "rob/stuff," just after the ADC. This block is required, because the drift in sampling instant will eventually be larger than the sampling period. When this happens, the "rob/stuff" block will either "stuff" a duplicate sample or "rob" one sample from the signal, depending on whether the receiver clock is faster or slower than the transmitter clock. This process prevents the receiver sampling instant from drifting so much that the symbol timing would be incorrect. The "ROTOR" block performs the required phase corrections with the information provided by the Digital Phase-Locked Loop (DPLL) that estimates the sampling frequency error.

Frequency Synchronization

One of the main drawbacks of OFDM is its sensitivity to carrier frequency offset. The effect of carrier frequency error on SNR was introduced in Chapter 1, where the main differences between multicarrier and singlecarrier systems were discussed. The degradation is caused by two main phenomena: reduction of amplitude of the desired subcarrier and ICI caused by neighboring carriers. The amplitude loss occurs because the desired subcarrier is no longer sampled at the peak of the sinc-function of DFT. The sinc-function is defined as sinc $(x) = \frac{\sin(x)}{x}$. Adjacent carriers cause interference, because they are not sampled at the zero-crossings of they sinc-functions. The overall effect on SNR is analyzed in Pollet et al. [18], and for relatively small frequency errors, the degradation in dB was approximated by

$$SNR_{Loss} = \frac{10}{3\ln 10}(\pi T f_\Delta)^2 \frac{E_s}{N_0} \text{ dB} \tag{2.25}$$

where f_Δ is the frequency error as a fraction of the subcarrier spacing and T is the sampling period. The performance effect varies strongly with the modulation used; naturally, constellations with fewer points can tolerate larger frequency errors than large constellations. Figure 2.13 illustrates the effect for QPSK and 64-QAM constellations. The figure shows that the 64QAM, the largest constellation in IEEE802.11a, cannot tolerate more than 1% error in the carrier frequency for a negligible SNR loss of 0.5dB, whereas QPSK modulation can tolerate up to 5% error for the same SNR loss.

The analysis above would seem to indicate that large constellations are exceedingly difficult to use with an OFDM system. However, keep in mind that a large constellation automatically implies higher operating SNR than with a small constellation. This directly improves the performance of the frequency error estimators, as is shown in Equations 2.41 and 2.57.

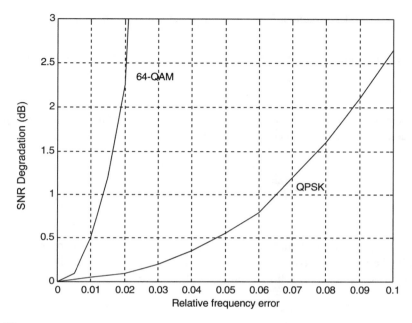

FIGURE 2.13

Symbol error rate (SER) degradation due to frequency offset at SER = 10^{-4}. *© 1995 IEEE. Adapted from Daffara and Adami [5].*

In Hsieh and Wei [8], the various algorithms that have been developed to estimate carrier frequency offsets in OFDM systems are divided into three types:

Type 1 Data-aided algorithms; these methods are based on special training information embedded into the transmitted signal.

Type 2 Nondata-aided algorithms that analyze the received signal in frequency domain.

Type 3 Cyclic prefix based algorithms that use the inherit structure of the OFDM signal provided by the cyclic prefix.

For WLAN applications, type 1 is the most important. The preamble allows the receiver to use efficient maximum likelihood algorithms to estimate and correct for the frequency offset, before the actual information portion of the packet starts. The algorithms belonging to types 2 and 3 are better suited for broadcast or continuous transmission type OFDM systems. Owing to the nature of this book, we will focus on data-aided frequency synchronization algorithms in this section.

Time Domain Approach for Frequency Synchronization

We first derive a data-aided maximum-likelihood estimator that operates on the received time domain signal. This method has been presented in several papers in slightly varying forms [2, 21]. The training information required is at least two consecutive repeated symbols. As a note, the preamble of the WLAN standards satisfies this requirement for both the short and long training symbols.

Let the transmitted signal be s_n, then the complex baseband model of the passband signal y_n is

$$y_n = s_n e^{j2\pi f_{tx} n T_s} \tag{2.26}$$

where f_{tx} is the transmitter carrier frequency. After the receiver downconverts the signal with a carrier frequency f_{rx}, the received complex baseband signal r_n, ignoring noise for the moment, is

$$r_n = s_n e^{j2\pi f_{tx} n T_s} e^{-j2\pi f_{rx} n T_s} \tag{2.27}$$

$$= s_n e^{j2\pi (f_{tx} - f_{rx}) n T_s} \tag{2.28}$$

$$= s_n e^{j2\pi f_\Delta n T_s} \tag{2.29}$$

where $f_\Delta = f_{tx} - f_{rx}$ is the difference between the transmitter and receiver carrier frequencies. Let D be the delay between the identical samples of the two repeated symbols. Then the frequency offset estimator is developed as follows, starting with an intermediate variable z

$$z = \sum_{n=0}^{L-1} r_n r_{n+D}^* \tag{2.30}$$

$$= \sum_{n=0}^{L-1} s_n e^{j2\pi f_\Delta n T_s} \left(s_{n+D} e^{j2\pi f_\Delta (n+D) T_s} \right)^* \tag{2.31}$$

$$= \sum_{n=0}^{L-1} s_n s_{n+D}^* e^{j2\pi f_\Delta n T_s} e^{-j2\pi f_\Delta (n+D) T_s} \tag{2.32}$$

$$= e^{-j2\pi f_\Delta D T_s} \sum_{n=0}^{L-1} |s_n|^2 \tag{2.33}$$

Equation 2.33 is a sum of complex variables with an angle proportional to the frequency offset. Finally, the frequency error estimator is formed as

$$\hat{f}_\Delta = -\frac{1}{2\pi D T_s} \angle z \tag{2.34}$$

where the $\angle z$ operator takes the angle of its argument.

Properties of the Time Domain Frequency Synchronization Algorithm

An important feature of the present method is its operating range. The operating range defines how large frequency offset can be estimated. The range is directly related to the length of the repeated symbols. The angle of z is of the form $-2\pi f_\Delta DT_s$, which is unambiguously defined only in the range $[-\pi, \pi)$. Thus if the absolute value of the frequency error is larger than the following limit

$$|f_\Delta| \geq \frac{\pi}{2\pi DT_s} = \frac{1}{2DT_s} \tag{2.35}$$

the estimate will be incorrect, since z has rotated an angle larger than π. This maximum allowable frequency error is usually normalized with the subcarrier spacing f_s. If the delay D is equal to the symbol length, then

$$\frac{1}{2DT_s} = \frac{1}{2}f_s \tag{2.36}$$

Thus the frequency error can be at most a half of the subcarrier spacing. It should be noted that if the repeated symbols include a cyclic prefix, the delay is longer than the symbol length, and hence the range of the estimator is reduced.

As an example we can calculate the value of this limit for the IEEE 802.11a system for both the short and long training symbols. For the short training symbols, the sample time is 50ns, and the delay $D = 16$. Thus the maximum frequency error that can be estimated is

$$f_{\Delta\max} = \frac{1}{2DT_s} \tag{2.37}$$

$$= \frac{1}{2 \cdot 16 \cdot 50 \cdot 10^{-9}} \tag{2.38}$$

$$= 625kHz$$

This should be compared with the maximum possible frequency error in an IEEE802.11a system. The carrier frequency is approximately 5.3 GHz, and the standard specifies a maximum oscillator error of 20 parts per million (ppm). Thus if the transmitter and receiver clocks have the maximum allowed error, but with opposite signs, the total observed error will be 40ppm. This amounts to a frequency error of $f_\Delta = 40 \cdot 10^{-6} \cdot 5.3 \cdot 10^9 = 212kHz$. Hence the maximum possible frequency error is well within the range of the algorithm. Now consider the long training symbols. The only significant difference is that the delay $D = 64$ is four times longer. Hence the range is

$$f_{\Delta\max} = \frac{1}{4 \cdot 2DT_s} \tag{2.39}$$

$$= 156.25kHz \tag{2.40}$$

Observe that this is less than the maximum possible error defined in the standard. Thus this estimator would not be reliable if only the long training symbols were used.

Beek et al. [2] show that in an AWGN channel the estimator $\hat{f}_\Delta$ is a maximum-likelihood estimate of the frequency offset. Additionally, under the same AWGN assumption, Schimdl and Cox [21] do an analysis of the performance of the algorithm and show that at high SNR the variance $\sigma^2_{\hat{f}_\Delta}$ of the estimator is proportional to

$$\sigma^2_{\hat{f}_\Delta} \sim \frac{1}{L \cdot SNR} \tag{2.41}$$

Hence the more samples in the sum, the better the quality of the estimator will be, as one would expect.

Post DFT Approach to Frequency Error Estimation

Frequency offset estimation can also be performed after the DFT processing [14]. As with the time domain algorithm, at least two consecutive repeated symbols are required. The preamble structure of WLAN standards has this property during the short and long training symbols, thus allowing the receiver to perform the frequency error estimation also after the DFT processing. Following the analysis in Moose [14], a maximum-likelihood frequency error estimator is derived as follows. The received signal during two repeated symbols is, ignoring noise for convenience,

$$r_n = \frac{1}{N}\left[\sum_{k=-K}^{K} X_k H_k e^{\frac{j2\pi n(k+f_\Delta)}{N}}\right] \qquad n = 0,1,\ldots,2N-1 \tag{2.42}$$

where X_k are the transmitted data symbols, H_k is the channel frequency response for subcarrier k, K is the total number of subcarriers, and f_Δ is the fractional frequency error normalized to the subcarrier spacing. Then calculating the DFT for the first received symbol, the value of kth subcarrier is

$$R_{1,k} = \sum_{n=0}^{N-1} r_n e^{\frac{-j2\pi kn}{N}} \qquad k = 0,1,\ldots,N-1 \tag{2.43}$$

and the DFT of the second symbol is

$$R_{2,k} = \sum_{n=N}^{2N-1} r_n e^{\frac{-j2\pi kn}{N}} \tag{2.44}$$

$$= \sum_{n=0}^{N-1} r_{n+N} e^{\frac{-j2\pi kn}{N}} \qquad k = 0,1,\ldots,N-1 \tag{2.45}$$

Now the crucial observation, from Equation 2.42, is that

$$r_{n+N} = \frac{1}{N}\left[\sum_{k=-K}^{K} X_k H_k e^{\frac{j2\pi(n+N)(k+f_\Delta)}{N}}\right] \tag{2.46}$$

$$= \frac{1}{N}\left[\sum_{k=-K}^{K} X_k H_k e^{\frac{j2\pi n(k+f_\Delta)}{N}} e^{\frac{j2\pi(k+f_\Delta)N}{N}}\right] \tag{2.47}$$

$$= \frac{1}{N}\left[\sum_{k=-K}^{K} X_k H_k e^{\frac{j2\pi n(k+f_\Delta)}{N}} e^{j2\pi(k+f_\Delta)}\right] \tag{2.48}$$

$$= \frac{1}{N}\left[\sum_{k=-K}^{K} X_k H_k e^{\frac{j2\pi n(k+f_\Delta)}{N}}\right] e^{j2\pi f_\Delta} \tag{2.49}$$

$$= r_n e^{j2\pi f_\Delta} \tag{2.50}$$

since $e^{j2\pi k} = 1$. Equation 2.50 implies that

$$R_{2,k} = R_{1,k} e^{j2\pi f_\Delta} \tag{2.51}$$

Thus every subcarrier experiences the same phase shift that is proportional to the frequency off-set. Hence the frequency error can be estimated from this phase shift. Using an intermediate variable z again

$$z = \sum_{k=-K}^{K} R_{1,k} R_{2,k}^* \tag{2.52}$$

$$= \sum_{k=-K}^{K} R_{1,k}\left(R_{1k} e^{j2\pi f_\Delta}\right)^* \tag{2.53}$$

$$= e^{-j2\pi f_\Delta}\sum_{k=-K}^{K} R_{1,k} R_{1,k}^* \tag{2.54}$$

$$= e^{-j2\pi f_\Delta}\sum_{k=-K}^{K} \left|R_{1,k}\right|^2 \tag{2.55}$$

Thus z is a complex variable, for which the angle is defined by the frequency error. Finally the estimator is

$$\hat{f}_\Delta = -\frac{1}{2\pi}\angle z \tag{2.56}$$

which is quite similar in form to the time domain version.

Properties of the Post DFT Frequency Error Estimation Algorithm

The estimator uses the angle of the complex variable as the basis for the estimate, thus the same $[-\pi, \pi)$ unique range applies as for the time domain estimator. The frequency error f_Δ was defined as a fractional value normalized to the subcarrier spacing, hence the maximum estimable frequency error is again a half of the subcarrier spacing. Otherwise the angle of z will rotate over the $\pm\pi$ limit. This implies that the frequency range is the same for both the time domain and frequency domain estimators.

A somewhat counterintuitive property of this estimator is that the ICI introduced by calculating the DFT of the signal with frequency offset is actually useful information for the estimator. Thus there is no performance penalty compared to the time domain algorithm. In fact, the variance $\sigma^2_{\hat{f}_\Delta}$ is shown [14] to be proportional to

$$\sigma^2_{\hat{f}_\Delta} \sim \frac{1}{L \cdot SNR} \tag{2.57}$$

which is the same result as for the time domain algorithm.

Exercise 3 *The simulation tool implements the time domain frequency error estimation algorithm. Write a Matlab script for the frequency domain algorithm and compare the performance of the algorithms.*

Comments on Frequency Error Estimation Algorithms

Figure 2.4 suggests a two-step frequency estimation process with a coarse frequency estimate performed from the short training symbols and a fine frequency synchronization from the long training symbols. The rationale for this can be explained with the estimation range of the time domain algorithm and the post DFT algorithm. As was shown in Equation 2.38, either estimator could not reliably estimate the frequency error only from the long training symbols. The two-step process would then proceed by first acquiring a coarse estimate of the frequency error from the short training symbols, and then correcting the long training symbols with this estimate. The accuracy of the coarse estimate should easily be better than the 156.25kHz range of the estimator during the long training symbols. Hence a second estimation step could be done from the long training symbols to improve the estimate. Whether the second step is necessary depends on the accuracy of the first estimate. If enough data samples are used to calculate the first estimate from the short symbols, a satisfactory accuracy can usually be reached. Hence the second estimation would be unnecessary.

The main disadvantage of frequency domain estimation is that the DFT has to be calculated for both repeated symbols. Compared to the time domain estimator, the DFT operations mean additional computations without any advantages. Thus the time domain method is preferable for a

WLAN receiver, which in general has very little time to complete all the necessary synchronization functions during the preamble.

Alternative Techniques for Frequency Error Estimation

Hsieh and Wei [8] present a technique to remedy the ±0.5 subcarrier estimation range. The idea is to take advantage of the correlation of the channel frequency response between adjacent subcarriers. The algorithm first uses training data to estimate the channel frequency response. The next step is to calculate the autocorrelation function of the channel estimate. Since the frequency offset shifts the received signal in frequency, the autocorrelation function will have its maximum at the lag corresponding to the frequency offset. The authors show that in an OFDM system with 1,024 subcarriers frequency offsets up to ±200 subcarrier spacings can be estimated, which is a significant improvement from the ±0.5 subcarrier spacing limit.

Traditional single carrier receivers usually employ some kind of phase locked loop to track the carrier phase. The main difficulty in using phase locked loops for OFDM carrier phase tracking is the nature of the OFDM waveform. It is not easy to design a phase error detector, a main component of a phase locked loop, for an OFDM system. A carrier frequency tracking technique for OFDM that resembles single carrier frequency recovery loop has been proposed [13]. The proposed method is composed of two steps: acquisition and tracking. The acquisition step is performed from known synchronization symbols. Tracking mode is a frequency control loop that has been modified for OFDM waveform. The main advantage of this method is its quite large acquisition range, compared to the two estimators presented above. This advantage is significant for broadcast systems like DVB and DAB, which place subcarriers very close to each other; for example, the minimum subcarrier spacing for DAB is 1 kHz. Thus a half subcarrier spacing acquisition range of the estimator practically renders the presented time domain and post DFT methods useless. In the paper, the crucial phase error detection is performed by detecting and remodulating the received data, and then comparing the remodulated signal to the received signal. A similar technique is also investigated in Daffara and Chouly [4]. The structure of the phase error detector of the previous two papers is simplified [5] by exploiting the cyclic prefix to detect the phase error.

Carrier Phase Tracking

Frequency estimation is not a perfect process, so there is always some residual frequency error. The SNR loss due to the ICI generated should not be a problem if the estimator has been designed to reduce the frequency error below the limit required for a negligible performance loss for the used modulation. The main problem of the residual frequency offset is constellation rotation. The analysis of the post DFT frequency error estimator also shows that the constellation rotation is the same for all subcarriers. To illustrate the effect in an IEEE 802.11a system, Figure 2.14 shows how much a QPSK constellation rotates during 10 OFDM symbols with a 3kHz frequency error.

This error corresponds to only 1% of the subcarrier spacing, thus the effect on SNR is negligible as shown earlier. The figure shows that after only 10 symbols, the constellation points have just rotated over the decision boundaries shown as solid lines, thus correct demodulation is no longer possible.

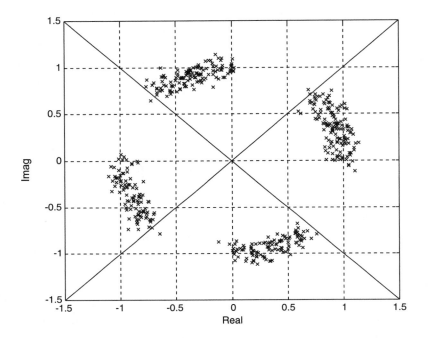

FIGURE 2.14
Constellation rotation with 3kHz frequency error during 10 symbols.

This effect forces the receiver to track the carrier phase while data symbols are received.

Data-Aided Carrier Phase Tracking

The simplest method is data-aided tracking of the carrier phase. IEEE 802.11a and HiperLAN/2 include four predefined subcarriers among the transmitted data. These special subcarriers are referred to as *pilot* subcarriers. The main purpose of these pilots is exactly to help the receiver to track the carrier phase. After the DFT of the nth received symbol, the pilot subcarriers $R_{n,k}$ are equal to the product of the channel frequency response H_k and the known pilot symbol $P_{n,k}$, rotated by the residual frequency error.

$$R_{nk} = H_k P_{nk} e^{j2\pi n f_\Delta} \tag{2.58}$$

Assuming an estimate $\hat{H}_k$ of the channel frequency response is available, the phase estimate is

$$\hat{\Phi}_n = \angle \left[\sum_{k=1}^{N_p} R_{n,k} \left(\hat{H}_k P_{n,k} \right)^* \right] \tag{2.59}$$

$$= \angle \left[\sum_{k=1}^{N_p} H_k P_{n,k} e^{j2\pi n f_\Delta} \left(\hat{H}_k P_{n,k} \right)^* \right] \tag{2.60}$$

If we assume that the channel estimate is perfectly accurate, we get the estimator

$$\hat{\Phi}_n = \angle \left[\sum_{k=1}^{N_p} |H_k|^2 |P_{n,k}|^2 e^{j2\pi n f_\Delta} \right] \tag{2.61}$$

$$= \angle \left[e^{j2\pi n f_\Delta} \sum_{k=1}^{N_p} |H_k|^2 \right] \tag{2.62}$$

In this case we need not worry about the $[-\pi, \pi)$ phase range, because the pilot data are known, thus the phase ambiguity is automatically resolved correctly. Note that in practice the channel estimates are not perfectly accurate, thus they contribute to the noise in the estimate.

Nondata-Aided Carrier Phase Tracking

The phase error can be estimated without the help of the pilot symbols. Recall that the phase error resulting from the frequency offset is identical for all the subcarriers; this property (identical frequency offset) allows the development of a nondata-aided estimator for the phase error. Figure 2.15 shows how the data subcarriers have rotated for a single BPSK modulated OFDM symbol after the channel effect has been corrected. The angle Φ shown in the figure is the result of the frequency offset.

The angle Φ can be estimated without any knowledge of the data by performing hard decisions $\hat{X}_{n,k}$ on the received data symbols $R_{n,k} = H_k X_{nk} e^{j2\pi n f_\Delta}$ after they are corrected for the channel effect. Then the angle between a hard decision and the corresponding received symbol is used as an estimator.

$$\hat{\Phi} = \angle \left[\sum_{k=-K}^{K} R_{n,k} \left(\hat{X}_k \hat{H}_k \right)^* \right] \tag{2.63}$$

$$= \angle \left[\sum_{k=-K}^{K} H_k \hat{H}_k^* X_{n,k} \hat{X}_{n,k}^* e^{j2\pi n f_\Delta} \right] \tag{2.64}$$

$$= \angle \left[\sum_{k=-K}^{K} |H_k|^2 |X_{n,k}|^2 e^{j2\pi n f_\Delta} \right] \tag{2.65}$$

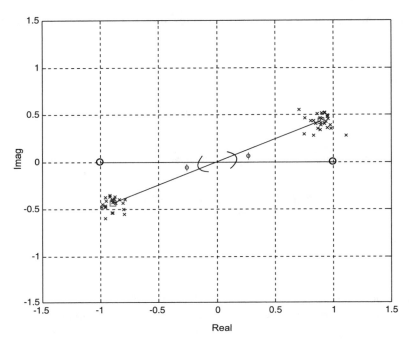

FIGURE 2.15

BPSK single symbol rotation.

In Equations 2.63-2.65, we have assumed that all the hard decisions are correct and that the channel estimates are perfect. In reality, neither condition is true, but if the number of data carriers is large the effect of incorrect hard decisions will not have a significant impact.

It should be noted that the total rotation angle increases from symbol to symbol, hence it is necessary to compensate this angle before the hard decisions are performed. Without the compensation the rotation angle will eventually cross the decision boundaries of the constellation, and then all the hard decisions will be incorrect. As a result, the phase estimate will also be worthless. This sounds like a circular argument: How can the angle be compensated before it has been estimated? A simple tactic is to keep track of the total rotation up to the previous symbol, and correct the data with this value, before the hard decisions are performed. The rotation from symbol to symbol is quite small, thus the probability of incorrect hard decisions is not increased significantly. After the angle has been estimated, the total rotation angle is updated for the next symbol.

Exercise 4 *The simulation tool implements the data-aided carrier phase tracking algorithm. Write a Matlab script for the nondata-aided algorithm and compare the performance of the algorithms. Try to implement a method to combine both algorithms to achieve improved performance.*

Channel Estimation

Channel estimation is the task of estimating the frequency response of the radio channel the transmitted signal travels before reaching the receiver antenna. The impulse response of a time varying radio channel is usually [20] represented as a discrete time FIR filter

$$h(\tau;t) = \sum_n \alpha_n(t)e^{-j2\pi f_c \tau_n(t)}\delta(\tau - \tau_n(t)) \qquad (2.66)$$

WLAN applications generally assume that the channel is *quasistationary*, that is, the channel does not change during the data packet. With this assumption the time dependency in Equation 2.66 can be dropped

$$h(\tau) = \sum_n \alpha_n e^{-j2\pi f_c \tau_n(t)}\delta(\tau - \tau_n) \qquad (2.67)$$

Then the discrete time frequency response of the channel is the Fourier transform of the channel impulse response

$$H_k = DFT\{h_n\} \qquad (2.68)$$

Hence the channel estimation process outputs the $\hat{H}_k$, an estimate of the channel frequency response for each subcarrier.

Channel estimation is mandatory for OFDM systems that employ coherent modulation schemes. Otherwise correct demodulation would not be possible. Knowledge of the channel can also improve the performance OFDM with noncoherent modulation schemes, although the $\hat{H}_k$ are not needed for demodulation in this case. The improvement can be achieved when an error control code is used in the system, in which case the channel knowledge can help the code decoder do a better job.

Frequency Domain Approach for Channel Estimation

Frequency domain channel estimation can be performed with two main approaches. The first method uses training data transmitted on every subcarrier. This method is applicaple to WLAN systems. The second method uses correlation properties of the frequency response of a multipath channel, and training information that is transmitted on a subset of the subcarriers. This approach is used in broadcast OFDM systems.

Channel Estimation Using Training Data

The long training symbols in the WLAN preamble, Figure 2.4, facilitate an easy and efficient estimate of the channel frequency response for all the subcarriers. The contents of the two long training symbols are identical, so averaging them can be used to improve to quality of the channel estimate. DFT is a linear operation, hence the average can be calculated before the DFT. Then only one DFT operation is needed to calculate the channel estimate. After the DFT processing, the received training symbols $R_{1,k}$ and $R_{2,k}$ are a product of the training symbols X_k and the channel H_k plus additive noise $W_{l,k}$.

$$R_{l,k} = H_k X_k + W_{l,k} \tag{2.69}$$

Thus the channel estimate can be calculated as

$$\hat{H}_k = \frac{1}{2}(R_{l,k} + R_{2,k})X_k^* \tag{2.70}$$

$$= \frac{1}{2}(H_k X_k + W_{1,k} + H_k X_k + W_{2,k})X_k^* \tag{2.71}$$

$$= H_k|X_k|^2 + \frac{1}{2}(W_{1,k} + W_{2,k})X_k^* \tag{2.72}$$

$$= H_k + \frac{1}{2}(W_{1,k} + W_{2,k})X_k^* \tag{2.73}$$

where the training data amplitudes have been selected to be equal to one. The noise samples $W_{1,k}$ and $W_{2,k}$ are statistically independent, thus the variance of their sum divided by two is a half of the variance of the individual noise samples.

Channel Estimation Using Pilot Subcarriers and Interpolation

If the subcarriers are very close to each other, like in broadcast standards (e.g. DVB) the frequency domain correlation of the channel frequency response can be used to estimate the channel, even if training data is not available for all the subcarriers. The *coherence bandwidth* of the channel is usually approximated [20] as the inverse of the total length of the channel impulse response

$$(\Delta f) \approx \frac{1}{\tau_{max}} \tag{2.74}$$

When the subcarrier spacing is much less than the coherence bandwidth, the channel frequency response on neighboring subcarriers will be practically identical. For example, the DVB standard takes advantage of this by not sending training information on all subcarriers, hence more data can be transmitted. The pilot subcarriers in DVB are divided into two sets. The first set is regular pilot subcarriers that are similar to the WLAN pilots subcarriers; known data is constantly transmitted on them. The second set is called *scattered* pilots; known data is transmitted only intermittently transmitted on the subcarrier. Then the channel estimation is performed by interpolating the frequency response of the subcarriers that do not have training information from the known subcarriers. We do not describe this algorithm in detail, a description of a method can be found in Speth et. al. [25].

Time Domain Approach for Channel Estimation

The channel estimation can also be performed using the time domain approach, before DFT processing of the training symbols. In this case, the channel impulse response, instead of the channel frequency response, is estimated. The following derivation of the channel estimator uses IEEE 802.11a standard training symbols as an example, but the same approach can be applied to any OFDM system that includes training symbols. The received time domain signal during the two long training symbols is

$$r_{1,n} = h * x_n + w_{1,n} \tag{2.75}$$

The time domain convolution can be expressed as a matrix vector multiplication. The circular convolution matrix is formed from the training data as

$$X = \begin{bmatrix} x_1 & x_{64} & x_{63} & \cdots & x_{64-L+2} \\ x_2 & x_1 & x_{64} & & x_{64-L+3} \\ \vdots & & \vdots & & \vdots \\ x_{63} & x_{62} & & & x_{64-L} \\ x_{64} & x_{63} & & \cdots & x_{64-L+1} \end{bmatrix} \tag{2.76}$$

The parameter L defines the maximum length of the impulse response that can be estimated, and X is in general a rectangular matrix. The channel impulse response vector is

$$h = \begin{bmatrix} h_1 \\ h_2 \\ h_3 \\ \vdots \\ h_L \end{bmatrix} \tag{2.77}$$

Then the convolution is expressed as

$$r_{1,n} = h * x_n + w_{1,n} = Xh + w_l \tag{2.78}$$

The channel impulse response estimate can then be formed by

$$\hat{h} = \frac{1}{2} X^\dagger (r_{1,n} + r_{2,n}) \tag{2.79}$$

$$= \frac{1}{2} X^\dagger (Xh + w_1 + Xh + w_2) \tag{2.80}$$

$$= X^\dagger Xh + \frac{1}{2} X^\dagger (w_1 + w_2) \tag{2.81}$$

$$= h + \frac{1}{2} X^\dagger (w_1 + w_2) \tag{2.82}$$

where $X^\dagger$ denotes Moore-Penrose [22] generalized inverse of X. The channel frequency response estimate is then formed by calculating the DFT of the impulse response estimate

$$\hat{H} = DFT\{\hat{h}\} \tag{2.83}$$

Exercise 5 *The simulation tool implements the frequency domain channel estimation algorithm. Write a Matlab script for the time-domain algorithm and compare the performance of the algorithms.*

Exercise 6 *The simulation tool allows to run simulations with perfect synchronization or with partial or full synchronization. Experiment how the performance of the system degrades compared to perfect synchronization as the various synchronization algorithms are activated.*

Analysis of the Time Domain and Frequency Domain Approaches for Channel Estimation

The advantage of the time domain approach is improved performance, when the maximum length of the impulse response can be limited to a number significantly less than the number of subcarriers. The rationale is that the frequency domain estimator has to simultaneously estimate all the subcarriers, whereas the time domain estimator needs to estimate only the taps of the impulse response. When the number of subcarriers is large compared to the number of channel taps, the signal energy used to estimate each H_k is significantly less than the signal energy used to estimate each h_n. In other words, it is easier to estimate fewer parameters given a fixed amount of data. For example, in the IEEE 802.11a system the number of subcarriers is 52, and the maximum length of the channel can be assumed to be less than the cyclic prefix length of 16 samples. Thus the frequency domain algorithm estimates more than three times the number of parameters than the time domain algorithm.

The drawback of the time domain method is that additional computations are required. The $\frac{1}{2} X^{\dagger}(r_{1,n} + r_{2,n})$ operation requires $64 \cdot L$ multiplications, which are not needed at all in the frequency domain estimator. This is the usual engineering trade-off; better performance usually implies higher costs in one form or another.

Enhancing the Channel Estimate

The correlation of the channel frequency response between different subcarriers can be used to further improve the quality of the channel estimate. Figure 2.16 shows an example of the channel amplitude response for a IEEE802.11a system. It can be seen that the neighboring subcarriers are highly correlated. We will not go to the details of this method, but refer to [12] for a full discussion. The paper shows that in some conditions performance very close to ideal channel estimation can be achieved. Unfortunately, this improvement does not come without a price; significantly more computations are required than to calculate the simple frequency domain channel estimator.

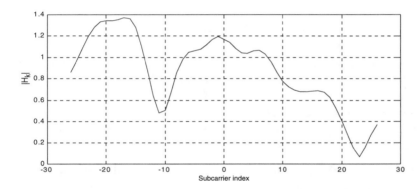

FIGURE 2.16

Example of a channel amplitude response.

Clear Channel Assessment

Clear Channel Assessment (CCA) is not strictly an OFDM synchronization algorithm, but a network synchronization method. However, it is closely related to packet detection problem and thus it is included in this chapter. The overall system performance of IEEE 802.11 WLAN is crucially dependent on high quality CCA algorithm, so the algorithm has to be carefully designed. The IEEE 802.11a standard has two different requirements for the CCA algorithm. The first is the detection probability when a preamble is available and the second is the detection probability when the preamble is not available. The requirement for the first case is that the CCA algorithm shall indicate a *Busy* channel with >90% probability within $4\mu s$ observation window, if a signal is received at −82 dBm level. For the second case, when the known preamble structure is not available, the requirement is relaxed by 20dB. Thus a signal detection probability of >90% within $4\mu s$ observation for a received signal level of −62dBm is required.

The first requirement can be approached using any of the packet detection algorithms presented in this chapter. The methods that use the known preamble structure are capable of reaching the performance level required in the standard. The only possible approach for the second requirement is to use the received signal energy detection method. The reason is the maximum allowed length of $4\mu s$ for the observation time. This is equal to the symbol length in the IEEE802.11a system. Thus, during the $4\mu s$ time, the receiver might receive one whole OFDM symbol or the end of one symbol and the start of the next one. In this case, there is no available signal structure that could be taken advantage of to improve the detection probability. The OFDM waveform itself resembles white noise, and inside $4\mu s$ windows it cannot be guaranteed that a whole OFDM symbol is received, which would allow to use the cyclic prefix in the CCA algorithm. As a conclusion, the receiver can only measure the total received energy and test whether it is above the specified limit.

Signal Quality

Signal quality estimation is not strictly a synchronization algorithm, but a network performance issue. WLAN systems define several data rates that can be used to transmit data; thus, to achieve the best overall network performance, data should be transmitted on the highest rate that can be reliably transmitted under the current channel conditions. For the transmitter to be able to decide what data rate to use, an accurate estimate of the quality of the channel has to be available. This is the task of the signal quality algorithm.

The double sliding window algorithm showed how its output could be used to estimate the received *SNR* in Equation 2.7. This is a quite simple method if the receiver implements the double sliding window detector. However, the form of the estimator does not take into account fading channel conditions. Only the total received signal energy is considered. In some cases, this behavior can lead to an overly optimistic estimate of the signal quality. For example, the total channel impulse response energy may be quite high, indicating high SNR, but the frequency response of the channel can have very deep nulls. In this case, the actual quality of the channel could be significantly less than the estimate given by double sliding window algorithm.

A quite different approach to the signal quality problem can be taken by using the convolutional error control code specified in the IEEE802.11a system. The convolutional error correcting code used in IEEE 802.11a standard is described in Chapter 3, "Modulation and Coding." The standard method to perform convolutional code decoding is the Viterbi algorithm that is described in Chapter 1, and in more detail in [20]. We will not describe the algorithm, but assume knowledge of its basic principles. Essentially the Viterbi algorithm calculates the distance between the maximum-likelihood transmitted code word and the received data. This distance can be used as an indication of the quality of the channel. When the channel is in good condition, the distance between the transmitted and received signal is small; this is indicated by the Viterbi algorithm as a small cumulative minimum distance at the end of the decoding process. When the channel is in a bad state, the distance between the transmitted and received signal is larger, and the cumulative minimum distance will be large. Figure 2.17 shows the probability density functions of the cumulative minimum distance for several different *SNRs*. The *SNR* estimator is formed by dividing the cumulative minimum distance into ranges according to the value of the PDFs. The *SNR* value corresponding to the PDF that has the largest value at a given cumulative minimum distance is the estimate of the signal quality. For example, a cumulative minimum distance between 2.2 and 2.9 indicates a 13dB SNR. From Figure 2.17 it can be seen that for a large range of received *SNRs* a very good accuracy of 1dB resolution can be achieved.

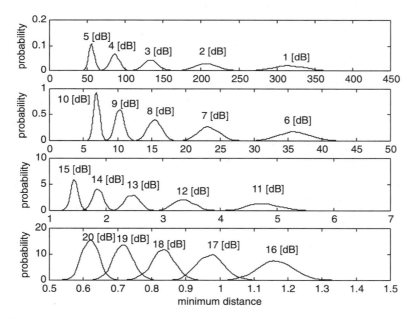

FIGURE 2.17

Cumulative minimum distance in Viterbi decoding.

Bibliography

[1]   J.-J. van de Beek, M. Sandell, M. Isaksson and P.O. Borjesson, "Low-complex frame synchronization in OFDM systems," in Proceedings of IEEE Internatial Conference Universal Personal Communications, Toronto, Canada, Sept. 27–29, 1995, pp. 982–986

[2] J-J. van de Beek, M. Sandell, P. O. Börjesson, "ML Estimation of Time and Frequency Offset in OFDM systems," IEEE Transactions on Signal Processing, Vol. 45, No. 7, July 1997

[3] G. Casella, R. Berger, "Statistical Inference," Duxbury Press, California, 1990

[4] F. Daffara, A. Chouly, "Maximum Likelihood Frequency Detectors for Orthogonal Multicarrier Systems," Proceedings of IEEE International Conference on Communications, Geneva, Switzerland, May 22–26, 1993, pp.766–771

[5] F. Daffara, O. Adami, "A New Frequency Detector for Orthogonal Multicarrier Transmission Techniques," Proceedings of IEEE Vehicular Technology Conference, Chicago, IL, July 25–28, 1995, pp.804–809

[6] S. A. Fechtel, "OFDM Carrier and Sampling Frequency Synchronization and its Performance on Stationary and Mobile Channels," IEEE Transactions on Consumer Electronics, Vol. 46, No. 3, August 2000, pp. 438–441

[7] HiperLAN/2, "Broadband Radio Access Networks (BRAN); HIPERLAN Type 2; Physical (PHY) layer," ETSI TS 101 475 V1.2.1 (2000–11)

[8] Meng-Han Hsieh and Che-Ho Wei, "A Low-Complexity Frame Synchronization and Frequency Offset Compesation Scheme for OFDM Systems over Fading Channels," in IEEE Transactions on Vehicular Technology, Vol. 48, No. 5, September 1999

[9] IEEE 802.11a, "Wireless LAN Medium Access Control (MAC) and Physical Layer (PHY) specifications: High-speed Physical Layer in the 5 GHZ Band," IEEE Std 802.11a-1999

[10] Steven M. Kay, "Fundamentals of Statistical Signal Processing: Detection Theory," Prentice Hall, New Jersey, 1998

[11] D. K. Kim, S.H. Do, H. B. Cho, H. J. Choi, K. B. Kim, "A New Joint Algorithm of Symbol Timing Recovery and Sampling Clock Adjustment for OFDM Systems," IEEE Transactions on Consumer Electronics, Vol. 44, No. 3, August 1998, pp. 1142–1149

[12] Y. Li, L. J. Cimini, N. R. Sollenberger, "Robust Channel Estimation for OFDM Systems with Rapid Dispersive Fading Channels," IEEE Transactions on Communications, Vol. 46, No. 7, July 1998

[13] M. Luise, R. Reggiannini, "Carrier Frequency Acquisition and Tracking for OFDM Systems," IEEE Transactions on Communications, Vol. 44, No. 11, November 1996

[14] P. H. Moose, "A Technique for Orthogonal Frequency Division Multiplexing Frequency Offset Correction," IEEE Transactions on Communications, Vol. 42, No. 10, October 1994

[15] R. van Nee and Ramjee Prasad, "OFDM for Wireless Multimedia Communications," Artech House Publishers, 2000

[16] M. Okada, S. Hara, S. Komaki, N. Morinaga, "Optimum Synchronization of Orthogonal Multi-Carrier Modulated Signals," Proceedings IEEE PIMRC, Taipei, Taiwan, Oct. 15–18, 1996, pp. 863–867

[17] T. Pollet, M. Peeters, "Synchronization with DMT Modulation," IEEE Communications Magazine, April 1999, pp.80–86

[18] T. Pollet, M. van Bladel, M. Moeneclaey, "BER Sensitivity of OFDM Systems to Carrier Frequency Offset and Wiener Phase Noise," IEEE Transactions on Communications, Vol. 43, Issue 2, Part 3, February, March, April 1995, pp. 191–193

[19] T. Pollet, P. Spruyt, M. Moeneclaey, "The BER Performance of OFDM Systems using Non-Synchronized Sampling," IEEE Global Telecommunications Conference 1994, pp. 253–257

[20] J. G. Proakis, "Digital Communications," McGraw-Hill, Boston, 3ed., 1995

[21] T. M. Schmidl, D.C. Cox, "Low-Overhead, Low-Complexity [Burst] Synchronization for OFDM," IEEE International Conference on Communications, Vol. 3., 1996, pp 1301–1306

[22] S. R. Searle, "Matrix Algebra Useful for Statistics," John Wiley & Sons, New York 1982

[23] M. Speth, D. Daecke, H. Meyr, "Minimum Overhead Burst Synchronization for OFDM based Broadband Transmission," IEEE Global Telecommunications Conference, Vol. 5, 1998, pp. 2777–2782

[24] M. Speth, S. A. Fechtel, G. Fock, H. Meyr, "Optimum Receiver Design for Wireless Broad-Band Systems Using OFDM-Part I," IEEE Transactions on Communications, Vol. 47, No. 11, November 1999, pp. 1668–1677

[25] M. Speth, S. Fechtel, G. Fock, H. Meyr, "Optimum Receiver Design for OFDM-Based Broadband Transmission-Part II: A Case Study," IEEE Transactions on Communications, Vol. 49, No. 4, April 2001, pp. 571–578

2

SYNCHRONIZATION

Modulation and Coding

IN THIS CHAPTER

- Modulation   88
- Interleaving   102
- Channel Codes   106
- Bibliography   120

Modulation and channel coding are fundamental components of a digital communication system. Modulation is the process of mapping the digital information to analog form so it can be transmitted over the channel. Consequently every digital communication system has a *modulator* that performs this task. Closely related to modulation is the inverse process, called *demodulation*, done by the receiver to recover the transmitted digital information. The design of optimal demodulators is called *detection* theory. An OFDM system performs modulation and demodulation for each subcarrier separately, although usually in a serial fashion, to reduce complexity.

Channel coding, although not strictly speaking mandatory for digital communication, is essential for good performance. After Claude Shannon published his groundbreaking paper [16] that started *information theory* as a scientific discipline and established the fundamental law equation 3.1 of the capacity C of an AWGN communication channel with bandwidth W and signal to noise ratio SNR, communication scientists and engineers have been searching for methods on how to reach the capacity of the channel.

$$C = W \log_2(1 + SNR) \tag{3.1}$$

Shannon's proof of the channel capacity formula was nonconstructive, and thus did not provide a method to actually reach the capacity C. As a consequence, *coding theory* got started as a discipline that research methods to design a communication system that has performance close to the fundamental limit C. The methods developed under coding theory have different names; channel coding, forward error correction (FEC), and error control coding are the most usual. Channel coding and basic types of FEC codes were introduced in "Channel Coding" in Chapter 1. Note that channel coding and source coding, introduced in the "Source Coding" section in Chapter 1, although related, are quite different topics.

Our goal in this chapter is to discuss modulation, detection, channel coding and interleaving from an OFDM system of point of view. Channel coding is such an important component of OFDM systems that the term Coded Orthogonal Frequency Division Multiplexing (COFDM) is sometimes used. The reasons for this emphasis on channel coding for OFDM systems will become apparent in the channel coding section of this chapter. Modulation and demodulation or detection are discussed in depth in several books [11, 17, 18]. Channel coding is the topic of a wide variety of books [10, 20] and also books that concentrate on specific types of FEC codes [7, 9].

Modulation

As was discussed in "Modulation" in Chapter 1, modulation can be done by changing the amplitude, phase or frequency of the transmitted Radio Frequency (RF) signal. For an OFDM system, the first two methods can be used. Frequency modulation cannot be used because subcarriers are orthogonal in frequency and carry independent information. Modulating subcarrier frequencies would destroy the orthogonality property of the subcarriers; this makes frequency modulation unusable for OFDM systems.

The main design issue of the modulator is the *constellation* used. Constellation is the set of points that can be transmitted on a single symbol. The used constellation affects several important properties of a communication system; for example, bit error rate (BER), peak to average power ratio (PAPR), and RF spectrum shape. The single most important parameter of a constellation is *minimum distance*. Minimum distance (d_{min}) is the smallest distance between any two points in the constellation. Therefore d_{min} determines the least amount of noise that is needed to generate a decision error. Actual BER or P_b of a constellation can in many cases be calculated using the Q-function defined in Equation 3.2. The value of the Q-function is equal to the area under the tail of the Probability Density Function (PDF) of a zero mean and unit variance normal random variable.

$$Q(x) = \frac{1}{\sqrt{2\pi}} \int_x^\infty e^{-\frac{t^2}{2}} dt \quad x \geq 0 \tag{3.2}$$

P_b is a function of energy per bit to noise ratio $\frac{E_b}{N_o}$ or signal energy to noise ratio $\frac{E_s}{N_o}$; these ratios are related by a simple scaling factor that depends on the number of bits k transmitted per symbol $E_s = kE_b$. The usefulness of $\frac{E_b}{N_o}$ as a measure of the signal quality will became apparent when different coding schemes are discussed in "Channel Codes" later in this chapter. Then a general form of P_b equations for several important constellations in terms of the Q-function is shown in Equation 3.3.

$$P_b \sim Q\left(\sqrt{\frac{E_b}{N_o}}\right) \tag{3.3}$$

The value of the Q-function gets smaller for larger arguments, hence Equation 3.3 shows that large $\frac{E_b}{N_o}$ implies better performance. Different constellations have different d_{min} values for the same $\frac{E_b}{N_o}$. The constellation with the largest d_{min} for a given $\frac{E_b}{N_o}$ has the best performance. In P_b equations like 3.3, this effect results in scaling of the value and the argument of the Q-function.

Minimum distance depends on several factors: number of points M, average power P_{ave} and shape of the constellation. The most important is the number of points in the constellation, which is directly dependent on the number of bits k transmitted in one symbol $M = 2^k$. Average power P_{ave} scales the constellation smaller or larger, depending on the transmitted power. Consequently, to make comparisons between different constellations fair, P_{ave} is usually normalized to one when d_{min} of a constellation is calculated. Average power of a constellation is evaluated simply by averaging the power of all the M points c_k of the constellation as shown in Equation 3.4.

$$P_{ave} = \frac{1}{M} \sum_{k=1}^M |c_k|^2 \tag{3.4}$$

3

MODULATION
AND CODING

Another important factor that influences d_{min} is the shape of the constellation. A constellation is basically a set of points located in one dimension or larger space spanned by the transmitted symbols. Traditional constellations are either one or two dimensional. In principle, these points can be located in any shape whatsoever. Naturally, for communication purposes care must be taken to ensure good performance and practical implementation. There are two main goals when constellation shapes are designed. The first is constant amplitude of the transmitted signal. In this case, all the points in the constellation are required to have equal amplitude. The second goal is to improve d_{min}. This is an optimization problem that tries to place all the points such that d_{min} is maximized for a finite P_{ave}. For the usual case of a two dimensional constellation with large number of points, this results in a circular constellation. Forney and Wei [4] give a through analysis of the behavior of d_{min} for different constellation types.

Coherent Modulations

Coherent modulation can be used by a communication system that maintains a phase lock between the transmitter and receiver RF carrier waves. Coherent modulation improves performance, but requires more complex receiver structure compared to *non-coherent* systems that are discussed later in this chapter. The performance gain of coherent modulation is significant when the system uses large constellations. High speed communication systems, like IEEE 802.11a, are usually coherent. The following sections describe the most common coherent modulations and their performance.

Amplitude Shift Keying

Amplitude Shift Keying (ASK) modulation transmits information by changing the amplitude of the carrier. Equation 3.5 shows the carrier waveform of ASK modulation. The A_k term does the actual modulation by multiplying the carrier wave by the selected amplitude level. The transmitted bits determine which of the possible symbols $\{A_1, \ldots, A_M\}$ is selected.

$$s(t) = A_k \cos(\omega_c t) \tag{3.5}$$

Figure 3.1 shows several different ASK modulations; (a) is a 2-ASK or BPSK, (b) is a 4-ASK, and (c) is a 8-ASK. In the figure, all the modulations have the same minimum distance $d_{min}^2 = 4$, however the average power of the constellations is not equal. To perform fair comparison of the ASK constellations, Table 3.1 shows the normalized d_{min}^2 and the required increase in *SNR* to maintain the same BER when changing to a one-step-larger constellation. The *SNR* increase converges to about 6 dB for each additional bit in the constellation; for this reason, large ASK modulations are rarely used in practice. The 2-ASK modulation does not have an *SNR* increase value, because it is the smallest possible constellation. The IEEE 802.11a system uses only the smallest 2-ASK modulation; for larger constellations, Phase Shift Keying and Quadrature Amplitude Modulations are used in practice. These two methods are the topics of the next sections.

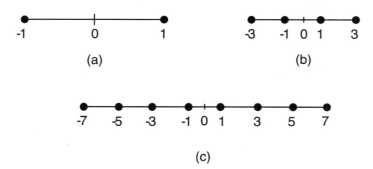

FIGURE 3.1

ASK modulations, (a) 2-ASK, (b) 4-ASK, (c) 8-ASK.

TABLE 3.1 Distance Properties of ASK Modulations

Modulation	P_{ave}	d^2_{min} Normalized	SNR Increase
2-ASK	1	4	–
4-ASK	5	$\frac{4}{5}$	6.99 dB
8-ASK	21	$\frac{4}{21}$	6.23 dB

Bit error rate P_b of binary ASK is the most basic error probability (see Equation 3.6). The P_b of 2-ASK is plotted in Figure 3.2. It is useful to memorize a reference point from this curve, like $P_b = 2 \cdot 10^{-4}$ at 8.0 dB $\frac{E_b}{N_o}$ or $P_b = 10^{-5}$ at 9.6 dB $\frac{E_b}{N_o}$. These points can serve as a quick check to validate simulation results. As the number of points in the constellation increases, exact analytic P_b equations become quite complicated, therefore either formulas for symbol error rate P_s or approximations to P_b are more commonly used.

$$P_b = Q\left(\sqrt{\frac{E_b}{N_0}} \right) \tag{3.6}$$

Symbol error rate P_s of M-ary ASK modulations is equal to Equation 3.7. Bit error rate P_b can be approximated by dividing P_s by the number of bits per symbol as in Equation 3.8. The formula for P_b is an approximation, because generally the number of bit errors that occur for each symbol error can be more than one. Equation 3.8 assumes that each symbol error causes only one bit error. However, with the help of Gray coding, which is discussed in the section "Labeling Constellation Points," for most symbol errors the number of bit errors is equal to one. The quality of this approximation improves at high signal to noise ratios.

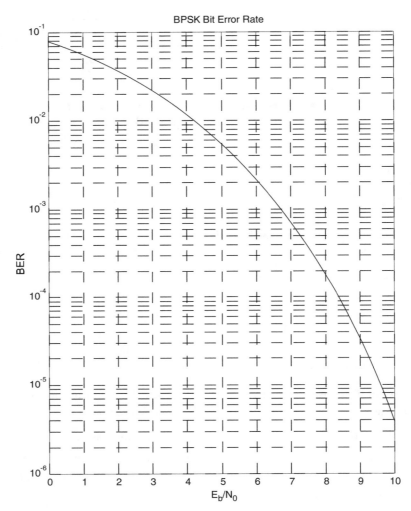

FIGURE 3.2
BPSK bit error rate.

$$P_s = 2\frac{M-1}{M}Q\left(\sqrt{\frac{A^2}{2N_0}}\right) \qquad (3.7)$$

In Equation 3.7, A is the amplitude difference between symbol levels. For example, in the constellation in Figure 3.1, $A = 2$.

$$P_b \approx \frac{P_s}{\log_2 M} = \frac{P_s}{k} \tag{3.8}$$

Phase Shift Keying

Phase Shift Keying (PSK) modulations transmit information by changing the phase of the carrier, the amplitude is kept constant; hence PSK modulations are also called *constant amplitude modulations*. Equation 3.9 shows the carrier waveform of PSK signal. Modulation is done by the ϕ_k term.

$$s(t) = \cos(\omega_c t + \phi_k) \tag{3.9}$$

The main benefit of constant amplitude modulation is the peak-to-average power ratio (PAPR) that is practically equal to one. However, this is only true for a single carrier systems. An OFDM signal that is a sum of several modulated subcarriers does not have a constant amplitude, even if the individual subcarriers do. The main benefit of constant amplitude modulation is simplified RF chain design for both the transmitter and receiver. An OFDM signal can never have a constant amplitude, hence having a constant amplitude constellation does *not* benefit OFDM systems. Several techniques to mitigate the large amplitude variations of OFDM signals are discussed in Chapter 5.

Figure 3.3 shows the three smallest PSK constellations, (a) is 2-PSK or binary PSK (BPSK), (b) is 4-PSK or quadrature PSK (QPSK), and (c) is 8-PSK. Note that BPSK is identical to 2-ASK. The figure shows how PSK modulations use both the *Inphase (I)* and *Quadrature (Q)* carrier waves, hence the modulation is two dimensional. This increase in dimensionality of the constellation improves the behavior of $d_{\min}^2$ as the number of points in the constellation increases.

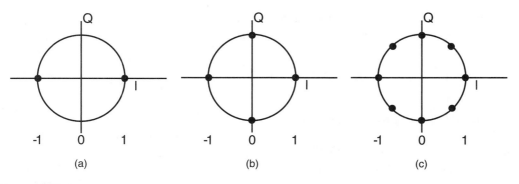

FIGURE 3.3
The three smallest PSK modulations, (a) BPSK, (b) QPSK, (c) 8-PSK.

Table 3.2 shows the required increase in *SNR* for 2- to 16-point PSK constellations. Note particularly that the increase from BPSK to QPSK is only 3 dB, compared to 2-ASK to 4-ASK increase of 6.99 dB. However, as the number of points is increased to 16, *SNR* increase for one additional bit per symbol converges towards the 6 dB figure as for ASK modulation. This behavior can be attributed to the fact that although PSK constellation is two dimensional, it still has only one degree of freedom: the phase of the carrier. Thus PSK does not fully use the two-dimensional space to locate the points of the constellation. Therefore larger than 8-point PSK modulations are not commonly used.

TABLE 3.2 Distance Properties of PSK Modulations

Modulation	P_{ave}	d^2_{min} Normalized	SNR Increase
BPSK	1	4.00	–
QPSK	1	2.00	3.00 dB
8-PSK	1	0.5858	5.33 dB
16-PSK	1	0.1522	5.85 dB

Symbol error rate of PSK modulations can be derived exactly for BPSK and QPSK; the former case was already shown in Equation 3.6. For QPSK, the P_s expression is somewhat more complicated than BPSK as shown in Equation 3.10.

$$P_s = 2Q\left(\sqrt{2\frac{E_b}{N_0}}\right)\left[1 - \frac{1}{2}Q\left(\sqrt{2\frac{E_b}{N_0}}\right)\right] \tag{3.10}$$

Higher order PSK modulation P_s can be approximated by Equation 3.11. Bit error rate can again be approximated by dividing P_s by the number of bits $k = \log_2 M$ in the constellation.

$$P_s = 2Q\left(\sqrt{\frac{E_s}{N_0}}\right)\sin\left(\frac{\pi}{M}\right) \tag{3.11}$$

Quadrature Amplitude Modulation

Quadrature Amplitude Modulation (QAM) changes both the amplitude and phase of the carrier, thus it is a combination of both ASK and PSK. Equation 3.12 shows the QAM signal in so-called *IQ*-form that presents the modulation of both the *I*- and *Q*-carriers. QAM can also be described by Equation 3.13 that shows how amplitude and phase modulations are combined in QAM.

$$s(t) = I_k \cos(\omega_c t) - Q_k \sin(\omega_c t) \tag{3.12}$$

$$= A_k \cos(\omega_c t + \phi_k) \tag{3.13}$$

The amplitude and phase terms of Equation 3.13 are calculated from Equations 3.14 and 3.15.

$$A_k = \sqrt{I_k^2 + Q_k^2} \tag{3.14}$$

$$\phi_k = \tan^{-1}\left(\frac{Q_k}{I_k}\right) \tag{3.15}$$

Figure 3.4 shows three QAM constellations: (a) 4-QAM or QPSK, (b) 8-QAM, and (c) 16-QAM. Especially QPSK and 16-QAM are very common modulations. On the other hand, 8-QAM is not used as often, probably due to its somewhat inconvenient shape; instead 8-PSK is commonly used when 8-point constellations are required. Figure 3.4 (b) is not the only possible shape for a 8-QAM constellation.

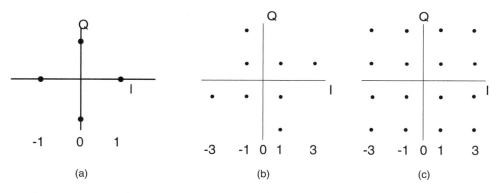

FIGURE 3.4

QAM constellations, (a) QPSK, (b) 8-QAM, (c) 16-QAM.

Table 3.3 shows how the d_{min}^2 of QAM behaves as a function of the constellation size. The step from QPSK to 8-QAM is somewhat anomalous, and it is actually possible to improve the minimum distance of our example 8-QAM modulation. However, we have used the present example because of its regular form. The step from 16-QAM to 32-QAM shows a 3 dB increase in required SNR to maintain constant BER. This 3 dB SNR increase for each additional bit per symbol is a general rule for QAM constellations.

Symbol error rate of QAM modulation is approximated by considering QAM as two independent ASK modulation on both *I*- and *Q*-carriers. This is shown in Equation 3.16.

$$P_s \approx 4\left(1 - \frac{1}{\sqrt{M}}\right) Q\left(\sqrt{\frac{3E_s}{(M-1)N_0}}\right) \tag{3.16}$$

TABLE 3.3 Distance Properties of QAM Modulations

Modulation	P_{ave}	d^2_{min} Normalized	SNR Increase
QPSK	1	2.00	–
8-QAM	6	0.67	4.77 dB
16-QAM	10	0.40	2.22 dB
32-QAM	20	0.20	3.01 dB

Labeling Constellation Points

Labeling constellation points means assigning a bit pattern to all the points. The selected labeling scheme has an impact on the performance and thus must be optimized. Figure 3.5 shows two common ways to assign bit patterns to 16-QAM constellation points: (a) is called natural order, and (b) is called Gray coding. Figure 3.5 shows the decimal value of the label above the point and binary value below the point. Natural ordering has appeal in its straightforward assignment of labels using decimal numbers from 0 to 15 to the points. The disadvantage of natural ordering is in the actual bit patterns representing constellation points.

3	2	1	0		2	6	14	10
0011	0010	0001	0000		0010	0110	1110	1010
7	6	5	4		3	7	15	11
0111	0110	0101	0100		0011	0111	1111	1011
11	10	9	8		1	5	13	9
1011	1010	1001	1000		0001	0101	1101	1001
15	14	13	12		0	4	12	8
1111	1110	1101	1100		0000	0100	1100	1000
	(a)					(b)		

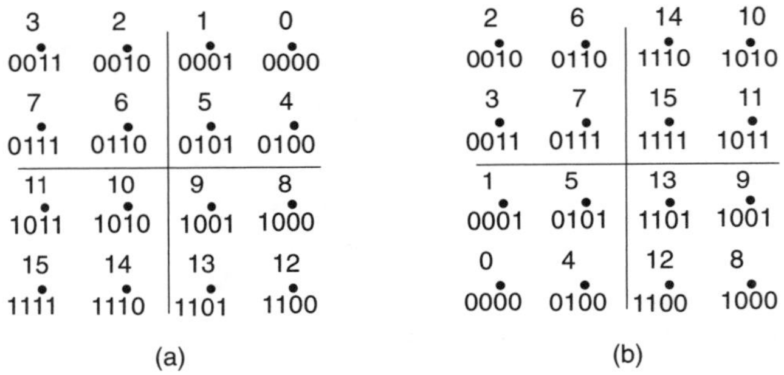

FIGURE 3.5

(a) QAM natural order and (b) Gray coded labeling schemes.

For example, consider an error where point number 1 was transmitted, but it was received as 2. This mistake between neighboring points is the most common type error the receiver does. Now look at the bit patterns representing 1 (0001) and 2 (0010); two bits have changed resulting in two bit errors for one symbol error. Gray coding eliminates all these two-bit errors for symbol errors between neighboring points, thus reducing bit error rate for the same symbol error rate. In the Gray coded constellations the points of the previous example are labeled 14 (1110) and 6 (0110); note that only left most bit is different. All the constellations in IEEE 802.11a and HiperLAN/2 standards are Gray coded.

Exercise 1 *Plot the different bit error probability functions corresponding to the modulations used in IEEE 802.11a and compare the curves with simulation results.*

Exercise 2 *Compare the performance difference predicted by minimum distace values of different constellations to the analytical bit error probability curves.*

Detection of Coherent Modulations

After the receiver has performed all the required synchronization operations, discussed in Chapter 2, the next job is to decide what was actually received. This is done by a detector or demodulator that decides for each received symbol the most likely transmitted bits. The decisions are divided into *hard* and *soft* decisions, depending on how much information about each transmitted bit is produced. Both types of detectors are discussed next.

Hard Decision Detection

A hard decision *demodulator* or *slicer* makes a definite determination of whether a zero or one bit was transmitted, thus the output of the demodulator are zeros and ones. A hard decision demodulator is also defined based on the number of possible inputs to the modulator in the transmitter. If this number is equal to the number of possible outputs from the demodulator in the receiver, the demodulator uses hard decision. If the demodulator can output more information than the input to the modulator, the system uses soft decision, which is discussed later. Figure 3.6 shows the *decision boundaries* for QPSK constellation. The decision boundaries determine how received symbols are mapped to bits. Essentially, the maximum-likelihood decision is the constellation point that is closest to the received symbol, and the hard decisions are the bits assigned to that constellation point. For example, in Figure 3.6, the *x* marks the location of the received symbol; it is closest to the constellation point on the positive *I*-axis, hence the hard decision bits are 00.

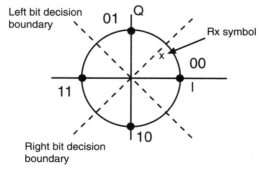

FIGURE 3.6
Hard decision boundaries for QPSK constellation.

3

MODULATION
AND CODING

Soft Decision Detection

Soft decision demodulator outputs *"soft"* bits, that in addition to indicating a zero or one bit retain information about the reliability of the decision. This additional information can greatly improve the performance of channel coding schemes; the effect will be discussed in "Channel Codes." To perform soft decisions, the demodulator has to consider the received bits individually. Consider again the received symbol in Figure 3.6. It is located very close to the decision boundary between symbols corresponding to bits 00 and 01. For the left bit to change to 1, the symbol would have to move over the left bit decision boundary. The received symbol is quite far from this boundary, hence the left bit is quite reliable. On the other hand, the right bit changes from 0 to 1; if the received symbol would be above the right bit decision boundary, instead of just below it. This flip does not require much additional noise, hence the right bit is quite unreliable. To reflect this difference of reliability of the soft decision, the soft bits have different values: a large absolute value for the first bit and a small value for the second bit. The sign of the soft decision indicates a 0 or 1 bit. The absolute value of each soft decision is the distance to the decision boundary. We will show the performance effect of using either hard or soft decision with the convolutional error correcting code used in IEEE 802.11a in "Channel Codes."

Non-Coherent Modulations

Non-coherent modulations can be used by a communication system that does not maintain a phase lock between transmitter and receiver, or have knowledge of the amplitude change of the transmitted symbol caused by the channel. This means that the received symbols are rotated and scaled arbitrarily compared to the transmitted symbol. Therefore the ASK, PSK, or QAM modulations cannot be used because they require the received symbol phase and amplitude to be very close to that transmitted phase and amplitude. The solution is to use differential PSK (DPSK) or differential APSK (DAPSK) modulation. Differential modulations encode the transmitted information to a phase, or phase and amplitude change from one transmitted symbol to the next. This encoding introduces memory to the signal, because transmitted symbols depend on previous symbols. As a consequence, the demodulator has to consider two consecutive symbols when making decisions. The next two sections describe these two modulation methods.

The main benefit of differential encoding is significantly simplified receiver structure. Several of the synchronization algorithms presented in Chapter 2 are not needed in a non-coherent receiver. Specifically, phase tracking and channel estimation are not needed, because absolute knowledge of carrier phase and the channel effect is not needed. Carrier frequency estimation could also be removed, if the system can tolerate the performance due to intercarrier interference caused by lost orthogonality between the subcarriers. Regardless of these simplifications in receiver design, non-coherent modulations have not achieved popularity among high speed communications systems. All the IEEE 802.11a and HiperLAN/2 modulations are coherent. The main reason is unavoidable performance loss associated with differential approach. In contrast, low data rate systems do use differential techniques, mainly DPSK modulations. For example, the European Digital Audio Broadcasting (DAB) system uses differential modulation.

Differential Phase Shift Keying

Differential phase shift keying changes the carrier phase from its current value according to the data bits. For binary DPSK, the encoding operation can be expressed at bit level, as in Equation 3.17, which shows how the transmitted bit b_n is calculated from the data bits d_n using binary XOR operation.

$$b_n = d_n \oplus d_{n-1} \tag{3.17}$$

Alternatively, encoding can be expressed directly as carrier phase change as in Equation 3.18

$$s(t) = \cos(\omega_c t + \Delta\phi_n + \phi) \tag{3.18}$$

where ϕ is unknown phase difference between transmitter and receiver and $\Delta\phi_n = \phi_n - \phi_{n-1}$ is the phase difference of two PSK modulated signals. DPSK is used in communications systems that require simple receiver structures. The constellation for M-DPSK modulation is identical with the corresponding M-PSK constellation; only the mapping of bits to constellation points is changed.

Differential Amplitude Phase Modulation

Differential Amplitude Phase Modulation (DAPSK) combines differential phase and differential amplitude modulation. Figure 3.7 shows a 32-point DAPSK constellation that uses three bits or eight levels for phase modulation and two bits or four levels for amplitude modulation. The differential phase modulation is analogous to the regular DPSK. Differential amplitude modulation, on the other hand, has to change the constellation shape compared to coherent amplitude modulation. The reason is the unknown scaling of the amplitude of the transmitted symbol caused by the channel. The receiver cannot correctly detect the symbols unless this unknown scaling is removed. Equation 3.19 shows a received OFDM subcarrier symbol R_k when the transmitted symbol was X_k and the subcarrier frequency response is H_k.

$$R_k = H_k X_k \tag{3.19}$$

To recover the amplitude modulation the receiver is only concerned with the amplitude of the received symbol, as shown in Equation 3.20.

$$|R_k| = |H_k X_k| = |H_k||X_k| \tag{3.20}$$

A general assumption when differential modulation is used is that the channel and carrier phase are constant during two consecutive symbols. Therefore we can cancel the effect of the channel by dividing two consecutive symbols, as shown in Equations 3.21 – 3.23.

3

MODULATION AND CODING

$$Y_k = \frac{|H_k||X_k|}{|H_{k-1}||X_{k-1}|} \tag{3.21}$$

$$= \frac{|H_k||X_k|}{|H_k||X_{k-1}|} \tag{3.22}$$

$$= \frac{|X_k|}{|X_{k-1}|} \tag{3.23}$$

The multiplicative scaling of the channel prevents using additive differential amplitude modulation, whereas for DPSK the channel effect on received symbol phase is additive, hence it can be canceled by subtraction instead of division. The next question is how the amplitude levels of the constellation are selected. This is illustrated in Figure 3.7, which shows amplitude levels $1, a, a^2, a^3$. The information is encoded as a jump from one amplitude level to another; for example, bits 01 could mean a jump of one amplitude level. Differential amplitude encoding done with multiplication such as

$$Y_k = D_k Y_{k-1} \tag{3.24}$$

where $D_k \in \left\{ \frac{1}{a^3}, \frac{1}{a^2}, \frac{1}{a}, 1, a, a^2, a^3 \right\}$. The fractional values are required, because amplitude multiplication is not naturally periodic like phase addition in the case of DPSK modulation. The actual value of D_k depends on the input bits and the value of Y_{k-1}. The value of D_k is selected such that the amplitude jumps wrap around after a^3. For example, if $Y_{k-1} = a^2$ and a two amplitude level jump is needed, then $D_k = \frac{1}{a^2}$, so $Y_k = a^2 \frac{1}{a^2} = 1$. The two amplitude level jump is then $a^2 \rightarrow a^3 \rightarrow 1$.

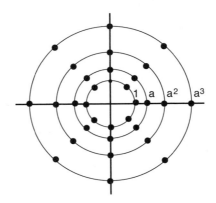

FIGURE 3.7
32-point differential amplitude and phase modulation.

The multiplication encoding method forces the points in the middle of the constellation quite close to each other. This is an unavoidable disadvantage of differential amplitude modulation. The effect is reduced minimum distance for the points in the middle, hence they experience a performance loss compared to the points on the outer amplitude levels.

Detection of Differential Modulations

Detection of differential modulation is done in two steps. First the differential encoding is removed from the signal and then a normal demodulation is performed as explained for regular PSK and QAM constellations. Equations 3.25 and 3.26 show how the differential encoding is removed in DPSK detection by calculating the phase difference of two consecutive symbols. Equation 3.26 also show the reason for the performance loss of differential encoding compared to coherent modulations. Differential detection has to use two symbols, therefore the amount of noise per detected symbol is approximately doubled.

$$\hat{\theta}_k = \angle(R_k + N_k) - \angle(R_{k-1} + N_{k-1}) \tag{3.25}$$

$$= \theta_k - \theta_{k-1} + \tilde{N}_k + \tilde{N}_{k-1} \tag{3.26}$$

The performance loss of DPSK compared to coherent modulation varies with the size of the modulation [11], for DBPSK it is between 1-2dB, for DQPSK about 2.3dB and for larger constellations 3dB.

Linear and Nonlinear Modulation

Different modulation methods are generally divided into linear and nonlinear modulations. The differentiating property is whether the transmitted signal can be expressed as a sum of the individual symbols a_k with pulse shape $p(t)$ as in Equation 3.27.

$$s(t) = \sum_{k=-\infty}^{\infty} a_k p(t - kT) \tag{3.27}$$

Nonlinear modulation usually contains memory in the modulator, like differential modulation, so that the transmitted symbols are dependent and cannot be simply delayed and summed together to form the transmitted waveform. Differential modulation is one application of nonlinear modulation; another common one is *continuous phase modulation* (CPM). The main goal of CPM is to control the spectrum of the transmitted signal by forcing the phase of the carrier wave to change continuously between symbols. This narrows the spectrum of the signal, because the change between symbols is less abrupt than without carrier phase control. CPM is not very useful for OFDM, because the spectrum shape is determined by the multicarrier nature and has a brick-like shape, even with linear modulation. Another difficulty in applying CPM to OFDM is that the signal would have to have a continuous phase for all the subcarriers. This is difficult or impossible to achieve, because of the cyclic prefix added to OFDM symbols. Therefore CPM is not used with OFDM systems.

Interleaving

Interleaving aims to distribute transmitted bits in time or frequency or both to achieve desirable bit error distribution after demodulation. What constitutes a desirable error distribution depends on the used FEC code. What kind of interleaving pattern is needed depends on the channel characteristics. If the system operates in a purely AWGN environment, no interleaving is needed, because the error distribution cannot be changed by relocating the bits. Communication channels are divided into *fast* and *slow* fading channels. A channel is fast fading if the impulse response changes approximately at the symbol rate of the communication system, whereas a slow fading channel stays unchanged for several symbols.

WLAN systems generally assume a very slowly fading channel, also called *quasi-stationary*, that does not change during one packet. Another characterization of communications channels is as *flat* or *frequency selective* fading channels. A channel is flat fading if the frequency response is constant over the whole bandwidth of the transmitted signal. A frequency selective channel changes significantly within the band of the signal. WLAN systems are wide bandwidth systems, and therefore usually experience frequency selective fading channel. OFDM technology is well suited for communication over slow frequency selective fading channels.

Diversity is the single most important technique to improve the performance of a communication system in a fading channel. Diversity generally refers to methods that take advantage of several different realizations of the channel to make a decision on each received information bit. The more independent channel realizations can be used, the better the performance improvement will be. This is a consequence of the channel fading statistics. The more individual samples of the channel are combined, the less likely it is that all of them are in a faded state. There are several sources of diversity that can be used: time, frequency, and space are the most common ones. OFDM wireless LANs mainly exploit frequency diversity due to their wideband nature. Time diversity cannot be used, because of the slowly fading characteristics of the channel. When the channel is in a bad condition, it will remain so for the duration of the packet, and there is nothing the receiver can do about it. Space diversity is achieved by using multiple transmit and/or receiver antennas. This technique is discussed in detail in Chapter 4.

Interleaving necessarily introduces delay into the system because bits are not received in the same order as the information source transmits them. The overall communication system usually dictates some maximum delay the system can tolerate, hence restricting the amount of interleaving that can be used. For example, cellular telephone systems usually use time diversity, because the channels are fast fading. However the maximum phone to phone delay is usually constrained to 20ms or less, to prevent noticeable degradation in call quality. This means the maximum inter-leaving delay must be much less than 20ms to allow for other delay sources in the system.

Block Interleaver

Block interleaving operates on one block of bits at a time. The number of bits in the block is called *interleaving depth*, which defines the delay introduced by interleaving. A block interleaver can be described as a matrix to which data is written in columns and read in rows, or vice versa. For example, Figure 3.8 shows a 8×6 block interleaver, hence interleaving depth is 48. The input bits are written in columns as $[b_0, b_1, b_2, b_3, \ldots]$ and the interleaved bits are read by rows as $[b_0, b_8, b_{16}, b_{24}, \ldots]$. Block interleaver is simple to implement using random access memory (RAM) on current digital circuits.

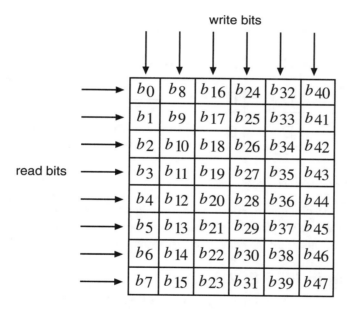

FIGURE 3.8

Bit write and read structure for a 8×6 block interleaver.

Deinterleaving is the opposite operation of interleaving; that is, the bits are put back into the orig-inal order. The deinterleaver corresponding to Figure 3.8 is simply a transpose of the original 8×6 matrix. The deinterleaver is a 6×8 matrix to which the received bits are written into columns and read from rows.

Convolutional Interleaver

A convolutional interleaver is another possible interleaving solution that is most suitable for systems that operate on continuous stream of bits. This interleaver structure was published by Ramsey [12]. Figure 3.9 shows the basic structure of a convolutional interleaver. The interleaver operates by writing the bits into the commutator on the left, and reading bits out from the commutator on the right. The delay elements D are clocked after each cycle of the commutators is completed; that is, after the last delay line has been written and read. The main benefit of a convolutional interleaver is that it requires approximately half of the memory required by a block interleaver to achieve the same interleaving depth. This saving can be significant for long interleaver depths.

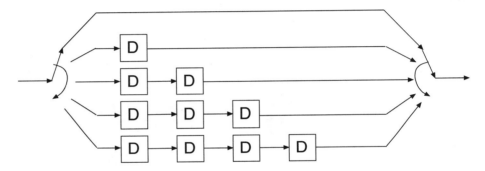

FIGURE 3.9
Basic structure of a convolutional interleaver.

Deinterleaving of convolutional interleaver is achieved by flipping the interleaver along its horizontal axis. The structure is otherwise identical except the longest delay line is at the top, and the no delay line is last. Otherwise the deinterleaving operation is identical to interleaving.

Interleaving in IEEE 802.11a

Interleaving is a very important component of the IEEE 802.11a standard. Interleaving depth has been selected to be equal to one OFDM symbol. Therefore it is naturally a block interleaver. The performance effect of interleaving in IEEE 802.11a is a consequence of frequency diversity. IEEE 802.11a is a wideband communications system and experiences a flat fading channel very rarely. This is an essential requirement to be able to exploit frequency diversity. The combined effect of interleaving and convolutional channel coding takes advantage of the frequency diversity provided by the wideband nature of the transmitted signal.

Interleaving depth is only one OFDM symbol, because the channel is assumed to be quasi-static; that is, the channel is assumed to stay essentially the same for the duration of a transmitted packet. Therefore no additional diversity gain can be achieved by interleaving in time. Additionally increasing the interleaving depth would increase the delay of baseband processing; the maximum delay possible is constrained by the IEEE 802.11 MAC level protocol's acknowledgement packet short interframe spacing (SIFS) timing requirements. The SIFS time is equal to $16\mu s$, hence after the packet ends, processing it has to be completed in less time. This is one of the most demanding implementation requirements of the IEEE 802.11a standard.

The interleaving depth measured in bits changes according the used modulation: BPSK, QPSK, 16-QAM, and 64-QAM have interleaving depths of 48, 96, 192, and 288 bits, respectively. The interleaving depth for each modulation is calculated by multiplying the number of data subcarriers by the number of bits per symbol.

Figures 3.10 and 3.11 show BER and PER curves for IEEE 802.11a 12 Mbits/s mode in a Rayleigh fading channel that has 75ns root mean square (rms) delay spread. The effect of the interleaver is most striking for PER, at 1% the gain from interleaver is approximately 5 dB. Figure 3.11 also shows how the slope of the curve is steeper with interleaving; this is a consequence of the diversity gain achieved.

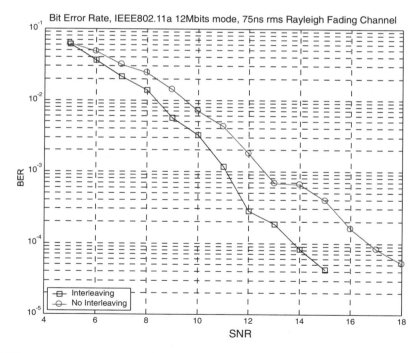

FIGURE 3.10

Bit error rate of IEEE 802.11a 12 Mbits mode with and without interleaving in 75ns rms delay spread Rayleigh fading channel.

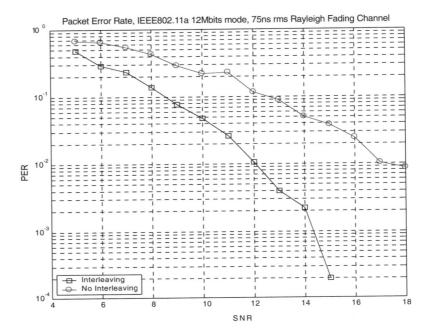

FIGURE 3.11
Packet error rate of IEEE 802.11a 12 Mbits mode with and without interleaving in 75ns rms delay spread Rayleigh fading channel.

Channel Codes

Channel codes are a very important component of any modern digital communication system, and they make today's effective and reliable wireless communications possible. There are several books that concentrate on different channel coding approaches [7, 9, 10, 17, 20]. The basic measure of channel coding performance is *coding gain*, which is usually measured in dBs as the reduction of required $\frac{E_b}{N_o}$ to achieve a certain bit error rate in AWGN channel. As an example, IEEE 802.11a could use two methods to achieve 12 Mbits/s data rate. The simplest way would be to use uncoded BPSK modulation on each subcarrier, therefore each OFDM symbol would carry 48 bits worth of information. The symbol time is $4\mu s$ or 250000 symbols per second, hence the overall data is 250000×48 = 12Mbits/s.

Another way to achieve the same data rate is to use channel coding. The IEEE 802.11a 12Mbits/s mode uses QPSK and rate 1/2 convolutional code. This results in a significantly lower $\frac{E_b}{N_o}$ or *SNR* to achieve a good BER performance. This is illustrated in Figure 3.12, which shows a coding gain of approximately 5.5dB at bit error rate of 10^{-5}. This means that to achieve the same performance, the system that does not use channel coding has to spend 5.5dB more energy for each transmitted bit than the system that uses channel coding. Figure 3.12 shows another typical behavior of channel codes, the uncoded and coded BER curves cross over at some point. However this happens at so high BER that channel coding practically always provides an improvement.

To make an even more striking demonstration of channel coding in action, Figure 3.13 shows packet error rate curves in a fading channel with the same parameters as the previous example. IEEE 802.11a is a packet-oriented system, hence PER is the most commonly used measure of its performance. In the figure, the curve without channel coding does *not* produce usable PER at all, hence the price paid for implementing channel coding is handsomely paid back. Over the 9dB increase in $\frac{E_b}{N_o}$, the performance of the coded system improves by two orders of magnitude, whereas the performance of the uncoded system only improves from 100% PER to about 80% PER. Flatness of the uncoded PER curves is explained by noting that even one bit error causes a packet error. The system is operating in a fading channel, hence typically some subcarriers experience very low SNR, and bit errors on these bad subcarriers cause packet errors.

The previous examples of channel coding options show another important parameter of channel coding, namely the *rate* of the code. Code rate is the ratio of bits input, called the *message word*, to the encoder to the bits output, called the *code word*, from the encoder. This ratio is always less than one; in the previous example, rate 1/2 means that twice as many bits are output from the encoder than were input. Therefore the coded system had to use QPSK modulation, instead of BPSK to achieve the same data rate. Channel coding always forces the system to use a larger constellation to keep the same data rate as an uncoded system. Going to a larger constellation reduces $d_{\min}$; this implies higher BER at the output of the demodulator. However, at the output of the channel code decoder, the bit error rate is significantly reduced.

The performance of channel codes is ultimately limited by the channel capacity formula, Equation 3.1. After about 50 years of research, *Turbo-codes* [7] have finally emerged as a class of codes that can approach the ultimate limit in performance. Another innovation, and a very active research area, are Low Density Parity Check (LDPC) codes, which also have performance very close to the capacity.

Convolutional codes have been the most widely used channel code in wireless systems for the past decades, hence this section concentrates on them and the performance of IEEE 802.11a system. Additional channel codes are Trellis-Coded Modulation (TCM) that is closely related to convolutional codes and algebraic Reed-Solomon (RS) codes. These coding schemes are described in sections "Trellis Coded Modulation" and "Block Codes," respectively.

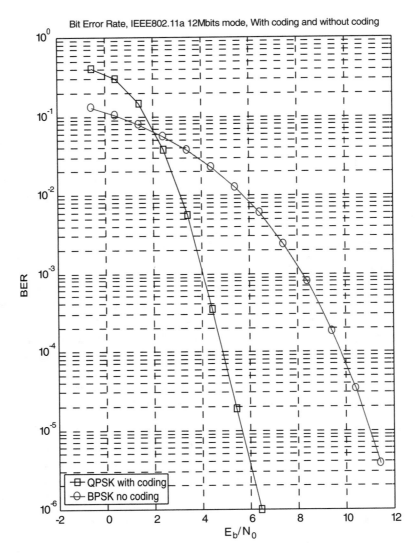

FIGURE 3.12

Coding gain in BER of 64 state rate 1/2 convolutional code in AWGN channel.

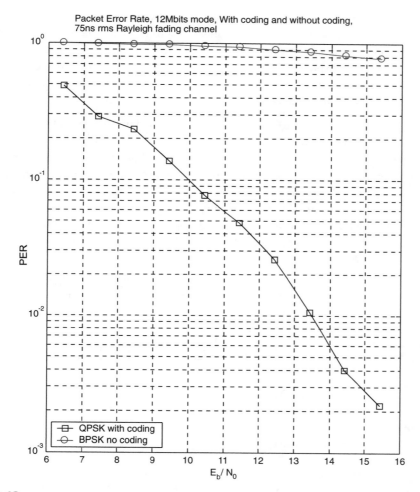

FIGURE 3.13

Coding gain in PER of 64 state rate 1/2 convolutional code in fading channel.

Convolutional Codes

Convolutional codes are one of the mostly widely used channel codes in today's systems; all the major cellular systems (GSM, IS-95) in use today use convolutional channel codes. IEEE 802.11a and HiperLAN/2 WLAN standards also use convolutional error correcting code, and IEEE 802.11b includes an optional mode that uses them. Convolutional codes owe their popularity to good performance and flexibility to achieve different coding rates.

A convolutional code is defined by a set of connections between stages of one or more shift registers and the output bits of the encoder. The number of shift registers k is equal to the nominator of the code rate and the number of output bits n is equal to the denominator. The rate of a convolutional code is generally expressed as $\frac{k}{n}$. The number of connections required to describe a code is equal to the product of k and n. For each output bit there are k connections that define how the value of the output bit is calculated from the state of the shift registers.

For example, Figure 3.14 shows the convolutional encoder used in IEEE 802.11a. This is a rate $\frac{1}{2}$ code with connections 133_8 and 171_8. The connections are defined as octal numbers, the binary representations are $001\,011\,011_2$ and $001\,111\,001_2$. The octal notation is used to shorten the expressions, when connections for different convolutional codes are tabulated. From the binary notation, the structure of the encoder is easily constructed. The connections are aligned to the end of the shift register, and a value of 1 means that the shift register stage output is connected to one of the output bits of the encoder using a binary XOR operation. In Figure 3.14 the connection 133_8 that defines values the even indexed bits b_{2n} and the connection 171_8 defines the values of the odd indexed bits b_{2n+1}.

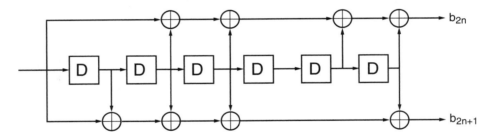

FIGURE 3.14
64 state rate 1/2 convolutional encoder used in IEEE 802.11a.

The end of shift register alignment for defining connection values is not universal. Several sources report the connection values by aligning them to the start of the shift register input. Using this notation the connection for the code in Figure 3.14 are 554_8 and 744_8 or in binary $101\,101\,100_2$ and $111\,100\,100_2$. The length of the binary representation is extended with zeros to be a multiple of three, so that the octal values are well defined. Connection values for several different convolutional codes can be found in coding theory text books [9, 10, 20]. These codes were all found using an exhaustive computer search for all possible convolutional codes of the specific rate and number of shift register elements.

The number of shift register elements determines how large a coding gain the convolutional code can achieve. The longer the shift registers, the more powerful the code is; unfortunately, the decoding complexity of the maximum likelihood Viterbi algorithm grows exponentially with the number of shift register elements. This complexity growth limits the currently used convolutional codes to eight shift register elements, and IEEE 802.11a uses only six, due to its very high speed data rates.

The performance of a convolutional code is determined by the minimum *free distance* of the code. Free distance is defined using the *Hamming distance* that is equal to the number of position in which two code words are different. Free distance of a convolutional code is the minimum Hamming distance between two different code words. An asymptotic coding gain at high SNR for a convolutional code can be calculated from the free distance and the rate of the code, as in Equation 3.1.

$$coding\ gain = 10\log_{10}(rate \cdot free\ distance) \tag{3.28}$$

For example, the code used in IEEE 802.11a has a free distance of 10 and rate $\frac{1}{2}$ that gives an asymptotic coding gain of $10\log_{10}\left(\frac{1}{2} \cdot 10\right) = 7.0dB$. However, this is an asymptotic result; Figure 3.12 showed that at 10^{-5} BER, the coding is equal to 5.5dB, and less for lower $\frac{E_b}{N_o}$. The asymptotic result is reached at such a high SNR that practical systems usually do not operate at that SNR region.

Puncturing Convolutional Codes

Usually communications systems provide a set of possible data rates; for example, IEEE 802.11a has eight different data rates: 6, 9, 12, 18, 24, 36, 48, and 54 Mbits/s. Now if the system could only change the data rate by adjusting the constellation size, and not the code rate, a very large number of different rates would be difficult to achieve as the number of constellations and the number of points in the largest constellation would grow very quickly. Another solution would be to implement several different convolutional encoders with different rates and change both the convolutional code rate and constellation. However this approach has problems in the receiver that would have to implement several different decoders for all the codes used.

Puncturing is a very useful technique to generate additional rates from a single convolutional code. Puncturing was first discover by Cain, Clark, and Geist [3], and subsequently the technique was improved by Hagenauer [6]. The basic idea behind puncturing is not to transmit some of the bits output by the convolutional encoder, thus increasing the rate of the code. This increase in rate decreases the free distance of the code, but usually the resulting free distance is very close to the optimum one that is achieved by specifically designing a convolutional code for the punctured rate. The receiver inserts dummy bits to replace the punctured bits in the receiver, hence only one encoder/decoder pair is needed to generate several different code rates.

The bits that are not transmitted are defined by a *puncturing pattern* . Puncturing pattern is simply a set of bits that are not transmitted within a certain period of bits. Figure 3.15 shows the two different puncturing patterns of IEEE 802.11a. The pattern (a) is used to generate rate $\frac{3}{4}$ code from the rate $\frac{1}{2}$ mother convolutional code. This puncturing pattern has a period of six bits, and bits 3 and 4 are punctured (not transmitted) from each period. The *puncturing rate* is equal to $\frac{4}{6} = \frac{2}{3}$ and the overall code rate is equal to $\frac{1}{2\frac{2}{3}} = \frac{3}{4}$, since $\frac{2}{3}$ of the original encoded bits are output from the puncturer. The other punctured code rate of IEEE 802.11a is a rate $\frac{2}{3}$ code. The puncturing pattern is shown in Figure 3.15 (b) has a period of 4 bits, and the fourth bit is punctured, the puncturing rate is $\frac{3}{4}$, hence the overall code rate is $\frac{1}{2\frac{3}{4}} = \frac{2}{3}$.

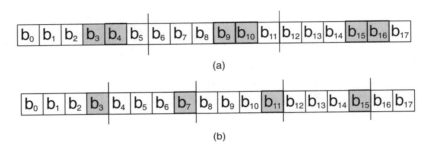

(a)

(b)

FIGURE 3.15
Puncturing patterns of IEEE 802.11a.

Table 3.4 shows the free distances and the asymptotic coding gains of the three code rates used in IEEE 802.11a. The table also shows the optimum rate $\frac{3}{4}$ and $\frac{2}{3}$ codes; as you can see, the performance loss due to using punctured codes, instead of the optimum ones, is very small. The rate $\frac{1}{2}$ is naturally the optimum code, because the original code is a rate $\frac{1}{2}$ code. Therefore the table does not show the punctured free distance and coding gain values for this rate.

TABLE 3.4 Free Ddistances of the 64 State Convolutional Codes Used in IEEE 802.11a

Code Rates	Punctured Free Distance	Punctured Coding Gain	Optimum Free Distance	Optimum Coding Gain
$\frac{1}{2}$	—	—	10	7.0 dB
$\frac{2}{3}$	6	6.0 dB	7	6.7 dB
$\frac{3}{4}$	5	5.7 dB	6	6.5 dB

Before the punctured code can be decoded, the removed bits have to be inserted back into the bit stream, because the decoder of the original code expects them to be there. Depuncturing is done by simply inserting dummy bits into the locations that were punctured in the transmitter. The values of the dummy bits depend on whether the system uses hard or soft decisions. A hard decision system should insert randomly one and zero bits into the punctured locations. A soft decision receiver inserts a soft decision value of zero. For the usual case of decoding with the Viterbi algorithm, the zero-valued dummy bit does not have any effect on the outcome of the decoder.

Decoding Convolutional Codes

There are several algorithms that can be used to decode convolutional codes. The algorithms vary in complexity and performance, and more complexity means better performance. During recent years, the Viterbi algorithm has reached a dominant position as the method to decode convolutional codes, especially in wireless applications; other methods are practically nonexistent. The reason is that the Viterbi algorithm is a maximum-likelihood code word estimator; it provides the best possible estimate of the transmitted code word. The Viterbi algorithm was introduced in Chapter 1, and it is discussed in detail in any of the coding theory text books mentioned in the start of this section, so we assume you are familiar with it.

The Viterbi algorithm can easily be implemented using either hard or soft decision demodulation. Figures 3.16 and 3.17 show the performance improvement in BER and PER gained by using soft decisions. The gain is approximately 2dB at 10^{-3} BER and 10^{-1} PER. The gain increases to a little bit more than 2dB for higher SNRs. Therefore soft decision decoding is the recommended method to use with Viterbi decoding because the performance improvement it provides does not cost any communications resources.

A coherent OFDM system has to estimate the frequency response of the channel. The information about the amplitudes of the individual subcarriers can be incorporated into the Viterbi algorithm to provide performance improvement. Equation 3.29 shows how the path metrics p_n in the Viterbi algorithm are calculated by weighting the squared Euclidian distance between the soft decision $\hat{b}_n$ and the reference value b_n by the squared amplitude of the subcarrier k on which the bit was transmitted.

$$p_n = |H_k|^2 \left|\hat{b}_n - b_n\right|^2 \tag{3.29}$$

The performance effect of this weighting is significant in fading channel. Figure 3.18 shows the PER of IEEE 802.11a 12Mbits/s mode when the convolutional code decoding is done with using weighting in Viterbi or by using equal weight for all the path metrics. The impact of weighting on performance is very large. The reason is diversity; when the subcarrier is faded, its amplitude is small and the path metric will be scaled down to almost zero. This means that the bits that were transmitted on bad subcarriers have very little impact on the decision the decoder makes, hence improved performance.

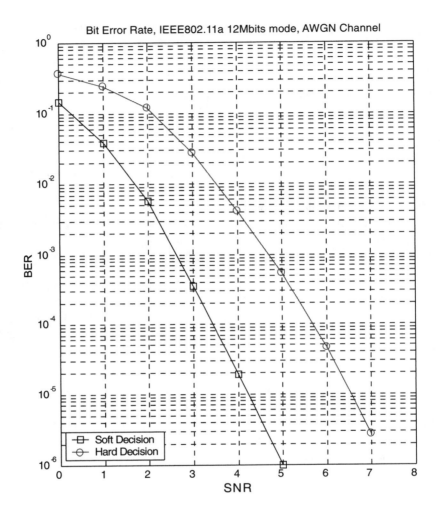

FIGURE 3.16
Bit error rate of IEEE 802.11a 12Mbits/s mode in AWGN channel using soft and hard decision decoding.

Performance of IEEE 802.11a

IEEE 802.11a offers eight different data rates from 6 Mbits/s to 54 Mbits/s with increasingly higher SNR required as the data rate increases. Figure 3.19 shows the SNR required for the 6 Mbits/s and 54 Mbits/s modes in AWGN channel. The total increase in SNR at 1% PER is about 17dB or about fifty fold increase in transmitted power. Another way to interpret the SNR increase is to look at the change of range of the system at different data rates. The range depends on the path loss the transmitted signal experiences, before it reaches the receiver antenna. The overall path loss L_p depends on many factors [18]. The range dependent factor is proportional to the distance d between the transmitter and receiver. The impact of d on path loss depends on path loss coefficient c, that determines how fast the signal power attenuates as it travels. This relationship is shown in Equation 3.30.

$$L_p \sim \frac{1}{d^c} \tag{3.30}$$

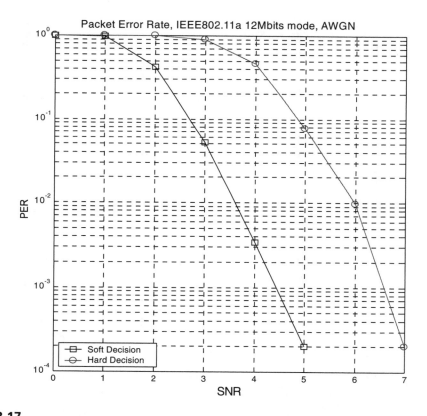

FIGURE 3.17

Packet error rate of IEEE 802.11a 12Mbits/s mode in AWGN channel using soft and hard decision decoding.

The value of the path loss coefficient is dependent on the environment and a large number of studies have been performed to determine its value in various cases [13]. The basic case is free space where $c = 2$; in an indoor environment, a value $c = 3$ can be used. We can use these two values to get an estimate of the range difference between the lowest and highest data rate of IEEE 802.11a. When $c = 2$, every doubling of range decreases the signal power to $\frac{1}{4}$ or by 6 dB, hence the 17 dB SNR range means approximately 7.2 factor in range. Therefore the 6 Mbits/s mode can function for a distance 7.2 times larger than 54 Mbits/s. The absolute range depends on many things, like transmitter power and receiver design. When we assume the indoor value $d = 3$, the transmitted power decreases to $\frac{1}{8}$ or by 9 dB for every doubling of range. This implies that range difference from 6 to 54 Mbits is about 3.7.

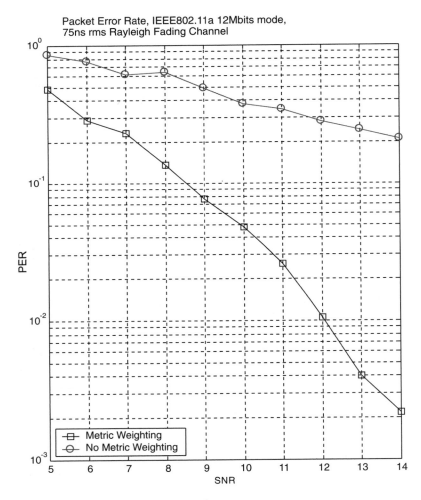

FIGURE 3.18

Packet error rate effect of metric weighting in Viterbi decoding of convolutional code for 12Mbits/s mode.

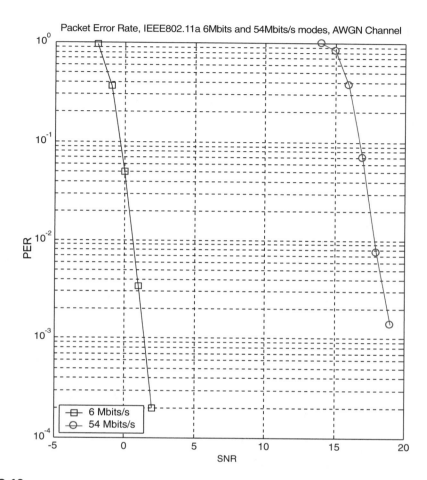

FIGURE 3.19
Packet error rate of IEEE 802.11a 6Mbits/s and 54 Mbits/s modes.

Exercise 3 *The performance of an OFDM system depends on the length of the impulse response of the channel. Simulate different rms delay spread values and note the PER performance. What is the explanation for the results?*

Exercise 4 *Simulate the 9 Mbits/s and 12 Mbits/s modes in both AWGN and fading channel. Compare the results and explain them using the convolutional code free distance and minimum distance of the constellations.*

3

MODULATION
AND CODING

Trellis Coded Modulation

Trellis coded modulation (TCM) was discovered by Ungerboeck [19]. Trellis Coded Modulation is the main subject of the book by Biglieri et al. [2]. The main idea of TCM is to merge channel coding and modulation into a single integrated component. The benefit of this approach is that the code design is optimized for the used constellation. The most significant benefits of this approach are reached in AWGN channel and with high spectral efficiencies; in other words, with large constellations. One of the first commercial applications of TCM was high speed telephone modems that use very large constellation sizes to reach data rates up 33 kbits/s over the telephone line.

A Trellis Coded Modulation encoder consists of two parts: a convolutional encoder and a modulator. Figure 3.20 shows a basic structure of a TCM encoder. The input bits to encoder are b_0, b_1, and b_2. The convolutional encoder in the figure has rate $\frac{2}{3}$, it encodes input bits b_0 and b_1. In general the convolutional codes used by TCM are of rate $\frac{k}{k+1}$. The three bits, c_0, c_1, and c_2, output from the convolutional encoder enter the modulator with one additional uncoded bit c_3, therefore the overall rate of the TCM code is $\frac{3}{4}$. In general the number of uncoded bits can vary from zero to several bits. These uncoded bits are TCM's Achilles' heel for using it in fading channels with packet radio system. Figure 3.13 showed how the PER really suffers in a fading channel when there are bits, like c_3 in Figure 3.20, that are not protected with channel coding. An error in a single uncoded bit causes a packet error, and the loss of the whole packet. For a practical TCM system to achieve the 54 Mbits/s data rate, it would have to include some uncoded bits in the encoder, thus TCM was not selected as the coding method for IEEE 802.11a. The detrimental effect of the uncoded bits can be reduced by increasing the diversity level of the system. This is discussed in more detail in Chapter 4.

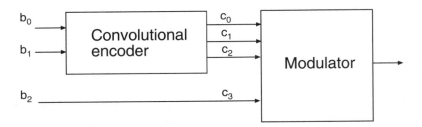

FIGURE 3.20

Trellis coded modulation encoder.

Block Codes

The first error correcting code, discovered by Hamming [5], was a block code. Block codes are different from convolutional codes in the sense that the code has a definite code word length n, instead of variable code word length like convolutional codes. The most popular class of block codes are Reed-Solomon (RS) codes discovered by Reed and Solomon [15]. Another important difference between block codes and convolutional codes is the block codes are designed using algebraic properties of polynomials or curves over finite fields, whereas convolutional codes are designed using exhaustive computer searches. Block codes have not gained wide acceptance in wireless systems, their performance does not reach the level of convolutional codes. The most famous application of Reed-Solomon codes is probably for compact discs that use RS codes to combat burst errors.

Concatenated Codes

Concatenated codes used to be the best performing error correcting codes, before the introduction of turbo codes that are discussed in next section. Concatenated codes are built by combining an outer code and an inner code, shown in Figure 3.21. The outer code is usually a Reed-Solomon block code and the inner code a convolutional code. Concatenated codes have reached performance that is only 2.2 dB from the channel capacity limit.

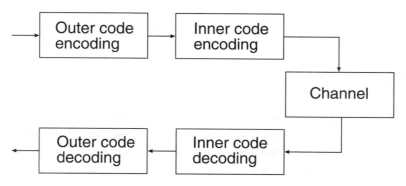

FIGURE 3.21
Basic structure of a concatenated channel coding system.

Turbo Codes

Turbo codes were a major discovery in 1993, when Berrou, Glavieux and Thitimajshima [1] released their results of a code that had performance only 0.6 dB from the channel capacity. Turbo codes are a combination of recursive systematic convolutional (RSC) codes, interleaving, and iterative decoding. Heegard and Wicker [7] provide a thorough treatment of these high performance codes. Figure 3.22 shows a basic structure of a rate $\frac{1}{3}$ turbo code encoder. The encoder outputs systematic bits b_{3n} that are identical to input bits, and two sets of encoded bits b_{3n+1} and b_{3n+2} that are encoded by different RSC encoders RSC1 and RSC2. The input to the RSC2 is an interleaved version of the input to the RSC1. The interleaver is an important component of a turbo code, and the code performance improves as the size of the interleaver is increased.

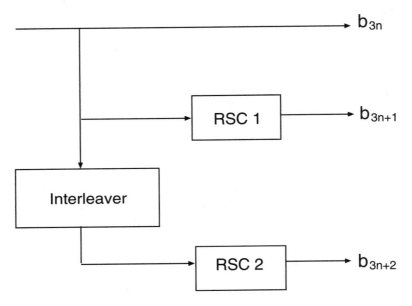

FIGURE 3.22

Rate 1/3 turbo code encoder structure.

Hoshyar, Jamali, and Bahai [8] studied a packet radio system with the same OFDM parameters as IEEE 802.11a, but replaced the channel code with turbo code. Surprisingly the results in a fading channel did not show similar performance gains as AWGN results would suggest, BER was stated to have equal performance, and PER performance was improved by 2.0 dB compared to the convolutional code.

Bibliography

[1] C. Berrou, A. Glavieux, P. Thitimajshima, "Near Shannon limit error-correcting coding and decoding: Turbo-codes," 1993 IEEE International Conference on Communications, Geneva, Volume: 2, 1993

[2] E. Biglieri, D. Divsalar, P. J. McLane, M. K. Simon, "Introduction to Trellis-Coded Modulation with Applications," Macmillan Publishing Company, New York, 1991

[3]   J. B. Cain, G. C. Clark Jr., and J.M. Geist, "Punctured Convolutional Codes of Rate (n-1)/n and Simplified Maximum Likelihood Decoding," IEEE Transactions of Information Theory, Vol. IT-25, pp. 97-100, January 1979

[4]   D. Forney, L.-F. Wei, "Multidimensional constellations. I. Introduction, figures of merit, and generalized cross constellations," IEEE Journal on Selected Areas in Communications, Volume: 7 Issue: 6, Aug. 1989, pp: 877–892

[5]   R. W. Hamming, "Error Detecting and Error Correcting Codes," Bell Systems Technical Journal, Vol. 29, pp. 147–160, 1950

[6]   J. Hagenauer, "Rate Compatible Punctured Convolutional Codes and Their Applications," IEEE Transactions on Communications, Vol. COM-36, pp. 389-400, April 1988

[7]   C. Heegard and S. B. Wicker, "Turbo codes," Kluwer Academic Publishers, 1999

[8]   R. Hoshyar, S. H. Jamali, A.R.S. Bahai, "Turbo coding performance in OFDM packet transmission," IEEE 51st Vehicular Technology Conference Proceedings, Tokyo, Volume: 2, pp. 805–810, 2000

[9]   L. H. Lee, "Error-Control Convolutional Coding," Artech House, 1997

[10]   S. Lin and D. J. Costello, "Error Control Coding: Fundamentals and Applications," Prentice-Hall, New Jersey, 2.ed, 1983

[11]   J. G. Proakis, "Digital Communications," McGraw-Hill, Boston, 3ed., 1995

[12]   J. L. Ramsey, "Realization of Optimum Interleavers," IEEE Transactions on Information Theory, Vol. IT-16, pp. 338-345, May 1970

[13]   T. S. Rappaport, "Wireless Communications: Principles and Practice," Prentice Hall, New Jersey, 1995

[14]   H. Rohling and K. Brüninhaus, "High Rate OFDM-Modem with quasicoherent DAPSK," IEEE 47th Vehicular Technology Conference, Volume: 3, pp: 2055–2059, 1997

[15]   I. S. Reed and G. Solomon, "Polynomial Codes over Certain Finite Fields," SIAM Journal on Applied Mathematics, Vol. 8, pp. 300–304, 1960

[16]   C. E. Shannon, "A Mathematical theory of communication," Bell Systems Technical Journal, 27, pp. 379–423, 623-656, 1948

[17]   M. K. Simon, W. C. Lindsey, S. M. Hinedi, "Digital Communication Techiques: Signal Design and Detection," Simon & Schuster Trade, 1994

[18]   B. Sklar, "Digital Communications: Fundamentals and Applications," Prentice-Hall, New Jersey, 2.ed, 2001

3

MODULATION
AND CODING

[19] G. Ungerboeck and I. Csajka, "On Improving Data Link Performance by Increasing the Channel Alphabet and Introducing Sequence Coding," 1976 International Symposium on Information Theory, Ronneby, Sweden, June 1976

[20] S. B. Wicker, "Error control coding," Prentice-Hall, New Jersey, 1995

Antenna Diversity

IN THIS CHAPTER

- Background   124
- Receive Diversity   131
- Transmit Diversity   136
- Bibliography   163

In this chapter, we explore the most underutilized resource in current wireless LAN systems, antenna diversity. Recent information theoretic results suggest that there is tremendous capacity potential for wireless communication systems using *antenna diversity*. Diversity is defined as multiple independent channels between transmitters and receivers; hence, antenna diversity or polarization discrimination occurs when the independent paths are spatial in nature. That is, there is sufficient spacing between the antenna elements at the transmitters and receivers such that there is no or very little correlation amongst their respective signals. The antenna diversity can be used to either improve the link performance of a signal or increase data throughput. The latter has been the subject of considerable research since it is generally believed that near Shannon capacity [61] might be achievable. The former has been and continues to be the study of research in error rate improvement. Both of these research areas have focused of various forms of antenna diversity techniques, which combines the multiple paths in such a way to improve the performance—either error rate or data rate—over that for a single transmit and receiver configuration. Throughout the remainder of this chapter, single transmit and receiver configuration shall be referred to as single-input, single-output (SISO) system.

The remainder of this chapter is organized as follows. First, the "Background" section provides the necessary relevant information required for a detailed discussion on antenna diversity. In the section, notation used throughout the remainder of the chapter is introduced. Most importantly, the fundamental limits of capacity that is achievable for various transmitter and receiver configurations are given. Remaining sections of the chapter are dedicated to antenna diversity techniques. More specifically, receive diversity and transmit diversity are discussed in the context of OFDM systems, respectively. The concepts presented in those sections are not easily grasped. Thus, in an effort to help the learning process, several examples are given throughout the sections to demonstrate particular concepts. This is a slight change from what has been heretofore presented in this text, but the complexity and the importance of this topic warranted additional learning aids. To maintain consistency with Chapters 2, 3, and 5, there are exercises provided that utilize the simulation tool at the Web site. As a final remark, the transmit diversity section is given more attention since additional hardware cost can be more easily accommodated at the access points (AP) rather than the mobile terminal (MT).

Background

In this section, we review the limits of capacity for fading environments, the channel model for multiple-input, multiple-output (MIMO) systems, and the concept of diversity. Each of these topics is needed to help in the understanding of the techniques used in antenna diversity. We begin with a treatment of capacity for fading environments. Foschini and Gans [20] have noted that OFDM systems are particularly well-suited for enhanced capacity using antenna diversity techniques. The report is summarized in the next section.

Limits of Capacity in Fading Environments

The report in [20] was motivated by the need for fundamental understanding of the ultimate limits of bandwidth efficient delivery of higher bit-rates in digital wireless communications. In addition, methods for achieving these limits are examined. The analysis assumes extremely limited mobility and a very slowly changing propagation environment such as a user at a desk within an office space. For this model, the channel is considered "quasi-static"; that is, the channel remains fixed during a burst and is allowed to randomly change from burst to burst. The burst is assumed to be of long enough duration that information theory offers meaningful results. Further, the results presented therein did not assume known channel characteristics at the transmitter, but the receiver knows the channel characteristic perfectly. The analysis is restricted to Rayleigh fading flat channels. Capacity is expressed in units of bits per second per Hertz (bps/Hz), or, equivalently, bits/cycle. The Rayleigh fading assumption stems from the fact that there are a large number of scatters within an indoor environment. Independence of the paths is assumed from the decorrelate on antennas spaced at least an half wavelength apart (polarization discrimination). Moreover, capacity in these analyses is treated as a random variable, and, as such, the *cumulative distribution functions* (cdf) are appropriate for assessing its performance. For instance, if we desire a 99% probability of achieving a particular performance, the cdf graphs provide the capacity curves and one can read off the SNR needed for a 1% outage probability. We briefly define the notation and basic assumptions that will be used throughout the remainder of this chapter:

- Number of transmit antennas and receive antennas are N and M, respectively
- Transmitted signal $s(t)$ is constrained to a total power P regardless of the value N
- The noise at each receiver $v_i(t)$ are independent identical distributed (i.i.d.) additive white Gaussian processes, whose power is equal to N_0
- The average SNR at each receiver is $\gamma = P / N_0$ independent of N
- Matrix channel impulse response $h(t)$ has N columns and M rows. $\mathbf{H}(f)^*$ will be used to denote the Fourier transform of $h(t)$
- Superscript T for vector transpose, superscript $\dagger$ for conjugate transpose, *det* for determinant, *tr* for trace of a matrix, and I_n for the $n \times n$ identity matrix

The received signal $r(t)$ at the ith antenna is given by

$$r_i(t) = h_i(t) \star s_i(t) + v_i(t) \tag{4.1}$$

Within the text, it will be convenient to drop the dependence of the power transfer characteristic on frequency for notational simplicity. The reader should assume that the discussion pertains to a particular frequency and uniformly applies to the other frequencies as well.

where $\star$ denotes linear convolution. The discretized versions of continuous variables such as $r(t)$, $s(t)$, and $h(t)$ will be denoted by sample time indexed variables such as $r(l)$, $s(l)$, and $h(l)$, respectively. For notational convenience, the dependence on the sampling time has been suppressed, e.g., $r(lT) \rightarrow r(l)$, where T is the sampling period.

Returning to the main discussion of this section, the standard capacity formula given by Shannon [61] can be expressed in bps/Hz as

$$C = \log_2\left(1 + \gamma|\mathbf{H}|^2\right) \quad bps \ / \ Hz \tag{4.2}$$

where H is just a complex scalar in this case.

For N statistically independent data streams with equal power and Gaussian distributed, the capacity becomes

$$C = \log_2\left[\det\left(I_M + \frac{\gamma}{N}\mathbf{H}\mathbf{H}^\dagger\right)\right] \quad bps \ / \ Hz \tag{4.3}$$

It is instructive to examine Equation 4.3 when $H = I_n$, i.e., parallel independent Gaussian channels; hence, the AWGN channel is found to be

$$C = n\log_2\left(1 + \frac{\gamma}{n}\right) \rightarrow \gamma \ / \ \ln(2) \quad as \ n \rightarrow \infty \tag{4.4}$$

Unlike the fading channels model (see Equation 4.2), the capacity scales linearly with increasing SNR for AWGN channels rather than logarithmically. Equation 4.4 hints at the benefits of parallel orthogonal transmission of independent information. One should, however, be careful not to forget that, in general, the various paths in a fading environment might not be orthogonal. In fact, there will tend to be correlation amongst the paths and thus they will interfere with each other. The equality in Equation 4.4 can be achieved by simply dividing the power equally among n independent paths and sending n equal rate independent signals.

When the channel is not AWGN but rather fading, diversity can be employed at the receiver; see the section on "Receive Diversity" for more details. It can be shown that multiple reception from a single transmitter can increase capacity. At the receiver, a linear combination of the antenna outputs are performed such that information contained in the input signal is maximized. This algorithm is called the *maximal ratio combining* (MRC) and is discussed in the "Maximal Ratio Combining" section of this chapter. The capacity resulting from MRC techniques is given by

$$C = \log_2\left(1 + \gamma\sum_{i=1}^{M}|\mathbf{H}_i|^2\right) \quad bps \ / \ Hz \tag{4.5}$$

where $\mathbf{H}_i$ is the channel matrix for the ith receive antenna.

Another receive diversity technique, which is commonly used but not optimum, is *selection diversity*. Selection diversity selects the receive antenna with the highest SNR The capacity offered by selection diversity is

$$C = \max_m \log_2\left[1 + \gamma|\mathbf{H}_m|^2\right] = \log_2\left[1 + \gamma \max_m |\mathbf{H}_m|^2\right], \quad m \in \{1, M\} \tag{4.6}$$

As implied previously, selection diversity is inferior to MRC diversity, yet it is much simpler to implement. Hence, it is attractive to use in that sense.

A brief point of clarification is in order here. Throughout the analysis presented heretofore in this section, the random channels considered have been Rayleigh channel models, which means that the elements of the $M \times N$ channel matrix $\mathbf{H}$ are i.i.d. complex, zero-mean, unit-variance Gaussian random variables. Further, it is well-known that the sum of the squares of k i.i.d. squared zero-mean unit-variance Gaussian random variables is a chi-squared random variable with k degrees of freedom.

The following equations examine some special Rayleigh channels using chi-squared variates.

Example 1 No Diversity: $M = N = 1$.

$$C = \log_2\left[1 + \gamma\chi_2^2\right] \tag{4.7}$$

So, the parameter γ multiplies a chi-squared variate with two degrees of freedom.

Example 2 Receive Diversity: $M = n, N = 1$.

$$C = \log_2\left[1 + \gamma\chi_{2n}^2\right] \tag{4.8}$$

Contrast Equation 4.8 with the capacity for selection diversity expressed using chi-squared variates,

$$C = \log_2\left[1 + \gamma \max\left(\chi_2^2\right)\right] \tag{4.9}$$

Example 3 Transmit Diversity: $M = 1, N = n$.

$$C = \log_2\left[1 + \frac{\gamma}{n} \chi_{2n}^2\right] \tag{4.10}$$

Compared with Equation 4.7, one can see that transmit diversity DOES NOT improve the SNR by $10\log_{10}(n)$, which is a common misconception. This would be true if we had not constrained

4

ANTENNA DIVERSITY

the overall transmit power independent of the number of transmitting antennas N. In other words, the average SNR over all channel realizations is the same at each receive antenna.

Example 4 Combine Transmit and Receive Diversity: It is required only that $N = M$, however, $N \geq M$ is easily accommodated, so it is included as well. The lower bound on the combined transmit and receive diversity case is given by

$$C = \sum_{k=N-(M-1)}^{N} \log_2\left[1 + \frac{\gamma}{N} \chi^2_{2k}\right] \tag{4.11}$$

Contrast Equation 4.11 with

$$C_{optimum} = \sum_{i=1}^{N} \log_2\left[1 + \frac{\gamma}{N} \chi^2_{2(M)_i}\right] \tag{4.12}$$

where i indexes statistically independent chi-squared variates each with $2M$ degrees of freedom. The capacity indicated by Equation 4.12 can only be achieved when the channel state information is known perfectly at both the transmitter and receiver simultaneously. The subject will be further pursued in the section "Water-Filling for Multi-Antenna Systems."

Example 5 Cyclic Delay Diversity: For this case, one transmitter of N transmit antennas is used at a time and detected by M receive antennas. All N transmit antennas are cycled through with period N. The cyclic mechanism avoids catastrophic interference and is simple to implement. The capacity formula for the cyclic delay diversity is given by

$$C = \frac{1}{N} \sum_{i=1}^{N} \log_2\left[1 + \gamma \chi^2_{2(M)_i}\right] \tag{4.13}$$

The first three examples, Equations 4.7–4.10, are simple applications of the generalized capacity formula and are easily derived. Equations 4.11 and 4.13 are more complicated, and interested readers are directed to reference [20] for the details of the proofs of the two formulas.

Exercise 1 *First, using the simulation tool provided at the Web site, determine the required SNR needed to transmit QPSK symbols encoded with the rate 1/2 convolutional code over a Rayleigh fading with reliability of 10^{-6} BER rate. Second, using Equation 4.2, determine the capacity in a Rayleigh fading for that SNR. Third, again using the capacity formula just mentioned, determine the SNR needed to obtain 1 bps/Hz. Finally, what can be said about the coding scheme, which corresponds to the 12 Mbps mode of the IEEE 802.11a standard, in terms of its efficiency with regards to optimum capacity?*

Exercise 2 *Which of the IEEE 802.11a standard modes is closest to optimum capacity in Rayleigh fading? Which is closest in AWGN?*

Channel Model for Multiple-Input/Multiple-Output (MIMO) Systems

In this section, we provide sufficient detail to generally characterize the channel for any multiple-input multiple-output (MIMO) systems employing an OFDM modulation; that is, we shall fully develop the expression given in Equation 4.1 of the previous section. The final form for the channel model shall be denoted in matrix/vector form for notational convenience. Now let's consider a communication link comprising N transmitter antennas and M receiver antennas that operates in a MIMO channel. Each receiver antenna responds to each transmitter antenna through a statistically independent fading path. The received signals are corrupted by additive noise that is statistically independent among the M receiver antennas and the transmission periods. For ease of presentation, discrete baseband notation shall be used; that is, at sample time index l, the complex symbol, $s_i(l)$, sent by the N transmit antennas and, subsequently, detected by kth receive antenna is denoted as $r_k(l)$. Then $r_k(l)$ can be expressed as

$$r_k(l) = \sqrt{\frac{P}{N}} \sum_{i=1}^{N} h_{ki}(l) \star s_i(l) + v_k(l), \quad 1 \le k \le M \tag{4.14}$$

where $h_{ik}(l)$ is the fading path between the ith transmitter antenna and the kth receive antenna at time index l. The noise samples at time index i, $v_k(l)$, are complex zero-mean spatially and temporally white Gaussian random variable with variance $N_0/2$ per dimension. It is further assumed that the transmitted signals $s_i(l)$ are normalized such that average energy for the signal constellation is unity. Recall in "OFDM WLAN Overview," in Chapter 1, for OFDM signal, the channel is made circulant by prepending a cyclic prefix (CP) to the data sequence prior to transmission. This simple mechanism allows for replacing the linear convolution in Equation 4.14 with a circular one. Hence, the frequency domain representation of Equation 4.14 using an L-point FFT is given by

$$R_k(m) = \sqrt{\frac{P}{N}} \sum_{i=1}^{N} \mathbf{H}_{ki}(m) \mathbf{S}_i(m) + V_k(m), \quad 1 \le m \le L \tag{4.15}$$

where $R_k(m)$, $\mathbf{H}_{ki}(m)$, $\mathbf{S}_i(m)$, and $V_k(m)$ denote the frequency domain representations of mth subcarrier of the received signal for the kth antenna, complex channel gains between ith transmitter antenna and the kth receive antenna, transmitted signal for the ith antenna, and noise signal for the kth receive antenna, respectively. If the channel gains are slowly fading, then it can be assumed that during a period of T time index the gains are constant and approximate the channel as a block fading channel. Thus, the received signal vector for the mth subcarrier using matrix notation is given by

$$\mathbf{R}(m) = \sqrt{\frac{P}{N}}\mathbf{H}(m)\mathbf{S}(m) + \mathbf{V}(m) \qquad (4.16)$$

where

$$\mathbf{R}(m) = [R_1(m), R_2(m), \cdots, R_M(m)]^T$$

$$\mathbf{H}(m) = \begin{bmatrix} H_{11}(m) & H_{12}(m) & \cdots & H_{1N}(m) \\ H_{21}(m) & \ddots & \cdots & H_{2N}(m) \\ \vdots & & \ddots & \vdots \\ H_{M1}(m) & \cdots & & H_{MN}(m) \end{bmatrix} \qquad (4.17)$$

$$\mathbf{S}(m) = [S_1(m), S_2(m), \cdots, S_N(m)]^T$$

$$S(m) = [V_1(m), V_2(m), \cdots, V_M(m)]^T$$

Hence, total received signal vector, again using matrix notation, can be written as

$$\tilde{\mathbf{R}} = [\mathbf{R}(1), \mathbf{R}(2), \cdots, \mathbf{R}(L)] \qquad (4.18)$$

which is simply a collection of the frequency domain received signals into a matrix.

Given this necessary mathematical framework, we can proceed to describe popular antenna diversity techniques.

Introducing Diversity

One way to improve the system performance over fading channels is to change its statistical characteristics. This is generally done by a technique called *diversity*. In fact, the effects of fading can be substantially mitigated through the use of diversity techniques in such systems via appropriately designed signal processing algorithms at both the transmitter and receiver. Practical, high-performance systems require that such diversity techniques be efficient in their use of resources such as power, bandwidth, and hardware cost; in addition, they often must meet stringent computational and delay constraints.

Three main forms of diversity are traditionally exploited in communication systems for fading channels: temporal, spectral, and spatial diversity. Temporal diversity is effective when the fading is time-selective. The degree to which this form of diversity can be exploited depends on delay constraints in the system relative to the coherence time of the fading process, which, in turn, is a function of, e.g., vehicle speeds in mobile applications [53]. "Interleaving" in Chapter 3 provides a detailed discussion of time diversity techniques.

Spectral diversity is effective when the fading is frequency-selective, i.e., it varies as a function of frequency. This form of diversity can be exploited when the available bandwidth for transmission is large enough that individual multipath components can begin to be resolved. Examples of systems that take advantage of frequency diversity are direct-sequence spread-spectrum communication, frequency-hopped spread-spectrum communication, and—the subject of this book—OFDM systems. The benefits of frequency diversity for OFDM have been documented in earlier chapters—"OFDM WLAN Overview" in Chapter 1 and "Interleaving" in Chapter 3—of this text while the spread-spectrum systems, on the other hand, are beyond the scope of this book.

Even in situations where the fading channel is nonselective, i.e., neither time selective nor frequency selective, or when system constraints preclude the use of these forms of temporal or spectral diversity, spatial diversity can be used to provide substantial improvement in system performance. Spatial diversity involves the use of multiple antennas sufficiently well-separated at the receiver and/or the transmitter that the individual transmission paths experience effectively independent fading. The extent to which this form of diversity can be exploited depends on issues such as cost and physical size constraints.

The two broad categories for antenna diversity are transmit and receive diversity.

We treat receiver diversity first because it is the simpler of the two concepts, and the remainder of the chapter is dedicated to transmit diversity.

Receive Diversity

The use of multiple antennas at the receiver, which is referred to as receive diversity, is fairly easily exploited. In essence, multiple copies of the transmitted stream are received, which can be efficiently combined using appropriate signal processing techniques. As the number of antennas increases, the outage probability is driven to zero, and the effective channel approaches an additive Gaussian noise channel. The two most popular receive diversity techniques are selection and maximal ratio combining.

Selection Diversity

The simplest receive diversity is selection diversity. Because of its simplicity, current IEEE 802.11b WLAN products employ selection diversity at the mobile terminal (MT) and access point (AP). Given M receive antennas, selection diversity entails choosing the receive antenna with the largest SNR in each symbol interval. Another attractive feature of selection diversity is that it does not require any additional RF receiver chain. In other words, all the receive antennas share a single RF receiver chains, which is key drive in keeping the cost down for the MT equipment.

The performance of selection diversity is easily computed by assuming each receive antenna is subject to *i.i.d.* Gaussian noise. Thus, selecting the antenna with the largest SNR is tantamount to selecting the receive antenna with the largest instantaneous power. Further, it assumes that the average reliability of each of the paths is equal. Thus, average SNR $\bar{\gamma}$ amongst the receive antennas is given by

$$\bar{\gamma} = \frac{\bar{\varepsilon}}{N_0} = E\left(h_l^2\right)\frac{\varepsilon}{N_0}, \quad l = 1, \ldots, M \qquad (4.19)$$

Naturally, the instantaneous SNR γ_l is therefore given by

$$\gamma = h_l^2 \frac{\varepsilon}{N_0}, \quad l = 1, \ldots, M \qquad (4.20)$$

The probability that the SNR for the *l*th receive antenna is lower than a threshold z is given by

$$Pr(\gamma_l \leq z) = \int_0^z f_{\gamma_l}(\beta)\partial\beta \qquad (4.21)$$

where $f_{\gamma_l}(\beta)$ denotes the probability density function (pdf) (see "Review of Stochastic Processes and Random Variables" in Chapter 1 for discussion) of γ_l, which is assumed to be the same for all antennas. With *M* independent receive antennas, the probability that all of them have an SNR below the threshold z is given by

$$Pr(\gamma_1 \leq z, \ldots, \gamma_M \leq z) = [Pr(\gamma_l \leq z)]^M \qquad (4.22)$$

and decreases as *M* increases. Not surprising, this is also the cdf of the random variable

$$\breve{\gamma} = \max\{\gamma_1, \ldots, \gamma_M\} \qquad (4.23)$$

Hence, $\breve{\gamma}$ is less than z if and only if (iff) $\gamma_1, \ldots, \gamma_M$ are all less than z. Therefore the pdf follows directly from the derivative of the cdf with respect to z. This result can be used to obtain the error probability of a digital modulation scheme in the presence of selection diversity by integrating the conditional error probability with respect to the $\breve{\gamma}$. To assess the benefit of selection diversity, we consider a QPSK modulation signal in a five-tap Rayleigh fading environment with 1, 2, and, 4 receive antennas. The error probability as a function of SNR is given in Figure 4.1.

From Figure 4.1, it is clearly evident that error rate performance improves with increasing number of receive antennas. Note for a BER of 1%, the improvement in error rate performance is between 2-3 dB for two receive antennas and 3-4 dB for four receive antennas. The caveat to this performance improvement is that each path for the receive antennas must be independent of the others.

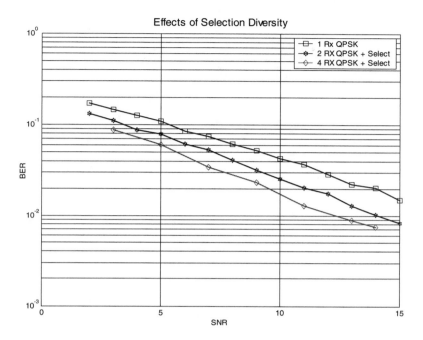

FIGURE 4.1

Error rate performance for selection diversity in Rayleigh fading.

To close, selection diversity is relatively easy to implement, as noted earlier, because it requires only a measure of the powers from each receive antenna and a switch. However, the simple observation that it disregards the information from all antennas but one leads us to conclude that is not an optimum combining technique.

Maximal Ratio Combining

In maximal ratio combining (MRC), the signals at the output of the M receive antennas are combined linearly so as to maximize the instantaneous SNR. The coefficients that yield the maximum SNR are found from straightforward application of optimization theory. Let's denote the received signal per antenna r_l as

$$r_l = h_l s_l + v_l \qquad (4.24)$$

with independent noise samples v_l and have the same power spectral density $2N_0$. Further assume perfect channel state information at each antenna. Finally, the transmitted signal s_l has been normalized such that the average signal energy equal 2ε.

MRC consists of using the linear combination

$$y = \sum_{l=1}^{M} w_l^* r_l = \sum_{l=1}^{M} w_l^* h_l s_l + \sum_{l=1}^{M} w_l^* v_l \tag{4.25}$$

prior to detection. The power spectral density S_v of the noise after MRC is given by

$$S_v = 2N_0 \sum_{l=1}^{M} |w_l|^2$$

while the instantaneous signal energy is

$$2\varepsilon \left| \sum_{l=1}^{M} |w_l^* h_l|^2 \right|$$

The ratio of these two quantities

$$\gamma = \frac{\varepsilon \left| \sum_{l=1}^{M} |w_l^* h_l|^2 \right|}{N_0 \sum_{l=1}^{M} |w_l|^2}$$

can be maximized as follows. Recall the Cauchy-Schwartz inequality defined as

$$\left| \sum_{l=1}^{M} |a_l^* b_l|^2 \right| \le \sum_{l=1}^{M} |a_l|^2 \sum_{l=1}^{M} |b_l|^2 \tag{4.26}$$

where the equality in Equation 4.26 is obtained for $w_l = h_l$ for all l, which provides the weighting coefficients for MRC. In plain English, each antenna is weighted proportionally by its corresponding fading attenuation. The heavily faded antennas, which are less reliable, are counted less than the less faded antennas, which are more reliable, and vice versa. The SNR provided by MRC is given by

$$\gamma_{MRC} = \frac{\varepsilon}{N_0} \sum_{l=1}^{M} |w_l|^2 \tag{4.27}$$

Noting that $\varepsilon |w_l|^2 / N_0$ is the SNR per antenna, then Equation 4.27 is just the sum of the SNRs for each antenna, which means γ_{MRC} can be large even when the individual SNRs are small. As an example of the improvement results from MRC, consider the same scenario as before with selection diversity. Rather than using selection diversity, we instead use MRC. The error performance of this system is shown in Figure 4.2.

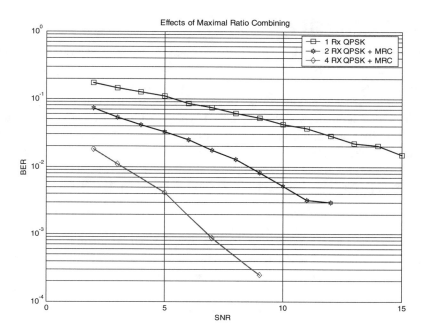

FIGURE 4.2

Error rate performance for MRC in Rayleigh fading.

The performance improvement is much more significant for MRC than selection diversity. For instance, at a BER of 1%, MRC with two receive antennas provides nearly 10 dB improvement, while for selection diversity, it was found to be between 2-3 dB. For four receive antennas, the improvement is nearly 15 dB!

In summary, the potential gain using MRC can be tremendous. This is not surprising since it is the optimum solution. The caveat to this is that perfect channel knowledge was assumed, which is not true in general. The accuracy of the channel estimation will depend somewhat on the operating SNR. The sensitivity of MRC to channel estimation error is left as an exercise to the readers.

Exercise 3 *Consider the case when the weights for the MRC are all equal to unity, referred to as equal gain diversity. How does this receive diversity technique compare to selection diversity and MRC? Modify the MRC module given at the Web site to perform this task and plot on the same graph selection diversity, equal-gain diversity, and MRC for the case scenario given in the selection diversity example.*

4

**ANTENNA
DIVERSITY**

Transmit Diversity

In the previous section, receive diversity techniques were reviewed. However, receive diversity can be impractical in a number of applications. In such scenarios, the use of multiple antennas at the transmitter, which is referred to as transmit diversity, is significantly more attractive. Multiple element transmitter antenna arrays have an increasingly important role to play in emerging wireless LAN networks, particularly at the AP. Indeed, when used in conjunction with appropriately designed signal processing algorithms, such arrays can dramatically enhance performance. This last statement begs the question, "How are good transmit diversity schemes designed?"

Transmit Diversity Design Criteria for Fading Channels

In this section, we explore different design criteria for transmit diversity schemes. As will be explained later, the design criteria depend heavily on how much is known about the channel at the transmitter and receiver. In general, a wireless communication system is comprised of N transmit antennas and M receive antennas. The information data is encoded using a channel code to protect it against imperfections caused by the channel. The encoded data stream is split into N parallel streams, each of which is modulated and then transmitted using separate antennas. Each path for the separate antennas is assumed *i.i.d.* and quasi-static; that is, the complex gains of the paths are constant over each data frame but changes from frame to frame.

We begin our analysis of transmit diversity design criteria by examining the single antenna case and then generalize the results for the multiple antenna case in the Trellis Space-Time Codes section. To develop codes that perform well over fading channels, we choose to minimize the pairwise error probability. That is, the probability that codeword $\mathbf{c}$ is transmitted over the channel and a maximum-likelihood (ML) receiver decides in favor of a different codeword $\mathbf{e}$. The ML receiver makes decoding decisions based on a performance metric $m(\mathbf{r}, \mathbf{c}, \mathbf{h})$ provided that estimates of the fading amplitudes, $\mathbf{h}$, are available at the receiver. Formally, the maximum likelihood criterion for the optimum decoder requires the conditional probability of receiving $\mathbf{r}$ given that codeword $\mathbf{c}$ was transmitted to be greater than the probability of receiving $\mathbf{r}$ assuming any other codeword $\mathbf{e}$ was transmitted, i.e.,

$$P(\mathbf{c} \rightarrow \mathbf{e} \mid \mathbf{h}) = \Pr[m(\mathbf{r}, \mathbf{e}; \mathbf{h}) \geq m(\mathbf{r}, \mathbf{c}; \mathbf{h}) \mid \mathbf{h}] \tag{4.28}$$

where

$$m(r_i, e_i; h_i) = \left| r_i - h_i e_i \right|^2 \tag{4.29}$$

and $\left| \cdot \right|^2$ represents the squared Euclidean norm. Note that since the performance metric $m(\mathbf{r}, \mathbf{c}; \mathbf{h})$ is just the distance between vectors, the total metric is simply the sum of the distances per dimension $m(r_i, e_i; h_i)$. The pairwise error probability is found by taking the statistical expectation of

Equation 4.28. Rather than solving for the exact pairwise error probability, which can only be evaluated numerically, an upper bound can be found for Equation 4.28 by using the Chernoff bound techniques [25]

$$P(\mathbf{c} \to \mathbf{e}) \leq \mathbf{E}_h\{\exp(\lambda[m(\mathbf{r}, \mathbf{e}; \mathbf{h}) - m(\mathbf{r}, \mathbf{c}; \mathbf{h})])\} \qquad (4.30)$$

$$P(\mathbf{c} \to \mathbf{e}) \leq \prod_{l=1}^{L} E_{h_l}\left\{\exp\left(\lambda\left[|r_l - h_l c_l|^2 - |r_l - h_l e_l|^2\right]\right)\right\} \qquad (4.31)$$

where $\lambda \geq 0$ is the Chernoff parameter to be optimized for the tightest bound. The equality in Equation 4.31 is obtained by invoking the additive property of the metric. The optimum Chernoff parameter to form the tightest bound can be found by first rewriting the multiplicands in Equation 4.31 as

$$\exp\left(\lambda\left[|r_l - h_l c_l|^2 - |r_l - h_l e_l|^2\right]\right) = \exp\left[-\lambda h_l^2 (1 - N_0 \lambda)|c_l - e_l|^2\right] \qquad (4.32)$$

Now, the optimum Chernoff parameter λ_{opt} is found by taking the derivative of the argument in Equation 4.32 with respect to λ to yield

$$\lambda_{opt} = \left(\frac{1}{2N_0}\right) \qquad (4.33)$$

Substituting Equation 4.33 into Equation 4.32 results in a optimized Chernoff bound

$$P(\mathbf{c} \to \mathbf{e}) \leq \prod_{l=1}^{L} E_{h_l}\left\{\exp\left(-\frac{h_l^2}{4N_0}|c_l - e_l|^2\right)\right\} \qquad (4.34)$$

Rician Channels

To evaluate the bound for a Rician channel, we average the result of Equation 4.34 over the Rician pdf [54] to obtain

$$P(\mathbf{c} \to \mathbf{e}) \leq \prod_{l=1}^{L} \int_0^\infty 2h_i(1+\kappa)\exp\left(-\left[\kappa + h_l^2(1+\kappa) + h_i^2\delta^2\right]\right) \qquad (4.35)$$

$$I_0\left(2h_l\sqrt{k(1+\kappa)}\right)\delta h_l \qquad (4.36)$$

where

$$\delta^2 = \frac{|c_l - e_l|^2}{4N_0}$$

and κ is the Rician factor defined as the ratio of energy in the spectral path to the diffuse path. This integral can be evaluated using [34]

$$\int_0^\infty t \exp\left(-at^2\right) \cdot J_0(\lambda t)\partial t = \frac{1}{2\alpha} \exp\left(\frac{-\gamma^2}{4a}\right) \tag{4.37}$$

where

$$J_0(jt) = I_0(t)$$

and $I_0(t)$ is the zeroth order modified Bessel Function [34] and $j = \sqrt{-1}$.

Thus the pairwise error probability for a Rician channel is given by

$$P(\mathbf{c} \rightarrow \mathbf{e}) \leq \Pi_{l=1}^L \frac{1+\kappa}{1+\kappa+\frac{1}{4N_0}|c_l - e_l|^2} \exp\left[\frac{-\kappa \frac{1}{4N_0}|c_l - e_l|^2}{1+\kappa+\frac{1}{4N_0}|c_l - e_l|^2}\right] \tag{4.38}$$

which simplifies for high signal-to-noise ratios (SNR) to

$$P(\mathbf{c} \rightarrow \mathbf{e}) \leq \Pi_{l \in \eta} \frac{(1+\kappa)\exp[-\kappa]}{\frac{1}{4N_0}|c_l - e_l|^2} \tag{4.39}$$

where η is the set of all l for which $c_l \neq e_l$. Denoting the number of elements in η as L_η, Equation 4.39 can be rewritten as

$$P(\mathbf{c} \rightarrow \mathbf{e}) \leq \frac{((1+\kappa)\exp[-\kappa])^{L_\eta}}{\left(\frac{1}{4N_0} d_P^2(L_\eta)\right)^{L_\eta}} \tag{4.40}$$

where $d_P^2(L_\eta)$ is the so-called squared product distance along the error event $(\mathbf{c}, \mathbf{e})$ path defined as

$$d_P^2(L_\eta) = \left(\Pi_{l \in \eta}|c_l - e_l|^2\right)^{\frac{1}{L_\eta}} \tag{4.41}$$

and L_η is the *effective length* of the error event $(\mathbf{c}, \mathbf{e})$.

Rayleigh Channels

For Rayleigh channels, κ is equal to zero and Equation 4.40 simplifies to

$$P(\mathbf{c} \rightarrow \mathbf{e}) \leq \Pi_{l \in \eta} \frac{1}{\frac{1}{4N_0}|c_l - e_l|^2} \tag{4.42}$$

Among all terms in Equations 4.40 and 4.42, the terms with the smallest effective length L_η and smallest product distance $d_P^2(L_\eta)$ dominate the error event probability at high SNR. Let's denote the minimum L_η by L and the corresponding squared product distance as $d_P^2(L)$ thus the error event probability for Rician channels is asymptotically approximated by

$$P(\mathbf{c} \to \mathbf{e}) \cong \alpha\left(L, d_P^2(L)\right) \frac{((1+\kappa)\exp[-\kappa])^L}{\left(\frac{1}{4N_0} d_P^2(L)\right)^L} \tag{4.43}$$

and, for Rayleigh channels,

$$P(\mathbf{c} \to \mathbf{e}) \cong \alpha\left(L, d_P^2(L)\right) \frac{1}{\left(\frac{1}{4N_0} d_P^2(L)\right)^L} \tag{4.44}$$

where $\alpha(L, d_P^2(L))$ is the average of number of code sequences having effective length L and squared product distance $d_P^2(L)$. Equation 4.44 says that the error event probability has two dominant factors: the product distance and its multiplicity—average number of occurrences $\alpha(L, d_P^2(L))$. So, not only must the product distance $d_P^2(L)$ be maximized, the number of low symbol Hamming weight code sequences $\alpha(L, d_P^2(L))$ must be kept as small as possible as well.

Delay Diversity

Just as selection diversity is the simplest of the receive diversity techniques, delay diversity is the simplest of the transmit diversity techniques. Consider a repetition code of length of N—a symbol is repeated N times on N transmit antennas. The N symbols are transmitted over the N different antennas at non-overlapping time instants or frequency bins of a DFT, i.e.,

$$\mathbf{S} = \begin{bmatrix} s_1 & s_2 & s_3 & s_4 & s_5 \\ 0 & s_1 & s_2 & s_3 & s_4 \\ 0 & 0 & s_1 & s_2 & s_3 \end{bmatrix} \tag{4.45}$$

where the rows correspond to transmit antennas and the columns correspond to symbol intervals. The received signal $r(l)$ is given by

$$r(l) = \sum_{i=1}^{N} \sum_{j=1}^{P} h_i(j) S_i(l-j) + v(l) \tag{4.46}$$

where the subscript ith indexes the individual paths. If this diversity code is subject to a frequency-selective channel, a minimum mean squared error (MMSE) decision feedback equalizer or a maximum likelihood sequence estimator (MLSE) is needed to resolve the multipath

4

ANTENNA
DIVERSITY

distortion. When implemented in an OFDM framework, the OFDM received signal for the kth subcarrier $R(k)$ becomes

$$R(k) = \sum_{i=1}^{N} H_i(k)S_i(k) + V(k) \tag{4.47}$$

where $H_i(k)$, and $S_i(k)$ are the frequency domain representations for the kth subcarrier and ith path of the channel impulse response and transmit signal, respectively; $V(k)$ is the additive noise process at the receiver. Assuming perfect knowledge of the channel at the receiver, the receiver must solve the following optimization problem for each subcarrier k,

$$\varepsilon_k = \min\left\| R(k) - \mathbf{H}(k)^{\dagger}\mathbf{S}(k) \right\|^2 \tag{4.48}$$

$$\mathbf{H}(k) = [H_1(k), H_2(k), \ldots, H_N(k)]^T \tag{4.49}$$

$$\mathbf{S}(k) = [S_1(k), S_2(k), \ldots, S_N(k)]^T \tag{4.50}$$

The MLSE requires a search over all possible transmit sequences and finds the sequence that yields the minimum of Equation 4.48.

Exercise 4 *Develop a Matlab script file using Equation 4.45 for a two-antenna delay diversity code within an OFDM frame with symbols drawn from a QPSK constellation. The receiver function shall be an MLSE, which requires that for every subcarrier, the sixteen possible combinations for two QPSK symbols are to be evaluated in Equation 4.48. Integrate the delay diversity encoder and decoder into the simulation environment at our Web site and compare the performance for this code with that of selection diversity and MRC with two receive antennas.*

Trellis Space-Time Codes

The foregoing analysis in the "Transmit Diversity Design Criteria for Fading Channels" section leads to a set of design parameters for good space-time codes (STC) over fading channels. To characterize these parameters, we consider the error event probability of STC over fading channels as the performance metric. Assuming ideal channel state information at the receivers and multiple transmit and receive antennas, the pairwise error probability, determined from the Chernoff bound in Equation 4.34, is given by

$$P(\mathbf{c} \rightarrow \mathbf{e}) \leq \exp\left(\frac{-d^2(\mathbf{c}, \mathbf{e})E_s}{4N_0}\right) \tag{4.51}$$

where $d^2(\mathbf{c}, \mathbf{e})$ represents the normalized accumulative distance between codewords $(\mathbf{c}, \mathbf{e})$ and is defined as

$$d^2(\mathbf{c}, \mathbf{e}) = \sum_{j=1}^{m} \sum_{l=1}^{L} \left| \sum_{i=1}^{n} h_{i,j}(c_i(l) - e_i(l)) \right|^2 \tag{4.52}$$

Using matrix notation, Equation 4.52 can be expressed as

$$d^2(\mathbf{c}, \mathbf{e}) = \sum_{j=1}^{m} \mathbf{h}_j^\dagger \mathbf{D}(\mathbf{e}, \mathbf{c})^\dagger \mathbf{D}(\mathbf{e}, \mathbf{c}) \mathbf{h}_j \tag{4.53}$$

where h_j is again the channel coefficient vector defined as

$$\mathbf{h}_j = \left[h_{1,j}, h_{2,j}, \cdots, h_{n,j} \right] \tag{4.54}$$

$\mathbf{D}(\mathbf{e}, \mathbf{c})$ is the codeword difference matrix defined as

$$\mathbf{D}(\mathbf{e}, \mathbf{c}) = \begin{bmatrix} c_1(0) - e_1(0) & c_1(1) - e_1(1) & \cdots & c_1(L) - e_1(L) \\ \vdots & \ddots & \vdots & \vdots \\ c_n(0) - e_n(0) & c_n(1) - e_n(1) & \cdots & c_n(L) - e_n(L) \end{bmatrix}^T \tag{4.55}$$

T denotes matrix transpose. Thus, substituting Equation 4.53 into Equation 4.51, the pairwise error probability in matrix notation becomes

$$P(\mathbf{c} \rightarrow \mathbf{e}) \leq \prod_{j=1}^{M} \exp \left(\frac{-\left[\mathbf{h}_j^\dagger \mathbf{D}(\mathbf{e}, \mathbf{c})^\dagger \mathbf{D}(\mathbf{e}, \mathbf{c}) \mathbf{h}_j \right] E_s}{4 N_0} \right) \tag{4.56}$$

The matrix $\mathbf{D}(\mathbf{e}, \mathbf{c})^\dagger \mathbf{D}(\mathbf{e}, \mathbf{c})$ is Hermitian; thus, it be can expressed in terms of a unitary matrix $\mathbf{V}$ whose columns are its eigenvectors $\mathbf{v}_i$ and a diagonal matrix Λ containing its eigenvalues, i.e.,

$$\mathbf{h}_j^\dagger \mathbf{D}(\mathbf{e}, \mathbf{c})^\dagger \mathbf{D}(\mathbf{e}, \mathbf{c}) \mathbf{h}_j = \sum_{i=1}^{n} \lambda_i \left| \mathbf{h}_j^\dagger \mathbf{v}_i \right| \tag{4.57}$$

We note that since channel coefficients $h_{i,j}$ are *i.i.d.* by assumption, an orthonormal transformation of the channel coefficients, $\beta_{i,j} = \mathbf{h}_j^\dagger \mathbf{v}_i$, is also *i.i.d.* Hence, we arrive at the upper bound on the average probability of error with respect to the $\beta_{i,j}$ for Rician and Rayleigh channels, respectively, by substituting Equation 4.57 into Equation 4.53 and using Equations 4.38 and 4.42,

$$P(\mathbf{c} \rightarrow \mathbf{e}) \leq \prod_{j=1}^{m} \prod_{i=1}^{p} \frac{(1 + \kappa_{i,j})}{1 + \kappa_{i,j} \frac{E_s}{4 N_0} \lambda_i} \exp \left[-\frac{\kappa_{i,j} \frac{E_s}{4 N_0} \lambda_i}{1 + \kappa_{i,j} \frac{E_s}{4 N_0} \lambda_i} \right] \tag{4.58a}$$

4

**ANTENNA
DIVERSITY**

$$P(\mathbf{c} \to \mathbf{e}) \le \left(\frac{E_s}{4N_0}\right)^{-pm} \left(\Pi_{i=1}^r \lambda_i\right)^{-m} \tag{4.58b}$$

where p is the rank of the codeword difference matrix $\mathbf{D}(\mathbf{e}, \mathbf{c})$. Inspection of (4.58b) leads to the design criteria we sought.

- **The Distance/Rank Criterion:** In order to achieve a diversity of pm in a rapid fading environment for any two codewords $\mathbf{c}$ and $\mathbf{e}$, the strings $c_1(l)\ c_2(l)\cdots c_n(l)$ and $e_1(l)\ e_2(l)\cdots e_n(l)$ must be different at least for p values of $1 \le l \le n$. In other words, the rank of $\mathbf{D}(\mathbf{e}, \mathbf{c})$ must be p to achieve a diversity of pm in a quasi-static flat fading environment.

- **The Product/Determinant Criterion:** Recall that η is the set of all l for which $c_l \ne e_l$. and let $|\mathbf{c}_l - \mathbf{e}_l|^2 = \sum_{i=1}^n [c_i(l) - e_i(l)]$. Then to achieve the most coding gain in a rapid fading environment, the minimum squared product distance $d_P^2(L_\eta)$ over η, as defined in Equation 4.41, must be maximized. For the case of a static fading channel, the minimum of pth roots of the sum of determinants of all $p \times p$ principal cofactors of $\mathbf{D}(\mathbf{e}, \mathbf{c})^\dagger \mathbf{D}(\mathbf{e}, \mathbf{c})$ taken over all pairs of distinct codewords $\mathbf{c}$ and $\mathbf{e}$ corresponds to the coding gain.

Improvement of the STC Design Criterion

D.M. Ionescu [43] demonstrated that the determinant criterion can be strengthened by requiring that the eigenvalues of $\mathbf{D}(\mathbf{e}, \mathbf{c})^\dagger \mathbf{D}(\mathbf{e}, \mathbf{c})$ be as close as possible, for any pair codewords $\mathbf{c}$, $\mathbf{e}$. Formally, the criterion was expressed as follows.

The Equal Eigenvalue Criterion: For N-transmit antenna system operating in i.i.d. Rayleigh fading with perfect channel state information (CSI), an upper bound to the pairwise error probability is made as small as possible *iff*, for all pair codewords $\mathbf{c}$, $\mathbf{e}$, the squared Euclidean distance $tr\left[\mathbf{D}(\mathbf{e}, \mathbf{c})^\dagger \mathbf{D}(\mathbf{e}, \mathbf{c})\right]$ are made as large as possible. Further, the non-square matrices $\mathbf{D}(\mathbf{e}, \mathbf{c})$ are semi-unitary—up to a scale factor—, i.e. $\mathbf{D}(\mathbf{e}, \mathbf{c})^\dagger \mathbf{D}(\mathbf{e}, \mathbf{c}) = \left(tr\left[\mathbf{D}(\mathbf{e}, \mathbf{c})^\dagger \mathbf{D}(\mathbf{e}, \mathbf{c})\right] / N\right) * I_N$. Essentially, maximizing $\min_{\mathbf{c}, \mathbf{e}} \det\left[\mathbf{D}(\mathbf{e}, \mathbf{c})^\dagger \mathbf{D}(\mathbf{e}, \mathbf{c})\right]$, as specified by the Determinant Criterion, requires maximizing the minimum eigenvalue product over all $\mathbf{D}(\mathbf{e}, \mathbf{c})^\dagger \mathbf{D}(\mathbf{e}, \mathbf{c})$.

Proof By Hadamard's theorem, the eigenvalue product for a square, positive definite matrix $\mathbf{A}$, with elements $a_{i,j}$ assumes its maximum value $\Pi_i a_{i,i}$, *iff* $\mathbf{A}$ is diagonal. Once $\mathbf{D}(\mathbf{e}, \mathbf{c})^\dagger \mathbf{D}(\mathbf{e}, \mathbf{c})$ is diagonalized, the product of its diagonal elements is maximized *iff* they are rendered equal and their sum, $tr\left[\mathbf{D}(\mathbf{e}, \mathbf{c})^\dagger \mathbf{D}(\mathbf{e}, \mathbf{c})\right]$, is maximized. Consider the arithmetric-mean geometric mean inequality [34], i.e.,

$$\sqrt[n]{\prod_{i=1}^n \lambda_i} \le \left(\frac{1}{n}\sum_{i=1}^n \lambda_i\right) \tag{4.59}$$

The astute reader will recognize that the left hand side of Equation 4.59 has the same form as the product distance given in Equation 4.41. Hence, the product distance $d_P^2(L)$ is upper bounded by the arithmetic mean of the eigenvalues of $\mathbf{D(e,c)}^\dagger \mathbf{D(e,c)}$ with equality achieved when all eigenvalues are equal.

D.M. Ionescu recognized that it might be difficult to enforce this condition for all pairs of codewords $\mathbf{c}$, $\mathbf{e}$ and thus proposed a sub-optimal solution to enforce the condition of the codewords corresponding to the shortest error event paths in the code trellis. Shortly, we will see that this new Determinant Criterion relates to block STC.

Using the original design criteria for STC, Tarokh *et al* [65, 67, 69] were able to generate a family of codes, which have received considerable attention. Tarokh *et al* claimed that these codes achieve near optimum *outage capacity* (rather than Shannon's capacity). Outage capacity is defined as the maximum constant information rate that can be maintained in all fading conditions with some nonzero probability of outage, assuming perfect receiver CSI. For these environments, it is more appropriate to use outage capacity rather than Shannon's capacity since some channels yield zero capacity using Shannon's formula. Hence, it is not a meaningful measure of the performance of these environments. Examples of outage capacity are when all the phone lines at your job are busy and your cell phone cannot get service. Hopefully, this doesn't occur to you very often. In fact, most communication systems strive to have greater than 99% availability to its customer or less than 1% outage probability. Previously reported performance results in [67], compared to outage capacity are reprinted here for inspection. The trellis structures examined are shown in Figures 4.3–4.5. The performance curves for these trellises are given for inspection and their corresponding performance in Figures 4.6–4.9.

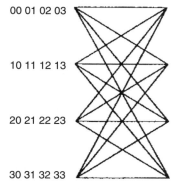

FIGURE 4.3

A fully connected four state STC using QPSK. © 1998 IEEE.

00, 01, 02, 03
10, 11, 12, 13
20, 21, 22, 23
30, 31, 32, 33
22, 23, 20, 21
32, 33, 30, 31
02, 03, 00, 01
12, 13, 10, 11

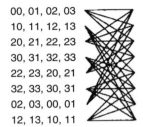

00, 01, 02, 03
12, 13, 10, 11
20, 21, 22, 23
32, 33, 30, 31
20, 21, 22, 23
32, 33, 30, 31
00, 01, 02, 03
12, 13, 10, 11
02, 03, 00, 01
10, 11, 12, 13
22, 23, 20, 21
30, 31, 32, 33
22, 23, 20, 21
30, 31, 32, 33
02, 03, 00, 01
10, 11, 12, 13

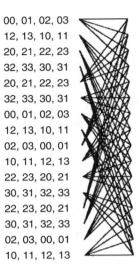

FIGURE 4.4

Trellises for 8 state and 16 state with diversity order 2. © 1998 IEEE.

00, 01, 02, 03, 04, 05, 06, 07

51, 52, 53, 54, 55, 56, 57, 50

22, 23, 24, 25, 26, 27, 20, 21

73, 74, 75, 76, 77, 70, 71, 72

44, 45, 46, 47, 40, 41, 42, 43

15, 16, 17, 10, 11, 12, 13, 14

66, 67, 60, 61, 62, 63, 64, 65

37, 30, 31, 32, 33, 34, 35, 36

15, 16, 17, 10, 11, 12, 13, 14

66, 67, 60, 61, 62, 63, 64, 65

37, 30, 31, 32, 33, 34, 35, 36

00, 01, 02, 03, 04, 05, 06, 07

51, 52, 53, 54, 55, 56, 57, 50

22, 23, 24, 25, 26, 27, 20, 21

73, 74, 75, 76, 77, 70, 71, 72

44, 45, 46, 47, 40, 41, 42, 43

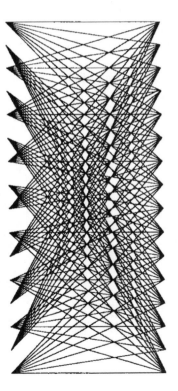

FIGURE 4.5

Trellis for 16 states, 3 bps/Hz STC. © 1998 IEEE.

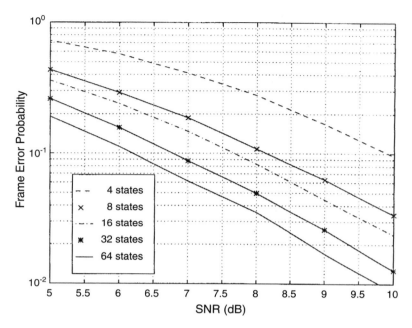

FIGURE 4.6

Codes for QPSK with rate 2 bps/Hz that achieve diversity order 4 with 2 rx and 2 tx antennas. © 1998 IEEE.

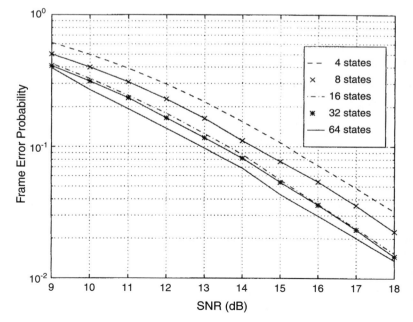

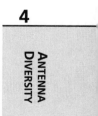

FIGURE 4.7

Codes for QPSK with rate 2 bps/Hz that achieve diversity order 2 with 1 rx and 2 tx antennas. © 1998 IEEE.

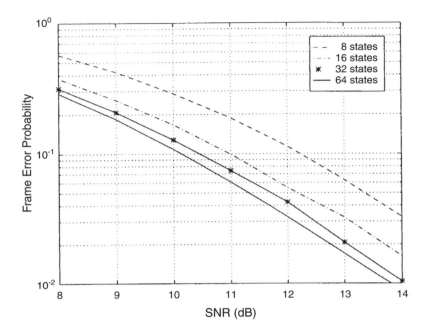

FIGURE 4.8

Codes for 8-PSK with rate 3 bps/Hz that achieve diversity order 4 with 2 tx and 2 rx antennas. © 1998 IEEE.

Layered Space-Time Codes

The Layered Space-Time Processing approach to STC was first introduced by Foschini [21] at Bell Labs. The basic concept behind layered STC is demultiplexing information bits into individual streams in a hierarchal manner, which are then fed into individual encoders. The outputs of the coders are modulated and fed to separate antennas, from which they are transmitted, using the same carrier frequency and symbol waveform. At the receiver, a spatial beam-forming process is used at the front end in order to separate the individual coded streams, and feed them to their individual decoders. After decoding the most important bits, they are used to decode less important bits and this goes till all the information is decoded.

Foschini considered this problem in [21]. He proposed a multilayered structure that in principle can achieve a tight lower bound on the capacity. If N transmit and N receive antennas are used, then at the receiver the transmitted signal from transmit antenna 1 is treated as the desired signal, while the signals transmitted from other transmit antennas are treated as interference. Linear processing is then used to suppress the interfering signals using N receive antennas, providing a diversity gain of one. Once the signal transmitted from antenna 1 is correctly detected, the signal transmitted from antenna 2 is treated as the desired signal while the signals transmitted from transmit antennas $3, 4, \cdots, N$ are treated as interference. Linear processing is then applied to suppress the interfering signals using N receive antennas. This provides a diversity gain of two. This process is repeated until all the transmitted signals are detected. Clearly, the dominant diversity in this architecture is associated with the first estimated signal. In this light, long frames of data combined with powerful coding techniques are needed to achieve the lower bound on outage capacity. The diversity level can be improved albeit at the expense of losing half of the rate [21].

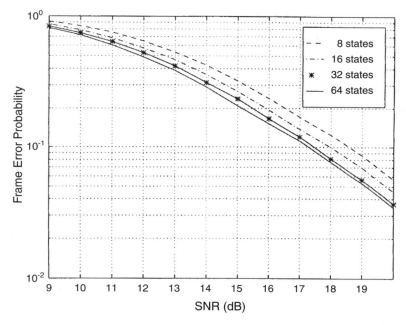

FIGURE 4.9

Codes for 8-PSK with rate 3 bps/Hz that achieve diversity order 2 with 1 rx and 2 tx antennas. © 1996 IEEE.

This approach is purely a signal processing one. Tarokh [65] attacked the problem from an array signal processing combined with channel coding perspective. Antennas at the transmitter are partitioned into small groups, and individual STCs, called the component codes, are used to transmit information from each group of antennas. At the receiver, an individual STC is decoded by a novel linear array processing technique, called the group interference suppression method [65], that suppresses signals transmitted by other groups of antennas by treating them as interference. Since the diversity in each decoding stage l is more than that of the previous decoding stage $l-1$, the transmit power out of each antenna at level l can be substantially less than that of the previous layer. Thus the transmitter should divide the available transmit power among different antennas in an unequal manner. Power allocation for this scenario is straightforward. In fact, powers at different levels could be allocated based on the diversity gains. In this way, the allocated powers may decrease geometrically in terms of the diversity gains.

4

ANTENNA DIVERSITY

This combination of array processing at the receiver and coding techniques for multiple transmit antennas provides reliable and very high data rate communication over wireless channels. One obvious advantage of the group interference suppression method over the architecture of Foschini [21] is that the number of receive antennas can be less than the number of transmit antennas [65].

Block Space-Time Codes

Trellis space-time coding combines signal processing at the receiver with coding techniques appropriate to multiple transmit antennas. Specific trellis space-time codes designed for two and four transmit antennas [67] perform extremely well in slow-fading environments (typical of indoor transmission) and come close to the outage capacity. However, when the number of transmit antennas is fixed, the decoding complexity of trellis STCs—determined by the number of trellis states in the decoder—increases exponentially with transmission rate.

In addressing the issue of decoding complexity, Alamouti [2] discovered a remarkable scheme for transmission using two transmit antennas. This scheme is much less complex than trellis space-time coding for two transmit antennas, but there is a loss in performance compared to trellis STCs. Despite this performance penalty, Alamouti's scheme is appealing in terms of simplicity and performance, and it motivated a search for similar schemes using more than two transmit antennas.

The novelty of Alamouti's block STC is the simple decoding system. Although it is shown [68] that the spectrum efficiency of this method is not as good as trellis STCs, the simplicity of the decoder is the motivation to use this method in practical systems. Maximum-likelihood decoding is achieved in a simple way through decoupling of the signals transmitted from different antennas rather than joint detection. This uses the orthogonal structure of the block STC and gives a maximum likelihood decoding algorithm, which is based only on linear processing at the receiver. Block STC are designed to achieve the maximum diversity order for a given number of transmit and receive antennas subject to the constraint of having a simple decoding algorithm.

A block STC is defined by an $N \times T$ transmission matrix X where its entries are linear combinations of the symbols $s_1, s_2, \cdots, s_k$ and their conjugates. It is designed in such a way that to get the maximum diversity gain of NM, but the coding gain is sacrificed to have a simple ML decoder. In fact, a block STC assigns a space-time signature to each symbol and its conjugate in such a way that these signatures generate the maximum diversity for all symbols. This condition results from the orthogonality property induced between signatures; hence, ML decoding is performed for symbols $s_1, s_2, \cdots, s_k$ independently. This results in a simplified decoder structure, which consists of a parallel bank of k simple ML decoders [66, 68].

The main properties of block space-time codes could be summarized as follows:

- There is no loss in bandwidth, in the sense that orthogonal designs provide the maximum possible transmission rate at full diversity.

- Because there is no coding gain obtained by block STC, the spectral efficiency of this method is less than trellis STC codes.

- There is an extremely simple maximum likelihood decoding algorithm which only uses linear combining at the receiver. The simplicity of the algorithm comes from the orthogonality of the columns of the orthogonal design. The above properties are preserved even if linear processing is performed at the transmitter. Therefore, the definition for orthogonal designs can be relaxed to allow linear processing at the transmitter. Signals transmitted from different antennas will now be linear combinations of constellation symbols.

Examples of real orthogonal designs are the 2×2

$$X = \begin{pmatrix} s_1 & s_2 \\ -s_2 & s_1 \end{pmatrix} \tag{4.60}$$

and the 4×4

$$X = \begin{pmatrix} s_1 & s_2 & s_3 & s_4 \\ -s_2 & s_1 & -s_4 & s_3 \\ -s_3 & s_4 & s_1 & -s_2 \\ -s_4 & -s_3 & s_2 & s_1 \end{pmatrix} \tag{4.61}$$

A point worth noting is that block STC guarantees satisfaction of the Equal Eigenvalue Criterion by M. Ionescu. Furthermore, the symbols $s_1, s_2, \cdots, s_k$ can be chosen to maximize the Euclidean distance for all pair codewords $\mathbf{c}, \mathbf{e}$. To compensate for poor spectral efficiency compared to trellis STC code, the symbols $s_1, s_2, \cdots, s_k$ can be generated from a spectrally efficient modulation such as trellis coded modulation (TCM) or block coded modulation (BCM). Researchers J. Terry *et al* [72] used this combination to produce a very high rate OFDM system. For OFDM systems, block STC can also be performed over the whole OFDM symbol. Consider the 2×2 complex block STC popularized by Alamouti [2], also known as the Radon Hurwitz (R-H) unitary transform defined as

$$R - H \begin{pmatrix} \mathbf{S}_1 \\ \mathbf{S}_2 \end{pmatrix} = \begin{bmatrix} -\mathbf{s}_1^* & \mathbf{s}_2 \\ \mathbf{s}_2^* & \mathbf{s}_1 \end{bmatrix}$$

If two consecutive OFDM symbols are referred to as $\mathbf{S}_o$ and $\mathbf{S}_e$, then at the first antenna $\mathbf{S}_o$ is transmitted in the first time epoch followed by $\mathbf{S}_e$ in the second time epoch while at the second transmitter $-\mathbf{S}_e^*$ is transmitted in the first time epoch followed by $\mathbf{S}_o^*$ in the second time epoch. The appeal, as mentioned earlier, of the block STC schemes is the ease in which decoding can be performed compared to trellis STCs. Denote the diagonal matrices containing the discrete Fourier Transforms (DFT) of the channel response vectors for transmitters 1 and 2 as $\mathbf{H}_1$ and $\mathbf{H}_2$, respectively. Assuming the channel is constant over the two consecutive time epochs, the demodulated received signals $(\mathbf{R}_1, \mathbf{R}_2)$ in the respective time slots are given by

$$\mathbf{R}_1 = -\mathbf{H}_1\mathbf{S}_0^* + \mathbf{H}_2\mathbf{S}_e^* \qquad (4.62)$$

$$\mathbf{R}_2 = \mathbf{H}_1\mathbf{S}_e + \mathbf{H}_2\mathbf{S}_0 \qquad (4.63)$$

Using simple substitution methods, the estimates of the consecutive OFDM symbols are

$$\hat{\mathbf{S}}_0 = \mathbf{H}_2^*\mathbf{R}_2 - \mathbf{H}_1\mathbf{R}_1^* \qquad (4.64)$$

$$\hat{\mathbf{S}}_e = \mathbf{H}_1^*\mathbf{R}_2 + \mathbf{H}_2\mathbf{R}_1^* \qquad (4.65)$$

Substituting Equations 4.62 and 4.63 into Equations 4.64 and 4.65 yield

$$\hat{\mathbf{S}}_0 = \left(|\mathbf{H}_1|^2 + |\mathbf{H}_2|^2\right)\mathbf{S}_0 \qquad (4.66)$$

$$\hat{\mathbf{S}}_e = \left(|\mathbf{H}_1|^2 + |\mathbf{H}_2|^2\right)\mathbf{S}_e \qquad (4.67)$$

Clearly from Equations 4.66–4.67, we understand why block STC technique improves the performance of TCM over fading channels. The envelope of the estimated symbols $\hat{\mathbf{S}}_0$ and $\hat{\mathbf{S}}_e$ are chi-squared variants with four degrees of freedom. Moreover, the chi-squared variates normalized by the number of degrees of freedom approach unity as the number of degrees of freedom approach infinity. In practice, this normalized chi-squared variates are nearly unity with four degrees of freedom. Another way to interpret this is that as the number of degrees of freedom increases, the randomness of the chi-squared variates decreases and, in the limit, approaches a constant. Thus, the code design should be targeted for an AWGN channel.

To summarize, both the Equal Eigenvalue Criterion and Rank Criterion are satisfied when block STC are concatenated with TCM. Since Ungerbock TCM codes are well known to be the best in terms of Euclidean distance, very powerful diversity codes are easily achieved using these two methods [3, 33].

For applications where good diversity performance on the base station link is required, trellis STCs seem to offer the best performance amongst the STC architectures. Yet, block space-time coding (STC) offers the best trade-off of performance versus complexity while layered STCs offer the simplest decoder complexity at the expense of poorest performance. This is largely due to the loss of diversity, which arises due to the antenna beamforming process, and error propagation effect.

Exercise 5 *Using the simulation tool at the Web site, compare the performances of a 2 × 2 block STC, i.e., Radon-Hurwitz, with QPSK modulation to the performances of two receive* *antenna selection diversity and MRC in five-tap Rayleigh fading chanels. Using Equation 4.61, modify the 2 × 2 block STC function and repeat the experiment above but now compare the performance to four receive antenna selection diversity and MRC.*

Multidimensional Space-Time Codes

The design criteria given earlier in the "Transmit Diversity Design Criteria for Fading Channels" section were derived starting with the pairwise error probability. This led to a determinant criteria for code design. To improve the performance of the coding gain of a constituent STC, the minimum squared distance of the signal constellation Δ_0^2 must be increased without increasing the average energy for the signal constellation. One simple way to accomplish this is to increase the dimensionality of the signal constellation.

Example 6 Consider a fully connected, two-antenna space-time trellis with Q states and Q transitions. This simple trellis is designed such that transitions leaving a state differ in the first symbol, and transitions entering a state differ in the second symbol. The codeword difference matrix for the shortest error event path in this trellis is easily shown to be

$$\mathbf{D}(\mathbf{c}, \mathbf{e}) = \begin{bmatrix} \Delta_0 & 0 \\ 0 & \Delta_0 \end{bmatrix} \tag{4.68}$$

Clearly, the outer product of matrix $\mathbf{D}(\mathbf{c}, \mathbf{e})$ is also diagonal with eigenvalues and geometric mean equal to Δ_0^2. Thus, increasing the minimum distance between codewords also increases the coding gain proportionately for this simple trellis.

In addition to maintaining the average energy, it is also desirable to minimize the peak to average power ratio (PAPR) of the transmitted symbols. A large PAPR requires the input signal power to the amplifier, located at the transmitter, to be "backed-off" from its saturation level, resulting in poor overall DC power efficiency. The combination of these two requirements lead to spherical codes as a natural choice for an OFDM system.

Spherical Coding

A k-dimensional *spherical code* is a set of points in $\mathbf{R}^k$ that lie on the surface of a k-dimensional unit radius sphere. Mathematically, the points on the surface of a unit radius k-dimensional Euclidean sphere are defined as

$$\Omega_k = \left\{ \begin{array}{l} \mathbf{x} = (x_1, x_2 \ldots, x_k) \in \mathbf{R}^k: \\ \|\mathbf{x}\|^2 = x_1^2 + x_2^2 + \cdots + x_k^2 = 1 \end{array} \right\} \tag{4.69}$$

Collectively, $(x_1, x_2 \ldots, x_k)$ is referred to as a *k-tuple*. The parameters of interest are *dimension, minimum distance,* and *size.* The dimension is the smallest integer k such that $\Theta \subset \Omega_k$. Usually, we describe the spherical code Θ with respect to the smallest possible basis, where the dimension equals the number of coordinates. The minimum squared distance of the code Θ is

$$d^2_{\min}(\Theta) = \min_{i \neq j} \|\mathbf{x}_i - \mathbf{x}_j\|^2 \tag{4.70}$$

The maximum theoretically attainable minimum squared distance is the quantity

$$\left(d^*_{\min}\right)^2 = \max_{\Theta}\left(d^2_{\min}\right) \tag{4.71}$$

The size, finally, is simply the number of points in the set Θ denoted by M.

Remark 1 *Any signaling scheme used in code construction should differ in all or as many coordinates as possible to improve diversity. Rotation of a spherical code Θ about its coordinate axes does not change $d^2_{\min}$ for the code. Therefore, diversity for a particular spherical code Θ is optimized when all coordinates differ for each symbol in the k-dimensional space.*

Remark 2 *Ideal coordinate interleaving for a k-dimensional spherical code provides a k-fold improvement in diversity level compared to ideal symbol interleaving.*

Remarks 1 and 2 lead the authors in [71] to believe that concatenation of spherical coding with STC, termed *spherical STC* (SSTC), will provide substantial diversity gains.

SSTC in an OFDM Framework

A simplified diagram of SSTC implemented in a conventional OFDM is shown in Figure 4.10. The spherical space-time decoder depicted in Figure 4.10 is comprised of the trellis STC decoder followed by a multidimensional symbol mapper. The latter function maps output code symbols of the trellis space-time encoder to points in $\mathbf{R}^k$ that lie on the surface of a k-dimensional unit radius sphere. L complex samples are formed from L pairs of coordinates from p output coded symbols, where

$$p = \left\lceil \frac{2L}{k} \right\rceil$$

and $\lceil \bullet \rceil$ represents the ceiling operation. The complex samples are interleaved and serially fed into the N–pt. IDFT, where $N \geq L$. After the IDFT operation, an cyclic prefix is prepended to the transformed symbols to form an OFDM symbol. Finally, each OFDM is transmitted over a separate antenna in every time epoch.

At the receiver, the cyclic prefix is removed. Next, the remaining complex samples are buffered and fed into a DFT. The output of the DFT is de-interleaved and the pairs of coordinates are re-grouped into *k*-tuples. The *k*-tuples are passed to the spherical space-time decoder that outputs an estimate of the transmitted data stream.

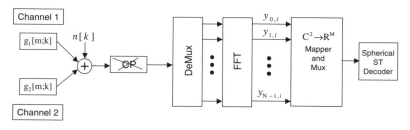

FIGURE 4.10

SSTC decoding in an OFDM framework.

To illustrate the benefits of SSTC, J. Terry and J. Heiskala compared the 24 Mbps mode of the IEEE 802.11a with a SSTC operating also at 24 Mbps. The system parameters for the SSTC were two transmit antennas, one receive antenna, 16-ary spherical code defined over four dimensions, and delay diversity STC trellis, i.e. Q states with Q transitions, which has no coding gain in AWGN channels. The spherical codes used for the signal mapper was found from a computer search based on maximizing the minimum Euclidean distance between symbols and symbol coordinates. The gain for this code is approximately 4.77 dB over uncoded. The systems are evaluated over an AWGN channel and a five-tap slowly fading indoor channel. The channel statistics follow a lognormal distribution and the taps are spaced 50 nanoseconds apart. Figure 4.11 demonstrates that the SSTC outperforms the considered 24 Mbits/sec mode of IEEE 802.11a for the error rates of interest. SSTC benefits from both coding gain and diversity gain as seen from the approximately 4 dB improvement over IEEE 802.11a in indoor fading channels and 2 dB over AWGN channels.

To summarize, the authors in [71] were able to demonstrate that a multidimensional signal mapper can be an effective method for providing both coding and diversity gains with STC. In general, as the dimensionality of the signal mapper is increased, the spectral efficiency decreases but the coding and diversity gains increase. Alternately, lattice codes rather than spherical codes can be investigated as multidimensional signal mappers. Based on the inherent structure of lattice codes, potentially simplified encoder and decoder structures can be conceived.

4

ANTENNA DIVERSITY

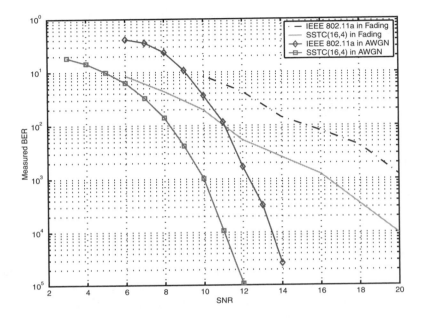

FIGURE 4.11

Performance comparison of 24 Mbit/sec modes for SSTC(16,4) and IEEE 802.11a.

Water-Filling for Single Antenna Systems

In this section, we consider a diversity technique referred to as *water-filling*, which assumes known channel state information at the transmitter. We begin with a review of the single antenna case in this section and generalize to the multi-antenna system in the next section. Note, when the channel frequency response is not ideal, the frequency components of transmitted signals observe different channel gain. This means that the frequency attenuation is not uniform for all the frequency components of the signal. Moreover, in channels which have severe nulls in their frequency response or there is powerful narrow-band noise, the signal frequency components are completely canceled out in those frequencies. It is obvious that transmitting energy in these frequencies is a waste of the power. Therefore, to approach the capacity of these channels, a kind of spectral shaping should be applied to transmitted signal. Correspondingly, new diversity schemes that are adapted to the frequency response of the channel are required [29, 30, 31, 72]. In other words, the output power and information should be distributed over frequency in such a way that achieve maximum capacity. This is the essence of water-filling. Typically, water-filling is performed in two steps: *power allocation* and *bit loading*.

Power Allocation

Let $P(f)$ and $N(f)$ denote the power spectral densities of the transmitted signal and the noise, respectively. Also, let $H(f)$ stand for the channel frequency response. The *channel SNR function* is defined as

$$\gamma(f) = \frac{|H(f)|^2}{N(f)} \tag{4.72}$$

Intuitively, the preferred transmission band is where $\gamma(f)$ is largest. Using information theory, the total capacity of the system is described by:

$$C = \int_B \log_2(1 + P(f)\gamma(f))df \tag{4.73}$$

where B is the channel bandwidth. Maximizing this capacity with respect to $P(f)$ subject to the following power constraint

$$\int_B P(f)df \leq P \tag{4.74}$$

and by employing Lagrange multipliers, results in an adaptive power distribution which is called "spectral water-filling" or power allocation and defined by

$$P_{Alloc}(f) = \left[u - \frac{1}{\gamma(f)}\right]^+, \quad f \in B \tag{4.75}$$

where μ is found such that, $P_{Alloc}(f)$ satisfies the power constraint in Equation 4.74 with equality; the function $[\cdot]^+$ clamps all the negative values to zero. Substituting $P_{Alloc}(f)$ in Equation 4.73 results the optimal capacity

$$C_{optimum} = \int_B [\log_2(\mu\gamma(f))]^+ df \tag{4.76}$$

The capacity-achieving band B is the most important feature of the water-filling spectrum. For many practical channels, B is a single frequency interval. However, in other cases, e.g., in the presence of severe narrow-band interference, it may consist of multiple frequency intervals as in an OFDM system.

Bit Loading

Let's assume that the channel has been decomposed into N disjoint subchannels, i.e., $B = N\Delta f$. Let P_i be the power assigned to subcarrier i, $1 \leq i \leq N$. Then, the total transmitted power is

4

ANTENNA DIVERSITY

$$P = \sum_{i=1}^{N} P_i \qquad (4.77)$$

It is obviously seen from Equation 4.75 that those subchannels which have higher SNR have been assigned more power and they are able to carry more information. The maximum amount of information in bps/Hz, which is possible to be sent reliably through each subchannel is determined from Equation 4.76. The total number of bits that can be supported by a particular channel realization $H(f)$ is $R_{Total} = C_{optimum}B$. Furthermore, since we are considering digital modulation schemes, we should find a set of integer bits per subchannel R_i such that the total number of bits sent for any channel realization is maximized, i.e.,

$$R_{Total} = \sum_{i=1}^{N} R_i \qquad (4.78)$$

with respect to P_i subject to Equation 4.77. The algorithm, which maximizes Equation 4.78 under the stipulated constraints, is referred to as bit loading.

If an M-ary QAM modulation set is combined with a channel code C_i to be used with subcarrier i, it can be shown that for a given error rate ε_i, power P_i, and $\gamma(i)$ for each subchannel, the maximum number of bits that can be transmitted through subchannel i, satisfying the given requirements is defined by [9, 48]

$$R_i = \log_2\left(1 + \frac{\gamma(i)P_i}{\Gamma(C_i, \varepsilon_i)}\right) \qquad (4.79)$$

where

$$\Gamma(C_i, \varepsilon_i) = \frac{3}{k_{eff}(C_i)\left[Q^{-1}\left(\frac{\varepsilon_i}{4}\right)\right]^2} \qquad (4.80)$$

is called the *capacity gap* , where k_{eff} and ε_i are the effective coding gain and required error rate, respectively. Q in Equation 4.80 denotes the *complementary error function* defined as

$$Q(x) = \frac{1}{\sqrt{2\pi}} \int_{-\infty}^{x} e^{-\frac{\tau^2}{2}} \partial\tau \qquad (4.81)$$

Therefore, the *inverse complementary error function* Q^{-1} is given by

$$Q^{-1}(x) = \sqrt{\ln\left(\sqrt{2\pi} \frac{\partial Q}{\partial x}\right)^{-2}} \qquad (4.82)$$

By increasing the reliability, the capacity gap increases and the spectral efficiency decreases.

To keep the overall error rate as small as possible, all the subcarriers should have the same error rate. Otherwise, the subchannel which has the maximum error rate will dominate. Assuming that the coding gain and error rate over all the subcarriers be the same and denoted by C and ε, respectively; let's define $\Gamma = \Gamma(C, \varepsilon)$ as the capacity gap over all subchannels. Now substituting Equation 4.79 in Equation 4.78, the total number of bits over all subchannels become

$$R_{Total} = \sum_{i=1}^{N} \log_2\left(1 + \frac{\gamma(i)P_i}{\Gamma}\right) \tag{4.83}$$

Maximizing this with respect to P_i's subject to the power constraint in Equation 4.77, we get [8, 19]

$$P_i = \left[\mu - \frac{\Gamma}{\gamma(i)}\right]^+, \quad i \in \{1, \cdots, N\} \tag{4.84}$$

This is similar to Equation 4.75 except the capacity gap that is defined by the required reliability and coding gain. It is analagous to saying that before applying water-filling, the SNR of all the subchannels $\gamma(i)$ should normalized by a constant Γ—indeed, prior even to selecting μ to satisfy the power constraint.

Water-Filling for Multi-Antenna Systems

Now consider a quasi static flat fading MIMO channel described by Equation 4.16. Recall, as mentioned in previous sections, when channel state information (CSI) is not available in transmitter (open loop systems), STCs should be used to get diversity and coding gain. Likewise to the single-input single-output (SISO) systems, when CSI is available in the transmitter, we can increase the efficiency of the system optimal power and rate adaptation in the transmitter.

Let the singular value decomposition of H be $H = U\Sigma V^H$, where U and V are unitary matrices and Σ be a diagonal matrix with positive real values on diagonal elements standing for the singular values of the channel. If the transmitted vector is premultiplied by V in transmitter and received vector is post multiplied by U^H in receiver, then (4.16) could be rewritten as

$$\tilde{\mathbf{y}} = \Sigma \mathbf{x} + \tilde{\eta} \tag{4.85a}$$

where $\tilde{\mathbf{y}}$ and $\tilde{\eta}$ denote the received vector and noise vector after postmultiplication by U. Note that because U is a unitary matrix, there is no noise amplification and the noise vectors remains spatially white. Thus, the error rate of maximum likelihood decoder remains the same as it was for decoding Equation 4.16, but its complexity is significantly reduced because the entries of $\mathbf{x}$ are decoded separately. If p denotes the rank of Σ, then this MIMO channel is a set of parallel of SISO channels

$$\tilde{y}_k = \sigma_k x_k + \tilde{\eta}_k \quad k = 1, \cdots, p \tag{4.85b}$$

where σ_k is the gain of kth channel and $\tilde{\eta}_k$ is white Gaussian noise.

The total capacity of the MIMO channel is equal to the aggregate capacity of all these SISO channels. Considering that if spatial water-filling is applied for this MIMO channel, the capacity of this MIMO channel is the sum of the capacities described by Equation 4.2. In the previous section, power allocation and bit loading were suggested for coding schemes achieving the maximum capacity over SISO fading channels. Here the capacity could be optimized by spatial-frequency waterfilling and bit loading. The spatial-frequency waterfilling would operate essentially as described in "Water-Filling for Single Antenna Systems." The next section explores potential bit loading algorithms.

Adaptive Modulation

Recall that in Chapter 3 several popular modulation and coding schemes were discussed. In that chapter, none of the modulation and coding techniques discussed adapted to fading conditions. These nonadaptive methods require a fixed link margin to maintain acceptable performance when the channel quality is poor. Thus, these systems are effectively designed for the worst case channel conditions, resulting in insufficient utilization of the full channel capacity. Adapting modulation to the signal fading allows the channel to be used more efficiently since power and rate can be allocated to take advantage of favorable channel conditions. For the purpose of our discussions, adaptive modulation shall function as the bit loading algorithm associated with multi-antenna water-filling techniques.

The basic idea behind adaptive transmission is to maintain a constant bit error rate by varying the transmitted power level, symbol transmission rate, constellation size, coding rate/scheme, or any combination of these parameters [29, 30, 72]. Thus, without sacrificing bit error rate (BER), these schemes provide high average spectral efficiency by transmitting at high speeds under favorable channel conditions, and reducing throughput as the channel degrades. Adaptive coded modulation does not require interleaving since error bursts are eliminated by adjusting the power, size, and duration of the transmitted signal constellation relative to the channel fading. However, adaptive modulation does require accurate channel estimates at the receiver which are fed back to the transmitter with minimal latency.

There are several practical constraints that determine when adaptive modulation should be used. If the channel is changing faster than it can be estimated and fed back to the transmitter, adaptive techniques will perform poorly, and other means of mitigating the effects of fading should be used. It has been shown in [30] that, to achieve a low target BER, the BER remains at its target level as long as the total delay of the channel estimator and feedback path is less than Doppler period $T_{Doppler}$, i.e.,

$$T_{Doppler} = \frac{\lambda}{v}$$

where v is the vehicle speed and λ is the signal wavelength. However, a higher BER target loosens the delay constraint. Furthermore, hardware constraints and pulse shaping considerations may dictate how often the transmitter can change its rate and/or power.

Cellular systems exploit the power falloff with distance of signal propagation to reuse the same frequency channel at spatially separated locations. While frequency reuse provides more efficient use of the limited available spectrum within a given area, it also introduces co-channel interference, which ultimately determines the data rates and corresponding BERs available to each user. Thus, although adaptive modulation techniques increase the spectral efficiency (bits/s/Hz) of a single channel, these techniques may also increase co-channel interference levels in a cellular system, thereby requiring a higher reuse distance to mitigate this increased interference power. Adaptive modulation may therefore reduce the area spectral efficiency [30]. As stated before, the inherent problem in fading channels is that the transmitted signal undergo a variable gain in transmission; this results to a time variant SNR in receiver. As a result, the instantaneous capacity is a random variable. Assuming that the fading gain is an ergodic random process, we can expect that the temporal average capacity of the channel be equal to the expected value of the instantaneous capacity.

If the channel state information (CSI) is not available at the transmitter, the optimal power allocation is to distribute it uniformly over time or subchannels. As the result, the achievable channel capacity is described by [5]:

$$C_{\text{RCSI}} = E_\gamma\{\log_2(1 + P_{av}\gamma)\} \tag{4.86}$$

$$= \int_0^\infty p_\gamma(\gamma)\log_2(1 + P_{av}\gamma)d\gamma \tag{4.87}$$

where $\gamma = \frac{v}{\sigma_\eta^2}$ is the channel SNR function and E_γ is the statistical expectation with respect to γ.

In contrast, if the CSI is available at the transmitter, it can adapt its output power P_x with respect to γ to increase the spectral efficiency. Therefore, under the power constraint $E\gamma\{P_x(\gamma)\} = P_{av}$, the maximum achievable capacity is achieved by temporal water-filling, which is described by

$$P_x^o(\gamma) = \left[\frac{1}{\gamma_0} - \frac{1}{\gamma}\right]^+ \tag{4.88}$$

where γ_0 is chosen so that $P_x^o(\gamma)$ satisfies the power constraint. This adaptation of the output power results in the following equation for channel capacity [5]:

$$C_{\text{TRCSI}} = E_\gamma\left(\left[\log_2\left(\frac{\gamma}{\gamma_0}\right)\right]^+\right) \tag{4.89}$$

4

ANTENNA
DIVERSITY

Channel Inversion

An alternate suboptimal approach is to invert the channel at the transmitter, referred to *channel inversion*. Channel inversion is very common in spread—spectrum systems with near—far interference imbalances. It is also very simple to implement, since the encoder and decoder are designed for an AWGN channel, independent of the fading statistics. However, it can exhibit a large capacity penalty in extreme fading environments. For example, in Rayleigh fading, the capacity gap $E\left(\frac{1}{\gamma}\right)$ is infinite, and thus the capacity with channel inversion is zero. The power adaptation for channel inversion $P_x^I(\gamma)$ is given by [31]

$$P_x^I(\gamma) = \frac{P_{av}}{\gamma E\left(\frac{1}{\gamma}\right)} \tag{4.90}$$

and the resulting achievable capacity for channel inversion power allocation C_{TRCSI}^I is

$$C_{\text{TRCSI}}^I = \log_2\left(1 + \frac{P_{av}}{E\left(\frac{1}{\gamma}\right)}\right) \tag{4.91}$$

Consequently, a truncated channel inversion policy that only compensates for fading above a certain cutoff fade depth level γ_0 is defined as [31]

$$P_\gamma^{TI}(v) = \begin{cases} \dfrac{P_{av}}{\gamma \int_{\gamma_0}^{\infty} \frac{1}{\gamma} p_\gamma(\gamma) d\gamma}, & \gamma \geq \gamma_0 \\ 0, \gamma < \gamma_0 \end{cases} \tag{4.92}$$

For decoding this truncated policy, the receiver must know when $\gamma < \gamma_0$. The maximum capacity in this case is obtained by maximizing over all possible γ_0

$$C_{\text{TRCSI}}^{TI} = \max_{\gamma_0} \log_2\left(1 + \frac{P_{av}}{\int_{\gamma_0}^{\infty} \frac{1}{\gamma} p_\gamma(\gamma) d\gamma}\right) \tag{4.93}$$

A more detailed analysis and also numerical simulation for each of these methods has been done by Goldsmith in [31]. Assuming the flat fading channel described by Equation 4.14, the general system model for an adaptive modulator that transmits message m from transmitter to receiver is illustrated in Figure 4.12. The message is encoded into the codeword x, which is transmitted over the time variant channel as $x(i)$ at time index i. The channel gain $g(i)$ changes over the transmission of the codeword. The perfect instantaneous channel power gain $g(i)$ is assumed to be known in both transmitter and receiver. This allows the transmitter to adapt $x(i)$ to the channel gain at time index i, and is a reasonable model for a slowly varying channel with channel estimation for transmitter feedback.

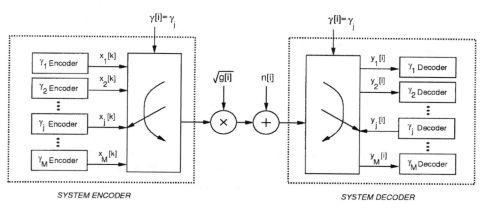

$\gamma[i] = \gamma_j$ $\gamma[i] = \gamma_j$

SYSTEM ENCODER   SYSTEM DECODER

FIGURE 4.12

General block diagram for an adaptive coding scheme. © 1997 IEEE.

The modulation scheme that the encoder should use is defined by the power adaptation method selected by transmitter. For example, if channel inverse power adaptation (Equation 4.90) is to be used, the encoder may use any modulation and coding schemes have been developed for AWGN channels. In the case, truncated channel inverse (Equation 4.92) is used for power adaptation, the encoder uses a kind of on/off channel encoder. However if the optimum power filling (Equation 4.88) is used, a more complex coding scheme is needed. It is obvious that the encoder for the first method has the least complexity and the encoder for the later one has the most complexity.

The general structure of an adaptive coded modulation, which has been introduced by Goldsmith [29], is shown in Figure 4.13. Specifically, a binary encoder operates on k uncoded data bits to produce $k + r$ coded bits, and the coset selector uses these coded bits to select one of the 2^{k+r} cosets from a partition of the signal constellation. For the nonadaptive modulation, $n - k$ additional bits are used to select one of the 2^{n-k} signal points in the selected coset, while in the adaptive modulator $n(\gamma) - k$, additional bits are used to select one of the $2^{n(\gamma)-k}$ preselected signal points out of the 2^{n-k} available signal points in the selected coset. The preselection is done in such a way that maximize the minimum distance between signals.

In a fading channel, the instantaneous SNR varies with time, which will cause the distance between signals to vary. The basic premise for using adaptive modulation with coset codes is to keep these distances constant by varying the size of the signal constellation relative to γ, subject to an average transmit power constraint P_{av}. Therefore, by maintaining a constant minimum distance d_{min}, the adaptive coded modulation exhibits the same coding gain as coded modulation designed for an AWGN channel with minimum coded distance d_{min}.

4

ANTENNA
DIVERSITY

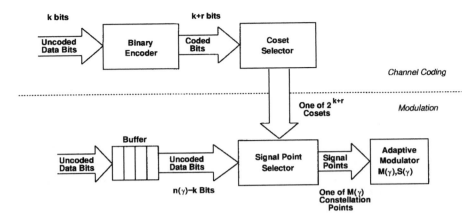

FIGURE 4.13

An adaptive trellis-coded modulation scheme. © 1998 IEEE.

The modulation segment of Figure 4.13 works as follows. The channel is assumed to be slowly fading so that γ_k is relatively constant over many symbol periods. During a given symbol period the size of each coset is limited to $2^{n(\gamma)-k}$, where $n(\gamma)$ is a function of channel fading gain. A signal in the selected coset is chosen using $n(\gamma) - k$ additional uncoded bits. The selected point in the selected coset is one of $M(\gamma) = 2^{n(\gamma)+r}$ points in the transmit signal constellation. By using an appropriate $M(\gamma)$ and $P_x(\gamma)$, it is possible to maintain a fixed distance between points in the received signal constellation corresponding to the desired minimum distance $d_{\min}$. The variation of $M(\gamma)$ with respect to γ causes the information rate to vary, so the uncoded bits should be buffered until needed. Since r redundant bits are used for channel coding, $\log_2 M(\gamma) - r$ bits are sent over each symbol period for a fading gain of γ. The average rate of the adaptive scheme is thus given by

$$R = \int_{\gamma_0}^{\infty} (\log_2 M(\gamma) - r)p_\gamma(\gamma)d\gamma \tag{4.94}$$

where $\gamma_0 \geq 0$ is a cutoff fade depth below transmission is suspended ($M(\gamma) = 0$). This cutoff value is a parameter of the adaptive modulation scheme. Since γ is known both in transmitter and receiver, the modulation and coding is suspended while $\gamma < \gamma_0$.

At the receiver, the adaptive modulation is first demodulated, which yields a sequence of received constellation points. Then the points within each coset that are closest to these received points are determined. From these points, the maximum-likelihood coset sequence is calculated and the uncoded bits from the channel coding segment are determined from this sequence in the same manner as for nonadaptive coded modulation in AWGN. The uncoded bits from the modulation segment are then determined by finding the points in the maximum-likelihood coset sequence which are closest to the received constellation points and applying standard demodulation to these points.

The adaptive modulation described above consists of any mapping from γ to a constellation size $M(\gamma)$, and output power $P_x(\gamma)$ for which $d_{\min}$ remains constant. Proposed techniques for adaptive modulation maintain this constant distance through adaptive variation of the transmitted power level and constellation sizes are available in [29]. It has been shown that for i.i.d. fading, using the channel information just in receiver has a lower complexity and the same approximate capacity as optimally adapting to the channel. However, for correlated fading, not adapting at the transmitter causes both a decrease in capacity and an increase in encoding and decoding complexity. It is also shown that the two suboptimal adaptive techniques channel inversion and truncated channel inversion, which adapt the transmit power but keep the transmission rate constant, have very simple encoder and decoder designs, but they exhibit a capacity penalty that can be large in severe fading.

To summarize the chapter, the trade-off between these adaptive and nonadaptive techniques is therefore one of both capacity and complexity. Assuming that the channel is estimated at the receiver, the adaptive techniques require a feedback path between the transmitter and receiver and some complexity in the transmitter. The optimal adaptive technique uses variable-rate and power transmission, and the complexity of its decoding technique is comparable to the complexity of decoding a sequence of additive white Gaussian noise (AWGN) channels in parallel.

For the nonadaptive technique, the code design must make use of the channel correlation statistics, and the decoder complexity is proportional to the channel decorrelation time. One of the various forms of STC is likely to be incorporated in a future high rate OFDM system in conjunction with one of the receive diversity techniques discussed. While optimal adaptive techniques always have the highest capacity, the increase relative to nonadaptive transmission using receiver side information only is small when the fading is approximately i.i.d. The suboptimal adaptive techniques reduce complexity at a cost of decreased capacity.

Lastly, antenna diversity, as mentioned in the introduction, will play an important role in future generation systems. The material presented herein is meant only to introduce some of the more popular techniques in the literature. It is by no means an exhaustive all-inclusive summary of all available techniques applicable to future generation systems.

Bibliography

[1]   D. Agrawal, V. Tarokh and N. Seshadri, "Space-time coded OFDM for high data-rate wireless communication over wideband channels," in *Proc. IEEE VTC*, pp. 2232–2236, 1998.

[2]   S. M. Alamouti, "A simple transmitter diversity scheme for wireless communications," *IEEE J. Select. Areas Commun.*, vol. 16, pp. 1451–1458, Oct. 1998.

[3]   Trellis coded modulation and transmit diversity: design criteria and performance evaluation, *ICUPC '98*, vol. 1, pp. 703–707, 1998.

[4]   E. Biglieri and G. Caire, and G. Taricco, "Limiting performance of block-fading channels with multiple antennas," *IEEE Trans. Inform. Theory*, vol. 47, pp. 1273–1289, May 2001.

[5]   E. Biglieri, J. Proakis, S. Shamai, "Fading channels: Information theoretic and communications aspects," *IEEE Trans. Inform. Theory*, vol. 44, pp. 2619–2692, Oct. 1998.

[6]   J. Bingham, "Multicarrier modulation for data transmission: an idea whose time has come," *IEEE Commun. Mag.*, pp. 5–13, May 1990.

[7]   A. R. Calderbank and N. J. Sloane, "New trellis codes based on lattice and cosets," *IEEE Transaction on Information Theory*, vol. IT-33, pp. 177–195, March 1987.

[8]   P. S. Chow, J. M. Cioffi, and A. C. Bingham, "A practical discrete multitone transceiver loading algorithm for data transmission over spectrally shaped channels," *IEEE Trans. Commun.*, vol. 43, pp. 773–775, Feb. 1995.

[9]   J. M. Cioffi, G. P. Dudevoir, M. V. Eyuboglu, and G.D. Forney, "MMSE Decision—Feedback Equalizers and Coding—Part II: Coding Results," *IEEE Trans. Commun.*, vol. 43, pp. 2595–2604, Oct. 1995.

[10]   J. H. Conway and N. J. A. Sloane, *Sphere Packings, Lattices and Groups*, 2nd ed. New York: Springer-Verlag, 1993.

[11]   D. J. Costello, J. Haganauer, H. Imai, S. B. Wicker, "Applications of error control coding," *IEEE Trans. Inform. Theory*, vol. 44, Oct. 1998.

[12]   D. Divsalar, M. K. Simon, "The design of trellis coded MPSK for fading channels: performance criteria," *IEEE Trans. Commun.,* vol. 36, pp. 1004–1012, Sept. 1988.

[13]   D. Divsalar and M.K. Simon, "The design of trellis coded MPSK for fading channels: Set partitioning for optimum code design," *IEEE Trans. Commun.*, vol. 36, pp. 1013–1021, Sept. 1988.

[14]   D. Divsalar and M. K. Simon, "Multiple trellis-coded modulation (MTCM)," *IEEE Trans. Commun.*, vol. 36, pp. 410–419, Apr. 1988.

[15]   A. Edelman, "Eigenvalues and condition numbers of random matrices," *M.I.T. PhD Dissertation*, 1989.

[16]   T. Ericson and V. Zinoviev, "Spherical codes generated by binary partition of symmetric pointsets," *IEEE Transactions on Information Theory*, vol. 41, no. 1, pp. 107–129, January 1995.

[17] F. R. Farokhi, G. J. Foschini, A. Lozano, R. A. Velenzuela, "Link optimal space time processing with multiple transmit and receive antennas," *IEEE Commun. Letter*, vol. 5, pp. 85–87, Mar. 2001.

[18] F. R. Farrokhi, G. J. Foschini, A. Lozano, R. A. Valenzuela, "Link-optimal BLAST processing with multiple-access interference," *VTC 2000*, 52nd, Vol. 1.

[19] R. F. H. Fischer and J. B. Huber, "A new loading algorithm for discrete multitone transmission," in *Proc. IEEE Globecom*, pp. 724–728, 1996.

[20] G. J. Foschini and M. J. Gans, "On limits of wireless communications in a fading environment when using multiple antennas," *Wireless Personal Communications 6*, pp. 311–335, 1998.

[21] G. J. Foschini, "Layered space-time architecture for wireless communication in a fading environment when using multi-element antennas," *Bell Labs Tech. J.*, vol. 1, pp. 41–59, 1996.

[22] G. D. Forney and G. Ungerboeck, "Modulation and coding for linear guassian channels," *IEEE Trans. Inform. Theory,* vol. 44, pp. 2384–2415, Oct. 1998.

[23] G. D. Forney, "Coset codes part I: Introduction and geometrical classification," *IEEE Trans. Inform. Theory*, vol. 34, pp. 1123–1151, Sept. 1988.

[24] G. D. Forney *et al.,* "Efficient modulation for band-limited channels," *IEEE J. Select. Areas Commun.*, vol. SAC-2, pp. 632–647, Sept. 1984.

[25] R. G. Gallager, *Information Theory and Reliable Communication.* New York: John Wiley & Sons, 1968.

[26] D. Gesbert, H. Bolcskei, D. Gore, and A. Paulraj, "MIMO wireless channels: Capacity and performance prediction," in *Proc. IEEE Globecom*, pp. 1083–1088, 2000.

[27] L. C. Godara, "Application of antenna arrays to mobile communications, part I: Performance improvement, feasability and system considerations," *Proc. IEEE*, vol. 85, pp. 1031–1060, July 1997.

[28] G. D. Golden, G. J. Foschini, R. A. Valenzuela, P. W. Wolniasky, "Detection algorithm and initial laboratory results using the V-BLAST space-time communication architecture," *Electronics Letters*, vol. 35, pp. 14–15, January 1999.

[29] A. J. Goldsmith and S. Chua, "Adaptive coded modulation for fading channels," *IEEE Trans. Commun.*, vol. 46, pp. 595–602, May. 1998.

[30] A. Goldsmith and S. Chua, "Variable-rate variable-power MQAM for fading channels," *IEEE Trans. Commun.*, vol. 45, pp. 1218–1230, Oct. 1997.

4

ANTENNA
DIVERSITY

[31] A. Goldsmith and P. Varaiya, "Capacity of fading channels with channel side information," *IEEE Trans. Inform. Theory*, pp. 1218–1230, Oct 1997.

[32] A. J. Goldsmith, "The capacity of downlink channels with variable rate and power," *IEEE Trans. Veh. Technol.*, pp. 569–580, Aug. 1997.

[33] Y. Gong and K. B. Letaief, "Analysis and design of trellis coded modulation with transmit diversity for wireless communications," in *Proc. IEEE WCNC* , vol.3, pp. 1356–1361, 2000.

[34] I. S. Gradshteyn and I. M. Ryzhik, *Table of Integrals, Series, and Products.* New York: Academic Press, 1980.

[35] J. Hamkins, "Design and analysis of spherical codes," Ph. D. dissertation, Univ. of Illinois at Urbana-Champaign, Sept. 1996.

[36] J. Hamkins and K. Zeger, "Asymptotically dense spherical codes—part I: wrapped spherical codes," *IEEE Transactions on Information Theory*, vol. 43, no. 6, pp. 1774–1785, November 1997.

[37] J. Hamkins and K. Zeger, "Asymptotically dense spherical codes—part I: wrapped spherical codes," *IEEE Transactions on Information Theory*, vol. 43, no. 6, pp. 1786–1798, November 1997.

[38] B. Hochwald, T. Marzetta, T. Richardson, W. Sweldens, and R. Urbanke, "Systematic design of unitary space-time constellations," *IEEE Trans. Inform. Theory* , vol. 46, pp. 1962–1973, Sept. 2000.

[39] B. Hochwald and T.Marzetta, "Unitary space-time modulation for multiple-antenna communications in Rayleigh flat fading, "*IEEE Trans. Inform. Theory* , vol. 46, pp. 543–564, Mar. 2000.

[40] R. Hoppe, "Bemerkung der Reduction," *Archiv Math. Phys.* (Grunert), vol. 56, pp. 307-312, 1874.

[41] J. Huber, U. Wachsmann, and R. Fischer, "Coded modulation by multilevel codes: Overview and state of the art," in *ITGFachbericht: Codierung fur Quelle*, Kanal und Ubertragung (Aachen, Germany, Mar. 1998), pp. 255–266.

[42] H. Imai and S. Hirakawa, "A new multilevel coding method using error correcting codes," *IEEE Trans. Inform. Theory* , vol. 23, pp.371–377, May 1977.

[43] D. M. Ionescu, "New results on space-time code design criteria," in *Proc. IEEE WCNC* , pp. 684–687, 1999.

[44] H. Jafarkhani, "A Quasi-Orthogonal Space-Time block code," *IEEE Trans. Commun.* , vol. 49, pp. 1–4, Jan. 2001.

[45] W. C. Jakes, *Microwave Communications, IEEE Press*, N.J. 1974.

[46] B. D. Jelicic and S. Roy, "Design of a trellis coded QAM for flat fading and AWGN channels," *IEEE Trans. Veh. Technol.*, vol. 44, pp. 192-201, Feb. 1995.

[47] V. K. Jones and G. G. Raleigh, "Channel estimation for wireless OFDM systems," in *Proc. IEEE Globecom* , pp. 980–985, 1998.

[48] I. Kalet, "The multitone channel," *IEEE Trans. on Commun.*, vol.37, pp. 119–124, Feb. 1989.

[49] V. I. Levenshtein, *Packing of polynomial metric spaces,* Proc. Third. Intern. Workshop on Information Theory, Sochi, 1987, pp. 271–274.

[50] —, *Packing and decomposition problems for polynomial association schemes, EJC* **14** (1993), 461–477.

[51] E. Lindskog and A. Paulaj, "A transmit diversity scheme for channels with intersymbol interference," in *Proc. IEEE ICC* , pp.307–311, 2000.

[52] A. Naurala, M. D. Trott, and G. W. Wornell, "Performance limits of coded diversity methods for transmitter antenna arrays," *IEEE Trans. Inform. Theory* , vol. 45, pp. 2418–2433, Oct. 1998.

[53] A. Narula, M. J. Lopez, M. D. Trott, and G. W. Wornell, "Efficient use of side information in multiple-antenna data transmission over fading channels," *IEEE J. Select. Areas Commun.*, vol. 16, Oct. 1998.

[54] A. Papoulis, *Probability, Random Variables, and Stochastic Processes.* New York: McGraw-Hill, 1984.

[55] S. S. Pietrobon, R. H. Deng, A. Lafanechére, G. Ungerboeck, and D. J. Costello, "Trellis-coded multidimensional phase modulation," *IEEE Transactions on Information Theory* , vol. 36, no. 1, pp. 63–89, January 1990.

[56] G. J. Pottie and D. P. Taylor, "Multilevel codes based on partitioning," *IEEE Trans. Inform. Theory* , vol. 35, pp. 87–98, Jan. 1989.

[57] G. G. Raleigh and J. M. Cioffi, " Spatio-Temporal coding for wireless communication," *IEEE Trans. Commun.*, vol. 46, pp. 357–366, Mar. 1998.

[58] G. G. Raleigh, V. K. Jones, "Multivariate modulation and coding for wireless communication," *IEEE J. Select. Areas Commun.*, vol. 17, pp. 851–866, May. 1999.

4

**ANTENNA
DIVERSITY**

[59]   J. Salz and J. Winters, "Effect of fading correlation on adaptive arrays in digital mobile radio," *IEEE Trans. Veh. Technol.*, vol. 43, pp. 1049–1057, Nov. 1994.

[60]   N. Seshadri, and C. Sundberg, "Multilevel trellis coded modulation for the rayleigh channel," *IEEE Trans. Commun.*, vol. 41, pp. 1300-1310, Sept. 1993.

[61]   C.E. Shannon, "A mathematical theory of communication," *Bell Labs. Tech. J.*, 27:379–423, 623–656, 1948.

[62]   C. E. Shannon, "Communication in the presence of noise," *Proc. IRE* , 37:10–21, 1949.

[63]   Q. H. Spencer and A. L. Swindlehurst, "Some results on channel capacity when using multiple antennas," in *Proc. IEEE VTC*, pp. 681–688, 2000.

[64]   R. Stridh, B. Ottersten, and P. Karlsson, "MIMO channel capacity on a measured indoor radio channel at 5.8 GHz," in *Proc. IEEE Conf. Signals Systems Computers*, pp. 733–737, 2000.

[65]   V. Tarokh, A. Naguib, N. Seshadri, and A.R. Calderbank, "Combined array processing and Space-Time coding," *IEEE Trans. Inform. Theory*, vol. 45, pp. 1121–1128, May 1999.

[66]   V. Tarokh, H. Jafarkhani, and A. R. Calderbank, "Space-Time block coding for high data rate wireless communications: Performance results," *IEEE J. Select. Areas Commun.*, vol. 17, pp 451–460, Mar. 1999.

[67]   V. Tarokh, N. Seshadri, and A. Calderbank, "Space-time codes for high data rate wireless communication: Performance criterion and code construction," *IEEE Trans. Inform. Theory*, vol. 44, pp. 744–765, Mar. 1998.

[68]   V. Tarokh, H. Jafarkhani, A. R. Calderbank, "Space-time block codes from orthogonal designs," *IEEE Trans. on Inform. Theory*, vol. 45, pp. 1456–1467, July 1999.

[69]   V. Tarokh, N. Seshadri, and A. R. Calderbank, "Low-rate multi-dimensional space-time codes for both slow and rapid fading channels," *The 8th IEEE International Symposium* on *PIMRC '97* , vol. 3, pp. 1206 -1210, 1997.

[70]   E. Teletar, "Capacity of multi-antenna Gaussian channels," *Tech. Rep* ., AT&T-Bell Labs, June 1995.

[71]   J. D. Terry and J.T. Heiskala, "Spherical space-time codes," *IEEE Communications Letters*, vol. 5, March 2001.

[72]   J. D. Terry, J. Heiskala, V. Stolpman, and M. Fozunbal, "On bandwidth efficient schemes for high rate OFDM system," to appear Eurasip 2002.

[73]   G. Ungerboeck, "Channel coding with multi-level/phase signals," *IEEE Trans. Inform. Theory* , vol. 28, pp. 55–67, Jan. 1982.

[74] G. Ungerboeck, "Trellis-coded modulation with redundant signal sets, part I and II," *IEEE Commun. Mag.*, vol. 25, pp. 5–21, Feb. 1987.

[75] L. F. Wei, "Coded modulation with unequal error protection," *IEEE Trans. Commun.*, vol. 41, pp.1439–1449, Oct. 1993 .

[76] L. F. Wei, "Trellis–coded modulation with multidimensional constellations," *IEEE Trans. Inform. Theory* , vol. 33, pp. 483–501, July 1987.

[77] J. Winters, "Smart antennas for wireless systems," *IEEE Personal Commun.*, vol. 5, pp. 23–27, Feb. 1998.

[78] J. Winters, "The diversity gain of transmit diversity in wireless systems with rayleigh fading," *IEEE Trans. Veh. Technol.*, vol. 47, pp. 119–123, Feb. 1998.

[79] A. Wittneben, "Basestation modulation diversity for digital simulcast," in *Proc. IEEE VTC*, pp. 848–853, 1991.

[80] P. W. Wolniansky, G. Foschini, G. Golden, and R. A. Valenzuela, " V-BLAST: an architecture for realizing very high data rates over the rich-scattering wireless channel," in *Proc. URSI Int. Symp. on Signals, Systems, and Electron.*, pp. 295–300, 1998.

[81] G. Wornell and M. D. Trott, "Efficient signal processing techniques for exploiting transmit antennas diversity on fading channels," *IEEE Trans. Signal Processing*, vol. 45, pp. 191–205, Jan. 1997.

4

ANTENNA DIVERSITY

RF Distortion Analysis for OFDM WLAN

IN THIS CHAPTER

- Components of the Radio Frequency Subsystem   172
- Predistortion Techniques for Nonlinear Distortion Mitigation   178
- Adaptive Predistortion Techniques   190
- Coding Techniques for Amplifier Nonlinear Distortion Mitigation   197
- Phase Noise   205
- IQ Imbalance   208
- Bibliography   210

In this chapter we examine the effects of nonlinear distortions on OFDM waveforms caused by the radio frequency (RF) subsystems. Earlier chapters focused on the baseband signal representation. But the true test of the practicality of the system design is measured by the performance of the bandpass signal under impairments caused by the RF subsystems. In this chapter, we will see that as robust as OFDM systems are to some synchronization errors, they are equally sensitive to some nonlinear distortions. The distortions examined are amplitude-to-amplitude (AM/AM) and amplitude-to-phase (AM/PM) distortions caused by large peak-to-average power ratio (PAPR) at the input of high power amplifiers, phase noise of the oscillators in the baseband converter, clipping noise from limiting the peak amplitude of the OFDM waveform, filtering at the transmitter to reduce out of band spectral emission, and, finally, the effects of imbalance of the inphase and quadrature components of the baseband signal. In addition, we review methods in the literature for mitigating some of these effects such as clipping noise and AM/AM distortion. The remaining portion of this chapter is organized as follows: first, components of the RF subsystem are introduced to familiarize readers with their basic operations and purpose; second, a brief review of topologies of amplifier design is presented and their corresponding distortions that are introduced; third, methods for mitigating the effects of clipping noise and AM/AM distortions are presented; and, finally, the latter two sections of this chapter briefly review the effects of phase noise and IQ imbalance.

Components of the Radio Frequency Subsystem

The RF subsystem consists of the in-phase and quadrature (IQ) modulator, power amplifier (PA), baseband converter, and spectral filter subsystems. The operations of the RF subsystem, proceeding from left to right in Figure 5.1, are the following. The IQ modulator takes the input data stream and split it into two separate data stream. One data stream x_I multiplies a sinusoidal waveform; the other data stream x_Q, a cosinusoidal waveform. These two waveforms are summed together to form a modulated intermediate frequency (IF) carrier. The envelope of the IF carrier, A, is given by

$$A = \sqrt{x_I^2 + x_Q^2} \tag{5.1}$$

The modulated IF carrier is converted to RF carrier frequency via the baseband converter, which is comprised of a multiplier and local oscillator. The spectrum of the modulated RF carrier is shaped using the spectral filter. The purpose of this filter is to limit the bandwidth of the modulated RF carrier and meet spectral emission requirements of the Federal Communications Commission (FCC). Finally, the PA serves to generate the required transmit power need for reliable transmission of the information. The next subsection discusses classifications of amplifiers and the resulting distortions associated with each classification.

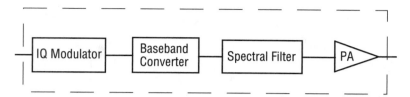

FIGURE 5.1

A block diagram of RF subsystem.

Amplifier Classification and Distortion

A brief overview of classifications of amplifiers and harmonic distortions are instructive to understanding the impacts of their nonlinear distortions on an OFDM signal. An amplifier is a three port device—collector, base, and emitter. The input of the amplifier is defined by its base and emitter ports; the output of the amplifier is defined by its collector and emitter ports. The classification of amplifier depends solely on the quiescent operating point of the amplifier, which is determined by its collector current I_c. The behavior of the collector current I_c shown in Figure 5.2 is governed by

$$I_c \approx I_o e^{V_{BE}/V_{Th}} \tag{5.2}$$

where I_o is the reverse saturation current that is device dependent, V_{Th} is the thermal voltage, which is a function of temperature, and V_{BE} is the input voltage of the amplifier. Interested readers are encouraged to read the text [20] for more details.

The most common classifications for an amplifier are A, AB, B, and C operations. Class A operation entails continuous flow of current at all time, which is depicted in Figure 5.2. Class A operates essentially over the linear portion of its power transfer characteristic. The linear portion of an amplifier is shown in Figure 5.3. The linear region of operation is the region over which the input power is related to the output power by a proportionality constant, either a loss or gain. The conversion efficiency for class A, however, is very poor. The conversion efficiency is a measure of an active device ability to convert DC power into AC power. Class A has a conversion efficiency of 25 percent. In other words, for every milliwatt of output power, 3 mW are consumed in DC power.

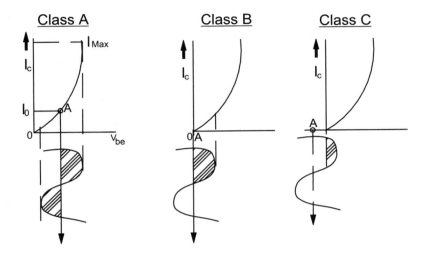

A = Operating Point

FIGURE 5.2

Illustrations of Class A, B, and C amplifier operating points.

Class B operation offers better conversion efficiency at the expense of linearity. During class B operation, current flows during half a sinusoidal period as depicted by the middle graph in Figure 5.2. During class B operation, the amplifier behaves more like a *rectifier** rather than a power amplifier. Again, with reference to the middle graph in Figure 5.2, it is illustrated the conduction cycles of the amplifier based on its bias point; conduction occurs during one half cycle, in the linear region of its power transfer curve, and shuts off during the next one half cycle, in the noise-limited region of the power transfer curve. The noise-limited region is the region where the minimum detectable signal is below the noise floor, which is given by

$$N_i = kTB \tag{5.3}$$

when matched to a resistive load. In Equation 5.3, k is Boltzmann constant ($k = 1.3806568 \times 10^{-23}\,\mathrm{JK}^{-1}$), T is room temperature in Kelvins, and B is the bandwidth of the amplifier. The advantages of class B as compared with Class A operation are greater power output and high conversion efficiency. For these reasons, in systems where the power supply is limited, Class B might be preferable if the harmonic distortions from rectification can be suffered. Class AB is not shown in Figure 5.2, since its operation is simply defined between the two extremes for class A

---

*A rectifier is a device whose output equals its input for positive input values and zero otherwise.

and Class B. Hence, the output signal is zero for part but less than one half of an input sinusoidal signal cycle. Finally, Class C operation is defined such that the output current is zero for more than one half of sinusoidal period. Again, as with the case of Class B operation, Class C is very efficiency however suffers from harmonic distortions.

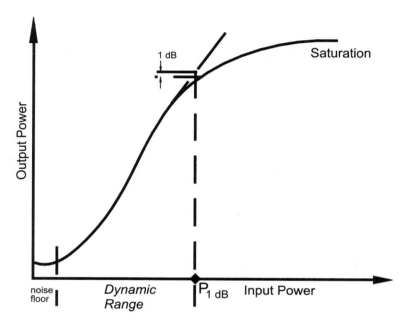

FIGURE 5.3
Power transfer function.

To better appreciate the effects of harmonic distortions, consider the case when two sinusoids are present in the passband of the amplifier. These signals mix with one another and generate inter-modulation products as seen at the output of the PA in Figure 5.4. From the figure, there is evidence of intermodulation (IM) products that occur very near to and far away from the two input sinusoids. These near-in IM products cause the most problems because of the difficulty with filtering them out. Another situation of equal importance is when the harmonic distortions are caused by the input signal driving the amplifier into its saturation region. In the saturation region, an increase in input drive level does not result in an increase in output power level. Most definitions for the beginning of the saturation region is specified relative to the 1 dB compression point. In Figure 5.3, the 1 dB compression point is labelled P_{1dB} and is defined as the point at which a 1 dB increase in input power results in 1 dB decrease in the linear gain of the amplifier. The dynamic range of amplifier, which also corresponds to the linear region of operation for an amplifier, is defined between the noise-limited region and the saturation region.

5

RF DISTORTION ANALYSIS

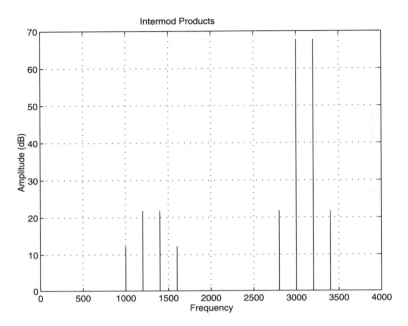

FIGURE 5.4

Example of intermodulation products caused by harmonic distortions.

Another perspective of harmonic distortions in terms of a modulated carrier can be seen from the AM\AM and AM\PM modulations onto a complex waveform. Consider a QPSK modulated carrier, whose input drive level operates in the saturation region of an amplifier. The output signal will experience modulation of its envelope and phase as illustrated in Figures 5.5 and 5.6. In general, the distortions caused by AM\PM are easily tracked and\or compensated using pilot tones or well-known phase recovery algorithms. AM\AM distortions are another matter entirely. AM\AM distortions are a major focus of research with OFDM systems. Because of the large number of carriers used in an OFDM system, the dynamic range for the output of the signal can be quite large. Thus, system designers are faced with the problem of minimizing the amount of harmonic distortions caused by driving the amplifier into saturation yet maintaining an efficient operating point as to not severely drain the DC power supply. Furthermore, many of the PAs used in communication systems that operate in the 1–5 GHz bands are subject to damage if a certain input drive level is exceed. Therefore, it is very important to limit input drive level of an amplifier not only for system performance but to protect the device as well. In the next section, a survey of the techniques that have been published in the literature to handle this problem is presented. These techniques can be broadly categorized as predistortion techniques or coding techniques. In an effort to help understand some of the concepts presented in this chapter, we suggest some simple exercises at the end of some sections that can be performed using the simulation tool on the Web site or Matlab directly.

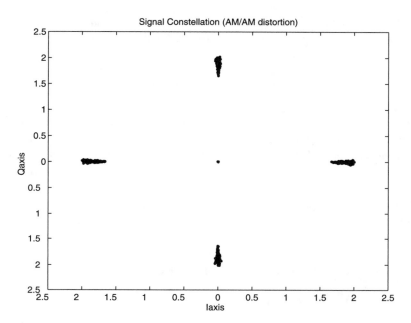

FIGURE 5.5

AM\AM distortion on a quaternary phase shifting keying signal.

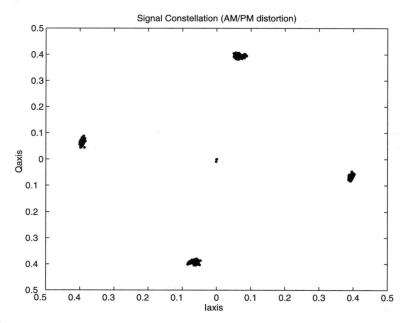

FIGURE 5.6

AM\PM distortions on a quaternary phase shifting keying signal.

Exercise 1 *The amount of distortion generated by amplifier depends on its input drive level and the number of frequencies present in its passband. Generate a signal, which is the sum of two sinusoidal wavesforms in Matlab, i.e.,*

$$s(nT) = A\sin(2\pi nf_1 T) + A\sin(2\pi nf_2 T) \tag{5.4}$$

Determine appropriate values for T, f_1, A, and, f_2 such that near-in IM product and the first harmonic of the appears in the power spectrum, as in Figure 5.4, when s(nT) is the input signal to the amplifier model provided at the website. Hint: Review the topics in "Source Formatting," in Chapter 1.

Exercise 2 *Reproduce Figures 5.5 and 5.6, using the amplifier model provided at the Web site, for 16QAM and 64QAM constellations, whose average energy is equal to $E(A^2)$ for the A found in Exercise 1.*

Predistortion Techniques for Nonlinear Distortion Mitigation

Predistortion techniques attempt to compensate for non-linear distortions by modifying the input signal characteristics. These modifications can be either non-adaptive or adaptive. The most common non-adaptive technique studied in the literature and used in practice is *amplitude clipping*. Amplitude clipping limits the peak envelope of the input signal to a predetermined value, or otherwise passes the input signal through unperturbed, i.e.,

$$L(x) = \begin{cases} x, & |x| \le A \\ Ae^{j\arg(x)}, & |x| > A \end{cases} \tag{5.5}$$

The distortions caused by amplitude clipping can be view as another noise source. Furthermore, the resulting noise caused by clipping falls both in-band and out-of-band. If clipping is performed on a Nyquist sampled signal (refer to "Source Formatting," in Chapter 1), all the *clipping noise* will fall in-band. On the other hand, if clipping is performed on an oversampled signal, then the in-band noise is reduced but out-of-band noise will be introduced. The in-band distortion cannot be reduced by filtering and results in degradation in the bit error rate (BER) performances while the out-of-band noise reduces the spectral efficiency. Filtering after clipping can reduce the out-of-band noise, but may also cause some peak regrowth. Clearly, extensive analyses are needed to quantify the effects of clipping with filtering on the performance of an OFDM wireless communication system.

Li and Cimini [18] examined the out-of-band noise caused by clipping and the effect of filtering. Evident in Figure 5.7 are the in-band signal attenuation and out-of-band noise emission power. Notice that for a clipping ratio (CR), defined as the ratio the clipping level A to the root mean squared value of the OFDM signal, of 1.4 the out-of-band emission is only 16 dB below the signal power. After filtering, the out-of-band emission power is greatly reduced as seen in Figure 5.8. The filtering, however, causes a 1 dB ripple across the band but does not cause any serious degradation when forward error-correcting codes are used as demonstrated in Figure 5.9 for $CR \geq 1.4$.

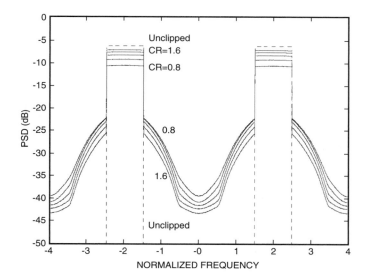

FIGURE 5.7
Power spectral density of unclipped and clipped OFDM signals. © 1998 IEEE.

As noted earlier, clipping causes in-band noise, which degrades the BER performance of the system. In Figure 5.9, the BER performance is shown as a function of signal-to-noise ratio (SNR), averaged across all the subchannels, with clipping and filtering over additive white Gaussian channels. For $CR \geq 1.4$, the penalty is less than 1 dB for a BER level of 10^{-2}. The degradation from clipping can become quite severe as evident from Figure 5.9. Hence, researchers have proposed several adaptive methods to recover the clipping amplitudes at the receiver.

Exercise 3 *Using the graphical user interface (GUI) provided at the website, select QPSK modulation, 16X oversampling, bandpass representation. Specify an IF equal to 4X the modulation rate. Plot the power spectrum of bandpass signal with and without a transmit pulse shaping filter. Hint: The pulse shaping filter can be generated using any of the following Matlab commands: rcosine, rcosfir, rcosiir.*

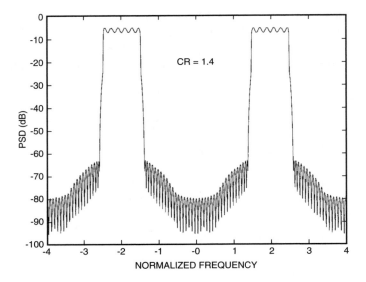

FIGURE 5.8

Power spectral density of the clipped and filtered OFDM signals with a CR=1.4. © 1998 IEEE.

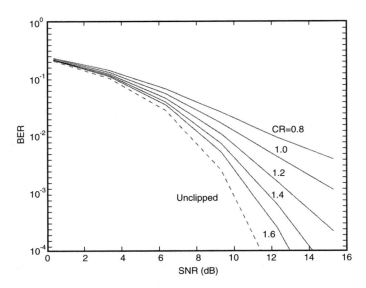

FIGURE 5.9

BER of clipped and filtered OFDM signals. © 1998 IEEE.

A Decision-Aided Method for Clipping Amplitude Recovery

Kim and Stüber [16] proposed a technique called *decision-aided reconstruction* (DAR) to mitigate the clipping noise. Assuming knowledge of the clipping amplitude A at the receiver, the algorithm is outlined as follows:

1. Given the received frequency domain signal $Z_n = \alpha_n H_n Y_n + W_n$, where H_n is the complex channel gain for the nth subchannel, Y_n is the transmitted modulation symbol, α_n is a multiplicative distortion factor from the clipping operation, and W_n is the additive white Gaussian noise process. The clipped signal $\tilde{y}_n$ is found and stored in memory by performing IFFT on $\tilde{Y}_n$, where

$$\tilde{Y}_n = \frac{Z_n}{H_n}, \quad 0 \le n \le N - 1 \tag{5.6}$$

2. Decisions on the transmitted symbols are made in the frequency domain as

$$\hat{X}_n^I = \min_X \left| Z_n^{(I)} - H_n X \right|, \, 0 \le n \le N - 1 \tag{5.7}$$

   where I represents an iteration number with an initial value of $I = 0$, and $Z_n^{(0)} = Z_n$.

3. The decisions in step 2 are converted back to the time domain using an IFFT, yielding $\left\{ \hat{x}_k^{(I)} \right\}$.

4. The clipped samples are detected and a new sequence $\left\{ \tilde{y}_k^{(I)} \right\}$ is computed as

$$\tilde{y}_n^{(I)} = \begin{cases} \tilde{y}_k, & \left| \hat{x}_k^{(I)} \right| \le A \\ \hat{x}_k^{(I)}, & \left| \hat{x}_k^{(I)} \right| > A \end{cases} \quad 0 \le k \le N - 1 \tag{5.8}$$

   where the sequence $\{ \tilde{y}_k \}$ is retrieved memory in step 1.

5. The sequence $\left\{ \tilde{y}_k^{(I)} \right\}$ is converted to the frequency domain yielding $\left\{ \hat{Y}_k^{(I)} \right\}$.

6. Increment the index number $I \leftarrow I = 1$ and compute

$$Z_n^{(I)} = H_n \hat{Y}_n^{I-1}, \quad 0 \le n \le N - 1. \tag{5.9}$$

7. Go back to step 2. Decisions are made yielding $\left\{ \hat{X}_n^I \right\}$. This completes the Ith iteration of the DAR algorithm.

8. Repeat steps 3-7 until algorithm converges.

Kim and Stüber offer this intuitive explanation for the DAR algorithm. When the clipping noise is large compared to the AWGN, the performance is limited by an error floor due to the clipping noise. However, even with this error floor, the clipping noise is mitigated significantly when the decisions are made in the frequency domain. When the symbol decisions are converted back to the time domain, the OFDM signal samples that were clipped will restore their original values prior to clipping. Hence, an improvement can be made by replacing the clipped samples with these decisions within the above algorithm. Since decisions made in the frequency domain are converted back to the time domain, the symbol estimates are noisy and may miss a few of the clipped samples (miss detection) or falsely replace unclipped samples (false detection).

Performance of DAR technique is difficult to analyze because of its highly nonlinear nature. From simulations shown in Figures 5.10–5.12, it was found that DAR technique achieves the most improvement when the number of clipped samples and decision errors within a block are not too large. It should be noted that the DAR technique rapid converges to a stationary point as indicative of the use only two iterations in these simulations. If the total of these two impairments exceed certain thresholds, the effect of decision error feedback becomes prominent and the improvement using DAR decreases. These thresholds are determined by the CR. The minimum CR of 4 dB was found experimentally for 16- and 64-QAM constellations.

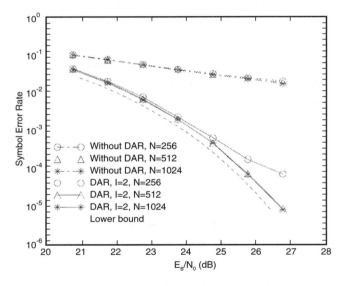

FIGURE 5.10

64-QAM over an AWGN channel with CR = 5 dB. The lower bound is achieved when clipping is not used. © 1998 IEEE.

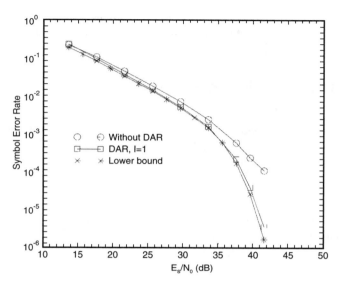

FIGURE 5.11

16-QAM over 6 tap static fading channel with CR = 4 dB, N = 1024. © 1998 IEEE.

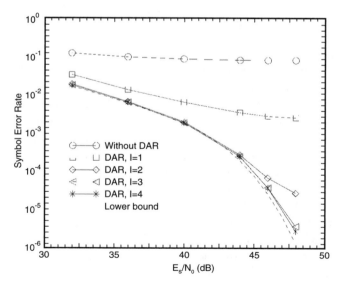

FIGURE 5.12

64-QAM over 6 tap static fading channel with CR = 4 dB, N = 1024. © 1998 IEEE.

5

RF DISTORTION ANALYSIS

Exercise 4 *Create a script file that performs the DAR algorithm. Add module to receive chain, per instruction at the Web site, and compute the BER performance of QPSK modulated signal with and without the DAR algorithm activated.*

Bayesian Inference Method for Clipping Amplitude Recovery

Declercq and Giannakis [7] proposed to model the clipping operation as a Bayesian inference. The received signal after channel equalization as in Equation 5.6 and conversion back to the time domain is given by

$$\tilde{y}_n = \tilde{x}_n + \varepsilon_n \tag{5.10}$$

where $\tilde{x}_n$ is the output of the clipping operation and ε_n is the additive complex white Gaussian noise process found from

$$\varepsilon_n = IFFT\left(\frac{W_n}{H_n}\right) \tag{5.11}$$

The presumption that ε_n is white Gaussian noise is predicated on precise knowlegde of the channel amplitudes H_n. The clipped amplitude $\tilde{x}_n$ is modelled as

$$\tilde{x}_n = x_n(1 - \ell_n) + Ae_n^{j\Psi_{x_n}}\ell_n \tag{5.12}$$

where ℓ_n is an indicator function, which specifies whether the sample at time n has been clipped ($\ell_n = 1$) or not ($\ell_n = 0$). Also, A is the amplitude saturation level of the soft limiter used to clip the signal. Declercq and Giannakis view ℓ_n as augmented random variables that need to be estimated jointly with the input signals x_n for $n \in [0 : N - 1]$. By modelling the clipping amplitude as in Equation 5.12, the nonlinear problem is converted into a conditionally linear problem. The disadvantage of the approach is that it increases the number of parameters to be estimated, which limits the use of maximum likelihood or maximum a posteriori (MAP) [2] estimators. The authors in [7] recognize that direct maximization of the full posterior distribution with respect to all variables is impossible since the parameter space is too large. Hence, Declercq and Giannakis considered iterative MAP algorithms that update the parameters sequentially. The first is the Monte Carlo Markov Chain (MCMC) [30] algorithm; the second, an extension of the stochastic Expectation Maximization (EM) strategy [8–9]. Although both of these algorithms provide estimates of all parameters, the only parameters of interest are X_m, the Fourier transform of $\tilde{x}_n$. Thus, a hybrid algorithm called Stochastic EM for Data Augmentation (SEM-DA) was proposed by the authors in [7]. Unfortunately, the algorithmic development presented therein [7] is well beyond the scope of this text. The basic principles governing the algorithm can be summarized as follows. First, prior densities for each of the parameters to be estimated were specified for the MAP estimators. Each parameter is updated by exploiting Bayes' theorem,[*] i.e.,

$$f_{\beta|\alpha}(\beta|\alpha) = \frac{f_{\alpha|\beta}(\alpha|\beta)f_\beta(\beta)}{f_\alpha(\alpha)} \tag{5.13}$$

in each iteration. In other words, the MAP estimator for each parameter is computed sequentially while holding the other parameters constant. This is continue until the SEM-DA algorithm converges. Note that convergence of SEM-DA to a stationary point of the posterior density is guaranteed, yet the stationary point is not necessarily the global maximum of the posterior density, which implies the algorithm is very sensitive to its initialization point. We now proceed to the results and comparison given in the paper.

Comparison of SEM-DA and DAR Algorithms

SEM-DA is compared to DAR algorithm, described earlier in this section, in terms of performance and complexity. DAR is computationally more attractive than SEM-DA since its complexity is of order $O(KN \log N)$, where K is the number of iteration and N is the FFT size. SEM-DA, on the other hand, has a complexity of order $O(KN(QN + \log N)) \simeq O(KQN^2)$. With regards to performance, DAR and SEM-DA were compared in terms of symbol error rate (SER) versus SNR over Rayleigh fading channels. The channel model consists of five complex Gaussian taps. The channel taps are normalized such that energy of the channel of unity. In Figures 5.13–5.14, the SER transmission with high power amplifier (HPA) is shown as the dashed lines. The improvements gained from using DAR and SEM-DA as well as the SER transmission over a linear channel. As expected, when the clipping is not too severe, as shown in Figures 5.13 with an input backoff (IBO) of 2.92 dB, the SEM-DA provides little improvement compared to DAR. For low SNR and small clipping effects, the DAR method is preferred because of its lower complexity and slightly performance degradation compared to SEM-DA. At high SNR, however, the DAR method interprets the clipping as noise while SEM-DA tries to compensate for it. SEM-DA is preferable to DAR when the clipping noise is significant relative to the background noise as illustrated in Figure 5.14 with an IBO of 1.58 dB at high SNR.

Let's summarize. Clipping is the simplest and most common non-adaptive predistortion technique used to mitigate nonlinear distortion associated with operating HPA in the saturation region. Although clipping helps limits the peak amplitude of the input signal, it also introduces an additional noise source called clipping noise. As it turns out, clipping noise can greatly degrade the BER and SER performances of a system. Thus, many researchers have attempted to produce methods to remove the effects of clipping noise at the receiver. The alternative is to reduce the

---

[*]In many iterative stochastic algorithms, the denominator of Equation 5.13 is ignored since it is assumed to remain constant throughout the iterative process.

amount clipping noise by increasing the clipping level of the soft limiter. This leads an increase in PAPR and, consequently, nonlinear distortions unless the amplifier is backed off. Thus, a vicious loop is established; reduction in nonlinear distortion from one source leads to the addition other nonlinear distortions from a different source. To avoid this cycle, the clipping amplitudes must be recovered at the receiver and then mitigated.

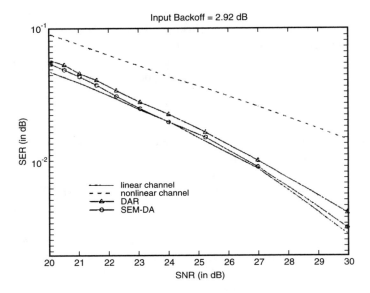

FIGURE 5.13

SER versus SNR with low clipping noise. © 2000 IEEE.

The DAR method works well in situations where the background noise is greater than the clipping noise, and the transmitted symbols are recovered with high probability. Using the estimates of the transmitted symbols enables us to estimate when clipping occurred at the transmitter and compensate for it. Note, however, that this method is subject to error propagates when incorrect decisions are used to estimate the clipping phenomenon. SEM-DA uses a different approach by modelling the transmitted sequence as a conditional linear estimation problem with a large parameter space. The SEM-DA is proposed in lieu of the full maximum likelihood solution which is intractable for this problem. Yet, SEM-DA remains more complex than the DAR method in terms of implementation. The benefits of SEM-DA are greatest when the clipping noise is large relative to the background noise, which is the situation when the DAR method fails or results in minor improvements in BER and SER performances. In this next section, we survey another adaptive receiver techniques used to mitigate nonlinear effects without amplitude clipping on the performance of OFDM systems.

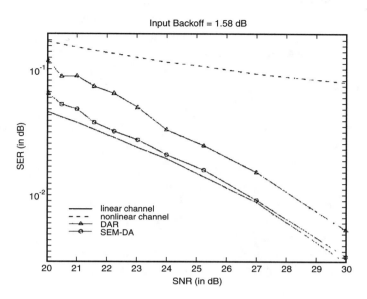

FIGURE 5.14

SER versus SNR with high clipping noise. © 2000 IEEE.

Effects of Amplifier Nonlinearities Without Amplitude Clipping

E. Costa et al [6] examined the effects of amplifier nonlinearities on OFDM transmission without clipping. The input-output relationship of the amplifier is given by

$$y(t) = G(|x(t)|)x(t) \tag{5.14}$$

where

$$G(|x(t)|) = \frac{AM/AM(|x(t)|)\exp\{jAM/PM(|x(t)|)\}}{|x(t)|} \tag{5.15}$$

The AM\AM distortion model [28] is given by

$$AM/AM(\tau) = \frac{\mu\tau}{\left[1 + (\alpha\tau/A)^{2p}\right]^{\frac{1}{2p}}}, \quad AM/PM \approx 0 \tag{5.16}$$

where A is the saturation level of the amplifier, μ is the small-signal gain, and p is an integer. As $p \to \infty$, the AM\AM curve approaches the ideal *soft limiter* nonlinear transformation described in previous sections, namely AM\AM$(\tau) = \mu\tau$, for $0 \leq \tau \leq \mu A$, and AM\AM$(\tau) = A$ for $\tau \geq \mu A$.

5

RF DISTORTION ANALYSIS

Nonlinear distortions depend on the *input backoff*, IBO, or *output backoff*, OBO. IBO is the difference in the current input drive level from that need to drive the amplifier into compression or saturation region while OBO measures the difference in current output power and the saturation power. Note that IBO and OBO can differ by several dBs for the same amount of distortion reduction. In other words, a 1 dB change in OBO does not result in 1 dB change in IBO, or vice versa.

Noting that OFDM signals are accurately modelled as bandlimited zero-mean Gaussian random processes and beginning with the basic definition of the autocorrelation of $x(t)$,

$$r_x(\xi) \triangleq E\{x(t+\xi)x^*(t)\} \tag{5.17}$$

the authors arrive at a complicated closed form equation for the output autocorrelation for a soft limiter, which is not repeated here. Interested readers can peruse the original paper for the derived equation for the autocorrelation function $r_x(\xi)$. The important point is that closed-form equation for the autocorrelation is used to compare with simulated data. The autocorrelation function $r_x(\xi)$ is then used to compute the power spectrum density, i.e.,

$$R_{x(t)} \triangleq FFT(r_x(\xi)) \tag{5.18}$$

The distortion only component $x_d(t)$ is given by

$$x_d(t) = y(t) - \eta x(t) \tag{5.19}$$

where η is a complex scalar factor accounting for the *AM\AM* and *AM\PM* distortions. Using the definitions of autocorrelation function (Equation 5.17) and power spectral density (Equation 5.18) and Equation 5.19, the power spectral densities of distortion signal $x_d(t)$, the input signal to the soft limiter $x(t)$, and output of the soft limiter $y(t)$ are given in Figure 5.15. The input backoff is IBO = 6 dB and the asymptotic phase distortion $AM\backslash PM_\infty \to \pi/3$. The dashed line represents the spectrum of the input OFDM signal, a perfect brickwall spectrum.

Reviewing Equation 5.19, we would like η to be chosen such that the distortion power is minimized. The straightforward solution is

$$\eta = \frac{r_y^*(0)}{r_x(0)} \tag{5.20}$$

The amplifier nonlinearity causes two effects on the detected samples:

- Constellation warping—amplitude and phase distortions as shown in Figures 5.5–5.6
- Nonlinear distortion that causes a cluster of received values around each constellation point rather than a single point

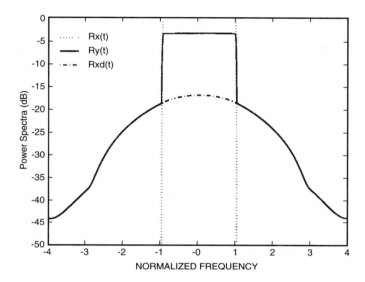

FIGURE 5.15

A comparison of the power spectra of the nonlinear distortion caused by amplifer, input, and output signals of the amplifier. © 1999 IEEE.

When the signal constellation points for each subchannel is drawn from a QAM constellation, both amplitude and phase distortions degrade the performance of the system. To overcome this effect, a one tap equalizer can be used. The optimum value for the tap is the reciprocal of η given in Equation 5.20. Figure 5.16 demonstrates theoretical predictions compared to simulated results. In the figure, various levels of IBO are examined with and without a one tap equalizer. Good agreement between theoretical and simulated results are shown. In closing, E. Costa et al were able to derive an analytical expression for predicting the effects of HPA on an OFDM waveform. The model was based on statistical propereties of the OFDM waveform and the resulting distortion introduced by the HPA. Since the OFDM waveform is well-approximated by a Gaussian pdf, E. Costa et al show that the autocorrelation of the output of the amplifier, $y(t)$, is given by a tetra-variant Gaussian pdf. The details of this development are left for the reader to investigate in the original paper. In this next section, we survey some of the adaptive predistortion techniques for OFDM systems.

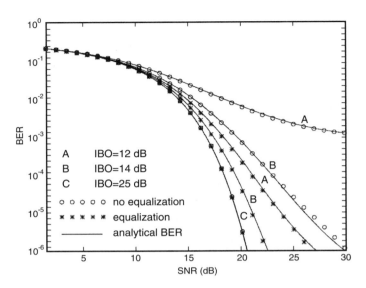

FIGURE 5.16

Simulated and analytical BER for an OFDM system with 16-QAM modulation scheme, solid state amplifier, with and without one tap equalization. © 1999 IEEE

Exercise 5 *Using the GUI provided at the Web site, select one of digital modulation available and enable the nonlinear amplifier in the transmit chain. Run an AWGN simulation using the GUI. Store simulation results and input/output of amplifier $x(t)$ / $y(t)$, respectively. Find η as in Equation 5.20. Create a script file that performs 1 tap equalization, i.e.,*

$$\hat{x}(t) = \frac{1}{\eta} y(t)$$

an add module in transmit chain, per Web site instructions, before simulating channel effects. Re-run AWGN simulation and plot against the earlier results. Investigate using the effects of varying the number of samples to compute η.

Adaptive Predistortion Techniques

Heretofore, the adaptive techniques presented have been receiver algorithms. These techniques were derived to mitigate the noise associated with clipping. Herein, we consider adaptive techniques at transmitter or adaptive predistortion algorithms. The first technique reviewed, developed by H. Kang et al in [14], considers a predistortions algorithm for a cascade of HPA and linear filter. In the approach, the memoryless HPA preceded by a linear filter, as shown in Figure 5.17, is modelled as a Wiener system [11]. Precompensation is achieved via adaptive algorithm derived using a stochastic gradient decent method [11].

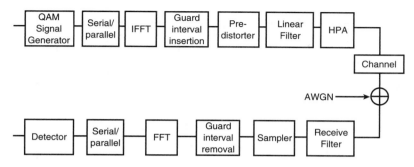

FIGURE 5.17

A simplified block diagram of the baseband equivalent OFDM transceiver. © 1995 IEEE.

Consider the simplified block diagram of the baseband equivalent system for an OFDM system shown in Figure 5.17. The serial-to-parallel block converts a QAM input data stream to a block of N symbols, which modulates the corresponding subcarrier. After the OFDM modulation is performed by the IFFT, the guard interval that is longer than the largest delay spread is inserted to remove the ISI and ICI. The linear filter in Figure 5.17 represents the transmitter pulse shaping filter. The HPA is widely used in wireless communications since it is considered a frequency independent memoryless nonlinearity. Thus, HPAs are completely characterized by their $AM\backslash AM$ and $AM\backslash PM$ conversions. The first step in the adaptive algorithm is a system classification or estimation performed by the system estimator block in Figure 5.18. The HPA is modelled by a memoryless nonlinear subsystem preceded by an adaptive linear filter, illustrated in Figure 5.18. The next step in the procedure is to develop an adaptive predistorter that compensates for the constellation warping and reduces ISI effects on the OFDM signal. Ideally, the adaptive predistorter is the inverse of the Wiener system found in the first step. To proceed, a polynomial approximation is used to model the HPA, i.e.,

$$\hat{y}(n) = \sum_{l=1}^{N_a} a(l) \left(\sum_{k=1}^{N_h} h(k)u(n-k) \right)^l \tag{5.21}$$

where N_h and N_a, respectively, denote the memory length of the linear filter $h(k)$, and the order of the nonlinear filter $a(l)$. Also, $u(n)$ denotes the input signal of the linear filter. Using only the input and output signals of the system, the coefficients of the system estimator $h(k)$ and $a(l)$ are adjusted to minimize the mean squared error (MSE), $\Gamma_1 = E\left\{ |e_1(n)|^2 \right\}$ where

$$e_1(n) = y(n) - \hat{y}(n) \tag{5.22}$$

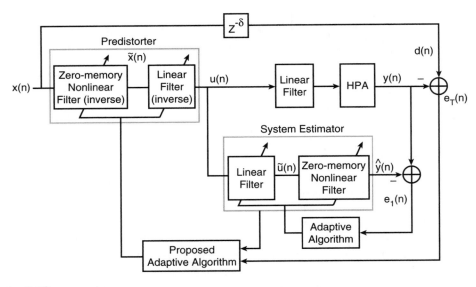

FIGURE 5.18

An adaptive predistorter for HPA preceded by a linear filter. © 1995 IEEE.

As an aside, there are well-known optimization techniques for minimizing Γ_1, but those techniques are beyond the scope of this book. Interested readers are directed to [11] as an excellent reference. After the correct parameters of the Wiener system have been estimated, the adaptive predistorter can be designed. An appropriate structure of the predistorter is easily shown to be the Hammerstein model [19]. The predistorter in Figure 5.18 is constructed by a memoryless nonlinear inverse filter followed by a linear inverse filter. Using a polynomial form of finite order for the memoryless nonlinear inverse filter, the predistorter can be expressed as

$$u(n) = \sum_{i=1}^{N_p} p(i) \sum_{j=1}^{N_s} s(j) x(n-i)^j \qquad (5.23)$$

where $x(n)$ is the input OFDM signal, N_p denotes the memory length of the linear inverse filter $p(i)$, and N_s denotes the order of the nonlinear inverse filter $s(j)$. The error of the total system is defined as

$$e_T(n) = d(n) - y(n) \qquad (5.24)$$

where the desired signal $d(n)$ is the delayed version of the input signal $x(n)$ by δ samples to account for causality of the predistorter. The coefficients of the predistorter are obtained by minimizing the MSE, $\Gamma_T = E\{|e_T(n)|^2\}$, of the system.

The validity of the proposed predistortion technique is demonstrated via computer simulation using a block-oriented model [14]. The serial to parallel converter in Figure 5.17 transfers a block of 1024 16-QAM symbols to the OFDM modulator, which uses an 800 of 1024 subchannels of IFFT to modulate them. The first and last 112 subcarriers are set to zero to avoid spectrum over-lapping. Effectively, this provides a 224 subcarrier guard band between adjacent OFDM systems. To monitor the effect of the predistorter, the channel is assumed perfectly equalized. The parameters of the Wiener system were first estimated by the system estimator. The order of the nonlinear filter is $N_a = 5$, and the memory length of the linear filter is $N_h = 3$. Figure 5.19 shows the learning curve of the system estimator, obtained by averaging 200 independent trials. The coefficients of the linear filter and the nonlinear filter, $h(k)$ and $a(l)$, respectively, are updated simultaneously using the stochastic gradient method [11]. The step-size constants, which determine convergence speed and MSE after convergence, were set to 0.0067 for the linear filter and 0.27 for the nonlinear filter. With zero initial conditions, about –45 dB in the MSE was obtained, resulting in a fairly accurate estimation of filter coefficients for the Wiener system under test.

After the checking for convergence of the Wiener system, the adaptive algorithm that minimizes the MSE of the system is applied. The order of the nonlinear inverse filter N_s and the memory length of the linear inverse filter N_P were set to numbers large enough to model inverse function, 7 and 10, respectively. The step-size parameters for the nonlinear inverse filter and linear inverse filter were set to 0.5 and 0.1, respectively. The input amplitude, output amplitude, and phase-shift are all quantized over six bits. The required memory used for this approach is 64 words of 12 bits each. By comparing the two curves in Figure 5.19, one can clearly see that proposed approach has a faster convergence speed and smaller fluctuation than the techniques reported in [15]. Figure 5.20 shows the BER comparison for the proposed approach with and without predistortion when the OBO = 6 dB. The effects of quantization is also demonstrated in Figure 5.20.

Although the results given by the authors are encouraging [15], there are several questions left unanswered. First, how much does the performance degrade when fading characteristics are considered in the problem. Second, is there sufficient time or data available for the various algorithms to converge in a real-time implementation? Finally, what happens if one of the adaptive algorithms misconverge to a local not global minimum? Hence, from an academic standpoint, adaptive predistortion of this type can help mitigate effects of nonlinearity in HPA. In practice, the actual benefits remain uncertain.

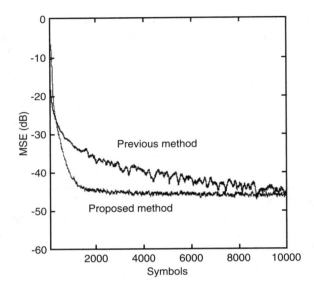

FIGURE 5.19

Learning curves for (a) system estimator with ($N_h = 3$, $N_a = 5$) and (b) predistorter with ($N_s = 7$, $N_p = 10$; OBO = 6 dB).
© 1995 IEEE.

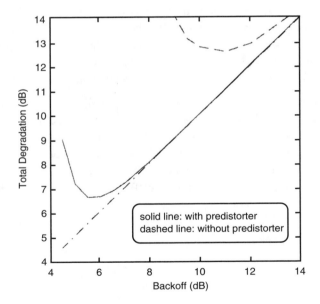

FIGURE 5.20

BER Performance for OBO = 6 dB. © 1991 IEEE.

Other researchers [12–15] have proposed methods for estimating the inverse characteristic for the HPA. The authors of [15] use Volterra series [10] to approximate the combined characteristics of the transmit filter and HPA. Using this model, the adaptive predistortion can be regarded as an inverse nonlinear estimation with memory problem. It is noted by the authors that the exact inverse of a nonlinear system with memory does not always exist, but existence of a finite-order inverse is guaranteed, where the pth-order inverse F_p is the system which, when cascaded with a nonlinear system G described by Volterra series, results in a system the first-order Volterra Kernel is a unit pulse. Further, the second- pth-order Volterra Kernels are all zero. The proof of this theorem and the remaining material presented [15] are beyond the scope of this text. The important outcome of this research is the interest it has sparked with other researchers [12, 14].

Finally, W. G. Jeon et al [12] noted that the approach in [15] is unsuitable when the input signal constellation is finite. The input levels of the HPA shown in Figure 5.17 can be nearly infinite depending on the size and type of the QAM constellations. By limiting the number of possibilities for the input levels of the HPA in Figure 5.17, the data predistortion problem becomes more tractable. In order to design data predistorter for the HPA in an OFDM system, the magnitude and phase of the input and output signals of the HPA is quantized uniformly over Q bits

$$0 \le i_n = \sum_{j=0}^{Q-1} b_{n,j} 2^j \le 2^Q - 1 \tag{5.25}$$

where the binary signal $b_{n,j}$ denotes the jth bit corresponding to the amplitude of the nth input signal x_n, which is a sampled version of the input $x(t)$. With reference to Figure 5.21, the complex input signal x_n can be re-written in polar form as

$$x_n = \rho_n e^{j\phi_n} \tag{5.26}$$

Ideally, the content of RAM(r_n, θ_n) addressed by the corresponding index i_n will represent the amplitude and phase required to linearize the HPA. Thus, the predistorted value applied to the HPA is

$$y_n = \gamma_n e^{j\psi_n} \tag{5.27}$$

where $\gamma_n = \rho_n r_n$ and $\psi_n = \theta_n + \phi_n$. Hence, the response of HPA to the predistorted signal is given by

$$z_n = R_n e^{j\Psi_n} \tag{5.28}$$

where $R_n = A(\gamma_n) + v_n$ and $\Psi_n = \Phi(\gamma_n) + \phi_n + w_n$. Here, $A(\cdot)$ and $\Phi(\cdot)$ are the AM\AM and AM\PM characteristic of the HPA, respectively; and v_n and w_n represent measurement noises for the amplitude and phase, respectively. The amplitude and phase errors ΔA_n and ΔP_n, respectively, are defined as the difference between the desired signal and the HPA output, i.e.,

$$\Delta A_n = \chi \rho_n - R_n \qquad (5.29)$$

$$\Delta P_n = \phi_n - \psi_n \qquad (5.30)$$

where χ denotes the desired gain, taking into account the linear gain of the HPA and the coupling factor of the sampling directional coupler. The least mean squared (LMS) algorithm [11] to update the RAM is given by

$$r_{n+1} = r_n + \mu_\alpha \Delta A_n \qquad (5.31)$$

$$\theta_{n+1} = \theta_n + \mu_\beta \Delta P_n \qquad (5.32)$$

denote step sizes for amplitude and phase, respectively. Once the step sizes for the LMS algorithms are fixed, the convergence rate of the predistorter is determined mostly by the size of the RAM since only the content of RAM corresponding to the input level is update each time. For an OFDM system with block size $N \geq 2^Q$, the content in each address will be updated $N/2^Q$ times during NT_s seconds (one block) on the average. For instance, for the OFDM system with $N = 512$ and $Q = 8$, each content will be updated twice per block on the average. This extremely slow convergence characteristic of the predistorter in the OFDM system limits its real-time implementation.

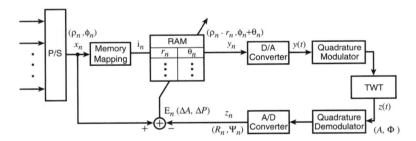

FIGURE 5.21

Block diagram of the proposed adaptive date predistorter using RAM or memory lookup. © 1995 IEEE.

The validity of the proposed adaptive data predistortion technique for compensation of an HPA in an OFDM system is demonstrated by computer simulation. For close examination of the proposed predistorter, only AWGN is assumed to be present in the channel. The block size N and the number of bits for quantization Q are set to 512 and 8, respectively. The convergence constants μ_α and μ_β are set to 0.04 and 0.08, respectively. The typical performance measure for quantifying the effect of nonlinear distortion in HPA is the total degradation (TD) in dB, defined as

$$TD = SNR_{HPA} - SNR_{AWGN} + OBO \quad \text{(dB)} \qquad (5.33)$$

where SNR_{HPA} represents the SNR to obtain a specific BER when the HPA is used, and SNR_{AWGN} is the required SNR to obtain the same BER over a AWGN channel without HPA. Equation 5.33 relates a linear degradation, OBO, to a nonlinear degradation, SNR_{HPA} via fixed system parameter, SNR_{AWGN}. Since the computer simulations are performed for a fixed BER, the SNR_{AWGN} also remains fixed. As the OBO is increased linearly in decibels, the SNR_{HPA} improves exponentially up to the SNR_{AWGN}. At which point, no further improvements in SNR_{HPA} is achieved, yet, to maintain the specified BER, more output power is needed to compensate for the OBO. In other words, every decibel of OBO requires a decibel of output power in the linear region of operation of the HPA to maintain the fixed SNR_{AWGN} requirement. Clearly from Figure 5.22, the effects of the predistorter can be seen from the lower TD for OBOs of 4-13 dB. The optimum backoff for this HPA is approximately 5.5 dB. Notice, also, that the OFDM system with the proposed data predistortion achieves a gain of 5 dB over a system without the data predistortion.

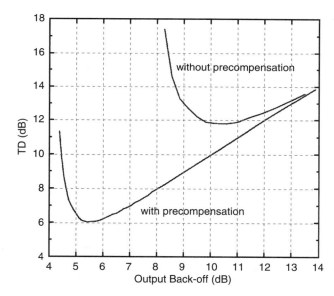

FIGURE 5.22
Total degradation versus HPA OBO (BER = 10^{-4}). © 1995 IEEE.

Coding Techniques for Amplifier Nonlinear Distortion Mitigation

In this section, the popular coding techniques for mitigating nonlinear distortion caused by HPA are reviewed. The three most popular techniques in the literature are *partial transmit sequences* (PTS), *selective mapping* (SLM), and block coding. Note that each of these methods require side information to be transmitted to the receiver.

Partial Transmit Sequence Techniques

PTS was first introduced by S. Muller and J. Hüber [21]. The concept is fairly simple and effective. The following notation is used throughout this development. The nth transmit symbol modulating the jth subcarrier is denoted by $X_j(n)$. The input data block at time instance n is formed as

$$\mathbf{X}(n) = \left[X_0(n), X_1(n), \ldots, X_{N-1}(n) \right]^T \tag{5.34}$$

and corresponding OFDM symbol is

$$\mathbf{x}(n) = IFFT\{\mathbf{X}(n)\} \tag{5.35}$$

Now, S. Muller and J. Hüber define an OFDM symbol crest factor as

$$\zeta_n \triangleq \frac{\max|\mathbf{X}(n)|}{\sqrt{E(|\mathbf{X}(n)|)}} \quad \text{for } n = 0, \ldots, N-1 \tag{5.36}$$

where $E(\cdot)$ denotes the statistical expectation. Note that the PAPR is simply the square of ζ_n. Finally, the performance criterion used to assess the algorithm is the complementary cumulative distribution function, P_ζ, i.e.,

$$P_\zeta(\zeta_0) \triangleq \Pr(\zeta_0 > \zeta_n) \tag{5.37}$$

The PTS algorithm is pictorially illustrated in Figure 5.23 and outlined as follows:

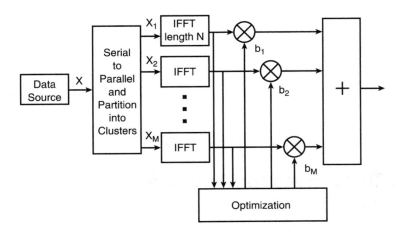

FIGURE 5.23

PTS functional block diagram. © 1997 IEEE.

Partiton the input data block $\mathbf{X}$ into M disjoint sets or clusters, denoted by $\mathbf{X}_m$, $m = 1, 2, \ldots, M$. For simplicity, the clusters are assumed contiguous and of equal size. Optimally combine the M clusters such that the crest factor ζ_n is minimized, i.e.,

$$\mathbf{X}' = \sum_{m=1}^{M} b_m \mathbf{X}_m \qquad (5.38)$$

where $\{b_m, m = 1, 2, \ldots, M\}$ are weighting factor of pure phase rotations. Computing the IFFT of $\mathbf{X}_m$ provides us with the so-called *partial transmit sequences*, i.e.,

$$\mathbf{x}' = \sum_{m=1}^{M} b_m \mathbf{x}_m \qquad (5.39)$$

Again, the phase rotations are chosen to minimize the crest factor of $\mathbf{x}'$. One immediately notices that one rotation factor can be set to unity without any performance, e.g., $b_1 = 1$. The remaining phase terms can be found from

$$\hat{b}_m = \arg\min\left(\max_{b_m}\left\{ b_1 \mathbf{x}_1 + \sum_{m=2}^{M} b_m \mathbf{x}_m \right\} \right), \quad m = 2, \ldots, M \qquad (5.40)$$

where $\arg\min(\cdot)$ achieves the global minimum for the peak power optimized transmit sequence.

Using four blocks of 128 subcarriers, QPSK modulation on each subcarrier, and phase factors limited to $\{\pm 1, \pm j\}$, the crest factor improves by 3 dB and 4 dB for $P_\zeta(\zeta_0) = 1\%$ and 10^{-5}, respectively. The authors [21] claim this improvement is accomplished with a surprisingly moderate additional complexity at the transmitter. The argument for this claim is that the IFFTs shown in Figure 5.23 can be performed in parallel. In addition, further computational saving can be gained if the transform makes use of the fact that a large fraction of input values are zero.

Modification of the PTS Algorithm

After publication of [21], other researchers [5, 29] have proposed refinements or modifications of the PTS algorithm. In [5], Cimini and Sollenberger proposed a suboptimal combining algorithm, which uses only binary weighting factors. The algorithm is summarized as follows:

1. Assume $b_m = 1$ for $m = 1, 2, \ldots, M$ and compute $\text{PAPR}^{(+)}$.
2. $m = 2$.
3. Invert: $b_m = -1$ and recompute the $\text{PAPR}^{(-)}$.
4. If $\text{PAPR}^{(+)} > \text{PAPR}^{(-)}$, retain $b_m = 1$; otherwise, $b_m = -1$.
5. $m = m + 1$.
6. Repeat Steps 3–5 until $m = m + 1$.

In Figure 5.24, the complementary cumulative distribution function P_ζ for an 256 carrier OFDM system partitioned into16 clusters each composed of 16 subcarriers. Each subcarrier is modulated with QPSK data symbols. The transmit signal is oversampled by a factor of four. In the simulation, 100,000 random OFDM blocks were generated to obtain the P_ζ as defined in Equation 5.37. The unmodified OFDM signal has PAPR which exceeds 10.4 dB for less than 1% of the blocks. By using the PTS approach with optimum binary phase sequence for combining, the 1% PAPR reduces to 6.8 dB. Moreover, the slope has been improved so that the reduction would be even greater at lower P_ζ values. The optimatization process has been reduced to 16 sets of 16 additions, a considerable saving over determining the optimum phase factors, while suffering only 1 dB lost in performance. The performance at each iterative step is greatly effected by the number of clusters and phase states as well as the data constellation size. Increasing the number of clusters and phase states impact the complexity of implementation. On the other hand, decreasing the number of clusters decreases the improvement. Yet, increasing the number of phase states, say from 2 to 4 using $\{\pm 1, \pm j\}$, with 16 clusters only nominally improve the performance. Finally, using a 16-QAM constellation rather than QPSK constellation on each subcarrier results in negligible difference from the QPSK case.

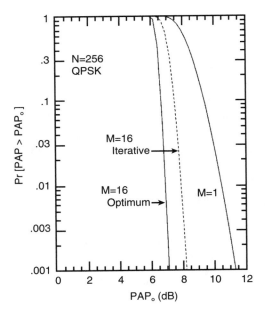

FIGURE 5.24

Comparison of iterative and optimum combining strategies. © 2000 IEEE.

C. Tellambura [29] argues that results obtained by Nyquist sampling does not lead to true *peak factor* (PF) rather, what they call the *low PF* or *discrete PF*. To get a better estimate, the input signal to the IFFT $\mathbf{X}_n$ needs to be oversampled by a factor of 8 to obtain the *true PF* (TPF). Furthermore, to make the optimization procedure tractable, the observation space is typically limited to discrete points as in [5–21]. Now, if we attempt to minimize the maximum of $|\mathbf{X}(n)|$ for $n = 0,\dots,N-1$, the TPF of $|\mathbf{X}(t)|$, Ω, will likely occur between sampling points. The performance, however, can be improved by using a bound on Ω, which is related to its aperiodic autocorrelation $r_x(k)$,

$$r_X(k) = \sum_{n=1}^{N-k} X(n+k)\mathbf{X}^*(n) \quad \text{for} \quad k = 0,\dots,N-1 \tag{5.41}$$

by

$$\Omega \le 1 + \frac{2}{N}\sum |r_X(k)| \tag{5.42}$$

Based on this bound, C. Tellambura proposes the following optimization criterion:

$$\hat{b}_m = \arg\min_{b_m}\left(\max\left\{\sum_{k=1}^{N-1}|r_X(k)|\right\}\right) \quad m = 2,\dots,M \tag{5.43}$$

This criterion entails computing the sum of autocorrelation sidelobe amplitudes of PTS for every possible phase factor combination of discretize phase weighting and selecting the phase factor that minimize the sum. To summarize, comparing this method to previously discussed version of PTS, both requires searching over L^{M-1} phase points; here it is assumed the phase factor have be quantized to L discrete values. On the other hand, computing the IDFT is less complex than computing the sum of the autocorrelation amplitudes. Yet, Equation 5.40 leads to the discrete PF or low PF. Thus, in terms of performance, C. Tellambura's algorithm is slightly superior; in terms of complexity, the methods presented in both [21] and [5] are superior. Based on the 0.5 dB performance improvement shown in Figure 5.25, it hard to justify the additional complexity of C. Tellambura's algorithm.

Exercise 6 *Create simple Matlab script files, which implements PTS and the modified PTS algorithms. Using QPSK modulation and four subgroups of IFFT, determine the sizes of the IFFT, where the each algorithm becomes intractable.*

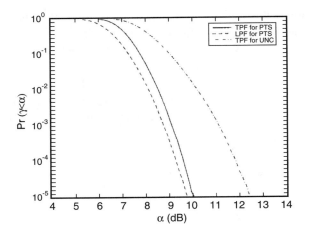

FIGURE 5.25

Comparison PTS using bounded PF and discrete PF optimizations. © 1998 IEEE.

Selective Mapping

The next coding scheme examined is selective mapping (SLM). R. W. Baümi *et al* first introduced SLM [3]. The concept is very straightforward. Given M statistically independent OFDM symbols conveying the same information, select the symbol with the lowest PAPR for transmission. The M statistically independent OFDM symbols are generated by weighting the OFDM symbols with M random sequences of length N. One possibility is to use Walsh sequences as suggested in [5]. Another possibility is to use a random interleaver on the data sequence as proposed in [3]. These two methods of SLM are compared with the iterative approach in [5] and shown in Figure 5.26. The results show that the use of 16 random sequences leads to the same performance of the iterative approach. The Walsh sequence of length 16 results in only additional 0.3 dB degradation. We conclude this section on coding techniques for amplifier nonlinear distortion mitigation with an examination of block coding techniques. The block coding approaches entail selecting only those codewords with small PAPR at the expense of increasing the transmission bandwidth needed for the coding redundancy [13]. In [1], it was noted that the proper design of the block code should provide error protection as well as PAPR reduction.

The system block diagram with the proposed block code is depicted in Figure 5.27.

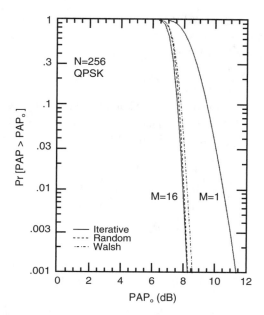

FIGURE 5.26

Comparison of SLM with PTS. © 1998 IEEE.

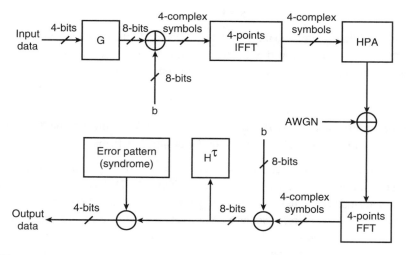

FIGURE 5.27

Functional block diagram of an OFDM system using the proposed block coding scheme.

The scheme achieves the minimum PAPR for a system using 4 subcarriers and QPSK modulation on each subcarrier. The rate of the block coding scheme is 4/8=1/2. The algorithm utilizes 4×8 generator matrix $\mathbf{G}^*$ followed by a 1×8 phase rotation vector $\mathbf{b}$ to yield the encoded output $\mathbf{x}$,

$$\mathbf{x} = \mathbf{uG} + \mathbf{B} \tag{5.44}$$

where $\mathbf{u}$ is the input data vector to be encoded. $\mathbf{G}$ and $\mathbf{b}$ are found by examining all possible, $4^4 = 256$, combinations of QPSK input sequences. Next, the 16 symbol combinations, which yield the minimum PAPR of 7.07 W after the IFFT, is selected. For this case,

$$\mathbf{G} = \begin{bmatrix} 1 & 0 & 0 & 1 & 0 & 1 & 1 & 0 \\ 0 & 1 & 0 & 1 & 0 & 1 & 0 & 1 \\ 0 & 0 & 1 & 1 & 0 & 0 & 1 & 1 \\ 0 & 0 & 0 & 0 & 1 & 1 & 1 & 1 \end{bmatrix} \tag{5.45}$$

and

$$\mathbf{b} = \begin{bmatrix} 0 & 0 & 0 & 0 & 0 & 0 & 1 & 1 \end{bmatrix} \tag{5.46}$$

In the receiver of the system, the inverse functions of the transmitter are performed as depicted in Figure 5.27. In particular, the proposed decoder $\mathbf{H}$ in Figure 5.27 is similar to a standard parity check matrix used for block decoding. That is to say that $\mathbf{H}$ is chosen such that

$$\mathbf{s} = \mathbf{GH}^T = 0 \tag{5.47}$$

where $\mathbf{s}$ is the syndrome vector and $\mathbf{0}$ is the 4x4 zero vector. In the proposed system, the effects of the phase rotation vector is removed prior to computing the syndrome of the received vector and error correction. For comparison, the PAPR for a conventional OFDM is provided,

$$PAPR = 10 \log_{10}(N) \quad \text{dB} \tag{5.48}$$

where N is the number of subcarriers. For $N = 4$, the PAPR for a conventional OFDM system is 6.02 dB compared to $10 \log_{10}\left(\frac{7}{4}\right) = 2.58$ dB for the proposed scheme.

In conclusion, the various coding techniques provide methods for PAPR reduction at the expense of bandwidth. The usefulness of these techniques are limited to OFDM systems with a small number of subcarriers and small constellation sizes; otherwise, the required exhaustive search for the block codes is intractable. Furthermore, to achieve PAPR reduction when there is a larger number of sub-carriers or large constellation size, the code rate becomes very low. Thus, the actual benefits of coding for PAPR reduction for practical OFDM systems of interest are extremely small.

---

[*]Herein, uppercase and lowercase boldface variable are used to denote matrix and vector quantities, respectively.

In the next two sections, we discuss other RF distortions—phase noise and IQ imbalance, which have not received the same attention in the literature as the amplifier nonlinearity has, but are as equally important.

Exercise 7 *Implement the block coding scheme described above and verify that is provides both PAPR reduction and coding gain for a QPSK modulated OFDM system.*

Phase Noise

Most of the discussions in this chapter have been presented with the baseband representation. Yet, to transmit information across a wireless channel, it is necessary to modulate the baseband information onto a RF carrier. Thus, an oscillator is required to generate the RF carrier. Like all real devices, the oscillator is a source of noise in the system. This section is dedicated to the development of this noise, and its effect on a OFDM system. To develop the noise associated with oscillators, a model is needed. D. P. Newkirk and U. L. Rohde [22] model an oscillator as a feedback system, which is comprised of a phase modulator cascaded with an amplifier and resonator as shown in Figure 5.28. The transfer characteristics of the phase modulator are determined by the flicker noise, which is a noise that varies inversely with frequency $(1/f)$, i.e,

$$S_\theta(\Delta f) = \frac{N_0}{P}\left(1 + \frac{f_z}{\Delta f}\right) \tag{5.49}$$

where N_0 is the noise density at the output of real unity gain amplifier, Δ_f is the frequency offset, and f_z is the corner frequency of zero in the magnitude response of the phase modulator. Recall from basic circuit design [20], the corner frequency is the frequency at which the idealized magnitude responses changes slopes by ±20 dB/decade for every zero and pole, respectively, in the magnitude response. The resonator has a lowpass transfer function depicted in Figure 5.29 and given by

$$L(\omega_m) = \frac{1}{1 + j(\omega_m / \omega_m)} \tag{5.50}$$

where f_p is the pole of resonator in radians/second and equal to half the bandwidth of the resonator. According to Equation 5.50, the phase noise passes unattenuated through the resonator up to the half-band width point. The closed loop response of the phase feedback loop for the system in Figure 5.29 is given by

$$\Delta\theta_{out}(\Delta f) = \left(1 + \frac{\omega_p}{j\omega_m}\right)\Delta\theta_{in}(\Delta f) \tag{5.51}$$

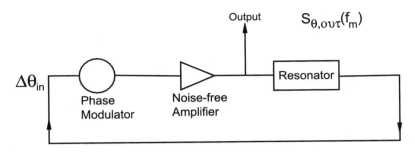

FIGURE 5.28

Oscillator functional block diagram.

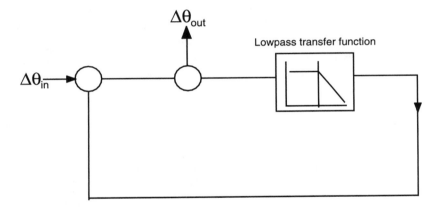

FIGURE 5.29

Equivalent lowpass representation for resonator.

Thus, the power spectral density of the phase noise at the output of the resonator becomes

$$S_{\theta,out}(\Delta f) = \left[1 + \left(\frac{f_p}{\Delta f}\right)^2\right] S_{\theta,in}(\Delta f) \tag{5.52}$$

which found by a directly applying the result of filtered random process given in "Filtering Random Processes," in Chapter 1. Substituting the definition for $S_{\theta,in}(\Delta f)$ given in Equation 5.49 yields the overal transfer characteristics

$$S_{\theta,out}(\Delta f) = \frac{N_0}{P}\left(1 + \frac{f_z}{\Delta f}\right)\left[1 + \left(\frac{f_p}{\Delta f}\right)^2\right] \tag{5.53}$$

Equation 5.53 does not account for the thermal noise floor, as seen in Figure 5.30, which is present in all physical devices.

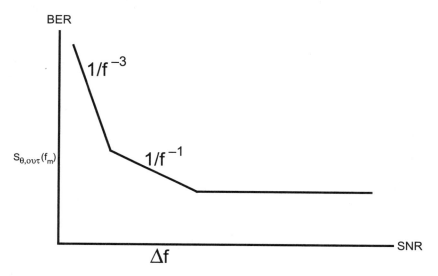

FIGURE 5.30

Power spectral density for phase noise.

We illustrate, in Figure 5.31, the performance degradation, which can occur from phase noise, by examining uncoded BPSK and 16 QAM with and without phase noise. The noise bandwidth of the resonator is set to 40 KHz and 100 KHz, the noise floor is set to −132 dBc/Hz,[*] and the slope of the phase noise power spectral density is −84 dBc/Hz. For BPSK, there is no perceivable degradation in performance for the phase noise generated. For 16 QAM, there is about 0.5 dB and 1.5 dB degradation at noise bandwidths of 40 KHz and 100 KHz, respectively. Partial compensation for phase noise can be done with phase lock loop (PLL) techniques, which is beyond the scope of this book; however, some techniques are outlined in the textbook [22].

Exercise 8 *Using the simulation tool provided at the website, vary the slope of the phase noise power spectral density and noise floor. Investigate the resulting degradation in BER for QPSK, 16QAM, and 64 QAM.*

---

[*]*dBc is the power in dB relative to the carrier.*

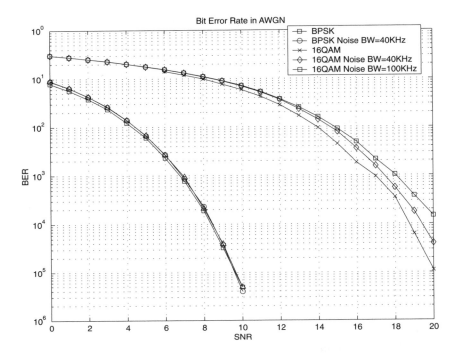

FIGURE 5.31

Performance evaluation of BPSK and 16 QAM with phase noise bandwidths of 40 KHz and 100 KHz.

IQ Imbalance

The final RF subsystem discussed in this chapter is the in-phase and quadrature (IQ) modulator shown in Figure 5.1. A functional block diagram of a real IQ modulator is shown in Figure 5.32.

The figure shows the DC offset that can occur on either the I or Q branch. Ideally, these values are zero. Also, the amplitude and phase imbalances are denoted by ε and ϕ, respectively. Let's examine the effects of these imbalance. Given an input data sequence $\mathbf{x}$. The ideal complex modulate carrier waveform $\mathbf{y}(t)$ is

$$\mathbf{y}(t) = \mathbf{x}_I(nT)\cos(\omega t) + j\mathbf{x}_Q(nT)\sin(\omega t) \tag{5.54}$$

while the IQ imbalanced modulated waveform $\tilde{\mathbf{y}}(t)$ is

$$\tilde{\mathbf{y}}(t) = \mathbf{x}_I(nT)\cos(\omega t) + \delta_I + \delta_Q - \varepsilon\mathbf{x}_Q(nT)\sin(\omega t + \phi) \tag{5.55}$$

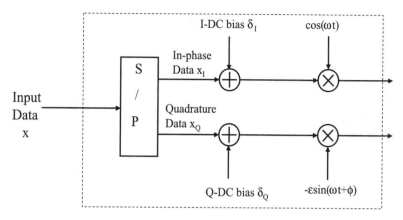

FIGURE 5.32

A block diagram of a real IQ modulator.

Equation 5.55 simplifies after adjustment for the DC offset terms to

$$\breve{y}(t) = \left[x_1(nT) - \varepsilon x_Q(nT) \sin(\phi) \right] \cos(\omega t)$$
$$- \varepsilon[1 + \cos(\phi)] x_Q(nT) \sin(\omega t) \breve{y}(t) = \tilde{y}(t) - (\delta_I + \delta_Q)$$

(5.56)

At the receiver, the synchronization must be performed with $\breve{y}(t)$ rather $y(t)$ (refer to Chapter 2 for more details on synchronization). The effects of IQ imbalance on a 16 QAM constellation is depicted in Figure 5.33. This is a severe case of IQ imbalance, but is, nonetheless, likely to occur if the IQ modulator is not properly designed.

The problem is further complicated since the imbalanced signal is in general subjected to frequency offset, channel fading, and received in the presence of additive white noise process. Recall in Chapter 2, the channel estimation, packet detection, and freqency offset algorithms exploit the phase information of the training sequence. Unfortunately, the phase of the imbalance signal ϕ_{IM}

$$\phi_{IM} = -\tan^{-1}\left(\frac{[x_I(nT) - \varepsilon x_Q(nT) \sin(\phi)]}{\varepsilon[1 + \cos(\phi)] x_Q(nT)} \right)$$

(5.57)

differs significantly from a properly balance signal ϕ_{BAL}

$$\phi_{BAL} = -\tan^{-1}\left(\frac{x_I(nT)}{x_Q(nT)} \right)$$

(5.58)

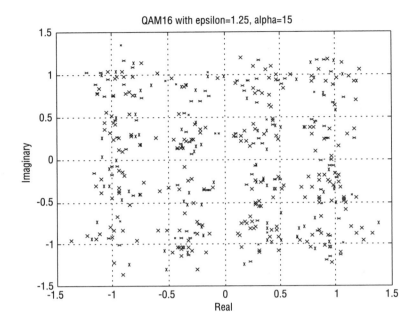

FIGURE 5.33

Impacts of IQ imbalance on the signal constellation.

Thus, potentially, IQ imbalance can limit the ability of the receiver to achieve synchronization, which would be devastating! One solution to combat this distortion is the perform the IQ modulation digitally. This requires the the baseband system to be sampled at a sufficiently high rate to generate an appropriate intermediate frequency (IF), which can be later modulated onto a RF carrier using a single conversion branch rather than two. The disadvantage to this approach is that additional processing is required to run at this high rate as well as impact the hardware design in several areas. Chapter 8 discusses some of those issues and interested readers are referred there for more detail. Other more sophisticated techniques can be used in the receiver to compensate for the IQ balance, but those techniques are well beyond the scope of this book.

Bibliography

[1]   H. Ahn, Y. Shin, and S. Im, "A block coding scheme for peak-to-average power ratio reduction in an orthogonal frequency division multiplexing system," *VTC* 2000, vol.1, pp. 56–60.

[2]   Y. Bar-Shalom and T. E. Fortmann, *Tracking and Data Association,* Mathematics in Science and Engineering, Volume 179, Academic Press, 1988.

[3] R. W. Baümi, R. F. H. Fischer, and J. B. Hüber, "Reducing the peak-to-average power ratio of multicarrier modulation by selective mapping," *Electronic Letters,* vol. 30, no. 22, October 1996.

[4] K. Chang, *Microwave Solid-State Circuits and Applications,* John Wiley & Sons, Inc. New York, 1994.

[5] L. J. Cimini, Jr. and N. R. Sollenberger, "Peak-to-average power ratio reduction of an OFDM signal using partial transmit sequences," *IEEE Communication Letters,* vol. 4, no. 3, March 2000.

[6] E. Costa, M. Midrio, and S. Pupolin, "Impact of amplifier nonlinearities on OFDM transmission system performance," *IEEE Communication Letters,* vol. 3, no.2, February 1999.

[7] D. Declercq and G. B. Giannakis, "Recovering clipped OFDM symbols with Bayesian inference," *IEEE International Conference on Acoustics, Speech, and Signal Processing,* 2000.

[8] A. P. Dempster, N. M. Laird, and D. B. Rubin, "Maximum likelihood from incomplete data via the EM algorithm," J. R. Statist. Soc., vol. 39, no. 1, pp. 1–38, 1977.

[9] J. A. Fessler and A. O. Hero, "Space-alternating generalized EM algorithm," IEEE Trans. Signal Processing, vol. 42, pp. 2664–2677, Oct. 1994.

[10] I.S. Gradshteyn and I.M. Ryzhik, *Table of Integrals, Series, and Products,* Academic Press, London, UK, 1994.

[11] S. S. Haykin, *Adaptive Filtering Theory*: Fourth Editions, Prentice Hall, Inc., Englewood Cliffs, N.J., 1995.

[12] W. G. Jeon, K. H. Chang, and Y. S. Cho, "An adaptive data predistorter for compensation of nonlinear distortion in OFDM systems," *IEEE Trans. on Communications,* vol. 45, no. 10, pp. 1167-1171, October 1997.

[13] A. E. Jones, T. A. Wilkinson, and S. K. Barton, "Block coding scheme for reduction of peak to mean envelope power ratio of multicarrier transmission scheme," *Electronic Letters,* vol. 30, no. 25, December 1994.

[14] H. W. Kang, Y. S. Cho, and D. H. Youn, "On compensating nonlinear distortions of an OFDM system using an efficient adaptive predistorter," *Trans. on Communications,* vol.47, no. 4, pp. 522–526, April 1999.

[15] G. Karam and H. Sari, "A data predistortion technique with memory for QAM radio systems," *IEEE Trans. on Communications,* vol. 39, pp. 336-344, February, 1991.

[16] D. Kim and G. J. Stüber, "Clipping noise mitigation for OFDM by decision-aided reconstruction," *IEEE Communications Letters,* vol. 2, no. 5, May 1998.

[17] M. Lampe and H. Rohling, "Reducing out-of-band emissions due to nonlinearities in OFDM systems," *VTC 1999,* vol 3, pp. 2255–2259.

[18] X. Li and L. J. Cimini, "Effects of clipping and filtering on the performance of OFDM," *IEEE Communications Letters,* vol. 2, no. 5, May 1998.

[19] S. Y. Mao and P. X. Lin, "A test of nonlinear autogressive models," in *Proc. Int. Conf. Acoustics, Speech, and Signal Processing,* New York, 1988, pp. 2276–2279.

[20] J. Millman, *Microelectronics: Digital and Analog Circuits and Systems,* McGraw-Hill Book Company, New York, 1979.

[21] S. H. Muller and J. B. Hüber, "OFDM with reduced peak-to-average power ratio by optimum combination of partial transmit sequences," *Electronic Letters,* vol. 33, no. 5, February 1997.

[22] D. P. Newkirk and U. L. Rohde, *RF/Microwave Circuit Design for Wireless Applications,* John Wiley & Sons, Inc. New York, 2000.

[23] H. Ochiai and H. Imai, "On clipping for peak power reduction of OFDM signals," IEEE *Global Telecommunications Conference*, 2000, vol. 2 , 2000.

[24] H. Ochiai and H. Imai, "Performance of the deliberate clipping with adaptive symbol selection for strictly band-limited OFDM systems," *IEEE Journal on Selected Areas in Communications,* vol. 18, no. 11, November 2000.

[25] H. Ochiai and H. Imai, "Performance of the deliberate clipping with adaptive symbol selection for strictly band-limited OFDM systems," *IEEE Journal on Selected Areas Communications,* vol. 18, no. 11, November 2000.

[26] R. A. Redner and H. F. Walker, "Mixture densities, maximum likelihood and the EM algorithm," SIAM Rev., vol. 26, pp. 195–239, Apr. 1984.

[27] R.Y. Rubinstein, *Simulation and the Monte Carlo Method.* John Wiley & Sons, 1981.

[28] A. A. Saleh, "Frequency independent and frequency dependent nonlinear models of TWT amplifiers," *IEEE Trans. on Communications,* vol. COM-29, pp. 1715–1720, Nov. 1981.

[29] C. Tellambura, "A coding technique for reducing peak to average power ratio in OFDM," *GLOBECOM* 1998, vol. 5, pp. 2783–2787.

[30] L. Tierney, "Markov chains for exploring posterior distributions," *Ann. Stat.,* 22, pp. 1701–1762, 1994.

[31] P. Vizmuller, *RF Design Guide: Systems, Circuits, and Equations,* Artech House Publishers, Boston, 1995.

[32] D. Wulich, N. Dinur, andA. Glinowiecki, "Level clipped high-order OFDM," *IEEE Trans. on Communications,* vol. 48, no. 6, pp. 928–930, June, 2000.

Medium Access Control (MAC) for IEEE 802.11 Networks

Venkatesh Vadde and Sridhar Ramesh

IN THIS CHAPTER

- MAC Overview   216
- MAC System Architecture   219
- MAC Frame Formats   222
- MAC Data Services   231
- MAC Management Services   239
- MAC Management Information Base   251
- Bibliography   256

The throughput of a WLAN is impacted not only by the channel quality, SNR, and diversity in the PHY layer but also by the medium access control (MAC) protocol. The MAC in IEEE 802.11a WLANs assumes significance owing to the specific nature of a wireless medium. Unlike in wired media, the channel in a wireless OFDM system changes dynamically, leading to unpredictable fading and to a high bit error rate (BER). The high BER often degrades further owing to the inability to detect an impending collision in a wireless medium [1, 2]. Typically, a packet error or collision incurs an expensive retransmission. These considerations imply that the throughput in a wireless LAN is limited largely by high error rates and packet retransmissions [3, 4]. Under such circumstances, the MAC layer, which is the focus of this chapter, can play a crucial role in enhancing the overall data throughput.

In addition to controlling medium access to enhance the data throughput, the MAC also acts as an interpreter of data moving between the physical (lower) and network (higher) layers. The MAC provides this seemingly less important but indispensable service by introducing structure and protocol into the communication process between two IEEE 802.11 mobile stations. Without the MAC, the physical layer merely specifies how to use the air interface to exchange bits of information. The MAC is the logical entity that adds grammar and syntax to the raw alphabet (bits and bytes) that the physical (PHY) layer helps transmit. In fact, no WLAN baseband design is considered complete unless it is accompanied with a MAC. The development of a MAC is as specialized as that of a baseband-PHY, and needs a significantly different approach as well as skill-set. From the world of complex number-crunching equalizers, encoders and decoders used in the PHY-layer, we transition to a world of protocols, rules, and nonlinear state-machines: the MAC layer.

In this chapter, the IEEE 802.11 MAC and its functional components are described. The emphasis is on the services provided by the MAC to support the communication process, as well as on the MAC frames that enable these services. For a systematic implementation of the MAC, the reader is advised to refer to the comprehensive Standard document.

MAC Overview

The MAC can be interpreted as an engine that works closely with the PHY to facilitate reliable and efficient data communication. Functionally, the MAC layer can be construed as a set of diverse services to accomplish information exchange, power-control, synchronization, and session management. These MAC services are implemented through the exchange of suitably defined MAC frames. Each MAC frame constitutes several bit fields which together encode the identity as well as purpose of the MAC frame. The different MAC frame types defined are data, control, and management frames. Typically, data frames are interspersed with control frames and management frames. The former serve to logically terminate data exchanges while the latter provide managerial support. Thus, the MAC can be viewed as providing vital data and management services for the network via well structured frame exchanges between stations. Finally, to store information regarding the dynamic state of the network on an ongoing basis, the MAC layer typically uses an information repository called the Management Information Base (MIB). The organization of the MAC layer can thus be succinctly specified in terms of three basic components:

- MAC Services
- MAC Frames
- MAC Information Management

The relationship between the three MAC components mentioned above is illustrated in Figure 6.1. In the sections that follow, the basic notions behind each of these components are introduced.

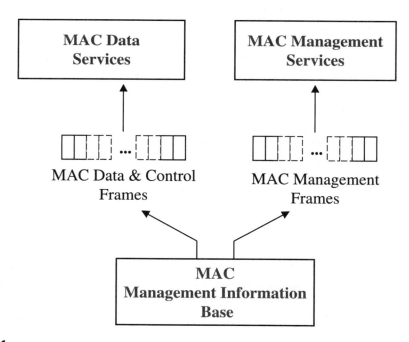

FIGURE 6.1

The interplay between MAC services, MAC frames and MAC management information base (MIB) is illustrated here. The MAC services are delivered by means of MAC frames based on the information stored in the MIB.

MAC Services

The term *MAC services* is typically used to refer to the services that are specifically provided by the MAC layer to other layers in the protocol stack or to sustain the normal operation of the network. There are several services that the MAC layer is designed to offer, all of which can be categorized under MAC data services and MAC management services. The OFDM-based WLAN is primarily attempting to effect data communication between stations (both asynchronously and synchronously). Asynchronous data communication typically involves the MAC allocating the channel to contending users based on a predetermined protocol. Synchronous data services, on the other hand, are often effected in a contention-free manner. The associated MAC functions are designated as MAC data services.

The MAC also offers several managerial services to the terminals communicating with each other. These managerial services range from simple session management and power management to synchronization. Session management refers to such book-keeping activities as association and authentication of a terminal to a network, address filtering upon data delivery, privacy and information protection. Power-management services are essential for two reasons. First, extending battery life takes precedence in portable devices, and WLANs are prime candidates. Second, power-control assumes even greater significance in an OFDM-based WLAN since the peak-to-average power ratio (PAPR) is often a problematic issue. At high PAPR, one is forced to operate at low powers leading, sometimes, to decreased data reliability. Conserving power for potential retransmissions is therefore very desirable. The wireless interface for data exchange makes privacy an important concern as tapping into RF waves is much simpler than into a sheathed cable. The MAC addresses this through encryption algorithms used for data protection, as part of MAC management services. Finally, synchronization between station clocks is of significance in just the same way as the PHY layer needs to keep a transmitter and receiver in sync. MAC services related to synchronization will be our other focus.

MAC Frames

As mentioned in the beginning of this section, MAC frames constitute the bricks and mortar used to implement the MAC protocol and to effect data communication. They come in three types: data frames, control frames, and management frames. The function of the latter two is to support the smooth and efficient exchange of data frames between stations. Within each type of MAC frame, there are several subtypes. Each frame subtype accomplishes a specific objective and identifies itself by encoding its subtype using a few bits within itself. These MAC frame subtypes will find mention again in the MAC data services as well as the overall MAC management services (i.e., power management, synchronization, session management and privacy) sections. Rather than describe all the frame types and subtypes in the frame formats section, an attempt is made to put the relevant MAC frames in context by mentioning the chief subtypes and their function soon after the MAC protocol pertaining to their function is described. For instance, the MAC data frames and MAC control frames get mentioned in the MAC data services since they directly pertain to exchange of data between stations.

MAC Information Management

The MAC layer needs to keep track of several variables that reflect the state of the network as a whole as well as that of any mobile station in question. The information of interest is different for a mobile station and an AP. A central repository that maintains a database of these network-related parameters is the MAC management information base, or MIB. In practice, there is a separate MIB for the PHY and the MAC layers. The MAC MIB itself is a collection of two sets of attributes. Some of them (station management attributes) configure MAC operation and help in station management, while others (MAC attributes) measure MAC performance and tune it in a desired direction. Notably, several of these attributes in the MIB can be probed and determined by an agent that is external to the station-MAC or AP-MAC that is housing the MAC MIB of interest. Some of the details of these attributes and the functions they control are described in greater depth in the "MAC Management Information Base" section, later in the chapter.

In the rest of this chapter, the MAC components outlined in this section are presented in their logical sequence. At the outset, system architectures from a MAC viewpoint are presented. MAC frames and frame formats (which constitute the MAC alphabet and vocabulary) will be presented before the MAC services and protocols (which constitute the language of the MAC) are discussed. This will hopefully give the reader a better appreciation of MAC frames and frame subtypes, while also setting ground for their usage in the different MAC services.

MAC System Architecture

Before details of the MAC service related protocols are presented, some architectural details of the system pertinent to the MAC layer will be briefly described. From an architectural standpoint, a WLAN can be configured as a basic service set or as an extended service set. Several potentially overlapping WLANs, each of which is a basic service set, constitute an extended service set.

Basic Service Sets

The WLAN in the most generic configuration comprises three entities: the station, the access point (AP), and the wireless medium. A collection of stations that communicate with one another is said to form a Basic Service Set (BSS). A simple BSS typically lacks an AP, and stations in the BSS directly communicate between themselves without mediation by an AP. Such an IEEE 802.11 WLAN configuration, illustrated in Figure 6.2, is often referred to as an independent BSS, and is limited in scope. For instance, two stations have to be within range of each other in order to be able to communicate. This is because stations do not relay data packets in an independent-BSS (Id-BSS). When the BSS is slightly more complex and is mediated by an AP, the setup is referred to as an infrastructure BSS (If-BSS). The AP in an If-BSS facilitates data exchange within the BSS (through relay of data packets) as well as acts as the gateway for communication with stations outside the BSS.

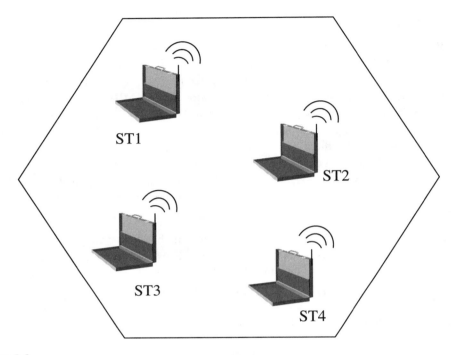

FIGURE 6.2

A Basic Service Set (BSS) is the simplest configuration in which an IEEE WLAN can exist, wherein a set of independent stations communicate directly with each other.

An infrastructure BSS with an AP is desirable for several reasons (as opposed to an independent BSS). Firstly, the reach of an infrastructure BSS is by design far greater, and of a longer-lived nature than an independent BSS. The presence of an AP can enable contention-free modes of operation. Such contention-free modes often form the basis of communication for delay-sensitive or real-time data between stations. Real-time data requires guaranteed Quality of Service (QoS) due to the very nature of the associated applications. By placing an AP in charge of medium access control and directing all traffic through it, reasonable guarantees of QoS are feasible in a WLAN setup. An AP can also enable vitally significant power-save modes that elongate battery life in portable stations. Since an AP is often better equipped than a station, it is capable of buffering data (in memory) for different stations belonging to an If-BSS, and delivering the data to the stations at a convenient time. The advantage of this scheme is that a majority of the stations can operate in power-save (sleep) mode, awakening to receive buffered data every once in a while. The obvious (and significant) benefit of this is longer battery life for typical WLAN users.

Extended Service Sets

The real potential of a portable device in finding ubiquitous connectivity is only fulfilled when several concomitant BSSs provide wide area coverage by communicating between each other through a backbone network. Such a configuration of interconnected BSSs is referred to as an Extended Service Set (ESS) and the associated backbone network is called the Distribution System (DS). An ESS can have potentially overlapping BSSs interconnected as shown in Figure 6.3, so long as adjacent BSSs use different frequency bands to avoid interference.

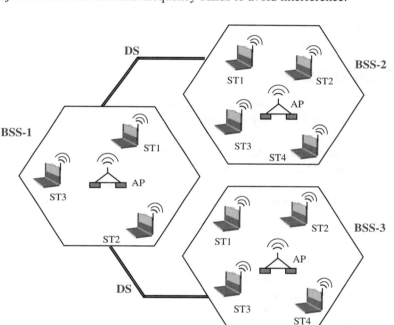

FIGURE 6.3

An Extended Service Set (ESS) is formed by several BSSs interconnected through a Distribution System (DS) which could be wired or wireless. The AP acts as the port of entry for each BSS within an ESS.

In the ESS model, multiple BSSs are interconnected via access points (APs). The AP acts as the entry point to the BSS, filtering and forwarding any frames coming from outside the BSS. Assuming all APs are on the same subnet, one can roam from one BSS to another without loss of connection. When an AP is used and the individual stations are put in infrastructure mode, each station associates with one AP, chosen as the one with the strongest signal. Furthermore, each AP has an ESSID (ESS Identifier) programmed into it, which is intended to represent the subnet the AP is attached to. Adjacent APs are set up so that their frequencies do not overlap with those of their neighbors, and thus interference is minimized. While in infrastructure mode, a station communicates only with its associated AP.

Each of the component BSSs uses the asynchronous communication protocol defined in the standard for medium access coordination. In addition, for synchronous data transfer, within every BSS the AP periodically polls each of its associated stations to see if they have anything to transmit. This allows each station to transmit non real-time as well as real-time traffic at some fixed, dependable rate for time-sensitive applications such as voice. It is the function of the APs within an ESS to forward data packets from one BSS to another, and to facilitate mobility of stations between adjacent BSSs. That is also why the MAC layer requires that each BSS in such an overlapping set be an If-BSS. The ESS could span any number of such If-BSSs, and the DS could potentially be wired or wireless. It is the duty of the IEEE MAC to ensure that these finer architectural details are taken care of during the BSS's setup and existence.

MAC Frame Formats

The IEEE 802.11 MAC fundamentally exists to facilitate exchange of data frames for different applications between two WLAN stations, employing the support of the PHY layer. A typical instance might be two stations exchanging a file using the FTP program. The FTP program is then the application, and the file to be exchanged is broken down into small data chunks called MAC service data units (MSDUs). The MAC layer accepts MSDUs and adds headers and trailers to create MAC protocol data units (MPDUs) and passes them over to the PHY layer for transmission. In the world of MAC frames, it is convenient to think of these MPDUs as so-called *data frames*.

The exchange of data frames with suitable headers and trailers enables the passage of raw information in a meaningful way from one station to another. However, the MAC world would fall apart if it were not for two other frame types—namely, control frames and management frames—that bring so much order to the MAC. Control frames assist in performing the handshakes that punctuate a typical exchange of data frames. Management frames, on the other hand, take care of bookkeeping functions that are such an integral part of any network of communicating entities. Together, control frames and management frames help accomplish exchange of data frames in an efficient and reliable manner.

Each MAC frame, whether it is data, control, or management type, is an aggregation of specific bit fields, along with a header and trailer. Details of the MAC frames and formats are discussed in the following sections.

IEEE 802.11 Frame Format

The general IEEE 802.11 frame format is shown in Figure 6.4. In the design of frame formats one attempts to balance two things: efficiency and functionality. The IEEE 802.11 standard MAC frame format is considered the best design balancing both efficiency and functionality.

Medium Access Control (MAC) for IEEE 802.11 Networks

CHAPTER 6

223

6

MEDIUM ACCESS
CONTROL (MAC)
FOR IEEE 802.11

	Header						Body	Trailer
Frame Control	Duration ID	Address 1	Address 2	Address 3	Sequence Control	Address 4	Frame Body	FCS
2	2	6	6	6	2	6	0-2312	4

Bytes

FIGURE 6.4

The general IEEE 802.11 MAC frame format is shown here. Each frame consists of a frame header, a frame body, and a frame trailer also called the frame check sequence. The frame body can take up to 2312 bytes when not encrypted.

The frame begins with a MAC header. The frame header consists of the frame control field, a duration ID field, three address fields followed by the frame sequence information and, finally, the fourth address field. It may appear that the MAC header is very long; however, not all these fields are used in all frames. Following the MAC header is the frame body. The frame body contains the MSDU from the higher layer protocols. The final field in the MAC frame is the frame check sequence. Each of these fields will be discussed below along with the pertinent subfields.

Frame Header

The following sections describe the component fields that make up the frame header.

Frame Control Field

The frame control field is a sixteen-bit field that comprises the information the MAC requires to interpret all of the subsequent fields of the MAC header. The subfields of the frame control field are the Protocol version, Frame Type and Subtype, To DS, From DS, More fragments, Retry, Power management, More data, Wired Equivalent Privacy (WEP), and Order. See Figure 6.5.

Protocol Version	Type	Subtype

To DS	From DS	More Frags	Retry	Power Mgmt	More Data	WEP	Order

FIGURE 6.5

Illustration of different components of the frame control field. This field encodes several important subfields that determine the frame type, subtype, whether the frame has been encrypted, whether it is the last fragment within a burst, and whether it came from within a BSS.

- Protocol Version Subfield

  The Protocol Version subfield is two bits in length. It is used to identify the version of the IEEE 802.11 MAC protocol used to construct the frame. The station uses this field to determine if the frame was constructed with a version of the protocol that the station understands.

- Frame Type and Subtype Subfields

  The Frame Type and Subtype fields identify the function of the frame and which other MAC header fields are present in the frame. There are three frame types: control, data, and management. The fourth frame type is currently reserved. Within each frame type there are several subtypes.

- To DS and From DS Subfields

  The To DS subfield is a single bit in length. It is used only in data type frames to indicate that the frame is destined for the DS. The From DS subfield is a single bit in length. It is also used only in data type frames to indicate that the frame is being sent from the DS. When both subfields are zero, the frame is a direct communication between two mobile stations. The other extreme, when both subfields are one, is used for a special case where an IEEE 802.11 WLAN is being used as the DS. These details are summarized in Table 6.1.

TABLE 6.1   Address Field Functions

Function	To DS	From DS	Address1	Address2	Address3	Address4
Id-BSS	0	0	RA = DA	SA	BSSID	N/A
From AP	0	1	RA = DA	BSSID	SA	N/A
To AP	1	0	RA = BSSID	SA	DA	N/A
Wireless DS	1	1	RA	TA	DA	SA

- More Fragments Subfield

  The More Fragments subfield is a single bit in length. This subfield is used to indicate that this frame is not the last fragment of a data or management frame that has been fragmented.

- Retry Subfield

  This subfield is a single bit in length. It is used to indicate whether a data or management frame is being transmitted for the first time or if it is a retransmission. The receiving MAC, to enable it to filter out duplicate received frames, uses this subfield, along with the sequence number subfield.

- Power Management Subfield

  This subfield is a single bit in length. A mobile station uses the power management subfield to announce its power management state. The value of the subfield indicates the power management state that the station will enter when a successful frame exchange is completed. A zero in this subfield indicates that the station is in the active mode and will be available for future communication. A one in this subfield indicates that the station will be entering the power management mode and will not be available for future communication.

- More Data Subfield

  The More Data subfield is a single bit in length. The AP uses this subfield to indicate to a mobile station that there is at least one frame buffered at the AP for the mobile station. In multicast frames, the AP may also set this subfield to one to indicate that there are more multicast frames buffered at the AP.

- WEP Subfield

  The WEP subfield is a single bit in length. When set to one, it indicates that the frame body of the MAC frame has been encrypted using the WEP algorithm. This subfield may be set to one only in data frames and management frames of subtype authentication. It is zero in all other frame types and subtypes.

- Order Subfield

  This subfield is a single bit in length. When set to one, this subfield indicates that the content of the data frame was provided to the MAC with a request for strictly ordered service. This subfield provides information to the AP and DS to allow this service to be delivered.

Duration/ID Field

The Duration/ID field is 16 bits in length. It alternately contains duration information for updating the NAV or a short ID, called the association ID (AID), used by a mobile station to retrieve frames that are buffered for it at the AP. Because of performance-related reasons, the maximum allowable value for the AID is 2007. All values larger than 2007 are reserved. When bit 15 of the field is zero, the value in bits 14-0 represent the remaining duration of a frame exchange. This value is used for virtual channel sensing to minimize the probability of collisions.

The value of the Duration/ID field is set to 32,768 (i.e., bit 15 is one and all other bits are zero) in all frames transmitted during the CFP. This value is chosen to allow a station that did not receive the beginning of the CFP to recognize that a CFP is ongoing and to prevent it from interfering.

Address Fields

The IEEE 802.11 MAC frame format contains up to four address fields. These additional address types are used to facilitate the level of indirection that allows transparent mobility and to provide a mechanism for filtering multicast frames. A single bit Individual/Group field allows to ascertain if a MAC frame is destined for an individual MAC or for a group (multicast). These important address subfields are described below with their purpose.

- BSS Identifier Subfield

  The BSS Identifier (BSSID) is a unique identifier for a particular BSS of IEEE 802.11 WLAN. In an If-BSS, the BSSID is the MAC address of the AP. In an Id-BSS, the BSSID is a locally administered, individual address that is generated randomly by the station that starts the BSS.

- Transmitter Address Subfield

  The transmitter address (TA) is the address of the MAC that transmitted the frame onto the wireless medium.

- Receiver Address Subfield

  The receiver address (RA) is the address of the MAC to which the frame is sent over the wireless medium. This address may be either an individual or group address.

- Source Address Subfield

  The source address (SA) is the address of the MAC that originated the frame. This address is always an individual address.

- Destination Address Subfield

  The destination address (DA) is the address of the final destination to which the frame is sent. This address may be either an individual or group address.

Sequence Control Field

The sequence control field is a 16-bit field comprising two subfields: The subfileds are a 4-bit fragment number and a 12-bit sequence number. As a whole, this field is used to allow a receiving station to eliminate duplicate received frames. The sequence number subfield holds the 12-bit sequence number assigned sequentially to each MSDU transmitted. The fragment number subfield holds the fragment number assigned to each fragment of an MSDU within a fragment burst.

Frame Body

The frame body field contains the information specific to the particular data or management frames. This field has variable length. It may be as long as 2304 bytes, without WEP encryption. The maximum length of this field is defined by the sum (MSDU + ICV + IV), where ICV and IV are the WEP encryption components.

There are a large number of frames for which the frame body is empty. These are control frames and management frames. Data frames typically have their frame body carrying the MSDU or fragments thereof. It is not unusual to use a Null Data frame in which the frame body is empty. Such a frame can be used to estimate the channel, expending very little overhead for the purpose.

Also, when a MAC frame body is carrying payload for a data frame, the frame is typically called a MAC service data unit, or MSDU. If it is carrying payload for a management frame, it is called a MAC management protocol data unit (MMPDU).

Frame Trailer

The frame trailer, also called frame check sequence (FCS) field, is 32 bits in length. It contains the result of applying the CCITT CRC-32 polynomial to the MAC header and frame body. This is the same polynomial used in other IEEE 802 LAN standards. The frame check sequence in an IEEE 802.11 frame is generated in the same way as it is in IEEE 802.3. The generator polynomial for the CRC is the standard polynomial of degree 32 given by

$$G(x) = x^{32} + x^{26} + x^{23} + x^{22} + x^{16} + x^{12} + x^{11} + x^{10} + x^8 + x^7 + x^5 + x^4 + x^2 + x + 1 \quad (6.1)$$

MAC Frame Subtypes

In what follows, the complete list of frame subtypes for data, management, and control frames are listed along with the context of usage for each subtype.

Data Frame Subtypes

Table 6.2 depicts the different forms in which data frames are employed along with the 4-bit subtype value in the frame control field for each frame. Notably, the format of individual data frames stays the same i.e., same as the canonical IEEE 802.11 frame format. In its simplest manifestation, a data frame consists of a header with an all-zero subtype value and has no payload in the frame body. Also called a Null-frame, the data frame in this form can be used for channel assessment by the PHY layer. The frame body can also be empty for the CF-ACK (no data), CF-Poll (no data), and CF-Ack+CF-Poll (no data) frames. Frames of subtype Data (see Table 6.2) are usable in contention as well as contention-free modes. All frames of subtypes Data+CF-X (where, X=ACK or Poll) are usable in the contention-free period. We note that there are several frame subtypes that have been reserved for as yet unseen purposes.

Control Frame Subtypes

Control frames are typically lightweight, punctuating frames that appear in between or following data frames. The motivation to keep them lightweight is to reduce the overhead imposed on MAC data by the transmission of these accompanying control frames. The Request to Send (RTS), Clear to Send (CTS), and Acknowledgment (ACK) frames are, as their names suggest, used to signal the impending transmission or successful reception of a data frame. The contention free (CF)-End and CF-End+CF-ACK frames are used within the contention-free periods to signal the end of the session and/or the reception of a data frame. Again, a good number of frames are reserved for future purposes. See Table 6.3.

TABLE 6.2   Data Frame Subtype Descriptions

Subtype Description	Type Description	Subtype Value	Type Value
Data	Data	0000	10
Data + CF-ACK	Data	0001	10
Data + CF-Poll	Data	0010	10
Data + CF-ACK + CF-Poll	Data	0011	10
Data + Null function (no data)	Data	0100	10
Data + CF-ACK (no data)	Data	0101	10
Data + CF-Poll (no data)	Data	0110	10
Data + CF-ACK + CF-Poll (no data)	Data	0111	10
Reserved	Data	1000-1111	10
Reserved	Data	0000-1111	11

TABLE 6.3   Control Frame Subtype Descriptions

Subtype Description	Type Description	Subtype Value	Type Value
Reserved	Control	0000-1001	01
Power Save (PS)-Poll	Control	1010	01
Request To Send (RTS)	Control	1011	01
Clear To Send (CTS)	Control	1100	01
Acknowledgement (ACK)	Control	1101	01
Contention Free(CF)-End	Control	1110	01
CF-End + CF-ACK	Control	1111	01

Management Frame Subtypes

For the purposes of network management, there are different management frames defined. For instance, the tasks of association, reassociation (one for request and one for response each), disassociation, and authentication are accomplished by the exchange of frames that go by the same names respectively. Timer synchronization and power-save modes are managed by the exchange of so called beacon and announcement traffic indication map (ATIM) frames. Finally, the task of scanning (which could be active or passive) is carried out by the exchange of probe frames (again, one for request and one for the response). The subtypes of all these management frames are defined in Table 6.4.

Medium Access Control (MAC) for IEEE 802.11 Networks

CHAPTER 6

229

6

MEDIUM ACCESS
CONTROL (MAC)
FOR IEEE 802.11

TABLE 6.4 Management Frame Subtype Descriptions

Subtype Description	Type Description	Subtype Value	Type Value
Association Request	Management	0000	00
Association Response	Management	0001	00
Reassociation Request	Management	0010	00
Reassociation Response	Management	0011	00
Probe Request	Management	0100	00
Probe Response	Management	0101	00
Reserved	Management	0110-0111	00
Beacon	Management	1000	00
Announcement TIM (ATIM)	Management	1001	00
Disassociation	Management	1010	00
Authentication	Management	1011	00
Deauthentication	Management	1100	00
Reserved	Management	1101-1111	00

Frame Fragmentation

We discussed upfront that the wireless nature of the connecting media in IEEE 802.11 WLANs poses some tough issues for the MAC as well as the PHY layer. These challenges are compounded by the presence of competing stations, overlapping BSSs, and other appliances in the global industrial, scientific, and medical (ISM) band at 2.4 GHz. Fragmentation is a MAC-level proposition that essentially tries to minimize the risk of suffering a frame error due to a difficult terrain presented by the PHY. The idea is that a longer frame is more error prone than a shorter frame in a noisy and interference ridden environment. So, the MAC layer chooses to transmit longer frames in several relatively short bursts by breaking up the frame into smaller fragments. This is called *frame fragmentation*. A frame being fragmented is shown in Figure 6.6.

Fragmentation

Fragmentation is a size related function, and is implemented for frames above a certain threshold size. The threshold size for fragmentation is specified by the dot11FragmentationThreshold, a MAC MIB parameter. The tradeoff, of course, (like in the RTS-CTS scheme) is that a slightly higher MAC overhead is incurred due to a greater number of ACK frames (in addition to MAC headers) that require to be transmitted with fragmentation.

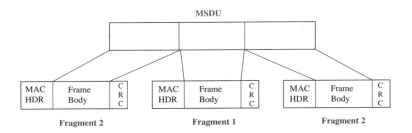

FIGURE 6.6

Fragmentation of a lengthy frame to decrease error probability at the expense of greater overhead is depicted. Notice how the overhead (MAC HDR + CRC) keeps adding up as we break down a single MSDU into several parts.

Frames longer than the fragmentation threshold are fragmented prior to the initial transmission into fragments no longer than the value of the dot11FragmentationThreshold MIB attribute. A frame thus gets split into one or more fragments equal in length to the fragmentation threshold and at most one fragment smaller than the fragmentation threshold. The default value of the fragmentation threshold is such that no frames will be fragmented. The value may be changed to begin fragmenting frames, depending on the nature of the PHY encountered. If the interference source is known, such as from an adjacent BSS or from an appliance in the same band, the value of the fragmentation threshold may be calculated from the transmission characteristics observed in the PHY. The process of transmitting a large frame in fragments is pictorially depicted in Figure 6.7. Typically, fragmentation is applied to unicast frames alone.

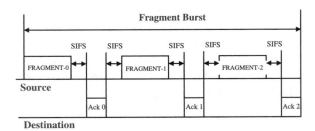

FIGURE 6.7

Transmission of large packets is broken down into multiple fragments to improve data reliability in an error-prone wireless medium. Each fragment is followed by an ACK frame separated only by a SIFS to ensure the burst takes place uninterrupted.[*]

Defragmentation

The process by which frame fragments (MPDUs) in a burst are recombined to form an MSDU or an MMPDU is termed defragmentation. Defragmentation is accomplished at every frame

---

[*]*From IEEE Std. 802.11a-1999. Copyright © 1999 IEEE. All rights reserved.*

Medium Access Control (MAC) for IEEE 802.11 Networks

CHAPTER 6

231

6

MEDIUM ACCESS
CONTROL (MAC)
FOR IEEE 802.11

reception point. In order to defragment a frame, all fragments must first be successfully received. Thus, the MAC allows for the usual ACK mechanism to ensure that a failed transmission is retried, until all fragments are received. The number of attempts before a fragmented MSDU or MMPDU is discarded is specified by the dot11ShortRetryLimit and aLongRetryLimit parameters. Each successfully transmitted fragment has a Sequence Control field consisting of a sequence number and fragment number. The More Fragments subfield of the Sequence Control field indicates if a fragment is the last one in the burst of fragments. Thus, the Sequence Control field is key to defragmentation. If a fragment is not delivered on the first attempt, subsequent fragments are not transmitted until the previous fragment has been acknowledged. If a fragment is not acknowledged, the normal rules for retransmission of frames apply.

MAC Data Services

In this section, MAC data services, which are responsible for carrying out data frame exchanges between WLAN stations, will be presented. First, the MAC data communication protocol will be described, for both non real-time and real-time data traffic. A special type of protocol using RTS and CTS control frames (typically used to reduce collision probability) will then be presented.

Distributed Coordination Function

The fundamental access method used by the MAC for an IEEE 802.11 OFDM WLAN is a distributed control mechanism, wherein each station (i.e., terminal) has a fair chance of accessing the medium. This technique, sometimes called distributed coordination function (DCF), is based on a carrier sense multiple access (CSMA) with collision avoidance (CA) or CSMA/CA protocol. The DCF constitutes the basic access mechanism in IEEE 802.11 LANs, and is the basis for all other protocols defined. In the CSMA/CA-based DCF, a station senses activity on the medium; if the medium is found idle, the station transmits data; if the medium is found busy, the station does not transmit so that a collision is avoided. In order to avoid a collision, the station (which attempts to transmit but detects activity) picks a random backoff time in multiples of slot-times and waits until the backoff clock reaches zero again. CSMA/CA is both equitable and suitable for a wireless network (where collision detection is not feasible).

Carrier Sense Mechanism

The physical mechanism to detect a carrier (i.e., transmission activity) on the medium constitutes the first step in the DCF. In practice, a station also has a virtual carrier sense mechanism built-in. This is by virtue of the Network Allocation Vector (NAV), which always has the latest information possible on scheduled transmissions on the medium. The NAV acts as a backup mechanism to avoid collisions—if perchance a carrier is not sensed by physical means (due to shadowing effects), the NAV can hopefully provide correct information on medium activity. Thus, a station does not attempt to transmit until both physical and virtual carrier sense mechanisms concur on the medium being idle.

Backoff Procedure

The DCF protocol mandates that every station that attempts to transmit (but just stops short of transmission upon sensing a busy medium) or successfully transmits a frame must execute a backoff. During backoff the station releases occupation of the medium for a random amount of time. This ensures low probability of collision and fair access opportunities for other aspiring stations. The value picked for the backoff clock is a uniformly distributed random number in the contention window [0, CWmax], where the units are slottimes. The backoff procedure is dictated by a binary exponential backoff algorithm, wherein each successive attempt to transmit the same packet is preceded by backoff within a window that is double the size used previously. A sample choice of backoff windows is illustrated in Figure 6.8. The backoff clock is decremented during a given slottime only if the medium is detected to be idle. Although it is an equitable procedure, the DCF is not very suited to real-time applications. A good performance evaluation of asynchronous data transfer protocols for WLANs, throughput studies and some basic improvements can be found in [5, 6].

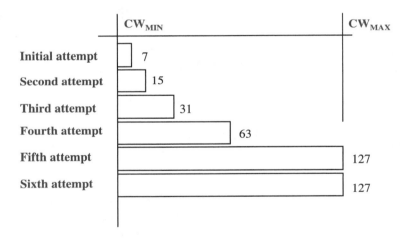

FIGURE 6.8

Illustration of the truncated binary exponential backoff algorithm: the doubling of backoff window with every successive attempt to transmit the same frame for typical asynchronous data transfer is shown. Normally, a frame is dropped if not transmitted within a finite (2-3) number of attempts.

Interframe Spacings

The notion of interframe spacings becomes immediately apparent when one is faced with a need to provide multiple priorities for medium access. For instance, in the next section, a method of medium access for real-time data called PCF is described which typically has higher priority over DCF (due to the data being time-sensitive). How does one ensure that stations implementing PCF have higher priority over DCF? The answer lies in the interframe spacings mandated by the MAC protocol.

Medium Access Control (MAC) for IEEE 802.11 Networks

CHAPTER 6

233

6

MEDIUM ACCESS
CONTROL (MAC)
FOR IEEE 802.11

According to the IEEE 802.11 MAC, successive frames must be separated by a minimum inter-frame spacing (or separation) defined as the short interframe spacing (SIFS). A SIFS is the minimum time-gap between any two frames, no matter what type. A DCF interframe spacing (DIFS) is the relevant IFS when applied to DCF stations. Thus, a frame sequence by any DCF station must begin at least a DIFS interval after any other frame sequence. Similarly, a PCF interframe spacing (PIFS) is the least spacing that must be allowed by a station implementing PCF, following any other frame sequence. Lastly, an extended IFS (EIFS) is the spacing required between a station's attempt to retransmit a failed packet and any preceding frame sequence.

Clearly, it would be desirable to have *SIFS < PIFS < DIFS < EIFS* to ensure a higher priority of PCF over DCF, and of a fresh DCF transmission over a DCF retransmission. Indeed, the value of SIFS = $16\mu S$, PIFS = $25\mu S$, DIFS = $34\mu S$, and EIFS = $43\mu S$ with an increment of a slottime = $9\mu S$ every step. Thus, as illustrated in Figure 6.9, by means of a suitable set of IFSs employed in the system, one ensures that different priorities are implicitly assigned to different requests for medium access.

Fragment Bursts

As seen in the previous section, "MAC Frame Formats," a large frame is often fragmented into smaller frames and sent out in a burst of successive fragments, separated by acknowledgment frames. The motivation for this is primarily to reduce the likelihood of the frame going in error (since longer frames are more error prone). The purpose of fragmentation is served by keeping a fragment burst uninterrupted, and this is accomplished by ensuring that consecutive frames in a fragment burst only need to be separated by a SIFS interval, the shortest possible IFS. Normal IFS rules take over once the fragment burst is over.

Relevant Frame Sequences

In Table 6.5, we summarize the list of valid frame sequences that can take place for data exchange during the DCF mode of operation. The shortest sequence constitutes a broadcast or multicast data frame. The longest frame sequence (i.e., with maximum overhead) comprises a fragment burst, with several interspersed acknowledgments, and starting with an RTS and CTS frame exchange (more of which in an upcoming subsection).

TABLE 6.5 Data frame exchange descriptions within DCF and RTS-CTS mode of operation. Items enclosed in [. .] may occur zero to many times, whereas items enclosed in {. .} may occur zero to one time in a sequence.

Frame Sequence	Frame Sequence Usage
Data (broadcast/multicast)	Broadcast or multicast MSDU
Data (dir)-ACK	Directed MSDU
[Frag-ACK-]Last-ACK	Directed MSDU or MMPDU
{RTS-CTS-}[Frag-ACK-]Last-ACK	Directed MSDU or MMPDU

Point Coordination Function

Apart from DCF, the other access method based on priority is a centrally controlled one. Referred to as the point coordination function (PCF), this technique employs a contention-free period during which stations with higher priority are permitted to access the medium. In this access method, control vests with a centralized coordinator, usually the access point. For this reason, the AP is also referred to as a point coordinator (PC), and PCF requires that a BSS be infrastructure type. PCF is preferred when supporting time-bound services. PCF works by polling stations for contention-free traffic, and if a station has any CF data, it is collected by the PC during PCF and routed to the destination within the same BSS or to another BSS.

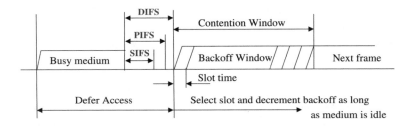

FIGURE 6.9

Different interframe spacings (IFS) in the distributed coordination function employed for asynchronous data transfer. The SIFS is the shortest spacing that needs to exist between any two frames; DIFS is used to start a DCF exchange, and PIFS is employed to begin a PCF exchange.[*]

Medium Access Mechanism

The basic access method during PCF is controlled by the PC resident in the AP. The PC gains control of the medium using DCF rules at the beginning of a CFP. It retains control of the medium throughout the CFP by waiting a SIFS shorter than the rest of the DCF stations (recall, *PIFS = DIFS–Slottime < DIFS*). Every station, whether it is party to the CFP or not, takes note of the CFP's intended length (i.e., maximum duration) from the PC and stores it in the NAV, and that helps in reducing contention during PCF. After the initial Beacon frame announcing the start of a CFP, the PC waits a SIFS period and transmits one of the following: a CF-Poll frame (polling stations for CF-data frames), a Data frame (transmitting buffered CF-traffic for a station), Data+CF–Poll frame (for buffered traffic in addition to a frame polling all stations), or a CF-End frame (to signal that the CFP is null, and that the CFP ends immediately). Following the CF-End frame, stations resume DCF functionality in contention mode again.

Medium Access Control (MAC) for IEEE 802.11 Networks

CHAPTER 6

235

6

MEDIUM ACCESS
CONTROL (MAC)
FOR IEEE 802.11

Contention-Free Polling

During the CFP, in an infrastructure BSS, the AP maintains a polling list which is simply a roster of all stations that are eligible to receive CF-Polls. Notably, the CF-Poll list helps the PC determine which station has (uplink) CF-data to be transmitted. The PC does not need a CF-Poll list to transmit (downlink) data to stations. The stations listed on the CF-Poll list are called CF-Pollable stations. The CF-Poll list is obviously a *logical* construct that is invisible to all but the MAC in the AP. The AP issues CF-Poll frames during the CFP in ascending order of Association ID (AID) value within the CF-Pollable stations. Different stations themselves are supposed to indicate their CF-Pollability within the Capability Information field of their Association and Reassociation Request frames while joining a BSS. Should their CF-Pollability status change, they are supposed to perform a reassociation and in the process indicate the change of status. In order to maximize the efficiency, the AP always considers piggybacking CF-Poll frames along with Data frames and acknowledgment frames sent in the downlink.

Frame Exchange Procedure

PCF stands in stark contrast to DCF in respect of frame exchange procedure and bandwidth efficiency. DCF offers truly distributed control, but access to the channel is subject to user-density (i.e., number of users in the BSS) as well as aggregate network traffic. Although DCF never guarantees access to the medium, it delivers a data packet to the destination in just one hop (in the best case), as shown in Figure 6.10. In contrast, PCF offers almost guaranteed access to the medium with assured QoS. However, from a bandwidth perspective, it is half as efficient as DCF since each data transmission is routed through the AP and takes two hops from source to destination: source station to AP and then AP back to destination station. Thus, one can trade off dependable access to the medium for bandwidth efficiency and vice versa by choosing the right protocol between DCF and PCF.

CFP Timing Structure

It is possible to have both DCF and PCF within the same network, with alternating time slots for DCF and PCF operation. In such a scenario, the PCF will have a higher priority over the DCF at all times. The ratio of contention-period and contention-free periods is typically fixed in proportion to the expected DCF and PCF traffic, respectively. In Figure 6.11, we illustrate how, ideally, the contention period and CFP alternate periodically with a period given by the CF repetition interval. Also notice how the NAV is set at the beginning of the CFP and reset at its end. Within each period (DCF and PCF), the fragment bursts are spaced a SIFS apart; however, the beginning of the DCF and PCF is marked by a DIFS and PIFS spacing as depicted in Figure 6.11. Also, within the PCF, notice that in the absence of a response to a CF-Poll (which is expected soon after a SIFS interval), the PC resumes CF-Polling other stations after a PIFS interval. All timing windows are carefully defined to provide prioritized access and to minimize contention where possible.

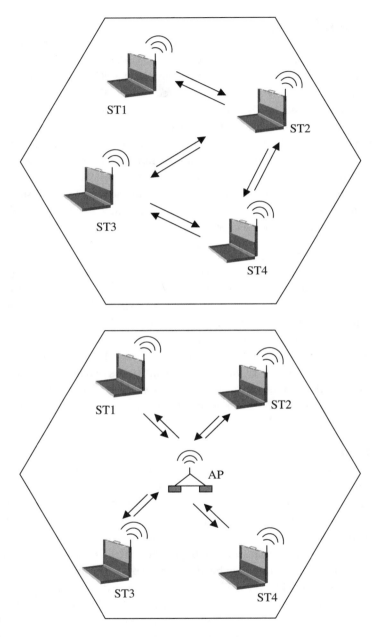

FIGURE 6.10

An Id-BSS and an If-BSS are contrasted in this diagram. Within an independent BSS, one trades off reliable medium access for better bandwidth efficiency when compared to an infrastructure BSS.

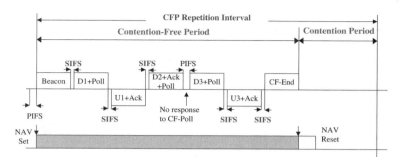

FIGURE 6.11

The timing structure of a CFP when it is overlaid on a regular system implementing pure DCF is shown. The sum of the contention-free period and the contention period determine the CFP repetition interval.[*]

Relevant Frame Sequences

The permitted frame sequences within the PCF mode of operation are listed in Table 6.6. We find that data frame sequences during the CFP tend to occur on a queried basis. A frame is sent up to the AP only in response to a CF-Poll, never otherwise. Also, every data frame needs an ACK, whether in the uplink or downlink. In order to minimize the MAC overhead associated with these additional frames, the MAC is designed to exploit piggyback modes whenever applicable, as opposed to sending individual data frames, CF-Polls or ACK frames.

TABLE 6.6 Data frame exchange descriptions within PCF mode of operation. Items enclosed in [. .] may occur zero to many times, whereas items enclosed in {. .} may occur zero to one time in a sequence.

Frame Sequence	Frame Sequence Usage
Data(dir)+CF-Poll{+CF-ACK}-Data(dir)+CF-ACK-{CF-ACK(no data)}	Poll and ACK sent with MPDUs
Data(dir)+CF-Poll{+CF-ACK}-CF-ACK(no data)	Poll of STA with empty queue, insufficient time for queued MPDU, or too little time remaining before dwell or medium occupancy boundary to send a queued frame
CF-Poll(no data){+CF-ACK}-Data(dir)-{CF-ACK(no data)}	Separate poll, ACK sent with MPDU
CF-Poll(no data){+CF-ACK}-Data(dir)-ACK	Polled STA sends to STA in BSS

Continued

TABLE 6.6   Continued

Frame Sequence	Frame Sequence Usage
CF-Poll(no data){+CF-ACK}- Null(no data)	Separate poll, STA queue empty, or insufficient time for queued MPDU or too little time remaining before a dwell or medium occupancy boundary to send a queued frame
Data(dir){+CF-ACK}-ACK	ACK if not CF-Pollable or not polled

Frame Exchange with RTS/CTS

The use of RTS/CTS handshaking messages is particularly advantageous in the presence of *hidden terminals*, i.e., pairs of terminals which may not directly hear one another due to signal fading and attenuation. RTS/CTS handshaking can be shown to improve MAC efficiency for larger MPDUs even when terminals are not hidden from each other. Consider the medium utilization overhead involved in RTS/CTS handshaking. This is given by the sum of length of the RTS and CTS frames and twice the SIFS, as seen in Figure 6.12. This leads to:

$$\text{Overhead}_{(RTS/CTS)} = RTS + CTS + 2SIFS$$

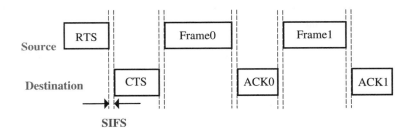

FIGURE 6.12

The use of RTS and CTS frames for a typical frame sequence is illustrated here. At the expense of a little overhead, the use of RTS/CTS can guarantee an uninterrupted channel leading to a high probability of successful frame transmission.

If RTS/CTS handshaking is not used, the MPDU may be transmitted immediately following the DIFS. However, when a collision occurs, the other stations waiting to transmit would require to wait for the entire MPDU to be transmitted, instead of merely the RTS message exchange. Thus, the extra duration of time which is wasted by transmitting the MPDU without an RTS/CTS exchange is given by $P_{coll} \times (MPDU - RTS)$, where P_{coll} represents the collision probability. Thus, it can be seen that when this expected time exceeds the RTS/CTS overhead, it is better to use RTS/CTS handshaking. Rearranging terms, one can see that RTS/CTS handshaking is profitable when

$$MPDU > RTS + \frac{RTS + CTS + 2SIFS}{P_{coll}} = MPDU_{thresh}$$

where $MPDU_{thresh}$ is a threshold value for the MPDU, exceeding which RTS/CTS handshaking may be used for greater efficiency.

MAC Management Services

In this section, the most significant MAC management functions from an OFDM-WLAN standpoint such as MAC power management, synchronization, MAC session management, and data privacy are described.

Power Management

Much effort has been devoted in recent times to make portable devices more power efficient. These efforts have been in designing efficient power amplifiers, designing low-power CMOS VLSI circuits to do baseband processing as well as designing batteries with longer life. An important step in the same direction has been the development of power-save algorithms. The incentives to save power are potentially significant because true portability requires standalone operation on battery power. The power management schemes listed in the IEEE 802.11 standard are arguably also the most complex. MAC power management allows mobile stations, in either an Id-BSS or an If-BSS, to enter low power modes of operation where they turn off their receivers and transmitters to conserve power.

The MAC power management services comprise mainly two parts which are distinctly different: MAC power management for an Id-BSS and MAC power management for an If-BSS. Let us recall that an Id-BSS can just be a set of communicating stations, whereas an If-BSS requires an AP. The frames used for the power management functions as well as the basic protocol are described below for the two setups.

Power Management in an Independent BSS

Power management in an Id-BSS is a fully distributed process, managed by the individual mobile stations. Power management is accomplished in two parts: a station announcing its intent to enter a low-power operating mode and the functions executed by the remaining stations of the Id-BSS to communicate with the station in power-save (PS) mode. An IEEE WLAN station enters a low-power operating state, wherein it turns off the receiver and transmitter to conserve power, when it successfully completes a data frame handshake with another station with the power management bit set in the frame header. There is no requirement on the other PS station to complete this handshake. If the station has no data to send, it may use the null function subtype of the data frame for this handshake. The station must remain awake until this frame handshake is completed successfully. A station may enter PS-mode any time it desires. Once the station has successfully completed the frame handshake with the power management bit set, it may enter the power saving state. In the PS state, the station is in touch with the network by waking up to every Beacon transmission. The station in fact stays awake for a period of time after each Beacon, called the *announcement* or *ad hoc traffic indication message* window (ATIM). The earliest moment that the station may go back to the PS state is at the ATIM window. It is during the ATIM window that other stations attempting to send frames to it will announce those frames. Upon receipt of a TIM frame, it is incumbent on the PS-station to acknowledge that frame and remain awake until the end of the next ATIM window, following the next Beacon frame, in order to allow the other station to send its data frame.

A natural question that arises is, how does one station desiring to send a frame to another station in an Id-BSS assess the PS-state of the latter? The estimate of the PS-state of another station may be based on the last data frame received from the station and on other information local to the sending station. How exactly the sending station creates its estimate of the PS-state of the intended destination is not described in the Standard. If the sending station determines that the intended destination is in the PS-mode, the sending station may not transmit its frame until after it has received an acknowledgment of an ATIM frame, sent during the ATIM window, from the intended destination. Once an acknowledgment of the ATIM is received, the station will send the corresponding data frame after the conclusion of the ATIM window. The sequence of frame exchanges for power-saving in an Id-BSS is illustrated in Figure 6.13.

Multicast frames must also be announced by the sending station during the ATIM window before they may be transmitted. The ATIM is sent to the same multicast address as the data frame that will be sent subsequently. Because the ATIM is sent to a multicast address, no acknowledgment will be generated, nor is one expected. Any stations that wish to receive the announced multicast data frame must stay awake until the end of the next ATIM window, after the next Beacon frame. The station sending the multicast data frame may send it at any time after the conclusion of the ATIM window.

It is evident that the power management protocol described above places a slightly heavier burden on the sending station than on the receiving station. Sending stations must send an announcement frame in addition to the data frame they desire to deliver to the PS-destination. Sending stations must also buffer the frames meant for the PS-destination until the PS-station awakens and acknowledges the ATIM. Because of the nature of the wireless medium, it may require several attempts before an ATIM is acknowledged. Each transmission of an ATIM consumes power at the sending station. The receiving station must awaken for every Beacon and ATIM window, but need not make any transmissions unless it receives an ATIM frame. Such a power management protocol could yield reasonable power savings in all mobile stations. However, there is a minimum duty cycle required of both senders and destinations, in the ratio of the time of the ATIM window to the time of the beacon period, that limits the maximum power savings that may be achieved.

Medium Access Control (MAC) for IEEE 802.11 Networks

CHAPTER 6

241

6

MEDIUM ACCESS
CONTROL (MAC)
FOR IEEE 802.11

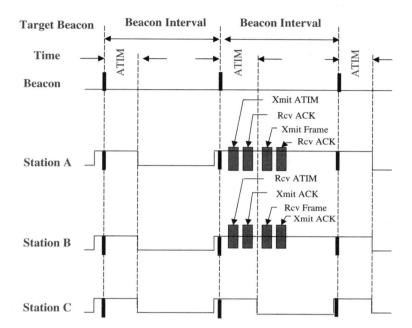

FIGURE 6.13

Power management illustrated for an independent BSS comprising several stations that alternately transmit Beacon frames and ensure that at least one station stays in the awake mode.[*]

Power Management in an Infrastructure BSS

In contrast to an Id-BSS, the AP in an infrastructure BSS holds the key to power management. While this necessitates the presence of a significantly more capable AP within the BSS, it takes the onus off from the stations to execute power-save protocols. An AP-centric power management protocol also allows significantly greater power savings for mobile stations than does the protocol used in Id-BSSs. The AP in an infrastructure BSS assumes all the burden of buffering data frames for power saving stations and delivering them when the stations request, allowing the mobile stations to stay in PS-modes for substantially longer periods.

The responsibilities of the mobile stations in an infrastructure BSS are to inform the AP, in its association request, of the number of beacon periods that the station will be in its power saving mode, to awaken at the expected time of a Beacon transmission to learn if there are any data frames waiting, and to complete a successful frame handshake with the AP, while the power management bit is set, to inform the AP when the station will enter the power saving mode. A mobile station can achieve much deeper power savings here than in the Id-BSS, because it is not required to awaken for every Beacon, nor to stay awake for any length of time after the Beacons for which it does awaken. The mobile station must however awaken at times determined by the AP, when multicast frames are to be delivered. This time is indicated in the Beacon frames as the delivery traffic indication map (DTIM). If the mobile station is to receive multicast frames, it must be awake at every DTIM. The process of power-control using DTIMs is shown in Figure 6.14.

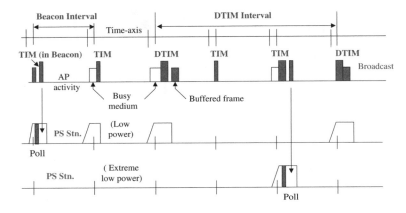

FIGURE 6.14

Power management in an infrastructure BSS wherein a DTIM-bearing Beacon frame is transmitted once every three TIM-bearing Beacon frames (i.e., DTIM interval = 3 × TIM interval). This allows sleep modes wherein a station can be in sleep mode most of the time, except when a DTIM-bearing Beacon is expected. [*]

The AP, as part of its responsibilities, will buffer data frames for each PS-mode station that it has associated with. It will also buffer all multicast frames if it has any stations associated that are in the PS-mode. The data frames will remain buffered at the AP for a minimum time not less than the number of Beacon periods indicated in the mobile station's association request. The IEEE 802.11 Standard specifies that an AP may use an aging algorithm to discard buffered frames that are older than it is required to preserve, although a specific algorithm is not described. Once the AP has frames buffered for a power saving station, it will indicate this in the traffic indication map (TIM) sent with each Beacon frame.

The actual mechanism used to indicate buffered traffic by the AP to the station is based on the AID field in the association response frame. Every station that is associated with the AP is assigned an AID during the association process. The AID indicates a single bit in the TIM that reflects the state of frames buffered for that station. When the bit in the TIM is set, there is at least

---

[*] *From IEEE Std. 802.11a-1999. Copyright © 1999 IEEE. All rights reserved.*

Medium Access Control (MAC) for IEEE 802.11 Networks

CHAPTER 6

243

6

MEDIUM ACCESS
CONTROL (MAC)
FOR IEEE 802.11

one frame buffered for the corresponding station. When the bit is clear, there are no frames buffered for the corresponding station. A special AID, AID zero, is dedicated to indicating the status of buffered multicast traffic. The AP will send the TIM, updated with the latest buffer status, with every Beacon.

If an AP has any buffered multicast frames, those frames are sent immediately after the Beacon announcing the DTIM. If there is more than one multicast frame to be sent, the AP will indicate this fact by setting the More Data bit in the Frame Control field of each multicast frame except for the last to be sent. Following the transmission of any buffered multicast frames, the AP will send frames to active stations and to those stations that have requested the delivery of frames buffered for them. A mobile station requests delivery of buffered frames by sending a PS-Poll frame to the AP. The AP will respond to each PS-Poll by sending one frame to the requesting station. In the Frame Control field of the frame sent in response to the PS-Poll, the AP will set the more data bit if there are further frames buffered for the station. The station is required to send a PS-Poll to the AP for each data frame it receives with the More Data bit set. This ensures that the station will empty the buffer of frames held for it by the AP. The Standard does not state any time requirement for the station to send the PS-Poll after seeing the More Data bit. Thus, some implementations may rapidly retrieve all buffered frames from the AP and others may operate at a more leisurely pace.

An AP that is also a point-coordinator running a contention-free period (CFP) will use the CFP to deliver buffered frames to stations that are CF Pollable. It may also use the CFP to deliver multicast frames after the DTIM announced.

Synchronization

In order to reliably communicate, stations within a BSS need to have their clocks synchronized (at least every so often). Synchronization is the process by which the MAC keeps station clocks in step. The process involves transmitting Beacon frames to announce the presence of a BSS, and stations scanning to find a BSS. Once a station finds a BSS as a result of the scan, it joins the BSS and thereafter keeps its clock in step with that of other members in the BSS. The process of keeping the clocks in step relies on a common timebase, provided by a timer synchronization function (TSF). The TSF maintains a 64-bit timer running at 1 MHz, and periodically updates it employing information from other stations.

Synchronization, as in power management, can be entirely distributed between the stations or it could be centrally coordinated by the AP. Thus, the procedure is distinctly different for independent and infrastructure BSSs. The tasks accompanying synchronization—namely, scanning and joining a BSS—tend to be similar in both independent and infrastructure BSSs. Synchronization procedures for the two types of BSSs will be presented first.

Timer Synchronization in an Infrastructure BSS

At the heart of synchronization is the periodic transmission of Beacon frames. In an infrastructure BSS (If-BSS), the AP is responsible for transmitting a Beacon frame periodically. The time between Beacon frames is called the beacon period and its value is embedded within the Beacon frame, in order to inform stations receiving the Beacon when to expect the next Beacon. The AP attempts to transmit the Beacon frame at the target Beacon transmission time (TBTT); i.e., when the value of the TSF timer of the AP, modulo the beacon period is zero. Note, however, that the Beacon is like any other frame, and is sent using the same rules for accessing the medium. Thus, the Beacon could be delayed beyond the TBTT owing to inaccessibility of the medium and back-off delays. In a lightly loaded BSS, the Beacon is usually sent at the TBTT and is spaced apart by exactly the beacon period. As the load increases in the BSS, the Beacon tends to get delayed beyond the TBTT more often.

The TSF timer within an AP is reset to zero upon initialization of the AP and is then incremented by the 1 MHz clock of the AP. At the time of each Beacon, the current value of the timer is inserted in the Beacon frame. A mobile station updates its TSF timer with the value of the timer in the Beacon frame from the AP, modified by any processing time required to perform the update operation. Thus, in an If-BSS, the timers in all the mobile stations receiving the Beacon are synchronized to that of the AP.

Timer Synchronization in an Independent BSS

In an independent BSS (Id-BSS), since there is no AP, the mobile station that starts the BSS begins by resetting its TSF timer to zero and transmits a Beacon, choosing a beacon period. That establishes the basic beaconing process for an Id-BSS. After the BSS has established, each station in the Id-BSS attempts to send a Beacon after the TBTT arrives. To ensure that at least one Beacon frame is sent during each beacon period, and to minimize collision of multiple Beacon frames on the medium, each station in the BSS chooses a random delay value which it allows to expire after the TBTT. This process of variable-delay beacon generation is illustrated in Figure 6.15. If the station receives a Beacon from another station in the BSS before the delay expires, the receiving station's Beacon transmission is cancelled. If, however, the expiry of the delay clock coincides with the station receiving a Beacon, the Beacon transmitter proceeds to send another beacon. The resulting collision of Beacons could potentially lead to poor reception of the Beacon for some receivers and good reception for others. Also, some receivers may receive more than one Beacon in a single beacon period. This operation is permitted in the Standard and causes no degradation or confusion in receiving stations.

Beaconing in an Id-BSS can also interact with power management algorithms. The Standard requires that the station, or stations, that send a Beacon frame must not enter power-save mode until they receive a Beacon frame from another station in the BSS. This simply ensures that there is at least one station in the Id-BSS awake and able to respond to Probe Request frames.

Medium Access Control (MAC) for IEEE 802.11 Networks

CHAPTER 6

245

6

MEDIUM ACCESS
CONTROL (MAC)
FOR IEEE 802.11

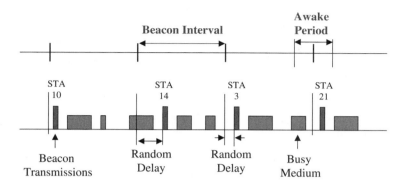

FIGURE 6.15

The generation of Beacons in an Id-BSS is subjected to CSMA deferrals, which can cause a perceptible deviation between actual Beacon arrivals and their nominal occurrence time.[*]

In an Id-BSS, a station updates its TSF timer with the value in the received Beacon frame if the received value, after modifying it for processing times, is greater than its current timer value. If the received value is less than (i.e., outdated compared to) the local timer value, the received value is discarded. The effect of this selective updating of the TSF timer and the distributed nature of beaconing in an Id-BSS is to spread the value of the TSF timer of the station with the fastest running clock throughout the Id-BSS. Clearly, the speed with which the fastest timer value spreads is dependent on the number of stations in the BSS and whether all stations are able to communicate directly. For a lightly loaded Id-BSS, the spread of the fastest timer is quick, and the propagation tends to slow down as the network load increases.

Scanning

For a station to begin communication, it must first locate either stations within an Id-BSS or an AP within an If-BSS. This process of finding another station or AP is called *scanning*. Scanning can be either a passive or an active process. Passive scanning typically involves only listening for IEEE 802.11 traffic, whereas active scanning requires the scanning station to transmit and elicit responses from other IEEE 802.11 stations and APs.

Passive scanning is designed to locate a BSS while minimizing the power expended. A station achieves this end by not transmitting, only listening. During passive scanning, a station moves to a channel and listens for Beacon and Probe response frames, extracting a description of a BSS from each of these frames received. The station repeats this operation by "scanning" different channels, until it finds lock with a BSS. While passive scanning conserves power, the process tends to be slow compared to active scanning.

Active scanning allows a station to find a BSS while minimizing the time spent scanning. The station achieves this by actively transmitting queries that elicit responses from stations in a BSS. In an active scan, the station moves to a channel and transmits a Probe Request frame. If there is a BSS on the channel that matches the SSID in the Probe Request frame, the station that sent the latest Beacon frame within the said BSS responds by sending a Probe Response frame to the scanning station. In an If-BSS, this would be the AP, while in an Id-BSS it would be the last station to send a Beacon.

Joining a BSS

A successful scan that results in location of one or more BSSs is usually followed by the station joining one of the BSSs. The joining process is a purely local process, and occurs entirely internal to the IEEE 802.11 mobile station.

Joining a BSS requires that all the portable station's MAC and PHY parameters be synchronized with the desired BSS. First, the station must update its TSF timer with the value of the timer from the BSS description, modified by adding the time elapsed since the description was acquired. This will synchronize the TSF timer to the BSS. In addition, the station needs to adopt the BSSID of the BSS, the parameters in the capability information field, the Beacon period, and the DTIM period. Once this process is complete, the mobile station is said to have joined the BSS and is ready to begin communicating with the other stations in the BSS.

Session Management

An IEEE 802.11 WLAN brings to fore issues not encountered previously in wired media. The convenience that a wireless medium provides is also accompanied with a vulnerability that requires special management capabilities in the MAC layer. These combined management capabilities supported by the WLAN's MAC are termed *session management* in this chapter simply because they assist in reliably and securely conducting a communication session within a BSS.

An intermittent connection to the wireless medium (unlike an "always ON" connection) constitutes the first challenge posed by the wireless medium in a WLAN. Exposure to potential eavesdroppers is the second challenge leading to the need for authentication of users and for data privacy or encryption. The third challenge is to handle the potential portability of a WLAN device across BSSs. To meet these challenges, the IEEE 802.11 MAC defines specific functions such as authentication, association, address filtering and privacy. Some of these topics will be the focus of this section and the next.

Authentication

In order to prevent unauthorized WLAN users to participate in the network, a WLAN provides for authentication, wherein a station proves its identity to another station in the WLAN. Authentication consists of an exchange of questions, proofs, assertions, and results. If the proofs exchanged are acceptable, each station would then tell the other that its assertion of identity is

Medium Access Control (MAC) for IEEE 802.11 Networks

CHAPTER 6

247

6

MEDIUM ACCESS
CONTROL (MAC)
FOR IEEE 802.11

believed. Authentication can be used between any two stations. However, it is most useful when used between a mobile station and an AP in an infrastructure LAN. In an If-BSS, the AP is the point of entry for any mobile station into the ESS and, possibly, into the wired LAN behind the ESS.

The IEEE 802.11 Standard makes two authentication algorithms available. The first algorithm, open system authentication, is not really an authentication algorithm at all. It is a placeholder for those users of IEEE 802.11 that do not wish to implement the WEP algorithms necessary for stronger authentication. Typically, station A would assert its identity to station B, and station B would respond with a successful result for the authentication. There is no verification of the identity of either station.

The second authentication algorithm is the shared key authentication algorithm. This algorithm depends on both stations having a copy of a shared WEP key. This algorithm uses the WEP encryption option to encrypt and decrypt a "challenge text" as evidence that the stations share the same key. Beginning the authentication process, station A sends its identity assertion to station B. Station B responds to the assertion with an assertion of its own and a request to station A to prove its identity by correctly encrypting the challenge text. Station A encrypts the challenge text (actually the entire frame body of the authentication management frame) using the normal WEP encryption rules, including use of default and key mapping keys, and sends the result back to station B. Station B decrypts the frame using the appropriate key and returns an authentication management frame to station A with the success or failure of the authentication indicated. If the authentication is successful, the standard says that each station is authenticated to the other.

Notably, this algorithm only authenticates station A to station B. The IEEE 802.11 Working Group believed that the AP somehow occupied a more privileged position than the mobile stations when it came to authentication, since it is always the mobile station that initiates the authentication process. It is for this reason that it is only the mobile station that performs the encryption operation on the challenge text. This leaves the IEEE 802.11 WLAN open to some potential security problems. In particular, a rogue AP could adopt the SSID of the ESS and announce its presence through the normal beaconing process. Once mobile stations manage to authenticate with the rogue, the rogue station can assume the role of the AP and deny access at will to other stations.

Association

A WLAN requires a station to "associate" itself with a BSS because, unlike in wired media, the stations can move from one BSS to another. Association is the process of a mobile station "connecting" (and, requesting for service) to an AP within a BSS, and through association, a station lets the network know of its current position in the ESS. Association may only be accomplished after a successful authentication has been completed. When a mobile station requests to be connected to the WLAN, it sends an association request to an AP. The association request includes information on the capabilities of the station, such as the data rates it supports, the high rate PHY options it supports, its contention-free capabilities, its support of WEP, and any request for contention-free services. The association request also includes information about the length of time that the station may be in a low-power operating mode. The information in an association request is used by the AP to decide whether to grant the association for the mobile station. The policies and algorithms used by the AP to make this decision are not described in the Standard. Considerations to granting association include supporting the required data-rate modes needed in the BSS, requirement for contention-free services, power-save modes desired by the station, the ability of the AP to provide buffering support, and the overall CFP traffic already being handled by the AP. When the AP responds to the mobile station with an association response, the response includes a status indication. The status indication provides the mobile station with the success or failure of the association request. If the request fails, the reason for that failure is in the status indication. Once a station is associated, the AP is responsible for forwarding data frames from the mobile station toward their destination.

Because the station is mobile and also because the medium is subject to both slow and fast variations, the mobile station will eventually lose contact with the AP. When this occurs, the mobile station must begin a new association in order to continue exchanging data frames. Because the DS must maintain information about the location of each mobile station, and because data frames may have been sent to an AP with which the mobile station no longer can communicate, a mobile station will use a reassociation request after its initial association. The reassociation request includes all of the information in the original association request, plus the address of the last AP with which the station was associated. The last AP's address allows the AP receiving the reassociation request to retrieve any frames at the old AP and deliver them to the mobile station. Once the AP grants the reassociation, the mobile station's older association is terminated. The mobile station is allowed to have only one location in the ESS so that there is no ambiguity as to where frames destined for that mobile station should be sent. Thus, the station is permitted only a single association.

Relationship Between States

The state of a given portable station in a WLAN from a MAC services perspective is threefold: [unauthenticated, unassociated], [authenticated, unassociated], and [authenticated, associated]. The current state of existence of two communicating IEEE MAC stations determines the scope of their relationship, and the frame exchanges possible between them. In Figure 6.16, we illustrate these possibilities, with the frames grouped into three classes; the states shown encircled refer to the state of the sending station with respect to the intended receiving station. As shown in Figure 6.16, the frames are most restricted (to Class-1 frames only) in State 1, and least restricted (permitting Class-1, Class-2 and Class-3 frames) in State 3. Class-1 frames are least restricted frames relating to very elementary functions such as RTS/CTS, ACK, Beacons etc., while Class-3 frames are most restricted such as data frames, deauthentication, and power-save mode (PS-Poll) frames. This hierarchy turns out to be logical with State 3 being the most privileged state.

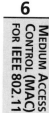

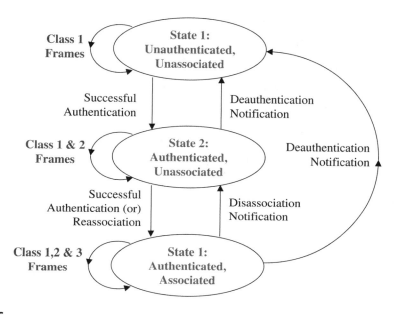

FIGURE 6.16

A hierarchical state diagram showing the valid frame exchanges possible under different states of authentication and association within a BSS. State 1 is the least privileged allowing minimal exchanges, while State 3 is most privileged permitting several types of frame exchanges. [*]

Address Filtering

The address filtering mechanism in the IEEE 802.11 WLAN is a bit more complex than that of other IEEE 802 LANs. In a WLAN, it is not sufficient to make receive decisions on the destination address alone. There may be more than one IEEE 802.11 WLAN operating in the same location and on the same medium and channel. In this case, the receiver must examine more than the destination address to make correct receiver decisions. IEEE 802.11 incorporates at least three addresses in each data and management frame that may be received by a station. In addition to the destination address, these frames also include the BSS identifier. A station must use both the destination address and the BSSID in making receive decisions, according to the standard. This ensures the station will discard frames sent from a BSS other than that which it is associated. Filtering on the BSSID is particularly important to minimize the number of multicast frames with which the station can deal.

Privacy

The need for secure communications is perhaps nowhere stronger than when a wireless medium is used. It is far easier to compromise the security of a wireless system employing a simple antenna and suitable transceivers following the RF chain. The IEEE 802.11 MAC-level incorporates privacy mechanisms to protect the content of data frames from eavesdroppers. The IEEE 802.11 Wired Equivalent Privacy (WEP) mechanism is designed to provide a protection level that is perceived as being equivalent to that of a wired LAN.

WEP is an encryption mechanism that takes the content of a data frame, and passes it through an encryption algorithm. The result then replaces the frame body of the data frame and is transmitted. The data frame so encrypted has its WEP bit in the frame control field of the MAC header set to indicate it is encrypted. The receiver of an encrypted data frame passes the encrypted frame body through the same encryption algorithm used by the sending station. The result is the original, unencrypted frame body. The receiver then passes the unencrypted result up to the higher layer protocols. Notably, only the frame body of data frames is encrypted. This leaves the complete MAC header of the data frame, and the entire frame of other frame types, unencrypted and available to even the casual eavesdropper. Thus, WEP alone offers no protection agains threats to a LAN such as traffic analysis.

The encryption algorithm used in IEEE 802.11 is RC4, which was developed at RSA Data Security, Inc. (RSADSI). RC4 is a symmetric stream cipher that supports a variable length key. A symmetric cipher is one that uses the same key and algorithm for both encryption and decryption. A stream cipher is an algorithm that can process an arbitrary number of bytes. This is contrasted with a block cipher that processes a fixed number of bytes. The key is the one piece of information that must be shared by both the encrypting and decrypting stations. It is the key that allows every station to use the same algorithm, but only those stations sharing the same key can correctly decrypt encrypted frames. RC4 allows the key length to be variable, up to 256 bytes, as opposed to requiring the key to be fixed at a certain length. IEEE 802.11 has chosen to use a 40-bit key.

The IEEE 802.11 Standard describes the use of the RC4 algorithm and the key in WEP. However, key distribution or key negotiation is not mentioned in the standard. This leaves much of the most difficult part of secure communications to the individual manufacturers of IEEE 802.11 equipment. In a secure communication system using a symmetric algorithm, such as RC4, it is imperative that the keys used by the algorithm be protected, that they remain secret. If a key is compromised, all frames encrypted with that key are also compromised. Thus, while it is likely that equipment from many manufacturers will be able to interoperate and exchange encrypted frames, it is unlikely that a single mechanism will be available that will securely place the keys in the individual stations.

Medium Access Control (MAC) for IEEE 802.11 Networks

CHAPTER 6

251

6

MEDIUM ACCESS
CONTROL (MAC)
FOR IEEE 802.11

Relevant Frame Sequences

In the preceding subsections, the various managerial duties of the IEEE MAC layer were described, with special consideration being given to power management, synchronization, session management and privacy. The frame subtypes employed to accomplish the associated tasks were summarized in Table 6.4. These frames are generally referred to as MAC management protocol data units (MMPDUs). The allowed frame sequences for MMPDUs are summarized in Table 6.7.

TABLE 6.7   Management frame exchange descriptions. Items enclosed in [. .] may occur zero to many times, whereas enclosed in {. .} may occur zero to one time in a sequence.

Frame Sequence	Frame Sequence Usage
Mgmt (broadcast)	Broadcast MPDU
Mgmt (dir)-ACK	Directed MMPDU
PS-Poll-ACK	Deferred PS-Poll response
PS-Poll-[Frag-ACK]Last-ACK	Immediate PS-Poll response
DTIM(CF)-[CF-Sequence]-{CF-End}	Start of Contention Free Period
Beacon(CF)	Beacon during Contention Free Period

MAC Management Information Base

The IEEE 802.11 management information base (MIB) can be construed as an SNMP Managed object with several configuration controls, option selectors, counters, and status indicators. These different attributes permit an external management agent to determine the status and configuration of an IEEE 802.11 station, as well as gauge its performance and tune its operation. The MIB in a station comprises two major sections, one for the MAC and one for the PHY. The focus of this section however will be on the MAC MIB. The MAC MIB is a collection of attributes arranged in tabular format, which together coordinate matters that are related to a single MAC function.

The MAC MIB consists of two sets of attributes: the station management attributes and the MAC attributes. While the station management attributes are associated with operation of MAC station management, the MAC attributes pertain to the operation of the MAC and its performance.

Station Management Attributes

Some station management attributes that assist in the MAC management of the station and configure the options of the IEEE 802.11 MAC are listed below.

dot11StationID: A 48-bit attribute that is designed to allow an external manager to assign its own identifier to a station, for the sole purpose of managing the station.

dot11MediumOccupancyLimit: This attribute provides a limit to the amount of time that the PC may control access to the medium. After the limit is reached, the PC must relinquish control of the medium to the DCF, allowing at least enough time to transmit a single maximum-length MPDU, with fragmentation, before taking control of the medium again.

dot11CFPollable: A Boolean flag that indicates the capability of the station to respond to the CF-Poll frame.

dot11CFPPeriod: Attribute defines the length of the CFP, in units of the DTIM interval, which, in turn is in units of the beacon period, that is measured in TU. To determine the time value of the CFP, multiply the value of this attribute by the DTIM interval (found in the Beacon frame) and multiply the result by 1024 microsecs.

dot11CFPMaxDuration: This attribute is modified by the MLME-Start.request primitive that is used to initiate a BSS.

dot11AuthenticationResponseTimeout: Attribute places an upper limit, in TU, on the time a station is allowed before the next frame in an authentication sequence is determined not to be forthcoming.

dot11PrivacyOptionImplemented: A Boolean indicator of the presence of the privacy option. This attribute simply indicates that the option is implemented, not that it is in use.

dot11PowerManagementMode: This attribute indicates the state of power management in the station. This attribute is would likely indicate to an external manager that the station is always in the active mode, never in the power saving mode.

dot11DesiredSSID: Indicates the SSID used during the latest scan operation by the station. Typically, this attribute will take the same value as the SSID of the IEEE 802.11 WLAN with which the station is associated.

dot11DesiredBSSType: Indicates the type of BSS that the station sought during the latest scan operation.

dot11OperationalRateSet: Is a list of data rates that may be used by the station to transmit in the BSS with which it is associated. The rates listed are a subset of those in the dot11SupportedRates in the PHY section of the MIB.

dot11BeaconPeriod: Controls the time that elapses between target beacon transmission times. This attribute is set by the MLME-Start.request primitive.

dot11DTIMPeriod: Controls the number of beacon periods that elapse between DTIMs. This attribute is also typically set by the MLME-Start.request primitive.

dot11AssociationResponseTimeout: Places an upper limit on the amount of time that a station will wait for a response to its association request.

dot11DisassociateReason: Indicates the reason code received in the most recently received disassociation frame. The dot11DeauthenticateReason and dot11DeauthenticateStation are used similarly to track deauthentications in the WLAN.

dot11AuthenticateFailReason and dot1lAuthenticateFailStation: Provide similar information about failures during the authentication process.

dot11AuthenticationAlgorithm: This holds an entry for each authentication algorithm supported by the station. Every station must support the open system algorithm. If the station also supports the shared key algorithm, the table will hold an entry for that algorithm.

dot11 WEPDefaultKeyValue: An attribute holding one of the WEP default keys. There can be as many as four default keys in a table in the station.

dotllKeyMappingWEPOn: A Boolean value which indicates whether the key mapping key is to be used when communicating with the station with the corresponding address. dotllKeyMappingValue is the key to be used when key mapping is used to communicate with the station with the corresponding address.

dotllPrivacyInvoked: A Boolean attribute that indicates when WEP is to be used to protect data frames.

dotllWEPDefaultKeyID: Identifies which of the four default keys are to be used when encrypting data frames with a default key.

dot11WEPKeyMappingLength: Indicates the number of entries that may be held in the key mapping table. The minimum value for this attribute is 10.

dot11ExcludeUnencrypted: A Boolean attribute that controls whether a station will receive unencrypted data frames. When this attribute is true, only received data frames that were encrypted will be indicated to higher layer protocols.

dotllWEPICVErrorCount: Attribute tracks the number of encrypted frames that have been received and decrypted, but for which the ICV indicates the decryption was not successful. This counter can indicate when an excessive number of decryption errors are encountered.

The station management portion of the MIB also includes three notification objects, the dot11Disassociate object, the dot11Deauthenticate object, and the dot11AuthenticateFail object which are activated when a station receives a disassociation frame, when the station receives a deauthentication frame, and when the station does not complete an authentication sequence successfully.

MAC Attributes

The MAC attributes monitor the performance of the MAC and tune the MAC protocol performance and provide identification of the MAC implementation. Some important MAC attributes and their basic purpose are listed below:

dotllMACAddress: This is the unique, individual address of the MAC. It is this address that the MAC considers to be its own and for which it will pass received frames to higher layer protocols.

dotllRTSThreshold: Controls the transmission of RTS control frames prior to data and management frames. The value of this attribute defines the length of the smallest frame for which the transmission of RTS is required; set by default to 2347 octets.

dot11ShortRetryLimit: Controls the number of times a frame that is shorter than the dotllRTSThreshold will be transmitted without receiving an acknowledgment before that frame is abandoned and a failure is indicated to higher layer protocols.

dot11LongRetryLimit: Controls the number of times a frame that is equal to or longer than the dotllRTSThreshold will be transmitted without receiving an acknowledgment before that frame is abandoned and a failure is indicated to higher layer protocols. The default value of this attribute is 4. It may be modified by local and external managers.

dot11FragmentationThreshold: Attribute defines the length of the largest frame that the PHY will accept. Frames larger than this threshold must be fragmented. The default value of this attribute is dependent on the PHY layer parameter aMPDUMaxLength. If the value of aMPDUMaxLength is greater than or equal to 2346, the default value is 2346. If the value of aMPDUMaxLength is less than 2346, the default value is one aMPDUMaxLength.

dotllMaxTransmitMSDULifetime: Controls the length of time that attempts to transmit an MSDU will continue after the initial transmission attempt. Because a frame may be fragmented and the retry limits apply to only a single frame of the fragment stream, this timer limits the amount of bandwidth that may be consumed attempting to deliver a single MSDU. The default value is 512 (Tus), or approximately 524 ms.

dotllMaxReceiveLifetime: Controls the length of time that a partial fragment stream will be held pending reception of the remaining fragments necessary for complete reassembly of the MSDU.

dot11ManufacturerID: A variable length character string that identifies the manufacturer of the MAC.

dot11ProductID: A variable length character string that identifies the MAC. This attribute may contain other information, at the manufacturer's discretion, up to the maximum of 128 characters.

dot11TransmittedFragmentCount: A counter that tracks the number of successfully transmitted fragments. An MSDU that fits in a single frame without fragmentation is also considered a fragment and will increment this counter. A successful transmission is an acknowledged data frame to an individual address or any data or management frame sent to a multicast address.

dot11MulticastTransmittedFrameCount: A counter that tracks only transmitted multicast frames. This counter is incremented for every frame transmitted with the group bit set in the destination MAC address.

dotllFailedCount: This counter tracks the number of frame transmissions that are abandoned because they have exceeded either the dot11ShortRetryLimit or dot11LongRetyLimit. This counter, along with the retry and multiple retry counters can provide an indication of the health of a BSS.

dot11RetryCount: A counter that tracks the number of frames that required at least one retransmission before being delivered successfully. The dot11MultipleRetryCount is a counter that tracks the number of frames that required more than one retransmission to be delivered successfully

dotllRTSSuccessCount: A counter that increments for each CTS received in response to an RTS.

Dot11RTSFailureCount: A counter that increments each time a CTS is not received in response to an RTS.

dotllACKFailureCount: A counter that tracks the number of times a data or management frame is sent to an individual address and does it result in the reception of an ACK frame from the destination.

dot11ReceivedFragmentCount: A counter that tracks the number of fragments received.

dot11MulticastReceivedCount: A counter that tracks the number of frames received by the station that match a multicast address in the group addresses table or were sent to the broadcast address.

FCSErrorCount: A counter that tracks the number of frames received, of any type, that resulted in an FCS error.

dot11TransmittedFrameCount: A counter that tracks the number of MSDUs that have been transmitted successfully. It increments only if the entire fragment stream required to transmit an MSDU is sent and an acknowledgment is received for every fragment.

dotllWEPUndecryptableCount: A counter that tracks the number of frames received without FCS errors and with the WEP bit indicating that the frame is encrypted, but that can not be decrypted due to the dot11WEPOn indicating a key mapping key is not valid or the station not implementing WEP. When this counter increments, it indicates either that the receiving station is misconfigured, has somehow gotten into a BSS that requires WEP, or has missed a key update for a key mapping station.

dot11ResourceTypeIDName: An attribute required by IEEE 802.1F. It is a read-only, fixed-length character string. Its default value is "RTID."

dot11ResounceInfoTable: Contains four more attributes required by IEEE 802.IF. These attributes are the dot11manufacturer, dotllmanufacturerName, dotl1manufacturerProductName, and dotl1manufacturerProductVersion. These attributes are read-only. dotl1manufacturerOUI contains the IEEE-assigned 24-bit organizational unique identifier that forms half of a globally administered MAC address. The dotl1manufacturerName is a variable length character string containing the name of the manufacturer of the MAC. The dotl1manufacturerProductName is also a variable length character string that identifies the version information for the MAC.

Bibliography

[1]   IEEE 802.11a Standard: Wireless LAN MAC and PHY Layer Specifications (1997).

[2]   Brian P. Crowe, Indra Widjaja et al, "IEEE 802.11 wireless LANs," IEEE Comm. Mag., Sept '97, 116-126 (1997).

[3]   Richard O. LaMaire, Arvind Krishna et al, "Wireless LANs and mobile networking: standards and future directions," IEEE Comm. Mag., Aug '96, 86-94 (1996).

[4]   Kwang-Cheng Chen, "Medium access control of wireless LANs for mobile computing," IEEE Network, Oct '94, 50-6 (1994).

[5]   Harshal S. Chhaya and Sanjay Gupta, "Performance of asynchronous data transfer methods of IEEE 802.11 MAC-protocol," IEEE Personal Communications, Oct'96, 8-15 (1996).

[6]   J. Weinmiller, H. Woesner, and A. Wolisz, "Analyzing and improving the IEEE 802.1-MAC protocol for WLANs," IEEE Proc. MASCOTS '96, 200-206 (1996).

Medium Access Control (MAC) for HiperLAN/2 Networks

CHAPTER

7

Mika Kasslin

IN THIS CHAPTER

- **Network Architecture**   259

- **DLC Functions**   260

- **MAC Overview**   261

- **Basic MAC Message Formats**   262

- **PDU Trains**   266

- **MAC Frame Structure**   269

- **Building a MAC Frame**   273

- **MAC Frame Processing**   274

- **Bibliography**   275

HiperLAN/2 is a 5 GHz WLAN standard specified in European Telecommunications Standards Institute (ETSI) Project Broadband Radio Access Networks (BRAN). The medium access control (MAC) for the IEEE 802.11 and HiperLAN/2 is the primary difference between the two OFDM WLAN standards. As discussed in Chapter 6, the IEEE 802.11 MAC is a carrier sense multiple access with collision avoidance (CSMA/CA) protocol, whereas the HiperLAN/2 MAC is a time division multiple access/time division duplexing (TDMA/TDD) protocol. In other words, the IEEE 802.11 MAC is a random access protocol, whereas the HiperLAN/2 MAC is a scheduled protocol based on transmission of fixed-size messages. That is why it has been regularly compared to a wireless asynchronous transfer mode (ATM) standard. The Mobile Multimedia Access Communication (MMAC) supports both of these protocols. This chapter focuses on the MAC layer and its functionalities. First we will describe the basic message formats. That is followed by the rules for the composition of the MAC frame and description of the basic MAC operation.

The basic approach taken with HiperLAN/2 was to standardize only the radio access network and some of the convergence layer functions to different core networks. The core network-specific functions were left to the corresponding forums (e.g., ATM Forum and IETF). As a result, the scope of the HiperLAN/2 Technical Specifications are limited to the air interface, the service interfaces of the wireless subsystem, the convergence layer functions, and the supporting capabilities required to realize the services. The HiperLAN/2 Technical Specifications describe the physical (PHY) and data link control (DLC) layers, which are core network independent, and the core network-specific convergence layer. The scope of the standard is illustrated in Figure 7.1.

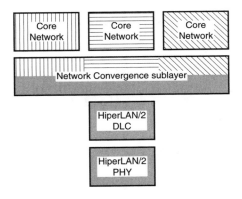

FIGURE 7.1

HiperLAN/2 standard scope [1].

The first set of all the specifications was published by spring 2000. The lowest layer of the open system interconnect (OSI) stack is defined in the physical layer specification [2]; the second layer for Data Link Control (DLC) consists of two basic specifications:

Part 1: Basic Data Transport Functions [3]

Part 2: Radio Link Control (RLC) Sublayer [4]

Extensions for different applications of the DLC are specified in DLC extension technical specifications:

Part 3: Extension for Business Environment

Part 4: Extension for Home Environment

Part 5: Profile for Home Environment

The interworking with higher layers is handled by convergence layers (CL) on top of the DLC layer. Packet and cell based convergence layers have been defined.

Network Architecture

HiperLAN/2 has two basic operation modes: centralized mode and direct mode. Centralized mode is used to operate HiperLAN/2 as an access network via a fixed access point (AP). All data transmitted or received by a mobile terminal passes the access point or centralized controller, even if the data exchange is between mobile terminals associated to the same access point or centralized controller.

In direct mode, an additional capability for direct link communication is provided. This mode is used to operate HiperLAN/2 as an ad-hoc network without relying on a cellular network infrastructure. In this case, a central controller (CC), which is dynamically selected among the portable devices, provides the same level of quality of service (QoS) support as the fixed AP. Data exchange between mobile terminals associated with the same AP or CC takes place without passing the AP or the CC. All the data exchanges are still under control of the AP or the CC. So, all the radio resource control and scheduling algorithms are always run in a centralized manner either in the access point or in the central controller.

The principle of the operation and the differences in the basic protocol in the two modes are illustrated in Figure 7.2. Even though the figure is a very simplified example of the operation it does bring out the basic differences between the two modes. No matter what is the mode of the operation, all the resources are centrally controlled. Only the data can be exchanged directly between terminals.

All the information exchange is based on transmissions over DLC connections. A DLC connection carries user or control data and is identified by a DLC connection identifier (DLCC ID) that is assigned to a connection by the AP RLC entity during connection setup. Before the MT is allowed to set up any connections, it has to associate [4] to the AP. During the association, an AP

RLC entity assigns each MT a MAC ID that is unique for the AP. This ID together with the DLCC ID forms a DLC User Connection ID (DUC ID), which is unique in a radio cell. It is used to identify which connection an MT is requesting and the AP/CC is granting resources.

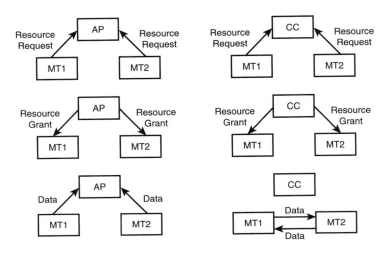

FIGURE 7.2

Information exchange principles in a centralized mode (left-hand row) and in a direct mode (right-hand row).

DLC Functions

The basic HiperLAN/2 DLC functions specified in [3] are for the purpose of transporting data and control information between HiperLAN/2 devices. These functions can be divided into two functional entities: Medium Access Control (MAC) and Error Control (EC). Their locations in the HiperLAN/2 protocol stack as well as relations to other functionalities are illustrated in Figure 7.3.

The EC is responsible for detection of and recovery from transmission errors on the radio link. Moreover, it ensures in-sequence delivery of data packets. The role of the MAC layer is to format information from higher layers into valid transmission packets to be delivered for the PHY layer for transmission, and vice versa.

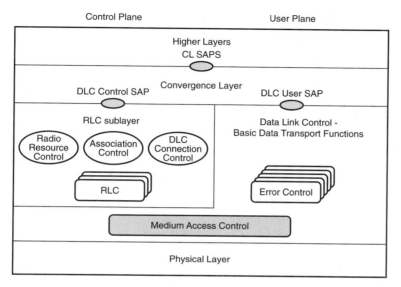

FIGURE 7.3

MAC in HiperLAN/2 protocol stack. [3]

MAC Overview

The MAC is based on a dynamic TDMA/TDD scheme with centralized control. The MAC frame appears with a period of two milliseconds (ms). The allocation of resources is controlled by an AP or CC. It is assumed that one MAC entity with one instance is provided per AP or per mobile terminal (MT). The MAC IDs are also used to administer broadcast and multicast services. The relation between MAC entities is created by a MAC ID, which is unique in a radio cell. To control the allocation of resources, the AP or CC needs to know the state of its own buffers and of the buffers in the MT. Therefore, the MTs report their buffer states in Resource Request (RR) messages to the AP or CC. Using this mechanism, the MTs request for resources from the AP, which are specified in terms of transmission capacity. Moreover, an optional feature is to negotiate a fixed capacity allocation over multiple frames. The AP allocates the resources according to the buffer states on a fair basis and, if required, takes quality of service parameters into account. The allocation of resources is conveyed by Resource Grant (RG) messages. RRs and RGs are defined on a per-connection basis. Data and control information are mapped onto transport channels. The transport channels are the basic elements to construct protocol data unit (PDU) trains that are delivered to and received from the physical layer. Six types of PDU trains are allowed: Broadcast, FCH-and-ACH, Downlink, Uplink with short preamble, Uplink with long preamble, and Direct Link PDU train.

Basic MAC Message Formats

MAC deals with all the information in three different formats. First, there are ten logical channels that are defined for different kinds of data transfer services offered by the MAC entity. Each logical channel type is defined by the type of information it carries and the interpretation of the values in the corresponding messages. Logical channels can be considered to operate between logical connection end points and between logical entities. They are referred to with four-letter abbreviations, e.g. BCCH. The names of the logical channels will mostly be used when message contents and their meaning are addressed and the names of the transport channels should reflect message lengths, rules to assemble a MAC frame, and access methods. In some other systems, logical channels are called simply messages with various message types and subtypes.

The logical channels are mapped onto transport channels that are referred to with three-letter abbreviations, e.g. BCH. They describe the basic message format, while the message contents and their interpretation are subject to the logical channels. Thus the transport channels are just a kind of link in information delivery from higher layers to the physical layer. They are useful in describing the mapping from logical channels onto radio bursts the physical layer deals with. "Logical Channels," Later in this chapter, describes the most important logical channels.

Transport channels are concatenated to construct PDU trains. PDU trains are used in data exchanges with the physical layer. The PHY layer maps the PDU trains provided by the MAC onto the PHY bursts. Six different kinds of PDU trains are defined to be used in different parts of the MAC frame. "Transparent Channels" provides a more detailed description of the transport channel.

All ten logical channels are listed in Table 7.1 and all six transport channels are listed in Table 7.2. The logical and transport channels are listed in Tables 7.1 and 7.2, respectively, as they appear within the frame. Figure 7.4 illustrates all the possible mappings between logical and transport channels for the downlink (DL), the uplink (UL), and the direct link (DiL) cases separately. The six PDU train types are listed in Table 7.3.

TABLE 7.1 Logical Channels in HiperLAN/2

Logical Channel	Abbreviation	Direction DL/UL/DiL
Broadcast Control Channel	BCCH	DL
Frame Control Channel	FCCH	DL
Random Access Feedback Channel	RFCH	DL
RLC Broadcast Channel	RBCH	DL/DiL
Dedicated Control Channel	DCCH	DL/UL/DiL

Medium Access Control (MAC) for HiperLAN/2 Networks

CHAPTER 7

263

7

MEDIUM ACCESS
CONTROL (MAC)
FOR HIPERLAN/2

TABLE 7.2   Continued

Logical Channel	Abbreviation	Direction DL/UL/DiL
User Broadcast Channel	UBCH	DL/DiL
User Multicast Channel	UMCH	DL/DiL
User Data Channel	UDCH	DL/UL/DiL
Link Control Channel	LCCH	DL/UL/DiL
Association Control Channel	ASCH	UL

TABLE 7.3   Transport Channels in HiperLAN/2

Transport Channel	Abbreviation	Direction DL/UL/DiL
Broadcast Channel	BCH	DL
Frame Channel	FCH	DL
Access Feedback Channel	ACH	DL
Long Transport Channel	LCH	DL/UL/DiL
Short Transport Channel	SCH	DL/UL/DiL
Random Channel	RCH	UL

TABLE 7.4   PDU Trains in HiperLAN/2

PDU train	Transport Channels	Direction DL/UL/DiL
Broadcast PDU train	BCH/FCH/ACH	DL
FCH-and-ACH PDU train	FCH/ACH	DL
Downlink PDU train	SCH/LCH	DL
Uplink PDU train with short preamble	SCH/LCH/RCH	UL
Uplink PDU train with long preamble	SCH/LCH/RCH	UL
Direct link PDU train	SCH/LCH	DiL

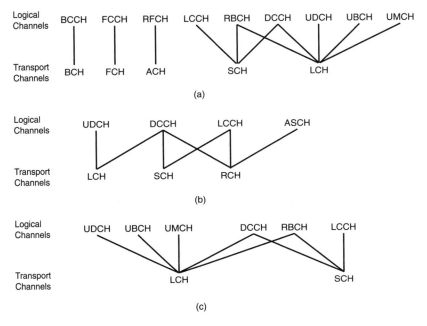

FIGURE 7.4

Mapping between logical channels and transport channels for (a) the downlink, (b) the uplink, and (c) the direct link.

Transport Channels

The transport channels are the basic elements to construct PDU trains and they describe the basic message format. In the case of the RCH, the random access method and the collision resolution scheme are also properties of the transport channel. Transport channels carry a fixed amount of data, except the FCH that can carry a variable amount. A short description of each transport channel and their characteristics are given in the following. Their characteristics are given in Table 7.4.

BCH: The BCH carries only the BCCH and is broadcasted in downlink direction. Its length is fixed and equal to 120 bits. One BCH is sent per MAC frame per sector antenna.

FCH: The FCH carries only the FCCH and is broadcasted in downlink direction. The FCH comprises of fixed size information element (IE) blocks. Every block contains three IEs, each with a length of eight octets, and a 24-bit CRC calculated over the three IEs of the block. The FCH structure is shown in Figure 7.5.

IEs carry resource grants in downlink direction. Resource grants are used to communicate resource allocation information to mobile terminals and are responses to resource requests from the terminals. All the IEs are discussed in more detail later in the chapter describing the logical channels. The access point or centralized controller determines the number of the blocks on the basis of the resource allocation status in the frame.

ACH: The ACH is used for sending RFCH in downlink direction. It has a total size of nine octets. The format is identical to the SCH format described below. ACHs are identified by a type field with binary coding 0110 at its beginning.

LCH: The LCH transports user data for the connections related to the granted user channels (UDCHs, UBCHs, and UMCHs). Further, it conveys control information for the connections related to the DCCH and RBCH. The LCH consists of 54 bytes. The two first bits indicate the LCH type. Only two types are defined: one for the logical channels mapped onto the LCH and another for a dummy LCH. The actual payload is always fixed in length and equals to 406 bits. The last three bytes of the LCH are for 24-bit CRC.

SCH: The SCH carries short control information for three control channels: DCCH, LCCH, and RBCH. It consists of nine bytes of which the first four bits are to determine the type of information in the channel. The following 52 bits are for information delivery and the last two bytes are for 16-bit CRC.

The SCH is primarily used to convey resource requests for both uplink and direct link, and to deliver RLC messages both in downlink and uplink. It is used also as a feedback channel in automatic repeat request (ARQ), and to deliver encryption information in downlink direction.

RCH: The RCH is used by a terminal to send control information to the access point or centralized controller when it has no granted SCH available. It consists of nine bytes and its format is identical to the one of the SCH. Only a subset of the SCH message types are defined for RCH transport. It is used to convey resource requests for both uplink and direct link. Further, it can be used to convey RLC messages to the access point or centralized controller.

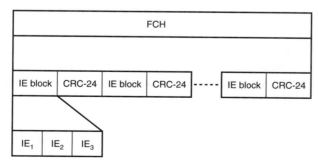

FIGURE 7.5
Data field structure of FCH frame.

TABLE 7.5 Transport Channel Characteristics

Transport Channel	PHY Mode	Length [bytes]
BCH	BPSK, r=1/2	15
FCH	BPSK, r=1/2	N^a*27
ACH	BPSK, r=1/2	9
LCH	Set in FCCH	54
SCH	Set in FCCH	9
RCH	BPSK, r=1/2	9

[a.] N is an integer.

PDU Trains

PDU trains represent the interface between the MAC and the PHY. They consist of a sequence of transport channels. Each of the six PDU trains listed in Table 7.3 is shortly described in the following.

Broadcast PDU Train

The format of the Broadcast PDU train depends on the number of sectors the access point uses. In the case of multiple sectors, each BCH is transmitted using an individual Broadcast PDU train. Otherwise, the PDU train consists of BCH, FCH, and ACH. Both these cases are illustrated in Figure 7.6.

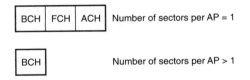

FIGURE 7.6
Possible Broadcast PDU trains.

FCH-and-ACH PDU Train

FCH-and-ACH PDU train is used only when the access point uses more than one sector. Then the AP transmits one FCH-and-ACH PDU train per each sector. The FCH is not transmitted if no traffic is scheduled for that sector in the current frame. Both of these cases are illustrated in Figure 7.7.

FIGURE 7.7
Possible FCH-and-ACH PDU trains.

Downlink PDU Train

Downlink PDU train consist of a sequence of SCHs and LCHs belonging all to the same terminal. All the SCHs belonging to a particular user connection are transmitted before the LCHs belonging to this connection. Only a single PDU train per terminal per MAC frame is transmitted. An example is shown in Figure 7.8.

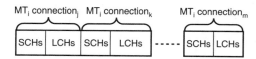

FIGURE 7.8
Possible Downlink PDU train.

Uplink PDU Train with Long/Short Preamble

Uplink PDU trains consist of a sequence of LCHs and SCHs belonging all to the same terminal, or a single RCH from the terminal. All the LCHs belonging to a particular user connection are transmitted before the SCHs belonging to this connection. The difference between the two Uplink PDU train types is in the length of preambles added by the PHY layer. The MAC layer doesn't specify the PDU train type. It is determined at the PHY layer. An example is shown in Figure 7.9.

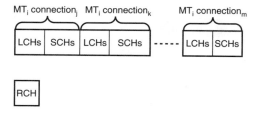

FIGURE 7.9
Possible Uplink PDU train.

Direct Link PDU train

A Direct link PDU train consists of all LCHs and SCHs belonging to the same pair of source and destination MAC entities. All the LCHs belonging to a particular user connection are transmitted before the SCHs belonging to this connection. Only one PDU train per terminal per MAC frame can be transmitted. An example is shown in Figure 7.10.

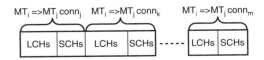

FIGURE 7.10

Possible Direct Link PDU train.

Logical Channels

Logical channels define the message contents and their interpretation. That's why in many systems they are called simply as *data messages* or *control messages*, depending on the content of the message. The most important logical channels are described below. Detailed message formats and descriptions about other logical channels can be found in [3].

Broadcast Control Channel (BCCH)

The Broadcast control channel is used in downlink direction to convey generic control information concerning the whole radio cell. Its length is fixed 120 bits containing information like frame counter, network, and AP identifier, and power control information. Additionally, it contains pointers to FCH and RCH transport channels for that sector.

Frame Control Channel (FCCH)

The frame control channel is used in downlink direction to convey information that describes the structure of the MAC frame visible at the air interface. The structure is announced by resource grants that are carried in information elements (IE) in the FCH transport channel (see Figure 7.5). There are IE-types for each of the three possible resource grants: downlink RG, uplink RG, and direct link RG. In all these cases, the schedule addressing is implemented with three basic parameters: start pointer, number of SCHs, and number of LCHs. All the SCHs are transmitted with the same PHY mode and there is an information field in the IE to signal that.

All the LCHs are also transmitted with the same PHY mode which, can be different from the one used with SCHs. Thus, there is a PHY mode indicator for the LCHs also in the IE. IEs are ordered in the FCCH according to the order of their occurrence in the MAC frame as shown in Figure 7.11. A more detailed and thorough description of the schedule addressing is given in "Schedule Addressing." The ordering is valid individually for each sector. The length of the FCCH is variable and depends on the amount of IEs sent per MAC frame per sector.

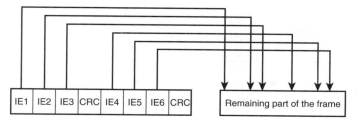

FIGURE 7.11

Order of the IEs in the FCCH and their occurrence in the MAC frame.

Random Access Feedback Channel (RFCH)

The random access feedback channel is used to inform the terminals that have used the RCH in the previous MAC frame about the result of their access attempts. It contains a 32-bit field in which each single bit indicates whether the respective RCH of the previous frame was received correctly or not (collision or idle channel). It is transmitted once per MAC frame per sector and carried over ACH transport channel.

User Data Channels

For unicast user data transmissions, the HiperLAN/2 standard has a user data channel (UDCH). It can be used both in centralized and direct mode and in all the links to transmit data from a source to a destination. The message format used is simple, containing just a sequence number for the error correction purposes and a 396-bit payload. The whole message is protected with a 24-bit CRC at the end of the message.

Other logical channels used for the user data transmission are user broadcast channel (UBCH) and user multicast channel (UMCH).

MAC Frame Structure

The basic MAC frame structure for a single sector system is shown in Figure 7.12 a. Each MAC frame consists of the transport channels BCH, FCH, ACH and at least one RCH. If user data is to be transmitted, a DL phase and/or an UL phase are provided. If direct mode is used and data has to be transmitted, it contains also a DiL phase between the DL and UL phase. The duration of the BCH is fixed. The duration of the FCH, DL phase, DiL phase, UL phase and the number of RCHs are dynamically adapted by the AP/CC depending on the current traffic situation.

The order of the subcomponents is BCH - FCH - ACH - DL phase - UL phase - RCHs for centralized mode, or BCH - FCH - ACH - DL phase - DiL phase - UL phase - RCHs for direct mode from the point of view of an MT. It's important to note that the given order is really from an MT point of view. The same strict order of DL and UL phases doesn't apply to the AP. An AP may, for example, have several DL and UL phases and mix phases randomly, as long as the order is kept for each individual MT.

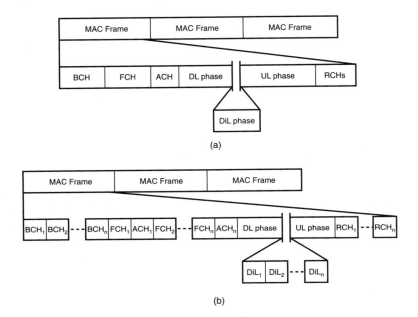

(a)

(b)

FIGURE 7.12

Basic MAC frame structure for (a) a single sector system, (b) multiple sectors (n=number of sectors used by the AP).

An example of the basic MAC frame structure from the AP's point of view in the case where multiple sectors are used is shown in Figure 7.12 b. Each MAC frame consists of a sequence of BCHs. The number of BCHs is equal to the number of sectors the AP is using. After the sequence of BCHs that have a fixed duration, a sequence of FCH-and-ACH PDU trains follows for each sector. The FCH shall not be transmitted if no traffic is scheduled for that sector in the current frame. A sequence of RCHs is located after the uplink phase. At least one RCH per sector is always present. The frame also contains at least one DL phase and/or UL phase for a particular sector if the corresponding FCH is present.

If direct mode is used and data is to be transmitted, the frame also contains a DiL phase. The DiL phase is located between the DL and UL phase. The duration of the FCH, DL phase, DiL phase, UL phase, and the number of RCHs are dynamically adapted by the AP depending on the current traffic situation.

Order of the Transport Channels

For a single sector in the AP/CC, the order of the transport channels from an MT's point of view is BCH - FCH – ACH – DL phase – (DiL phase) – UL phase – RCH. The DiL phase can only exist if both AP/CC and MT support it. All possible combinations of the MAC frame for an AP or CC using a single sector are depicted in Figure 7.13.

For an AP with n sectors, the sequence of channels is BCH1, BCH2, ..., BCHn, FCH1, ACH1, ..., FCH #k, ACH #n, DL #i, ..., DL #k, UL #i, ..., UL #k, RCHs #1, RCHs #2, RCHs #n. Several RCHs can be allocated for a particular sector. Support for multiple sectors is mandatory for MTs but optional for the AP.

No matter whether a single or multiple sectors are used, all granted LCHs and SCHs for a single MT are always grouped together. All RGs in the FCCH belonging to one MAC ID in CM, or belonging to the same pair of source and destination MAC IDs in DM, are grouped such that they result in a single PDU train.

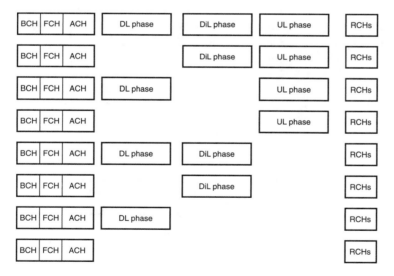

FIGURE 7.13

All possible combinations of a MAC frame for an AP using a single sector.

Schedule Addressing

The basic time unit of the MAC frame, called a *slot*, has duration of 400 ns. The position of the transmission of channels and messages in the MAC frame is indicated by pointers given in the FCCH and BCCH. The pointer in BCCH indicates the start position of the FCCH for the respective sector. Pointers in the FCCH indicate the start positions of the DLC connections of the terminal.

The reference point of an MT for all start pointers is the first sample of the first BCH preamble of a MAC frame. The first BCH preamble is addressed with a value of 0 in the start pointer. This applies also to the case with multiple sectors. This rule is illustrated in Figure 7.14.

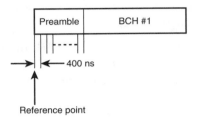

FIGURE 7.14

Reference point for the start of the preamble definition.

When calculating the pointers, the AP has to take both the PHY layer preambles and the needed guard times into account. The preambles are different for different PDU trains and they can be found in [2]. They have to be taken implicitly into account by the MT when evaluating the pointers. Three different guard times for radio settling and propagation delays are used: radio turn-around time, sector switch guard time, and propagation delay guard time. Maximum turn-around time is 6 ms and the maximum time to switch sectors is 800 ns. The guard time between different PDU train types and PHY bursts varies. They can be found in [2].

An example of pointers for the uplink and downlink phases is given in Figure 7.15.

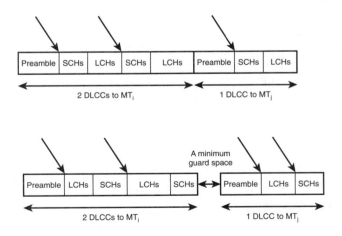

FIGURE 7.15

Pointers for the downlink and uplink.

Building a MAC Frame

Each MAC frame is started with a sequence of BCHs. The number of BCHs is equal to the number of sectors used by the AP. BCHs are transmitted according to the ascending sector identifier number. A single BCH is used per sector and they are transmitted periodically every two ms, except in cases where the AP is performing its own measurements related to the dynamic frequency selection (DFS) procedure [4]. In that case, some BCHs may be left out to allow the AP to perform measurements related to channel selection. BCHs are always transmitted using BPSK and coding rate 1/2.

The FCH follows directly after the BCH in the case of one sector. In the case of more than one sector, a pointer is used in the BCCH to identify the starting point of the FCH. If the FCH does not exist, the starting point in the BCCH identifies the location of the ACH. In the case the numbers of sectors field in the BCCH is set to 0, a single sectored antenna is applied and the FCH follows directly after the BCH. The pointer in the BCCH still points to the location of the FCH.

If a single sector is used, the FCH is present and has a minimum length of 36 µs. If there are not enough information elements to fill the FCH, one or more padding information elements is inserted. The minimum length of the FCH is 0 in the case where multiple sectors are used. FCH with length 0 is used for each sector where no Downlink, Uplink, or Direct Link PDU trains are allocated in FCCH.

Whenever padding information elements are to be inserted, they are allocated at the end of the IE blocks. Not more than one FCH per sector per MAC frame is transmitted. Information elements are ordered in the FCH according to the order of their occurrence in the MAC frame, i.e. with increasing start pointer values as shown in Figure 7.11. An exception is the information element for empty parts, which contain two start pointers. For this IE, the first start pointer is used for the purpose of ordering the IEs in the FCH. Not more than one RGs is used per user connections per direction per FCH. The ordering is valid individually for each sector.

The FCH is followed by an ACH (RCH feedback). The AP/CC prepares an ACH for every sector. The ACH is either part of the Broadcast PDU train (single sector AP) or part of the FCH-ACH-PDU train (multiple sector AP). The ACH uses BPSK and coding rate 1/2.

The ACH contains feedback to the RCHs of the previous frame. No explicit resource grant is needed for the ACH. An ACH that has not been received correctly, for whatever reason, leads to a behavior of an MT equal to that for an unsuccessful access attempt to an RCH and results in a new random access contention cycle.

Next in the transmission order within the MAC frame is the downlink phase, which consists of a sequence of SCHs and LCHs. The AP forms the respective PDU trains as defined and signaled in the FCCH. Same rule applies both to the direct link phase and the uplink phase. The FCCH transmitted early in the frame dictates the order and position of the SCHs and LCHs in these phases of the frame.

The last part of the frame is for RCH. At least one RCH is allocated per sector in each MAC frame. The RCHs for all sectors are clustered together; that is, the RCH phases for different sectors follow directly each other. The RCH uses BPSK with coding rate 1/2. Between RCHs there is a space for preamble and guard time. A terminal uses not more than one RCH per MAC frame.

MAC Frame Processing

The role of the MAC layer is to build valid TDMA/TDD MAC frames. TDMA/TDD MAC constructs frames based on the information elements and their formats given earlier in this chapter. Three parallel running processes can be identified:

- Scheduler
- Transmission and reception process
- Control information exchange between MAC entities

Scheduler is an algorithm that assigns the transmit and receive slots for MT, but its implementation is beyond the scope of the standard and this chapter. Its implementation is entirely up to the device manufacturer as long as all the rules given in the standard and described shortly in this chapter are followed.

Access Point

Before being able to start transmitting a MAC frame, the access point and the central controller have to calculate the frame composition according to the rules given earlier. After that, it can prepare and transmit the BCH, FCH, and ACH in appropriate PDU trains. A BCH contains the position and length of its associated FCH as well as the position and the number of the RCHs. With IEs of the FCH, it transmits resource grants for the transmission of PDUs in the logical channels of this frame. The IEs can also contain an indication of empty parts of a frame.

Next the AP/CC prepares an ACH for every sector. Depending on the number of sectors, the ACH is either part of the Broadcast PDU train or part of the FCH-and-ACH PDU train. ACHs are followed by PDUs from logical channels in downlink phase. The order and the location of the PDUs and logical channels are according to the current frame composition indicated in the FCH. If the CC is involved in direct mode operation, it also transmits PDUs from logical channels in the direct link phase.

After downlink and direct link transmissions, the AP/CC receives and processes the PDUs transmitted by the terminals in the uplink phase. If the CC is involved in direct mode operation, it also receives and processes the PDUs meant for itself which are transmitted by another terminal in the direct link phase.

At the end of the MAC frame, the AP/CC receives and processes PDUs transmitted by the terminals in the RCH.

Mobile Terminal

MAC frame processing in an MT is much more straightforward and simple than in an AP. While the AP has to determine the schedule to the MAC frames, the MT acts according to the generic and specific control information transmitted by the AP.

First, in the MAC frame, the MT receives and processes the BCH and the FCH. It evaluates the FCCH with respect to the logical and transport channels relevant to it. After that, if the MT has used the RCH in the previous frame, it evaluates the ACH to get feedback from the usage of the random channel. The final phase in reception mode of the MT is to receive and process PDUs transmitted either by the AP/CC during the downlink phase or by other MTs during the direct link phase. After receiving all the scheduled transmissions to it, the MT prepares to transmit PDUs from logical channels at the scheduled time. First in time are the transmissions in direct link. Finally after the uplink transmission the MT may access the RCH if needed.

To close, the HiperLAN/2 MAC is an efficient method for data transport, which provides a specified capacity resource for each user. This features makes it attractive for delay-sensitive traffic types such as streaming video or audio. In contrast, the IEEE 802.11 MAC is better suited for delay insensitive traffic types with large packet length. Since the overhead of the medium access protocol is independent of packet length, the frame efficiency—the ratio of the data bytes to the total frame length—increases as the packet length increases.

Bibliography

[1]   ETSI TR 101 683 (V1.1.1): "Broadband Radio Access Networks (BRAN); HIPERLAN Type 2; System Overview"

[2]   ETSI TS 101 475 (V1.2.2): "Broadband Radio Access Networks (BRAN); HIPERLAN Type 2; Physical (PHY) Layer"

[3]   ETSI TS 101 761-1 (V1.2.1): "Broadband Radio Access Networks (BRAN); HIPERLAN Type 2; Data Link Control (DLC) Layer; Part 1: Basic Data Transport Functions"

[4]   ETSI TS 101 761-2 (V1.2.1): "Broadband Radio Access Networks (BRAN); HIPERLAN Type 2; Data Link Control (DLC) Layer; Part 2: Radio Link Control Protocol Basic Functions"

Rapid Prototyping for WLANs

Dennis McCain

IN THIS CHAPTER

- **Introduction to Rapid Prototype Design   278**
- **Good Digital Design Practices   284**
- **Bibliography   298**

In the interest of quicker time-to-market, it is important to be able to rapidly prototype new technologies enabling the technology transfer necessary for product development. The rapid prototyping methodology reduces the risk involved when deciding whether to implement new algorithms for a product and allows the validation of research ideas in hardware long before production commitments. It is a relatively low-cost way of determining the viability of products prior to spending millions of dollars on full-scale production. Rapid prototyping also gives a company a lot of leverage in setting the standards for new technologies; it is difficult to argue with a working prototype. For these reasons, rapid prototyping is becoming a standard among leading technology companies trying to keep up with a rapidly changing marketplace.

This chapter is divided into three sections. In the first section, an overview of system modeling is presented along with a rapid prototype design flow which includes a description of the hardware and software tools involved with its implementation. In the second section, a short overview of good digital design practices is presented describing some of the implementation issues with taking a system design down to silicon and getting it to run real-time. In the last section, a case study is presented describing a rapid prototype design flow applied to the prototyping of a real-time implementation of an IEEE802.11a WLAN (Wireless Local Area Network) baseband radio system. The prototyping methodology presented in this chapter was developed in conjunction with a research project focused on advanced IEEE 802.11a baseband algorithms; these algorithms, which were validated in the prototype described in the case study served as the reference design for productization in an ASIC (Application Specific Integrated Circuit).

Introduction to Rapid Prototype Design

Rapid prototyping is any design methodology whereby a system-level design specified in a high-level description language like C is quickly translated to a hardware implementation. The essential aim of rapid prototyping is to quickly produce a working system without going through the traditional time-consuming process of separately defining a firm system specification and then handing it over to a design team to implement. A common problem in translating a system-level design to a hardware implementation is bridging the gap between system engineering and hardware design. System engineering traditionally specifies a system in the form of documentation, pseudo-code, and so on and defines the partition between hardware and software. These specifications are then handed off to the respective hardware design groups which translate the system-level specification to an HDL (Hardware Description Language) such as VHDL (Very high-speed integrated circuit Hardware Description Language) [11] or Verilog. The advantage of using an HDL like VHDL or Verilog is that it allows hardware designers to describe the architecture of their design without worrying about the transistor-level implementation. This requirement to redescribe the high-level system design in a hardware description language creates a rift between system engineers and hardware engineers since this is done in a different development environment and generally only the hardware engineers understand their HDL implementation. As well, the translation to HDL inherently creates the possibility for errors and inconsistencies in the design as hardware designers are forced to reverse engineer the high-level system design.

To bridge the gap between system engineering and hardware design, a lot of time and effort is expended to write the specifications as clearly as possible and resolve any inconsistencies in the design. In large projects with deliverables in the 12–24 month timeframe, this system flow has been used in many companies; however, in a rapid prototype design flow with deliverables in the 6–12 month timeframe, this process is not the most efficient. With rapid prototyping, it is critical to streamline this process so that system engineering comes closer to specifying the actual hardware implementation.

In an effort to bring system engineering and the hardware/software design closer, several EDA (Electronic Design Automation) companies have developed tools that make the translation from system algorithm to silicon design flow, creating the so-called system-on-chip (SoC), as seamless as possible. A number of leading system houses are supporting the Open SystemC Initiative (OSCI) [8], which uses a standardized subset of the C++ programming language to model hardware at the system level, behavioral level, and register transfer level (RTL). SystemC [9] provides a C++ based platform, which gives system engineers and hardware engineers a common development environment to model hardware at a high level of abstraction thereby bridging the communication gap between the two. This SystemC code-based hardware model can then be translated to HDL and then synthesized to a target hardware architecture. Because C/C++ lacks the syntax to adequately describe hardware, EDA companies have traditionally developed their own proprietary extensions to C/C++, which has fragmented the market for system level design tools. The OSCI seeks to make SystemC a standard for system-level design much like VHDL and Verilog are standards for hardware design. Once standardized, SystemC is an approach that can make rapid prototyping of new technologies and faster time-to-market a reality.

Another approach for system-to-silicon design that makes rapid prototyping possible is a graphical HDL entry design flow which allows designers to capture their high-level design in schematic-like block diagrams. Like the SystemC approach, this hierarchical, block diagram approach also attempts to bridge the gap between system engineering and hardware design by providing system and hardware engineers a common development environment in which to communicate. This common environment enables simple system model comparison and validation and ensures a more accurate hardware implementation. In the graphical entry approach, behavioral and architectural system design blocks are wired together graphically in a CAD (Computer Aided Design) environment and simulated for verification. Following the verification of the design, synthesizable RTL can then be generated to target a specific hardware architecture like an ASIC or FPGA (Field Programmable Gate Array). This design flow allows a fairly small group of system engineers to build complex systems in hardware without a thorough knowledge of hardware design. This design flow essentially allows the designers to focus on the design as opposed to the target hardware implementation. This rapid prototype design flow will be the primary focus for this chapter concluding with a case study of a project that successfully used the design flow in developing a real-time IEEE 802.11a baseband radio.

An Example of a Rapid Prototype Design Flow

An example of the rapid prototype design flow that is based on a graphical entry RTL tool called HDS (Hardware Design System) is shown in Figure 8.1. The design flow shown in the figure is the design flow used in the rapid prototype case study presented later in this chapter. The design flow begins with floating-point modeling and simulation in MATLAB (www.mathworks.com), which is a tool commonly used in the research and development of communication systems. MATLAB allows the rapid verification of communication algorithms before any fixed-point modeling is done where BER (Bit Error Rate) and PER (Packet Error Rate) curves are generated and compared to ideal system performance.

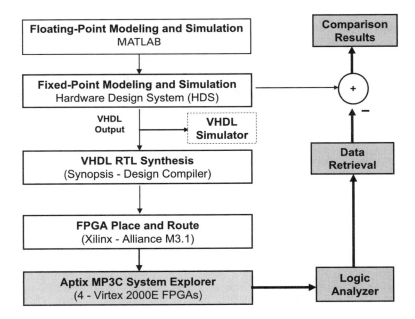

FIGURE 8.1

Example of a rapid prototype design flow.

Once algorithms have been optimized in the floating-point environment using MATLAB, the next step in the design flow is to do the fixed-point modeling of the floating-point algorithms. As described earlier, SystemC is one approach for translating the floating-point algorithms to fixed-point models and eventually HDL code. Another approach for doing fixed-point modeling is to directly translate the floating-point MATLAB code to HDL and perform simulations using an

HDL simulator. As described earlier, this approach creates a chasm between the system engineer and hardware designer because HDL is not a common language between the two. As a result, there is the possibility for errors in implementing the system design in hardware. This direct translation approach also requires a good knowledge of the chosen HDL language and the resources to code and simulate the HDL. Since creating HDL is a part of any prototype design flow that targets either an FPGA or ASIC, the issue becomes how to create it. The fixed-point model and simulation tool chosen in the example rapid prototype design flow is a graphical entry RTL tool called HDS (Hardware Design System), which utilizes the fixed-point library within Cadence's SPW (Signal Processing Worksystem) (www.cadence.com/datasheets/spw.html).

HDS offers the advantage of allowing the graphical entry of an RTL design similar to schematic capture and directly generating the HDL, either VHDL or Verilog, within the tool. This provides a common language for both system and hardware engineers that allows designers without a good knowledge of a particular HDL to design complex systems. For this reason, HDS is a good choice for a rapid prototype design flow because it bridges the gap between system engineering and hardware design. As shown in Figure 8.1, the HDL generated from HDS can also be simulated in any of the various HDL simulation tools on the market, such as Modelsim by Model Technology (www.model.com), which is owned by Mentor Graphics, and NC-VHDL by Cadence (www.cadence.com), prior to RTL synthesis. The one drawback is that the HDL generated within the tool provides few comments and is not easily read, so this VHDL is not readily transferable to other design groups. Since HDS is a component of SPW, mixed mode simulations with both floating-point and fixed-point blocks are also possible enabling the complete verification of system-level designs. The HDL generated within HDS can be directly synthesized to target a specific hardware architecture either an FPGA or ASIC. In the example design flow of Figure 8.1, Synopsys Design Compiler was chosen as the RTL synthesis tool based on the fact that Design Compiler is commonly used to synthesize ASIC designs from HDL.

The next step in the prototype design flow is to place and route the design on the target hardware using the vendor-specific tools. In the example design flow, Xilinx Virtex-E FPGAs [12] were chosen as the target hardware. Other high-density FPGA vendors include Altera, Lucent, and Atmel [5]. FPGAs are the ideal choice for a rapid prototype design flow. The real advantage FPGAs offer over ASICs is that FPGAs can be reprogrammed as the design changes, which is expected to happen several times in prototyping a new design. Changing an ASIC design requires a complete respin of the ASIC costing time and money. Also, FPGA technology has advanced to the point that very large digital designs can be routed on a single FPGA and run at real-time speeds. In terms of cost, FPGAs are much cheaper than ASICs in low volumes characteristic of prototype designs.

An FPGA essentially consists of several programmable logic blocks, each capable of implementing some arbitrary combinational function. It is these configurable logic blocks, along with the surrounding routing matrix, that are used to implement a digital design. In a rapid prototype

8

RAPID
PROTOTYPING
FOR WLANS

design flow, changes in the design need to be quickly verified in hardware so reconfigurable hardware such as SRAM (Static Random Access Memory)-based FPGAs [3] which can be reprogrammed many times make an ideal choice. In terms of speed, FPGAs are well-suited to the implementation of modern communication systems such as the IEEE 802.11a baseband design presented in the case study described in the next section. As specified in the IEEE 802.11a standard, the baseband can support data rates of up to 54 Mb/s. To support this high data rate, the baseband design requires at least 15 GOPS (giga operations per second). One of the fastest DSP processors available in 2001, the Texas Instruments C64x, supports less than 5 GOPS [10]. Current DSP microprocessors, even with advanced architectural extensions like VLIW (Very Long Instruction Word) or super-scalar processing, do not satisfy the arithmetic processing requirements of a modern communication signal processing engine. On the other hand, current FPGAs like the Xilinx Virtex series can support up to 20 GOPS due to the highly parallel processing nature of an FPGA. This makes FPGAs the logical choice for prototyping the IEEE 802.11a baseband design.

Another reason for choosing FPGAs in a rapid prototype design flow is design size. FPGA technology has come a long way in the last five years in terms of the size of the design that can be supported on a single FPGA. The size of digital designs is typically described in terms of the number of "equivalent gates" or just "gates." A "gate" is defined as a two-input NAND gate which equates to 4 CMOS (Complementary Metal Oxide Semiconductor) transistors; so, for example, a 10K gate FPGA design is equivalent to 10K NAND gates or 40K transistors [4]. In 1996, a high-end FPGA could support designs of around 25K gates. This number increased to 100K gates in 1997 and jumped to 2M gates in 2000. The Xilinx (www.xilinx.com) Virtex II family of FPGAs introduced in 2001 can support designs of around 10M system gates [13]. With this system-on-chip capability, current FPGAs can support the more complex DSP algorithms associated with the next generation wireless technologies. Being able to build an SoC design avoids the problems with partitioning the design over multiple FPGAs and/or platforms and makes system integration much easier. For the example rapid prototype design flow shown in Figure 8.1, the Xilinx Virtex-E FPGA [12] was chosen as the target hardware in the rapid prototype case study as it is currently one of the most advanced FPGAs on the market supporting large designs of around two million system gates. There are several over FPGA vendors offering similar SRAM-based FPGAs[5]. For example, Altera (www.altera.com) offers their APEX II family of FPGAs which supports large designs of around 4M gates. The choice of Xilinx over Altera or other FPGA vendors was based mainly on FPGA availability and compatibility with the Aptix system. Using a large FPGA like the Xilinx Virtex FPGA minimizes the partitioning of a baseband design, thereby reducing the complexity and greatly increasing the overall speed of the design. Xilinx place and route software is used to do the final routing of the synthesized netlist on the target Virtex FPGA before porting the design to hardware. The place and route software generates a mapping to the FPGA I/O and binary file for programming the FPGA.

The Aptix MP3C System Explorer (www.aptix.com) was chosen as the FPGA prototype platform in the rapid prototype design flow shown in Figure 8.1. The Aptix system provides the mechanism to program and route the FPGA modules enabling real-time functional verification of a digital design possibly partitioned across several FPGAs. Routing between FPGAs on the Aptix platform is constrained by the bus speeds on Aptix, which are currently around 35 MHz; faster speeds can be achieved by hardwiring the FPGAs together to bypass the Aptix internal routing. The Aptix system is an ideal choice for a rapid prototype design flow. The Aptix platform supports many of the high-density FPGAs currently available including Xilinx and Altera. The real advantage of using the Aptix system is that it provides for the flexible routing between FPGAs which allows the system and hardware designers to focus on the actual fixed-point design as opposed to the time-consuming board-level PCB (Printed Circuit Board) design and troubleshooting thereby decreasing the prototype development turnaround time. In addition to providing a platform for FPGA-based designs, the Aptix system allows the probing of signals within the design with a logic analyzer. The data captured from the Aptix system on the logic analyzer can be retrieved and compared to the fixed-point design in HDS. Any differences in the hardware implementation versus the fixed-point simulations, shown as comparison results in Figure 8.1, can then be resolved and the design flow can be repeated with a new design. This design flow allows several versions of an algorithm to be evaluated quickly. This last verification step in the rapid prototype design flow essentially closes the loop on the baseband design verification.

In summary, the design flow after the floating-point modeling and simulation in MATLAB is to first model and then simulate the fixed-point design in HDS. After the fixed-point design has been verified, synthesizable VHDL is generated within the HDS tool. This VHDL is then synthesized in Synopsys Design Compiler to target a vendor-specific FPGA. After completing synthesis, the resultant netlist is routed on the target FPGA using the vendor place and route software. The FPGA design files are then downloaded to the Aptix prototype platform using the Aptix software, which supports the download of the design files to the FPGAs, the routing between the FPGA modules, and the programming of the logic analyzer for capturing the data and comparing the data to HDS simulation results. With the aid of scripts, this design flow is very efficient in terms of the cycle-time to get a system-level design to hardware and reach closure in the design verification.

The slowest steps in the rapid prototype design flow described are the fixed-point modeling and simulation in HDS and the tool-driven place and route of the design on the target FPGA(s), which could take from a few minutes to several hours depending on the size of the design. Once a baseline system model is established at the fixed-point modeling level, changes can generally be made to the fixed-point model and verified in FPGAs on the Aptix platform in a single day, which is very fast considering it takes a few months to tape-out an ASIC or design a prototype evaluation board. The rapid prototype design flow is a way to reduce the risk in productizing new technologies. It is a relatively low-cost way to determine the viability of algorithms before committing to production. Projects with tight time-to-market schedules that require real-time verification would benefit greatly from rapid prototyping. A key aspect of the rapid prototype methodology is bridging the gap between system engineers and hardware designers to create a common language that is understood by both groups. This enables a very smooth transition from system-level design to hardware implementation.

Good Digital Design Practices

It is important to understand good design practices to improve the speed and reliability of designs. More extensive coverage of good digital design practices, as well as exercises to help the reader understand the concepts better, can be found in the references for this section. The design practices presented here can be applied to any digital design and should be followed early in the design flow to save time and effort later. These design practices should be considered in doing the fixed-point digital design regardless of whether the target hardware is an FPGA or ASIC. As described earlier, HDS, as part of a rapid prototype design flow, is a tool that is intended to be a common language between system and hardware engineers. Part of this language is understanding some of the implementation issues with regard to speed and reliability of the final design in hardware. Digital design engineers typically understand these implementation issues, but this may not be the case for system engineers. One of the biggest issues in any design is trying to get it to run in real-time. Depending on the design, typical FPGA implementations have maximum clock speeds of 40 to 50 MHz while ASIC implementations have typical operating speeds of 80 to 100 MHz [5]. For this reason, it is important to use good design practices that can help improve design speed especially for FPGAs. Poor design practices early in the design cycle can make a big difference in the final implementation.

One way to improve the speed of a digital design is through the use of pipelining whereby several stages of combinatorial logic are broken into sections separated by registers [3]. Pipelining is a common technique to accelerate the operation of critical datapaths in a design. Pipelining increases the overall speed of a design due to fewer combinatorial stages between registers at the cost of increased latency in the design. An example of pipelining is shown in Figure 8.2 where a pipeline stage is added in an HDS design to increase the speed of the implementation.

This example design without the pipeline stage synthesized to target an FPGA has 826 logic gates at a maximum clock speed after routing of 68 MHz. With the pipeline stage added, the design synthesized to 982 logic gates, and the maximum clock speed increased to 103 MHz. Using pipelining in this example design gave a 51% improvement in speed at the cost of an 18% increase in logic gates. More pipeline stages could be added to this example design to increase the speed even more. Adding extra pipeline stages for high-performance data paths makes sense in so far as the delays of the registers become comparable to the combinational logic delays [3]. Given this small example, it should be clear that using pipelining especially in large designs can give significant improvements in design speeds. This technique was extensively used in the rapid prototype case study described in the next section to achieve real-time system performance.

EXAMPLE HDS DESIGN

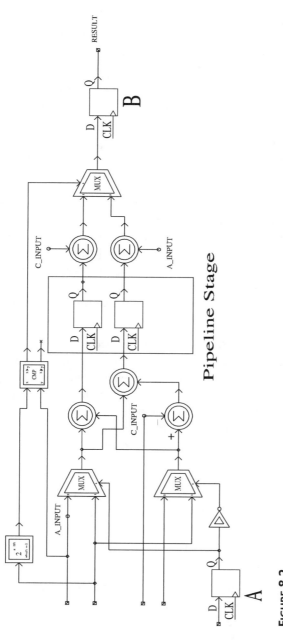

FIGURE 8.2

An example of pipelining.

Another technique that can improve the speed of a design is reducing fanout. Fanout is defined as the number of load gates that are connected to the output of a driving gate [3]. When a gate has a large fanout, the added load can degrade the performance of the driving gate, leading to problems with the speed and reliability of the overall design. One technique to reduce fanout is to insert a buffer between the driving gate and the fanout. A variation of this technique is shown in the HDS design of Figure 8.3 where the 1-bit RESET net is registered eight times and divided into eight separate nets.

In this case, the register acts like a buffer to drive the separate nets which reduces the fanout of the RESET net in the design. This technique was used in the rapid prototype case study described in the next section to improve the speed and reliability of the design.

There are some common design practices that can ensure the reliability of the final design. The first practice is registering the output of each block in a design hierarchy. This ensures the follow-on modules have a known timing budget with which to work [2]. Figure 8.4 shows the example HDS design from Figure 8.2 with the output at point "B" tapped directly off the output of the multiplexer as opposed to the register making the timing of the follow-on modules dependant on the variable combinatorial delay of the output as opposed to the known timing of the register. By registering the output, the designers of the follow-on modules have a known timing budget with which to design.

By not registering the output of a hierarchical block, logic synthesis becomes more complicated because appropriate timing constraints will need to be specified for all destinations receiving this output signal. Another design practice that should be avoided is having uninitialized storage devices in a design such as registers or RAMs. When storage devices are uninitialized, the initial state is unknown leading to possible errors in the implementation of the design. Different simulation tools handle the floating initial state problem differently. The HDS simulation tool used in the rapid prototype design flow presented earlier initializes all storage device states to 0, thereby hiding the problem of uninitialized blocks. Most RTL simulation tools, however, use what is called MVL (multi-value level) logic, which includes not only 0 and 1 but also indeterminate (X) and undefined (U) values. This allows designers to more easily troubleshoot this problem. This problem can be very difficult to debug in hardware because the initial state can vary from one implementation to another causing random errors. An example of a FIR (Finite Impulse Response) filter implemented as a TDL (tapped delay line) design with uninitialized registers is shown in Figure 8.5

Without resetting all the registers in the design, an unknown state is induced at the output of the filter. Although any initial errors in the filter would disappear after a few clock cycles, the uninitialized filter would no longer be linear or time-invariant.

FANOUT EXAMPLE

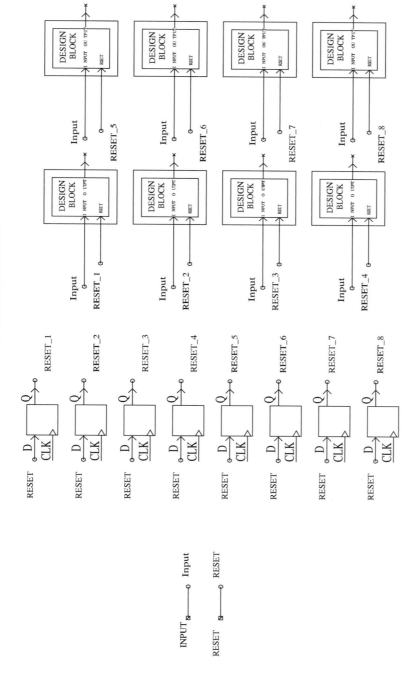

FIGURE 8.3

An example of fanout.

EXAMPLE HDS DESIGN

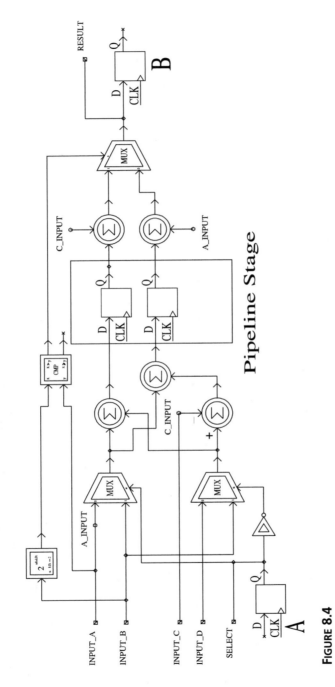

FIGURE 8.4

An example of unregistered input/output.

INITIALIZATION EXAMPLE

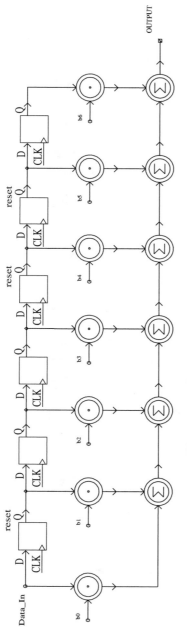

Tapped-Delay Line

FIGURE 8.5

An example of a design with uninitialized registers.

The design practices discussed are well-known techniques for increasing the speed and reliability of a digital design and should be followed when appropriate to improve design speed and save time in the debugging phase. Using good design practices early in the design process can save a lot of effort later in the implementation phase. All the techniques described were applied to the design in the case study in the next section to achieve real-time performance on FPGAs for the 54 Mb/s IEEE 802.11a baseband implementation.

Rapid Prototyping of a WLAN System

In this section, the rapid prototype methodology presented in the previous section is applied to the design of an IEEE 802.11a baseband radio. Briefly, IEEE 802.11a is a standard for WLAN radios in the 5GHz unlicensed band [1]. The standard based on OFDM (Orthogonal Frequency Division Multiplexing) uses 48 data subcarriers in a 20 MHz bandwidth to support data rates of 6 to 54 Mbps. The topic of OFDM and the IEEE 802.11a standard is covered in detail in earlier chapters. Following the rapid prototype design flow of Figure 8.1, the fixed-point design for the baseband radio is done in HDS based on the floating-point model and simulation in MATLAB. Once the HDS design is verified, VHDL is generated for each design block, which is then synthesized at the RTL synthesis stage to target an FPGA. After the place and route of the resultant netlist on the target FPGA, the design can be downloaded directly to the target FPGA for verification against the HDS model.

After some initial timing analysis in HDS, it was determined that the clock speed for the design needed to be at least 60 MHz to perform real-time signal processing. Reaching the target clock speed of 60 MHz would be a challenge in FPGAs since like most DSP designs, the WLAN baseband design uses several complex arithmetic operations that can slow down the final implementation. The RTL generated for the fixed-point arithmetic blocks (adders, subtracters, multipliers, and dividers) modeled in HDS are all combinatorial blocks where each operation is performed in one clock cycle. This results in a much slower implementation due to the number of operations that must be performed per clock cycle. A highly pipelined architecture in which the arithmetic blocks have registered outputs as well as internal registers between intermediate operations results in a much faster implementation at the cost of a few clock cycles of latency depending on the operation.

In order to meet the real-time speed requirement of 60 MHz for the IEEE802.11a baseband implementation in FPGAs, it was absolutely necessary to use a highly pipelined architecture in the design. To achieve this goal, most of the arithmetic blocks in HDS were replaced with FPGA core library math blocks, which are pipelined and optimized for the specific FPGA architecture. In HDS, these cores are modeled as "black boxes." Inside these "black boxes," the behavior of the actual cores are modeled for simulation purposes only and are not expanded until the FPGA place and route stage in the design flow. At the place and route stage, the actual netlist for the cores replace the "black boxes." The HDS simulations are bit and cycle-true simulations of the actual hardware implementation, so it is important to accurately emulate the timing and latency of the core "black boxes." If the core behavior is not modeled correctly in HDS, the resultant implementation will have timing errors causing unnecessary iterations through the design flow.

In the IEEE 802.11a prototype implementation, a lot of time was spent going through the design flow to optimize the design for speed and fixing timing errors in the FPGA implementation. In terms of optimizing the baseband design for speed, following good digital design practices, like pipelining, and using the FPGA core library blocks contributed to a 300 to 400 % improvement in overall design speed.

The motivation for choosing a 60 MHz clock speed was based primarily on the processing time required for the 64-point complex FFT (Fast Fourier Transform) block, which is used in both the transmitter and receiver of the IEEE 802.11a baseband. To eliminate the need to design the FFT in HDS, an FPGA core library FFT was chosen. Using an FFT core, provided a netlist which is optimized specifically for the target FPGA and guaranteed to run at 60 MHz. The IEEE 802.11a standard defines the IFFT / FFT period to be 3.2 microseconds, which is very difficult with current DSP technology due to the serial processing nature of DSPs; this is one reason FPGAs were chosen as the target hardware in this design flow. The core FFT provides a result vector every 192 clock cycles which equates to 3.2 microseconds at 60MHz. The chosen 64-point transform engine employs a Cooley-Tukey radix-4 decimation-in-frequency (DIF) FFT [7] to compute the DFT of a complex sequence. The input-data for the core is a vector of 64 complex samples where the real and imaginary components of each sample are represented as 16-bit 2's complement numbers.

In addition to the FFT core, another core that is used extensively in the baseband design is the core RAM and ROM blocks. The Xilinx Virtex FPGA chosen as the target hardware in this design has several on-chip RAM blocks (80 KB for the Virtex 2000E), which are optimized for speed; however, the RTL generated from HDS for RAM and ROM blocks is generic and does not specifically target these on-chip RAM blocks. So, the RAM blocks in HDS must be substituted with Xilinx core RAM blocks using the "black box" approach discussed earlier. To optimize the design for speed, this rule was also applied to all RAM, ROM, and dual-ported RAM blocks in the design.

A small group of research engineers was able to successfully implement the IEEE 802.11a baseband in real-time on FPGAs in less than 12 months using the rapid prototype methodology in Figure 8.1. Besides the actual fixed-point design in HDS, most of the effort in implementing the design on FPGAs was focused on optimizing the design to reach the 60 MHz target speed for real-time operation. The specific implementation of the IEEE 802.11a transmitter and receiver is presented in the next few sections.

IEEE 802.11a Transmitter

The baseband transmitter design is a straightforward implementation of the IEEE802.11a WLAN standard [1]. Each subcarrier is modulated using either BPSK, QPSK, 16-QAM, or 64-QAM modulations. The transmitter generates data symbols using these modulations and either a 1/2, 2/3, or 3/4 puncturing rate to support bit rates from 6 to 54 Mbps. The baseband transmitter block diagram is shown in Figure 8.6 with the estimated FPGA gate count for each block shown above the respective blocks. The transmitter data flow begins with bits being generated from a random bit generator as the input to a convolutional encoder with rate 1/2 and constraint length 7. A random bit generator is used to provide the input stimulus for the system instead of having data from a MAC (Medium Access Control) layer. The output from the encoder is punctured to either 1/2, 2/3, or 3/4 rate according to the IEEE 802.11a mode by removing bits from the encoded data stream. The data is then bit interleaved according to the interleaver pattern specified in the standard. This block is implemented using a LUT (Look-Up Table) ROM block for the interleaver patterns. The symbol mapper block maps the bits to BPSK, QPSK, 16-QAM, or 64-QAM constellation points depending on the mode. The symbol mapper outputs the 48 complex values comprising one OFDM symbol each consisting of an inphase (I) and quadrature (Q) component.

The add pilots block adds the four pilot symbols and zero-pads the OFDM symbol according to the standard prior to the 64-point inverse FFT. The inverse FFT outputs a symbol every 192 clock cycles, which meets the standard requirement of 3.2 microseconds with a clock speed of 60 MHz. The inverse FFT output is the time-domain representation of the frequency-domain OFDM symbol. In the add guard block, the last 16 data symbols are cyclically prepended to the beginning of the 64 data samples for a total of 80 data samples in one OFDM symbol. Finally, the preamble block generates the IEEE 802.11a preamble, which consists of long and short training symbols for packet detection, frequency offset, and channel estimation at the receiver. According to the standard, the transmitter is required to generate an OFDM data symbol every four microseconds which equates to a 20 MHz symbol rate. This output rate requires that the baseband transmitter operate at a system clock rate of 60 MHz due to the cycle latency of the 64-point FFT. In a separate FPGA, the output data is interpolated from 20 MHz to 60 MHz to match the sample rate of the DAC (Digital to Analog Converter) in the RF stage. This interpolated data is then filtered using a 24-tap FIR low-pass filter to remove the images generated from the interpolator. Finally, the resultant signal is amplitude-limited to limit the peak to average power of the output signal prior to going to the RF.

The IEEE 802.11a baseband transmitter shown in Figure 8.6 utilizes a total of 585K FPGA gates which includes 57K logic gates and 528K gates of FPGA core RAM blocks. The design uses 33 of the core 4Kb RAM blocks in a Virtex 2000E FPGA. Maximizing the use of the on-chip RAM blocks decreases reliance on the Virtex FPGA logic gates which are separate from the RAM blocks. The RAM blocks can be configured as single-port RAM, dual-port RAM, or ROM blocks and are used in various parts of the baseband transmitter design.

For example, ROM blocks are used for LUTs in the interleaver, puncturer, and add preamble blocks. Dual-port RAM blocks are used in the FFT core block. The transmitter design of 57K logic gates utilizes 14% of the available logic of a Virtex 1000 FPGA and utilizes 33 RAM blocks, but the Virtex 1000 only has 32 RAM blocks. Based on the number of RAM blocks, the design was migrated over to a Virtex 2000E which has about 33% more logic gates and 160 RAM blocks. In a Virtex 2000E, the transmitter design utilizes 9% of the available logic and 21% of the available RAM blocks. After placement and routing on the Virtex 2000E FPGA, the transmitter meets the 60 MHz system clock speed required for real-time operation.

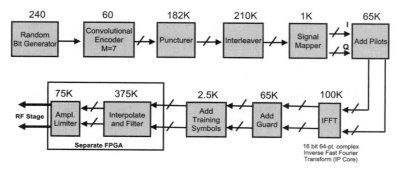

FIGURE 8.6

IEEE 802.11a baseband transmitter with FPGA gate counts.

IEEE 802.11a Receiver

The received IEEE 802.11a packet consists of short and long training symbols, a signal field followed by data symbols. The training symbols are used for packet detection, frequency offset, and channel estimation. The signal field contains the rate and packet length information for the packet. The input to the receiver comes from the ADC (Analog-to-Digital Converter) in the analog baseband. The input from the ADC is 10 bits inphase and quadrature channels at 60 MHz. In a separate FPGA, the data is decimated to 20 MHz and sent through a low-pass filter similar to the one used in the transmitter. The digital baseband receiver block diagram is shown in Figure 8.7 with the approximate FPGA gate counts for each block. The first block in the receiver chain performs the functions of packet detection, time synchronization, and removal of the symbol cyclic prefix or guard interval. This first block detects the beginning of the packet using a windowed moving average correlation with the IEEE 802.11a short training symbols. With a properly set threshold, the algorithm can detect the start of a packet within a few samples. This block generates the processing control signals for the received packet which resets the receiver and triggers the fine-time-synchronizer block also within the first block. The fine-time-synchronizer block determines the exact start point of the received packet's long training symbols by correlating the incoming packet with the known long training symbols. Finally, the cyclic prefix of the data symbols is removed. The block also changes the data rate by buffering one OFDM symbol, so the output is synchronized at 60 MHz which is the processing rate for the baseband receiver.

After the fine-time-synchronizer block, the synchronized signal goes to the FFT block. Like the inverse FFT in the transmitter block, this block performs a 64-point fixed-point complex FFT in 192 clock cycles. The synchronized long training symbols at the output of the FFT are used in the frequency-offset estimation and channel estimation blocks. The frequency offset estimation block estimates the amount of frequency modulation caused by the clock skew between the transmitter and the receiver. It does this by calculating the phase shift in the long training symbols then taking the arctangent of this phase to obtain the corresponding frequency offset. The arctangent operation is performed by using a LUT. A sinusoidal waveform generated with another ROM LUT is then used to generate the compensation signal to the front-end of the receiver to correct the frequency offset in the frequency correction block. The channel estimator block estimates the channel impulse response by comparing the received long training symbols at the output of the FFT with the known long training symbols. The channel estimation result calculated from the preamble is then used for the entire packet. The remove pilots block removes the pilot carriers and reorders the data carriers from the FFT block. The channel correction block corrects the channel distortion by dividing the data carriers by the estimated channel impulse response determined in the channel estimator block.

In parallel, the phase error for the received data symbols is determined in the phase tracker block by comparing the received pilots with the known pilots. The phase error is removed by multiplying the data carriers by a correction vector. The demodulator demodulates the corrected signal into the four different IEEE 802.11a modes either BPSK, QPSK, 16-QAM, and 64-QAM. The 4-bit soft decisions are determined by the distance between the carrier and several decision thresholds based on the signal constellation. The demodulated soft decision vector then goes to the deinterleaver which uses a LUT to determine the order for the bit deinterleaving reversing the interleaver operation in the transmitter. The depuncturer block inserts dummy zeros in the soft-decision stream according to the designated puncturing scheme either no puncturing, 2/3 puncturing, or 3/4 puncturing. The output of the depuncturer is two 4-bit soft-decision data streams which are the input to the Viterbi decoder. The Viterbi decoder designed in HDS is a 64-state 4-bit soft-decision decoder with a traceback length of 64. The Viterbi decoder uses the input soft decisions to calculate the path metrics; the hard decisions are determined using the traceback through the trellis.

The IEEE 802.11a baseband receiver utilizes a total of 948K FPGA gates, which includes 228K gates of logic and 720K gates associated with the core RAM blocks. The design uses 45 of the core 512 byte RAM blocks in the Virtex FPGA. The FPGA gate count for each block in the baseband receiver is shown in Figure 8.7. Like the transmitter design, the receiver design maximizes the use of the on-chip RAM blocks which decreases reliance on the Virtex FPGA logic gates. The receiver design utilizes 81% of the available logic of a Virtex 1000 FPGA and 45 RAM blocks.

The high logic utilization for a Virtex 1000 makes routing difficult, and the Virtex 1000 FPGA has only 32 on-chip RAM blocks. Because of this, the design was migrated over to a Virtex 2000E [12].

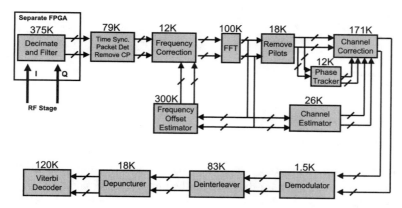

FIGURE 8.7

IEEE 802.11a baseband receiver with FPGA gate count.

In a Virtex 2000E, the receiver design utilizes 52% of the available logic and 28% of the available RAM blocks. A lot of time was spent optimizing the design for speed by reducing fanout and using a more pipelined architecture especially in the HDS implementation of the Viterbi decoder. As a result of this optimization effort, the design speed increased from less than 20 MHz to the target speed of 60 MHz, which enabled real-time data processing.

IEEE 802.11a Baseband Demonstrator

With the completion of the IEEE 802.11a digital baseband design, the next logical step was to integrate a discrete-component RF front end to the design with the goal being to build a complete IEEE 802.11a baseband radio. Using this demonstrator system, it was possible to characterize the performance of the baseband algorithms in an actual system prior to transferring the design to a production group. The IEEE 802.11a baseband demonstrator with the interface to the RF boards is shown in Figure 8.8. It is composed of the IEEE 802.11a digital baseband design implemented in Xilinx Virtex FPGAs on separate FPGA platforms with a parallel port interface to a laptop computer to set the mode and packet length information for the transmitter and to capture the BER (Bit Error Rate) and PER (Packet Error Rate) performance at the receiver. The laptop also has an interface to control the AGC and program the PLL (Phase Lock Loop) on the RF boards to set the LO (Local Oscillator) to 5.785 GHz on the transmit and receive RF boards. The FPGA platform used in the demonstrator is the Aptix MP3C System explorer which provides the programming and routing of the Xilinx Virtex FPGAs used in the design flow.

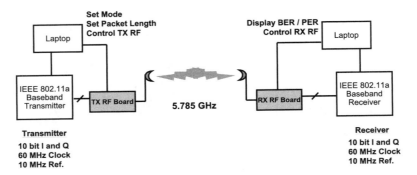

FIGURE 8.8

IEEE 802.11a baseband demonstrator.

For the baseband interface to the RF boards, 10-bit Inphase and Quadrature channels with a sampling rate of 60 MHz were chosen for the DAC on the transmitter RF and ADC (Analog-to-Digital Converter) on the receiver RF. Since the output rate of the transmitter is 20 MHz, a 60 MHz sample rate equates to three times oversampling. The LO for the RF boards was specified to be 5.785 GHz which is the upper end of the 5 GHz unlicensed band [1]. Due to the sample rate of the DAC, the data from the transmitter had to be interpolated to 60 MHz which requires the insertion of 0's between data samples followed by the application of a LPF (Low Pass Filter). This LPF was implemented as a 24-tap FIR filter. This interpolation and filter block is followed by an amplitude limiter block which limits the peak-to-average power of the transmitted OFDM symbol. These blocks shown in Figure 8.6 were designed on a separate FPGA as the interface to the DAC on the transmitter RF board. Likewise, in the receiver shown in Figure 8.7, there is a decimation and LPF block on a separate FPGA to decimate the incoming ADC data from 60 MHz down to 20 MHz for the baseband receiver processing. So, there are 2 FPGAs used on the transmit and receive platforms, one for the interface to the RF and one for the baseband processing.

From the digital baseband side, one of the key issues in designing the baseband demonstrator was clearly specifying the digital baseband interface to the RF including ADC output, DAC input, AGC (Automatic Gain Control), sample/reference clock(s), and enable/disable controls. These issues should be addressed during the RF board design and obviously effect the digital baseband design. For the basic IEEE 802.11a baseband demonstrator shown in Figure 8.8, the baseband interface only includes the 10-bit I and Q channels, the ADC and DAC sample clocks, and a 10 MHz reference clock. For simplicity in the baseband demonstrator, all the remaining RF inputs are controlled from a laptop interface, which allows the user to set the AGC level and program the LO. Among the issues to consider in designing the baseband-to-RF interface is DC offset, which could be seen at the output of the ADC due to the cumulative effects of the RF components. This DC offset causes problems in the receiver baseband as it changes the threshold level at which a packet is detected. Since the accumulated data samples from the ADC should add to zero, the DC offset correction can be implemented by accumulating the data samples and subtracting the result from each data sample.

With this IEEE 802.11a demonstrator, it was possible to characterize the performance of the baseband implementation in a working system. Using attenuators after the receiver antenna, it was possible to adjust the SNR (Signal to Noise Ratio) and plot the associated BER and PER. With the demonstrator setup shown in Figure 8.8, where the resultant BER/PER data is captured and processed on a laptop at the receiver, it was possible to run five IEEE 802.11a packets per second with up to 4KB of data per packet which is faster than the MATLAB system simulation. Actual BER and PER performance points were generated from this system and compared to the floating-point model in MATLAB. Some interesting results were found when these comparisons were made. In comparing the PER results for the QPSK and 16QAM modes in the final demonstrator, there was about a 5 dB implementation loss which is to be expected in any fixed-point implementation. In the course of developing the baseband radio demonstrator, numerous fixed-point implementation errors were found and corrected in the FPGA implementation while intermittent random errors did not appear until several thousand packets were run through the baseband demonstrator and PER performance was evaluated. These random errors were usually caused by overflow in fixed-point arithmetic operations. In cases where the PER performance of the demonstrator was far worse than expected, the fixed-point algorithms were reevaluated and fixed accordingly. Final performance data gathered from the demonstrator was used to further improve the baseband algorithms and make recommendations to product groups on the deployment of the system prior to production. The development and evaluation of this IEEE 802.11a baseband demonstrator proves the value of rapid prototyping as the design and deployment recommendations could avoid costly production commitments.

The real-time implementation of the IEEE 802.11a baseband demonstrates the viability of rapid prototyping as a means to test new algorithms and make the transfer of technology from research to product development much faster. The complete IEEE 802.11a baseband design was implemented in FPGAs in less than 12 months by a small group of research engineers, which shows the efficiency of rapid prototyping as a design methodology. This baseband design was taken a step further by integrating it with an RF as part of a baseband radio demonstrator. The performance data captured from this baseband demonstrator was used to make recommendations on the viability of the IEEE 802.11a radio system prior to production, which shows the value of rapid prototyping from a business strategy point of view.

Although rapid prototyping with FPGAs has been the focus of this chapter, there are other issues to consider in a product design flow targeting an ASIC in a product. Although the cost and reconfigurability of FPGAs make an ideal choice for prototyping a new technology, the cost in volume and power efficiency may not be ideal for productization since ASICs are cheaper in large volumes and much more power efficient than FPGAs [4]. As well, the recommended design practice of piplining to increase the speed of an FPGA design is not necessarily applicable to ASIC designs, which are inherently faster. FPGA designs can be changed, so complete verification of all test cases is not critical, but if an ASIC is the goal, the verification of the design prior to fabrication must be exhaustive to avoid the added cost and time associated with a redesign. As a result, the ASIC design methodology should include several verification checkpoints to ensure first-pass silicon. The issues of chip size, package type, power consumption, designing for testability, and the inclusion of other processor cores, among others, should also be considered for the final product. In terms of the design, a prototype can have artificialities like the laptops in the baseband demonstrator to control the RF boards; whereas, in an ASIC design, the functionality necessary to integrate the baseband to the MAC and RF boards should be addressed. Although the rapid prototype design flow presented in this chapter has advantages in terms of efficiently verifying a new design in FPGAs, it may not be the most complete design methodology for taking a system-level design to an ASIC for a product.

Bibliography

[1] "Wireless LAN Medium Access Control (MAC) and Physical Layer (PHY) specifications: High Speed Physical Layer in the 5 GHz Band," P802.11a/D7.0, July 1999.

[2] "HDS Design Methodology: Design of an IS-95 Transmit FIR Filter," Cadence Design Systems Publication, Michael Sturgill, January 20, 1999.

[3] "Digital Integrated Circuits, A Design Perspective," Jan M. Rabaey, 1996.

[4] "Application-Specific Integrated Circuits," Michael John Sebastian Smith, April 1999.

[5] "High-Density FPGAs Take on System ASIC Features and Performance Levels," Electronic Design, September 18, 2000.

[6] "FPGA High-Level Design Methodology Comes Into Its Own," Electronic Design, June 14, 1999.

[7] "An Algorithm for the Machine Calculation of Complex Fourier Series," Math. Comput., Vol. 10, pp. 297-301, April 1965.

[8] "An Introduction to System Level Modeling in SystemC 2.0," Stuart Swan, Cadence Design Systems, May 2001.

[9] "Functional Specification for SystemC 2.0" available at www.systemc.org.

[10] "TMS320C64X Technical Overview" available at www.ti.com.

[11] "The Designer's guide to VHDL," Peter J. Ashenden, December 1995.

[12] "Xilinx Virtex-E Data Sheet," v2.0, April 2, 2001.

[13] "Xilinx Virtex II Platform FPGA Data Sheet," v1.5, April 2, 2001.

INDEX

SYMBOLS

16-QAM symbol, 37

64-QAM symbol, 37

A

access points (APs), 219-222, 234, 274

Acknowledgement (ACK) frames, 227

active scanning, 245-246

ad hoc traffic indication message (ATIM), 240

adaptive modulation, 158-164

    channel inversion, 160-164

    fundamentals, 158-160

adaptive predistorter (diagram), 192

address fields, 225-226

address filtering in IEEE 802.11, 249

Alamouti's block STC, 148

amplifier classification and distortion, 173-178

amplifier nonlinear distortion mitigation

coding techniques, 197-205

partial transmit sequence techniques, 198-199

PTS algorithm, modification of, 199-202

selective mapping, 202-205

predistortion techniques, 178-190

amplifier nonlinearities, 187-190

Bayesian inference method, 184-187

decision-aided method, 181-184

amplitude clipping

amplifier nonlinearities and, 187-190

Bayesian inference method and, 187-190

decision-aided method and, 187-190

defined, 178

Amplitude Shift Keying (ASK), 90-93

analog signals, 12-13

analog-to-digital (A/D) converters, 13-14, 62

announcement traffic indication map (ATIM) frames, 228

antenna diversity, 124-169

background, 124

capacity limits in fading environments, 125-129

channel model for MIMO systems, 129-130

diversity, introduction to, 130-131

receive diversity, 131-135

maximal ratio combining, 133-135

selection diversity, 131-133

transmit diversity, 136-164

adaptive modulation, 158-164

block space-time codes, 148-151

delay diversity, 139-140

fading channels, 136-139

layered space-time codes, 146-148

multidimensional space-time codes, 151

spherical coding, 152

SSTC in OFDM framework, 152-154

trellis space-time codes, 140-146

water-filling (multi-antenna systems), 157-158

water-filling (single antenna systems), 154-157

Aptix platform, 283

architecture, network (HiperLAN/2), 259-260

ASK modulations, 91

association ID (AID), 225

association, station, 247-248

attributes

MAC, 254-256

station management, 251-253

authentication, station, 246-247

automatic gain control (AGC), 38

B

backoff procedure, 232

baseband demonstrator (IEEE 802.11a), 295-298

Basic Data Transport Functions, 259

Basic Service Sets (BSSs). *See* BSSs (Basic Service Sets)

Bayesian inference method, 184-187

Bit Error Rate (BER), 19, 216, 280, 295-296

bit loading (water-filling), 156-157

bits, information, 12

black boxes, 290-291

block codes (channel codes), 119

block interleaver, 103

block space-time codes, 148-151

BPSK symbol, 37

Broadcast control channel (BCCH), 268

Broadcast PDU train, 266

BSSs (Basic Service Sets), 219-220

Identifier subfields, 226

Independent, 244-245

Infrastructure, 244

joining, 245-246

C

capacity gap, 157

capacity limits in fading environments, 125-129

carrier phase tracking, 73-76

data-aided, 74-75

nondata-aided, 75-76

carrier sense mechanism, 231

causality, 8

CDMA (code division multiple access) techniques, 27-28

CFP timing structure, 235-237

channel amplitude response (example), 81

channel codes, 19-24, 106-120

block codes, 119

concatenated codes, 119

convolutional codes, 22-24, 109-114

decoder, 24

defined, 19

fundamentals, 106-109

IEEE 802.11a, performance of, 114-117

linear block codes, 20-21

Trellis Coded Modulation (TCM), 118

turbo codes, 119-120

channel estimation, 77-81

enhancing channel estimate, 81

frequency domain approach for, 77-79

using pilot subcarriers and interpolation, 78-79

using training data, 77-78

time and frequency analysis, 80-81

time domain approach for, 79-80

channel impulse response (sample), 62

channel inversion, 160-164

channel models

MIMO systems, 129-130

multipath, 28-31

channel state information (CSI), 38

Chernoff parameters, 137

classes of amplifiers

class A, 173

class B, 174-175

class C, 175

clear channel assessment (CCA), 35

Clear to Send (CTS) frames, 227

clipping noise, 178

clock tracking, sample, 62-66

basics, 62-64

sampling frequency errors, 64-66

co-channel reuse ratio (CRR), 26

codes

codewords, 20, 107

concatenated, 119

convolutional, 22-24

linear block, 20-21

rates, 107

coding

gain, 106

and modulation. *See* modulation and coding

nonlinear distortion techniques, 197-205

partial transmit sequence, 198-199

PTS algorithm, modification of, 199-202

selective mapping, 202-205

theory, 88

coherence bandwidth (channels), 30-31

coherent detection (RF carriers), 25

coherent modulations, 90-98

Amplitude Shift Keying (ASK), 90-93

constellation points, labeling of, 96-97

hard decision detection, 97

Phase Shift Keying (PSK), 93-94

Quadrature Amplitude Modulation (QAM), 94-96

soft decision detection, 98

communication resource hyperplane, 27

complementary error function, 157

complex exponential, defined, 7

concatenated codes (channel codes), 119

constant amplitude modulations, 93

constellations

modulations and, 89

points, labeling of, 96-97

constraint length, 22

contention-free (CF) polling, 235

Continuous Phase Modulation (CPM), 101-102

continuous transmission systems, 62

control frame subtypes (MAC), 227-228

control messages, 268

convergence layers (CL), 259

convolutional codes

decoding, 113-114

definition and basics, 109-111

fundamentals, 22-24

puncturing, 111-113

convolutional interleaver, 104

correlation and covariance, 4-5

coset leaders, 20-21

CSMA/CA protocol, 231

cumulative distribution functions (cdf), 125

D

DAR and SEM-DA algorithms, 185-187

data frame subtypes (MAC), 227, 228

data frames, 222

data messages, 268

data services (MAC), 231-239

distributed coordination function (DCF), 231-233

backoff procedure, 232

carrier sense mechanism, 231

fragment bursts, 233

frame sequences, 233

interframe spacings, 232-233

frame exchange with RTS/CTS, 238-239

point coordination function (PCF), 234-238

CFP timing structure, 235-237

contention-free polling, 235

frame exchange procedure, 235

frame sequences,
237-238

medium access mecha-
nism, 234

**DCF interframe spacing
(DIFS), 233**

**decision-aided method
(clipping amplitude),
181-184**

**decision-aided reconstruc-
tion (DAR), 181-182**

decoder, 24

**decoding convolutional
codes, 113-114**

defragmentation, 230-231

deinterleaving, 103-104

delay diversity, 139-140

**delay power spectrum
(channels), 30**

**delays, interleaving and,
102-103**

**delivery traffic indication
map (DTIM), 242**

demodulation, 88

**demodulator, hard deci-
sion, 97**

design practices, digital

fanout example, 286-287

HDS design example,
284-285, 288

initialization example, 289

**Destination Address (DA)
subfields, 226**

detection theory, 88

deterministic signals, 2

**DFT (Discrete Fourier
Transform), 11-12**

**Differential Amplitude
Phase Modulation
(DAPSK), 99-101**

**differential encoding,
98-99**

**differential modulations,
detection of, 101**

**Differential Phase Shift
Keying (DPSK), 99**

**digital communication
systems, 12-31**

basic elements, 13

channel coding, 19-24

channel model, 28-31

divide and conquer
strategy, 12

modulation, 25

multiple access techniques,
25-28

quantization and encoding,
16-17

sampling and reconstruc-
tion, 14-15

source coding, 18-19

source formatting, 13-14

digital design practices

fanout example, 286-287

HDS design example,
284-285, 288

initialization example, 289

**Digital to Analog
Converter (DAC), 62**

Direct link PDU train, 268

**direct link resource grant
(RG), 268**

**Discrete Fourier
Transform (DFT), 11-12**

discrete peak factor, 201

**discrete-time signal pro-
cessing, 6-12**

Discrete Fourier Transform
(DFT), 11-12

discrete-time signals, 6-7

discrete-time systems, 7-8

filtering random processes,
9-11

**distance/rank criterion,
142**

distortion analysis. *See*
**WLAN RF distortion
analysis**

**distributed coordination
function (DCF)**

backoff procedure, 232

carrier sense mechanism,
231

fragment bursts, 233

frame sequences, 233

interframe spacings,
232-233

**Distribution System (DS),
221**

diversity. *See* **antenna
diversity**

**divide and conquer
strategy, 12**

DLC (Data Link Control) functions (HiperLAN/2), 258-261

double sliding window packet detection, 51-53

Downlink PDU train, 267

downlink resource grant (RG), 268

DSP microprocessors, 282

duration I/D fields, 225

E

encoding and quantization, 16-17

ensemble averages, 3-6

equal eigenvalue criterion, 142-143, 149, 150

ergodic processes, 6

Error Control (EC), 260

ETSI/BRAN standard, 36

European Digital Audio Broadcasting, 99

Expectation Maximization (EM) strategy, 184

expected value (random variables), 3-4

extended interframe spacing (EIFS), 233

Extended Service Sets (ESSs), 221-222

F

fading channels
Rayleigh channels, 138-139
Rician channels, 137-138

fading environments, capacity limits in, 125-129

fanout design (example), 286-287

fast fading channels, 102

FCC (Federal Communications Commission), 26

FCH-and-ACH PDU train, 266-267

FDMA (frequency division multiple access) techniques, 25

FFT (Fast Fourier Transform) blocks, 291

filtering random processes, 9-11

fine-time-synchronizer blocks, 293-294

Finite length Impulse Response (FIR) systems, 9

flat selective fading channels, 102

FPGA (Field Programmable Gate Array), 279, 281-284

fragment bursts, 233

fragmentation, defined, 229-230

Frame control channel (FCCH), 268-269

frame formats (MAC)
fragmentation and defragmentation, 229-231
IEEE 802.11 format, 222-227
  body field, 226-227
  header, 223-226
  trailer field, 227
MAC frame subtypes
  control frames, 227-228
  data frames, 227
  management frames, 228-229

Frame Type and Subtype subfields, 224

frames
body fields, 226-227
check sequence, 223
control fields, 223-225
exchange procedure, 235
headers, 223-226
  address fields, 225-226
  duration I/D field, 225
  frame control field, 223-225
  sequence control field, 226

MAC

building, 273-274

processing, 274-275

sequences

distributed coordination function (DCF), 233

for MMPDUs, 251

point coordination function (PCF), 237-238

structure (MAC), 269-272

order of transport channels, 271

schedule addressing, 271-272

trailer fields, 227

frequency domain approach

time approach comparison, 80-81

using pilot subcarriers and interpolation, 78-79

using training data, 77-78

frequency errors

effects, 41-44

estimation of

alternative techniques for, 73

estimation algorithms, 72-73

post DFT approach to, 70-71

frequency selective fading channels, 102

frequency shift keying (FSK) modulation, 31

frequency synchronization, 66-76

carrier phase tracking

data-aided, 74-75

nondata-aided, 75-76

error estimation

algorithms, 72-73

alternative techniques, 73

post DFT approach to, 70-71

time domain approach, 67-70

From DS subfields, 224

G-H

gates, 282

guard bands, 26

Hammerstein model (predistorter), 192

Hamming distance, 21, 111

Hamming weight, 21

hard decision detection (coherent modulations), 97

harmonic distortions, 176

HDL (Hardware Description Language), 278-279

HDS design (example), 288

HDS (Hardware Design System), 281

hidden terminals, 238

HiperLAN/2 (High Performance Local Area Network type 2)

basics, 32-33

MAC protocol for. *See MAC protocol for HiperLAN/2 networks*

preambles, 54, 56-57

receivers, 49

hyperplane, communication resource, 27

I

IEEE 802.11

networks, MAC for. *See MAC protocol for IEEE 802.11 networks*

standard, 36-37, 59

IEEE 802.11 frame format (MAC), 222-227

body field, 226-227

headers, 223-226

address fields, 225-226

duration I/D fields, 225

frame control fields, 223-225

sequence control fields, 226

trailer field, 227

IEEE 802.11a

baseband demonstrator, 295-298

interleaving in, 104-106

performance of, 114-117

preambles, 54-57

receiver, 293-295

transmitter, 292-293

Independent BSS (Id-BSS)

power management in, 239-241

timer synchronization in, 244-245

Infinite length Impulse Response (IIR) systems, 9

information theory, 88

Infrastructure BSS (If-BSS)

power management in, 241-243

timer synchronization in, 244

initialization design (example), 289

Inphase (I) carrier waves, 93

input backoff (IBO), 188

interframe spacings, 232-233

interleaving, 102-106

block interleaver, 103

convolutional interleaver, 104

delays and, 102-103

depth, 103

diversity and, 102

in IEEE 802.11a, 104-106

inverse complementary error function, 157

inverse DFT (IDFT), 11

IQ imbalance, 208-210

IQ modulator (diagram), 209

J-K-L

jitters, timing, 40-41

k-tuples, 20, 22

lattice codes, 154

layered space-time codes, 146-148

linear and nonlinear modulation, 101-102

linear block codes, 20-21

linear shift-invariant (LSI) systems, 7

linearity, 8

link adaptation scheme, 36

logical channels

Broadcast control channel (BCCH), 268

Frame control channel (FCCH), 268-269

HiperLAN/2, 262-263

random access feedback channel (RFCH), 269

user data channels, 269

Low Density Parity Check (LDPC) codes, 107

low peak factor, 201

M

MAC (Medium Access Control) protocol

attributes, 254-256

frame subtypes

control frame subtypes, 227-228

data frame subtypes, 227

management frame subtypes, 228-229

frames, basics of, 218

information management, 219

services (IEEE 802.11), 217-218

for WLAN standards, 32-36

MAC message formats (HiperLAN2)

basic formats, 262-266

logical channels

Broadcast control channel (BCCH), 268

Frame control channel (FCCH), 268-269

random access feedback channel (RFCH), 269

user data channels, 269

PDU trains

Broadcast PDU train,
266

Direct link PDU train,
268

Downlink PDU train,
267

FCH-and-ACH PDU
train, 266-267

Uplink PDU train, 267

MAC protocol data units
(MPDUs), 222, 227

MAC protocol for
HiperLAN/2 networks,
258-275

building MAC frames,
273-274

DLC functions, 260-261

frame structure, 269-272

fundamentals, 269-270

order of transport chan-
nels, 271

schedule addressing,
271-272

fundamentals, 258-259

message formats

logical channels,
262-263, 268-269

PDU trains, 263,
266-268

transport channels, 263,
264-266

network architecture,
259-260

overview, 261

processing MAC frames

access point (AP), 274

mobile terminal (MT),
275

MAC protocol for IEEE
802.11 networks,
216-256

data services, 231-239

defined, 49

frame formats, 222-231

frame fragmentation,
229-231

frame subtypes,
227-229

IEEE 802.11 format,
222-227

management information
base (MIB), 251-256

management services. *See*
management services
(MAC for IEEE 802.11)

overview

frames, 218

information
management, 219

services, 217-218

system architecture

basic service sets,
219-220

extended service sets,
221-222

MAC protocol manage-
ment information base
(MIB)

MAC attributes, 254-256

station management
attributes, 251-253

MAC service data units
(MSDUs), 222, 227

management frame sub-
types (MAC), 228-229

management information
base (MAC)

attributes, 254-256

station management
attributes, 251-253

management services
(MAC for IEEE 802.11),
239-251

power management

in Independent BSS,
239-241

in Infrastructure BSS,
241-243

privacy, 250-251

session management

address filtering, 249

association, 247-248

authentication, 246-247

states, relationship
between, 248-249

timer synchronization

in Independent BSS,
244-245

in Infrastructure BSS,
244

joining a BSS, 245-246

scanning, 245-246

MATLAB, 280

maximal ratio combining (MRC), 126, 133-135

maximum likelihood sequence estimator (MLSE), 139-140

mean squared value (random variables), 4

medium access control (MAC) protocol. See MAC (Medium Access Control) protocol

medium access mechanism, 234

memoryless sources, 19

message formats, MAC (HiperLAN/2), 262-266

logical channels in HiperLAN/2, 262-263

PDU trains, 266-268

PDU trains in HiperLAN/2, 263

transport channels, 263, 264-266

message word, 107

MIMO (multiple-input/multiple-output) systems, 129-130

minimum distance (constellations), 89

MMAC (Mobile Multimedia Access Communications), 32-36, 258

mobile terminals (MTs), 275

modulation

defined, 25

symbols, 37

modulations and coding, 88-122

channel codes, 106-120

block codes, 119

concatenated codes, 119

convolutional codes, 109-114

fundamentals, 106-109

IEEE 802.11a, performance of, 114-117

Trellis Coded Modulation (TCM), 118

turbo codes, 119-120

coherent modulations, 90-98

Amplitude Shift Keying (ASK), 90-93

constellation points, labeling, 96-97

hard decision detection, 97

Phase Shift Keying (PSK), 93-94

Quadrature Amplitude Modulation (QAM), 94-96

soft decision detection, 98

constellations and, 89

definitions and background, 88

interleaving, 102-106

block interleaver, 103

convolutional interleaver, 104

delays and, 102-103

diversity and, 102

in IEEE 802.11a, 104-106

linear and nonlinear modulation, 101-102

non-coherent modulations, 98-101

basics, 98-99

Differential Amplitude Phase Modulation (DAPSK), 99-101

differential modulations, detection of, 101

Differential Phase Shift Keying (DPSK), 99

Monte Carlo Markov Chain (MCMC), 184

More Data subfields, 225

More Fragments subfields, 224

multi-antenna systems (water-filling), 157-158

multi-carrier modulation (MCM), 31

multidimensional space-time codes, 151

multidimensional symbol mapper, 152

multipath (multiple transmission path)

effects on transmitted signal, 28-31

intensity profile, 30

spread (channels), 30

symbol timing and, 59-62

multiple access techniques, 25-28

CDMA (code division multiple access) techniques, 27-28

FDMA (frequency division multiple access) techniques, 25

TDMA (time division multiple access) techniques, 26-27

N

N-point DFT, 11

Network Allocation Vector (NAV), 231

network architecture (HiperLAN/2), 259-260

non-coherent detection (RF carriers), 25

non-coherent modulations, 98-101

basics, 98-99

Differential Amplitude Phase Modulation (DAPSK), 99-101

differential modulations, detection of, 101

Differential Phase Shift Keying (DPSK), 99

nonlinear and linear modulation, 101-102

Null Data frame, 226, 227

Nyquist Sampling Theorem, 14

O

OFDM (orthogonal frequency division multiplexing)

standards, parameters of, 36

system (block diagram), 203

transceiver (diagram), 191

WLAN overview

MAC for WLAN, 32-36

physical layer specifications for WLAN, 36-38

open system interconnect (OSI) stack, 258

OpenSystemC Initiative (OSCI), 279

Order subfields, 225

oscillator, 205-206

outage capacity, 143

output backoff (OBO), 188

P

packet detection, 49-57

double sliding window, 51-53

fundamentals, 49-50

HiperLan/2 preambles, 56-57

preamble structure, using for, 53-56

received signal energy detection, 50-51

packet error rate (PER) effect, 107, 116-117, 280, 295-296

partial transmit sequences (PTS), 197-199

passive scanning, 245-246

PCF interframe spacing (PIFS), 233

PDU trains (HiperLAN/2)

Broadcast PDU train, 266

Direct link PDU train, 268

Downlink PDU train, 267

FCH-and-ACH PDU train, 266-267

Uplink PDU train, 267

peak factor (PF), 201

peak-to-average power ratio (PAPR), 218

phase lock loop (PLL) techniques, 207, 295

phase noise, 205-208

phase references, noisy, 41-44

Phase Shift Keying (PSK), 93-94

physical layer specifications (WLAN standards), 36-38

pilot subcarriers, 64, 74, 78-79

pilot symbols, 62, 64

pipelining technique, 284-285

point coordination function (PCF), 234-238

   CFP timing structure, 235-237

   contention-free polling, 235

   frame exchange procedure, 235

   frame sequences, 237-238

   medium access mechanism, 234

point coordinator (PC), 234

post DFT frequency error estimation algorithm, 72

power allocation (waterfilling), 155-156

power management

   in Independent BSS, 239-241

   in Infrastructure BSS, 241-243

Power Management subfields, 225

preamble structure, for packet detection, 53-56

predistortion techniques

   adaptive, 190-197

   nonlinear distortion mitigation, 178-190

      amplifier nonlinearities, 187-190

      Bayesian inference method, 184-187

      decision-aided method, 181-184

privacy in wireless systems, 250-251

Probe Request frames, 244-246

product determinant criterion, 142

protocol data units (PDUs), 33-34

Protocol Version subfield, 224

PSDU (Physical Layer Service Data Unit), 35

pseudonoise (pseudorandom signals), 28

PSK modulations, distance properties of, 94

PTS algorithms, 199-202

puncturing convolutional codes, 111-113

Q-R

QAM modulations, distance properties of, 96

QPSK symbol, 37

Quadrature Amplitude Modulation (QAM), 94-96

Quadrature (Q) carrier waves, 93

quantization, encoding and, 16-17

quasi-stationary channels, 102

radio frequency (RF) carriers, 25-26

radio frequency subsystems (components)

   amplifier classification and distortion, 173-178

   basics, 172-173

Radio Link Control (RLC), 259

Radon Hurwitz (R-H) unitary transform, 149

RAM blocks, 292-293

random access feedback channel (RFCH), 269

random signals and variables, 2-3

rapid prototype design

basics, 278-280

design flow example, 280-284

Rayleigh channels, 30, 125, 127-128, 138-139

RC4 algorithm, 250

receive diversity, 131-135

maximal ratio combining, 133-135

selection diversity, 131-133

received signal energy detection, 50-51

Receiver Address (RA) subfields, 226

receivers (IEEE 802.11a), 293-295

Reed-Solomon (RS) codes, 119

Request to Send (RTS) frames, 227

resonator, 205-206

Resource Grant (RG) messages, 261

Resource Request (RR) messages, 261

Retry subfields, 224

RF distortion analysis. *See* **WLAN RF distortion analysis**

Rician channels, 137-138

"rob/stuff" block, 66

RTS/CTS handshaking, 238-239

S

sampled data signals, 13

sampled waveform spectrum, 15

sampling

frequency error, correcting, 65-66

frequency error, estimating, 64-65

reconstruction and, 14-15

scanning, station, 245-246

scattered pilots, 78

schedule addressing (MAC frames), 271-272

selection diversity, 127, 131-133

selective mapping (SLM), 197, 202-205

SEM-DA (Stochastic EM for Data Augmentation) algorithm

DAR algorithm comparison, 185-187

defined, 184-185

Sequence Control fields, 226, 231

session management (MAC)

address filtering, 249

association, 247-248

authentication, 246-247

states, relationship between, 248-249

Shannon's capacity, 143

shift-variance, 8

short interframe spacing (SIFS), 233

sifting property, 7

signal-to-noise ratio (SNR). See SNR (signal-to-noise ratio)

signals

analog, 12-13

deterministic and random, 2

fade in strength of, 28

pseudonoise or pseudorandom, 28

sampled data, 13

single antenna systems (water-filling), 154-157

bit loading, 156-157

power allocation, 155-156

single carriers versus OFDM systems, 38-44

frequency errors, effects of, 41-44

fundamentals, 38-40

synchronization errors, 40-41

"single-shot" synchronization, 48

SISO (single-input/single-output) system, 124

slicer, hard decision, 97

slot (time unit), 271

slow fading channels, 102

SNR (signal-to-noise ratio), 16-18, 44

soft decision detection (coherent modulations), 98

Source Address (SA) subfields, 226

source coding, 18-19

source entropy, 18-19

source formatting, 13-14

space-time codes (STC)

    block, 148-151

    layered, 146-148

    multidimensional, 151

    trellis, 140-146

spacial diversity, 130-131

spectral diversity, 130-131

spherical coding, 152

SSTC in OFDM framework, 152-154

stability, system, 8-9

standard arrays, 21

states (stations), 248-249

station clocks, synchronization of, 243-246

station management attributes (MAC), 251-253

stationary random processes, 6

STC design criterion, 142-146

stochastic processes, 2-6

    ensemble averages, 3-6

    random variables, 3

surviving paths, 24

symbol timing, 57-62

    in continuous transmission systems, 62

    defined, 57-58

    in multipath channels, 59-62

    for WLAN receivers, 58-59

symbols, pilot, 62

synchronization

    errors, 40-41

    timer, 244-246

synchronization algorithms, 48-85

    channel estimation, 77-81

        enhancing channel estimate, 81

        frequency domain approach, 77-79

        time and frequency domain analysis, 80-81

        time domain approach, 79-80

    clear channel assessment (CCA), 81-82

    frequency synchronization, 66-76

        carrier phase tracking, 73-76

        frequency error estimation, 70-73

        time domain algorithm, 68-70

        time domain approach, 67-68

    signal quality, 82-83

    timing estimation, 49-66

        packet detection, 49-57

        sample clock tracking, 62-66

        symbol timing, 57-62

syndromes, defined, 20-21

Synopsis Design Compiler, 281

system architecture (MAC)

    Basic Service Sets (BSSs), 219-220

    Extended Service Sets (ESSs), 221-222

system-on-chip (SoC), 279

T

tapped-delay line, 289

target Beacon transmission time (TBTT), 244

TDMA (time division multiple access) techniques, 26-27

temporal diversity, 130-131

time domain algorithms, 68-70

time domain approach

channel estimation, 79-80

frequency approach comparison, 80-81

for frequency synchronization, 67-68

timer synchronization

in Independent BSS, 244-245

in Infrastructure BSS, 244

joining a BSS, 245-246

scanning, 245-246

timer synchronization function (TSF), defined, 243

timing errors (jitters), 40-41

timing estimation, 49-66

packet detection, 49-57

double sliding window, 51-53

fundamentals, 49-50

HiperLAN/2 preambles, 56-57

preamble structure, using for, 53-56

received signal energy detection, 50-51

sample clock tracking, 62-66

basics, 62-64

sampling frequency errors, 64-66

symbol timing, 57-62

in continuous transmission systems, 62

defined, 57-58

in multipath channels, 59-62

for WLAN receivers, 58-59

To DS subfields, 224

transceiver, OFDM (diagram), 191

transmit diversity, 136-164

adaptive modulation, 158-164

channel inversion, 160-164

fundamentals, 158-160

block space-time codes, 148-151

delay diversity, 139-140

fading channels

Rayleigh channels, 138-139

Rician channels, 137-138

layered space-time codes, 146-148

multidimensional space-time codes, 151

spherical coding, 152

SSTC in OFDM framework, 152-154

trellis space-time codes, 140-146

distance/rank criterion, 142

equal eigenvalue criterion, 142-143

product determinant criterion, 142

STC design criterion, 142-146

water-filling (multi-antenna systems), 157-158

water-filling (single antenna systems), 154-157

bit loading, 156-157

power allocation, 155-156

Transmitter Address (TA) subfields, 226

transmitters (IEEE 802.11a), 292-293

transport channels (HiperLAN/2), 264-266, 271

Trellis Coded Modulation (TCM), 107, 118, 162

trellis diagrams, 23-24

trellis space-time codes, 140-146

distance/rank criterion, 142

equal eigenvalue criterion, 142-143

product determinant criterion, 142

STC design criterion, 142-146

true peak factor (TPF), 201

turbo codes (channel codes), 107, 119-120

U-V

unicast users, 269

uninitialized registers (design example), 289

unit sample, defined, 7

unit step, defined, 7

unregistered input/output (example), 288

Uplink PDU train, 267

uplink resource grant (RG), 268

user broadcast channel (UBCH), 269

user data channels, 269

user multicast channel (UMCH), 269

variance, symbol timing and, 61

VHDL (Very High-speed Hardware Description Language), 278

Viterbi algorithm, 82-83, 110-111, 113

Viterbi decoding, 24, 83, 294

W-Z

water-filling

multi-antenna systems, 157-158

single antenna systems, 154-157

bit loading, 156-157

power allocation, 155-156

WEP subfield, 225

wide-sensory stationary (WSS) randon processes, 6

Wired Equivalent Privacy (WEP) mechanism, 250

Wireless Local Area Network (WLAN). *See* **individual WLAN(s) entries**

WLAN RF distortion analysis, 172-213

coding techniques, 197-205

partial transmit sequence, 198-199

PTS algorithm, 199-202

selective mapping, 202-205

IQ imbalance, 208-210

phase noise, 205-208

predistortion techniques (adaptive), 190-197

predistortion techniques (nonlinear), 178-190

amplifier nonlinearities, 187-190

Bayesian inference method, 184-187

decision-aided method, 181-184

radio frequency subsystems (components)

amplifier classification and distortion, 173-178

basics, 172-173

WLAN receivers, symbol timing for, 58-59

WLAN standards, overview of, 1-46

digital communication systems (components), 12-31

discrete-time signal processing, 6-12

OFDM WLAN overview, 31-38

single carriers versus OFDM, 38-44

stochastic processes, 2-6

**WLANs rapid prototyping,
278-298**

applied to WLAN system,
290-298

*IEEE 802.11a base-
band demonstrator,
295-298*

*IEEE 802.11a receiver,
293-295*

*IEEE 802.11a transmit-
ter, 292-293*

digital design practices,
284-290

*fanout example,
286-287*

*HDS design example,
284-285, 288*

*initialization example,
289*

rapid prototype design,
278-284

basics, 278-280

*design flow (example),
280-284*